INSPECTED, RATED, & APPROVED

Bed & Breakfasts ♛ Country Inns

Second Edition

Publisher: Sarah W. Sonke
Chief Editor: Beth Stuhlman
Cover Design: Beth Stuhlman

The American Bed & Breakfast Association
Midlothian, Virginia, USA

ISBN: 0-934473-21-8

Manufactured in the United States of America
Second edition/First printing

Cover photograph is of the Captain Mey's Inn in Cape May, New Jersey. The photograph is courtesy of George Gardner who is well known in the B&B industry as an experienced professional photographer of B&Bs and country inns throughout the United States.

CONTENTS

Introduction..1

Reservation tips, definitions of the various types of B&B accommodations, and explanation of the ratings will help you determine which B&B is best for you.

The American Bed & Breakfast Association.............................3

Purpose of the association, its Code of Ethics and inspection and rating system.

Sample Listing..6

Reservation Agencies..7

A list of reservation agencies throughout the region who can assist you in making reservations at a variety of B&B accommodations.

B&B Listings

Descriptions of B&B accommodations throughout the United States and Canada.

Introduction

What's so special about bed and breakfast accommodations? Ask any B&B traveler and he or she is sure to fire back with a story drawn from personal experience.

If you ask Sue Trefry and Lori Limacher, you'll hear about their B&B trip to Montreal one summer. Soon after settling into a comfortable guest room, they were invited to come downstairs to meet an unexpected visitor, former Canadian Prime Minister Pierre Trudeau, a personal friend of their host.

Eileen Rodan, an experienced B&B hostess from New Jersey, has many happy B&B experiences to share. Imagine her surprise on Christmas Eve one year when a former guest at her B&B returned from Canada with a diamond ring and a proposal of marriage for her daughter. The wedding reception was held (where else?) but in Mrs. Rodan's B&B home overlooking the yacht harbor.

While every B&B stay might not be as dramatic as these, one thing is certain - the hospitality and unique surroundings of each B&B provide a truly memorable experience for the traveler. And because of the people-to-people contact involved, it often ends up being the highlight of a vacation.

Bed & breakfast has come a long way in North America since its humble beginnings a little over a decade ago. With an estimated 15,000 accommodations now available throughout the United States and Canada, there is a B&B for everyone's taste and budget.

The variety of accommodations can range from a lobsterman's island home off the coast of Maine to a beach house in California. From an elegant high-rise apartment in New York City to an Alaskan farm with a trout stream where the host promises, "if you catch 'em and clean 'em, I'll cook 'em for breakfast." For the adventurous, there's B&B on a tugboat. If you're a history buff, you'll enjoy the many restored antique homes, from Southern antebellum mansions to a quaint New England sea captain's house. Nature lovers might enjoy staying at a working cattle ranch out West or visiting a new cedar lodge overlooking a pure mountain river in West Virginia which is a ninety minute trip from the nearest paved road by four-wheel drive.

Definitions

The large number of bed and breakfast accommodations now available can be divided into three distinct categories: private B&B homes, guest houses and cottages, B&B inns, and country inns with restaurants. When planning your B&B stay, determine which type best suits your individuality, style, and pocketbook.

1

Introduction

B&B Homes: The "at-home-style of bed & breakfast," B&B homes are hosted by individuals who enjoy meeting other people, sharing their homes and communities, and perhaps even showing off in the kitchen with their favorite breakfast recipes. Hosts generally have jobs outside the home during the day but enjoy taking occasional guests when their schedules allow. Guests are made to feel part of the family in this people-to-people hospitality concept, which has thrived in Europe for decades. Reservations at many B&B homes are made in advance through B&B reservation agencies, and rates for two generally range from $45 to $75, depending upon location and amenities.

B&B Guest houses and cottages: Guest houses and cottages are private, separate buildings located on the property near the main house where hosts live. Breakfast is often brought to the building in a basket each morning, although guests may sometimes join hosts for breakfast in the main house. Reservations may be made directly with the guesthouse or indirectly through a B&B reservation agency.

B&B and Country Inns: B&B inns and country inns are commercial lodgings that pride themselves on providing personal attention and clean, comfortable accommodations. A wide variety of inns are available, from historic homes to contemporary mansions, each having established their own unique individuality and charm. Many inns are graced by abundant antiques and period decor. Others are particularly celebrated for fine cuisine, special weekend events, or romantic atmosphere. Rates for inns generally range from $75 to over $100, depending upon location and amenities. Reservations are usually made directly with the inn but sometimes through a B&B reservation agency.

B&B Reservation Agencies: These are businesses that arrange all of the details of a B&B stay for guests who wish to choose from a variety of accommodations but prefer to make only one phone call. Reservation agencies also develop and train B&B hosts, personally visit host homes, publicize B&B, screen guests and match guests to appropriate B&Bs, and generally handle all of the administrative details of arranging a B&B stay.

Tips in Choosing a bed & breakfast

The key to an enjoyable stay at a bed and breakfast is to choose one that matches your individuality, style, and pocketbook. As a potential guest, you should let your specific desires be known. Some of the points you should consider before making reservations include:

1. Location: Is the B&B location suitable for your purposes? Is parking available if you are arriving by car?
2. Purpose of your visit: If the purpose of your visit is a week-end

2

getaway, be sure to mention this, especially if you'd like a romantic room with a fireplace and Jacuzzi. If you are traveling on business you may want to request a quiet room with a private telephone, television, desk, and good lighting.

3. Guest rooms & baths: Do you prefer a large guest room? Do you insist upon a private bath? What decor do you prefer? Check whether the room is air-conditioned if this is important to you. If you are traveling to a scenic location check if there is a room available with a view.

4. Price: What price range do you have in mind? Would spending an additional $10 get you an upgraded room? Does the B&B accept credit cards. What is their cancellation policy?

5. Special considerations: If you are traveling with children or pets be sure to mention this on the telephone. Some bed and breakfasts do have handicapped facilities but many do not have this provision so be sure to check in advance if you have special needs. Also, be certain to discuss any special dietary needs you may have.

Once you have made reservations here are some pointers to help ensure a happy stay at a bed and breakfast:

• Call your host and give the approximate time of arrival. Get specific directions from the host that will aid you in easily finding the B&B.

• When there's an unexpected delay and you're going to be late, telephone your host and let them know in case special arrangements need to be made.

• Adhere to your host's policies regarding smoking, children, and pets.

• If you must cancel your trip contact your host immediately. Cancellation policies differ from one host to the next but if you're able to give reasonable notice, most B&Bs will return your deposit less a small service charge.

• After your visit provide feedback to your host or the reservation agency handling your accommodations. Your B&B experience reflects on the entire industry and comments and suggestions are appreciated.

American Bed & Breakfast Association

The American Bed & Breakfast Association (AB&BA) was founded in 1981 and serves as a central clearinghouse for B&B travel and trade information in North America. Objectives of the association are:

1. To encourage and support B&B travel in North America.
2. To gather and distribute reliable B&B travel information.
3. To encourage public and private sector efforts to promote B&B.
4. To unite the diverse components of the B&B industry and implement programs that support common goals.
5. To provide a forum for addressing industry-wide issues.

6. To provide services, conduct studies, disseminate information, and provide networking opportunities for the benefit of its membership.

All members of the association must meet the specific requirements of the AB&BA's Quality Assurance Program as well as agree to abide by the Member Code of Ethics.

American Bed & Breakfast Association - Code of Ethics

1. We acknowledge ethics and morality as inseparable elements of doing business and will test every decision against the highest standards of honesty, legality, fairness, impunity, and conscience.
2. We will conduct ourselves personally and collectively at all times such as to bring credit to the service and tourism industry at large.
3. We will concentrate our time, energy, and resources on the improvement of our own product and services and we will not denigrate our competition in the pursuit of our own success.
4. We will treat all guests equally regardless of race, religion, nationality, creed, or sex.
5. We will deliver standards of service and product with total consistency to every guest.
6. We will provide a safe and sanitary environment at all times for every guest and employee.
7. We will strive constantly, in words, actions, and deeds, to develop and maintain the highest level of trust, honesty and understanding among guests, clients, employees, employers and the public at large.
8. We will provide every employee at every level all of the knowledge, training, equipment, and motivation required to perform his or her own tasks according to our standards.
9. We will guarantee that every employee at every level will have the same opportunity to perform, advance, and will be evaluated against the same standard as all employees engaged in the same or similar tasks.
10. We will actively and consciously work to protect and preserve our natural environment and natural resources in all that we do.
11. We will seek a fair and honest profit.

Letters from B&B travelers are always welcome and can be sent to: AB&BA Editor, 1407 Huguenot Road, Midlothian, VA U.S.A. 23113.

The American Bed & Breakfast Association

The Association's Inspection and Rating System

The American Bed & Breakfast Association is the only organization within the bed and breakfast industry that has established national standards and a consumer rating system. Compliance with these standards is verified by an annual on-site inspection performed by trained evaluators. Every effort has been made to ensure that the ratings assigned to each bed and breakfast are fair and accurate. The ratings that appear with each bed and breakfast listed in this book are intended to give readers a true feel for the overall quality of the property, the level of hospitality, cleanliness, and how well the building and its contents are maintained. There are five principal areas which are evaluated during the on-site inspection:

1. The exterior of the building and grounds.
2. All common areas such as parlors and dining rooms.
3. Guest rooms - cleanliness, comfort, furnishings, and decor.
4. Guest bathrooms - cleanliness, safety, function, and quality of materials.
5. Hospitality, guest services, and management policies.

The basic requirements and national standards of the AB&BA insist that every bed and breakfast who is a member of the association be clean, comfortable, well-maintained, safe, serve a wholesome breakfast which is included in the overnight room rate, and offer friendly hospitality. These are the basics requirements. Each rating level above the basic is an evaluation of how the property exceeds the basic requirements in areas such as quality of furnishings and accessories, room decor, and guest amenities and services.

The basic ratings in this book are similar to grades awarded in schools throughout the United States. The rating as well as the letter grade (which sometimes show a plus or minus sign) accompany each listing within the book:

♛ - "C" - Acceptable, meets basic requirements.
♛♛ - "B" - Good, exceeds basic requirements.
♛♛♛ - "A" - Excellent, far exceeds basic requirements.
♛♛♛♛ - "AA" - Outstanding.

The ♛♛♛♛ outstanding award is the highest award given for any property during 1992. A top ♛♛♛♛♛ is available starting in 1993 to any bed and breakfast who proves to be an exceptional property over a period of at least two years and will be used to designate the top two percent of bed and breakfasts throughout the United States and Canada.

All guest comments which appear in this book have been carefully verified and affidavits signed by the guests to vouch for the authenticity of their comments are on file with the American Bed & Breakfast Association.

Sample Listing

Here is a sample description of a B&B, followed by an explanation of each specific part:

Waterman[1]
Grandma's B&B
1200 Main Street
Waterman, WI 78435
(222) 222-2222[2]

Type of B&B: B&B Inn
Rooms: 3, 2 with private bath.[3]
Rates: 1/$45; 2/$55[4]

♛ ♛ ♛ - Excellent, far exceeds basic requirements.[5]

Victorian home[6] built in 1910 is located 5 miles from downtown off Route 144.[7] Choose from three guest rooms, two with private bath.[8] Each room features individual decor, antique furnishings, and a small balcony overlooking the river. The large fireplaced parlor is a gathering place each afternoon for tea and dessert and for quiet reading or board games in the evening. Visit nearby antique and craft shops, galleries, and historic settlements. Enjoy four-season recreation nearby including fishing and boating.[9] Full breakfast includes specialties such as walnut French toast or Grandma's super-duper eggs.[10] Wedding and meetings facilities available.[11] Families welcome.[12] Wheelchair access.[13] No smoking.[14] 1/$45; 2/$55.[15] AE, MC, V.[16] Travel agent.[17]

1. City in or near where the B&B is located.
2. Name of B&B, address, and telephone number to call for reservations.
3. Number of rooms and baths.
4. Rates.
5. Overall rating of the property.
6. Architecture.
7. Location.
8. Guest rooms and baths.
9. Special features, area attractions, and recreation opportunities in the area.
10. Type of breakfast.
11. Facilities for meetings, weddings, or social functions are available.
12. Children of all ages are welcome. If a listing does not state "Families welcome," there may be restrictions on the ages of children accommodated at the B&B.
13. Some guest rooms and baths have wheelchair access.
14. Smoking is prohibited.
15. Overnight rates for a single person or two sharing the same room. All rates include breakfast.
16. Credit cards are accepted for full payment.
17. You may book reservations at this B&B through your local travel agent.

B&B Reservation Agencies and Associations

Bed and breakfast reservation agencies are businesses that arrange all of the details of a B&B stay for guests who wish to choose from a variety of accommodations but prefer to make only one phone call. Reservation agencies also develop and train B&B hosts, personally visit host homes, publicize B&B, screen guests and match guests to appropriate B&Bs, and generally handle all of the administrative details of arranging a B&B stay.

The following B&B reservation agencies and associations are members of the American Bed & Breakfast Association and will handle reservations for a great number of B&B homes, guest houses, and inns throughout the United States and Canada.

Arizona

Mi Casa Su Casa
P.O. Box 950
Tempe, AZ 85281
(602) 990-0682 or (800) 456-0682
Fax: (602) 990-3390

Office hours: Daily 8 a.m. - 8 p.m.

Geographic area: Arizona, New Mexico, and Utah.

Inspections: Annually.

Deposit: A first night's deposit is required for stays under one week. For one-night stays, payment includes an extra $5.00 charge. For stays over seven nights, 20% of the total amount is required as a deposit.

Payment: Cash or traveler's checks only.

Guests write: *"The reservation agency was very helpful in selecting the inn considering our price range and needs. The B&B itself was a very warm, inviting place. Our room was large and well decorated in pine furniture. Our hosts greeted us with wine and cheese as we checked in during afternoon tea time."* (G. Grinis)

"We wanted to stay up for hours visiting with our lovely hosts. In the morning I was asked if we'd like to try their grapefruit. So our host went out to his tree, picked a grapefruit and we ate it. Now that was fresh! We're from the Midwest so this was very special. The smell of orange blossoms is heavenly. We trust Mi Casa Su Casa to find us a place to stay where we feel welcome and comfortable. They have never let us down." (A. Bush)

"Our hosts were absolutely the most friendly and hospitable people. We felt more like family or friends than paying guests. We were genuinely sorry to leave and have since thought about moving to Arizona. Bu we're not sure if it's for the weather or because of our hosts!" (E. Albrecht)

B&B Reservation Agencies and Associations

California

Eye Openers Bed & Breakfast Reservations
P.O. Box 694
Altadena, CA 91001
(213) 684-4428 or (818) 797-2055
Fax: (818) 798-3640

Office hours: Monday - Friday, 10 a.m. - 6 p.m.

Geographic area: Bed and breakfast homes and inns throughout the entire state of California.

Inspections: Annually.

Deposit: A $25.00 deposit is required to confirm reservations.

Payment: MC, V accepted for deposit and payments.

Travel agent commission available.

Guests write: *"We couldn't have wanted nicer hosts or more romantic places to stay. You really did an incredible job of matching us with just the right places. Our three favorites were the Garden Room in San Diego, the Beach House in Cambria, and the fantastic Victorian with the brass bed and woodburning fireplace in San Francisco. You made a memorable time even more exciting and romantic."* (J. Gallucci)

"We particularly were pleased with the B&B accommodations that were made for us by Eye Openers B&B Reservations. Our hostess was delightful and gracious in sharing her home with us. We would like to heartily recommend them as an alternative to the standard modes of lodging." (B. Pincince)

"You certainly handled my reservation to my satisfaction and I would highly recommend your service to others." (C. Miles)

"Both of our hosts were magnificent. They not only fulfilled the basic B&B functions, they both went out of their way to provide information, supplies, services, excellent food, tickets to a concert they could not attend, and on and on. A beautiful experience!" (K. Poll)

Georgia

Bed & Breakfast Atlanta
1801 Piedmont Avenue, Suite 208
Atlanta, GA 30324
(404) 875-0525, 875-9672 or 800-96-PEACH

Office hours: Monday - Friday, 9 a.m. to noon, 2-5 p.m.

Geographic area: Metropolitan Atlanta

Inspections: Annually

Deposit: A deposit equal to one night's stay is required to confirm reservations.

Payment: Personal check, AE, MC, V.

Established in 1979, this agency covers the geographic area of metropolitan Atlanta (site for the 1996 Olympics), and selected sites around Georgia.

Guests write: *"The carriage house is a lovely, peaceful retreat. I was in Atlanta for a very busy convention, so I particularly appreciated this oasis. The neighborhood was great for walking." (B. Steel)*

"We are absolutely delighted! Great beds, lovely room, good food. But, most of all, very warm, gracious, and real hosts. We have been pampered, welcomed, and made truly comfortable. Thank you!" (L. Driver)

"We originally opted for B&B because all of Atlanta's hotels were booked. We were pleasantly surprised to find that not only was B&B cheaper but it was extremely cozy and pleasant. My wife and I plan to return for a vacation. Our hostess was extremely gracious, helpful and a lot of fun. Overall, I have no complaints and nothing but praise for my host and this organization!" (J. Pazun)

"Our hosts were very gracious. Their home was everything as described and more. I would emphasize how very helpful the staff person was at B&B Atlanta. She not only knew the available inventory, but knew what made each home different and this helped us make a choice." (A. Farley)

B&B Reservation Agencies and Associations

Quail Country Bed & Breakfast Ltd.
1104 Old Monticello Road
Thomasville, GA 31792
(912) 226-7218 or 226-6882

Office hours: Monday - Friday, 9 a.m. - 9 p.m.

Geographic area: Thomasville and Grady County.

Inspections: Annually.

Deposit: A deposit of $25 is required to confirm reservations.

Choose from eight special B&B accommodations in Thomasville and Grady County which include Victorian farmhouses, plantations, and pool guest houses. Thomasville is a winter resort area with excellent recreation and hunting. It's also known as the City of Roses.

Hawaii

Bed & Breakfast Hawaii
P.O. Box 449
Kapaa, HI 96746
(808) 822-7771 or (800) 733-1632
Fax: 808) 822-2723

Office hours: Monday - Saturday, 8:30 a.m. - 4:30 p.m.

Geographic area: All islands in Hawaii.

Inspections: Annually.

Deposit: A deposit of 20% along with 4% excise tax is required to confirm reservations.

Payment: MC, V accepted for deposit only. Balance of payment should be cash.

10% travel agency commission available. A guidebook with 150 host listings is available for $10.00.

Guests write: *"We were given good service on short notice and greatly appreciated their help. The accommodations were very good, beds comfortable, and breakfast excellent." (J. Reid)*

Bed & Breakfast Honolulu (Statewide)
3242 Kaohinani Drive
Honolulu, HI 96817
(808) 595-7533 or (800) 288-4666
Fax: (808) 595-2030

Office hours: Monday - Friday, 8 a.m. to 5 p.m., and Saturday, 8 a.m. to noon.

Geographic area: All islands in Hawaii.

Inspections: Annually.

Deposit: 50% deposit for stays more than 3 days. Full payment is required in advance for stays of three days or less.

Payment: Cash, traveler's check, MC, V.

Car and inter-island air coupons are available at low rates. 10% travel agency commission available.

Indiana

Amish Acres Bed & Breakfast Agency
1600 West Market Street
Nappanee, IN 46550
(219) 773-4188 or (800) 800-4942
Office hours: Weekdays 9 am - 5 pm.

Geographic area: Reservations can be made for twenty bed and breakfast homes throughout Nappanee and some surrounding towns of Elkhart County. This area is convenient to Amtrak service out of Chicago. Most accommodations are in two-story frame houses. Guests may observe a working farm first hand as they stay with Amish, Mennonite, or non-Amish hosts.

Inspections: Annually.

Deposit: Reservations must be accompanied by a $15 deposit.

Payment: MC, V, D, accepted for full payment.

B&B Reservation Agencies and Associations

Kentucky

Kentucky Homes Bed & Breakfast
1507 South Third Street
Louisville, KY 40208
(502) 635-7341

Office hours: 4 p.m. - 8 p.m. each weekday and 9 a.m. - 5 p.m. on Saturdays.

Geographic area: Select from a variety of eighty B&B accommodations throughout Kentucky.

Inspections: Annually.

Deposit: A 25% deposit is required to confirm reservations.

Massachusetts

Bed & Breakfast Associates Bay Colony, Ltd.
P.O. Box 57166, Babson Park
Boston, MA 02157
(617) 449-5302 or (800) 347-5088

Office hours: Monday - Friday, 10 a.m. to 12:30 p.m. and 1:30 - 5 pm.

Geographic area: Reservations may be made for over 170 B&B accommodations in eastern Massachusetts including greater Boston, Cambridge, and the North and South shores.

Inspections: Annually.

Payment: AE, MC, V, Diner, and Carte Blanche.

5% travel agency commission available on bookings of 3 nights or more.

Guests write: *"Peggy was extremely pleasant. On arrival to her brownstone, she greeted us with chilled champagne and a thorough explanation of the best places to visit in Boston. We followed every suggestion and had a fabulous time! The brownstone was lovely. Our room was quite spacious and nicely furnished. Her buffet breakfasts were great. We felt very much at home. We appreciated the thorough and professional manner in which we were treated."* (L. Weinstein)

"Our hostess was a delight. Her hospitality and breakfasts were excellent. She loves people and it shows!" (B. Love)

"Can't wait to return. Very nice hosts, beautiful room. We were extremely comfortable. Breakfasts were great and they were helpful with information about Boston. I would recommend this place highly!" (J. Sullivan)

B&B Reservation Agencies and Associations

Be Our Guest Bed & Breakfast, Ltd.
P.O. Box 1333
Plymouth, MA 02362
(617) 837-9867

Office hours: Daily 10 a.m. - 7 p.m.

Geographic area: Over twenty B&B accommodations are located throughout Boston, Cape Cod, Plymouth, and south of Boston.

Inspections: Annually.

Payment: AE, MC, V.

Bed & Breakfast Cape Cod
P.O Box 341
West Hyannisport, MA 02672-0341
(508) 775-2772, FAX: (508) 775-2884

Office hours: Monday - Friday 8:30 a.m. to 6 p.m. Contact by fax or leave a message on the answering machine at other times.

Geographic area: Select from 90 B&B homes, country inns, and historic homes located on Cape Cod, Nantucket, and Martha's Vineyard islands, Gloucester at Cape Ann and south of Boston at Cohasset, Scituate, and Marshfield.

Deposit: A deposit of 25% of total room rate plus a $5.00 booking charge is required to confirm reservations.

Payment: MC, V, AE accepted for deposit or full payment.

Guests write: *"Our B&B in Scituate Harbor was an unforgettable experience - one that I could replicate neither before nor since. The house is beautiful and wonderfully situated, the hosts congenial and they know just how much to "host" and yet give you lots of privacy. The household cats, Victorian decor, and classical music all work together. The bedrooms are beautifully decorated, the towels plentiful and of good quality. I do hope to return." (A. Tonello)*

"This was a wonderful way to spend our first vacation in four years! The accommodations could not have been nicer, the food could not have been more delicious, the hosts could not have done any more to make guests feel at home." (J. McNair)

"I thank them so much for their advice and guidance in my choice of accommodations. They operate an excellent service with efficiency and expertise!" (M. Merkley)

B&B Reservation Agencies and Associations

Folkstone/Central Massachusetts Bed & Breakfast
Darling Road
Dudley, MA 01571
(508) 943-7118 or (800) 762-2751

Office hours: Monday - Friday, 9 a.m. - 5 p.m. Messages left on the answering machine are returned promptly.

Geographic area: Select from B&B accommodations located throughout central Massachusetts.

Inspections: Annually.

Deposit: A deposit equal to one night's stay is required to confirm reservations.

Payment: AE, MC, V accepted for deposit or full payment.

Mississippi

Lincoln, Ltd. Bed & Breakfast,
Mississippi Reservation Service
P.O. Box 3479
Meridian, MS 39303

(601) 482-5483, FAX: (601) 693-7447

Office hours: Monday - Friday, 9 a.m. - 5 p.m.

Geographic area: Select from a variety of B&Bs located throughout Mississippi, Natchez to Memphis, eastern Louisiana and southwest Alabama.

Inspections: Annually.

Deposit: A deposit equal to one night's stay is required to confirm reservations.

Payment: MC, V, AE accepted for full payment.

Travel agent commission available.

B&B Reservation Agencies and Associations

Missouri

Ozark Mountain Country Bed & Breakfast
P.O. Box 295
Branson, MO 65616
(417) 334-4720 or (800) 695-1546

Office hours: Weekdays 1 - 9 p.m. and weekends, 1 - 5 p.m.

Geographic area: Reservations are available at over eighty B&B homes, guest cottages, suites, and inns throughout southwest Missouri, northeastern Oklahoma, and northwest Arkansas.

Inspections: Annually.

Deposit: Reservations must be accompanied by a 50% deposit.

Payment: MC, V accepted with added fee of 5%.

10% travel agent commission available.

Montana

Bed & Breakfast Western Adventure
P.O. Box 20972
Billings, MT 59104-0972
(406) 259-7993.

Office hours: May through September, weekdays 9 a.m. - 5 p.m. and Saturday 9 a.m. to 1 p.m. Winter hours are weekdays 1 - 5 p.m.

Geographic area: Montana, Wyoming, Black Hills of South Dakota, and northeastern Idaho.

Inspections: Annually.

Deposit: A deposit equal to one night's stay is required to confirm reservations.

Payment: MC, V accepted for payment.

7% travel agency commission available on bookings of at least two nights.

Guests write: *"I'm a business traveler who prefers B&B to hotel/motels. All my comments come not as a vacationer but regarding a place to stay on business. I find B&Bs gearing up for people like me who like comfort and pampering. As a single, professional woman, B&Bs are the answer. There was a lovely selection of rooms to choose from. Hostess was very warm and friendly."* (T. Elliott)

"Karen is a charming hostess. She really makes you feel welcome with wonderful food. One of the nicest B&Bs we've visited!" (P. McPhee)

B&B Reservation Agencies and Associations

"The reservation process was prompt with excellent courtesy, assistance, and directions. Wonderful room and food. The town is lovely and the surroundings give you many things to do. The hostess was very helpful and friendly." (F. Thatcher)

"We always use B&Bs whenever we can and we have used B&B Western Adventure numerous times. We know we can always count on a home which has been inspected and we have always found the hosts most congenial and the accommodations most comfortable." (M. Thorndal)

New York

Abode Bed & Breakfast Ltd.
P.O. Box 20022
New York, NY 10028
(212) 472-2000

Office hours: Weekdays 9 a.m. - 5 p.m. and Saturday 11 a.m. - 2 p.m.

Geographic area: Reservations may be made for over one-hundred B&B accommodations throughout Manhattan, Park Slope, and Brooklyn Heights, New York. Also available are unhosted, fully equipped apartments in owner-occupied brownstones. Guests have total privacy in their own apartment and still enjoy the benefits of having hosts on hand for questions, information, advice, and whatever else they need.

Inspections: Annually.

Deposit: A deposit of approximately 25% of the stay is required to confirm reservations.

Payment: AE is accepted for deposit or full payment.

Restrictions: Minimum stay is two nights.

Guests write: *"I was greeted by a spotlessly clean facility, tastefully decorated, comfortably furnished, a cup of coffee in the waiting, and a dozen roses that lasted during my entire stay. The location was idea. My host offered us a tour - it was a nice and welcoming thing to do." (V. LaFrance)*

B&B Reservation Agencies and Associations

Bed & Breakfast & Books
35 West 92nd Street
New York, NY 10025
(212) 865-8740

Office hours: Weekdays 9:30 a.m. to 5 p.m.

Geographic area: Reservations can be made for over sixty B&B accommodations located throughout Manhattan - Upper West and East sides, Chelsea, Gramercy Park, Greenwich Village, and Soho.

Deposits: A deposit equal to one night's stay is required to confirm reservations.

5% travel agent commission available.

Ohio

Private Lodgings, Inc.
P.O. Box 18590
Cleveland, OH 44118
(216) 249-0400

Office hours: Weekdays 9 a.m. - noon, 3 - 5 p.m. Closed Wednesdays.

Geographic area: Reservations can be made for more than forty B&B homes and inns located throughout the Cleveland metropolitan area.

Inspections: Annually.

Deposit: A deposit of 50% is required to confirm reservations.

Payment: Cash and traveler's checks are accepted for full payment.

B&B Reservation Agencies and Associations

Pennsylvania

Bed & Breakfast Connections
P.O. Box 21
Devon, PA 19333
(215) 687-3565 or (800) 448-3619 (outside Pennsylvania)

Office hours: Monday - Saturday, 9 a.m. to 9 p.m. Phone messages left on the answering machine on Sundays will be returned.

Geographic area: B&Bs are located in Philadelphia, Main Line suburbs, Chestnut Hill, Germantown, Mt. Airy, Valley Forge, Brandywine Valley, Reading, and Amish area.

Inspections: Annually.

Deposits: A deposit equal to one night's stay is required to confirm reservations.

Payment: AE, MC, V accepted for full payment.

10% travel agency commission available.

Bed & Breakfast of Philadelphia
1616 Walnut Street, #1120
Philadelphia, PA 19103
(215) 735-1917 or (800) 220-1917

Office hours: Weekdays 9 a.m. - 6 p.m.

Geographic area: B&Bs are available throughout metropolitan Philadelphia and the surrounding five counties.

Inspections: Annually.

Deposits: A deposit equal to one night's stay or 25% of the total booking is required to confirm reservations.

Payment: AE, MC, V accepted for full payment.

10% travel agency commission available.

B&B Reservation Agencies and Associations

Bed & Breakfast of Southeast Pennsylvania
146 West Philadelphia Avenue
Boyertown, PA 19512
(215) 367-4688

Office hours: Monday - Saturday, 9 a.m. to 9 p.m.

Geographic area: B&Bs are available throughout the southeast area of the state, from Easton in the east, westward through Allentown and Reading, southwest in Lancaster County near the Susquehanna River.

Inspections: Annually.

Deposit: A deposit equal to one night's stay is required to confirm reservations. Rates will include a $5 booking fee and 6% state sales tax.

Payment: V, MC accepted for full payment.

Hershey Bed & Breakfast Reservation Service
P.O. Box 208
Hershey, PA 17033
(717) 533-2928

Office hours: Weekdays 10 a.m. - 4 p.m.

Geographic area: Choose from a variety of B&Bs located throughout the southeastern section of the state. Personalized service is offered in matching guests to just the right bed and breakfast whether the trip is for a family vacation, a farm experience, a long stay when transferring into the area, romantic honeymoons, or for a business retreat in a relaxing setting.

Inspections: Annually.

Deposit: A 25% deposit is required to confirm reservations.

Payment: AE, MC, V accepted for full payment.

5% travel agent commission available.

Rest and Repast Bed & Breakfast Reservation Service
P.O. Box 126
Pine Grove Mills, PA 16868
(814) 238-1484

Office hours: Weekdays and Saturday 8:30 a.m. - 10 a.m. Closed Sundays.

Geographic area: Select from over sixty B&B homes and inns located throughout Central Pennsylvania including the Penn Station area.

Inspections: Annually.

Deposit: A $20-50 deposit per night is required to confirm reservations.

Payment: Cash only.

Guests write: *"My B&B needs have changed dramatically in the 10 years since I left college, yet every year Rest & Repast places me with the perfect host. From my every penny counts years when they saved me $70 off the cheapest hotel room to my years when a crib and a host close to the action counted most, Rest & Repast comes through with flying colors! And the food ... it seems like Center County folks just like to cook. I don't think we've ever had fewer than 3 courses for breakfast. Our hosts have always been eager to please. One woman even had guests sign the tablecloth which she later embroidered."* (D. Painter)

"Our Rest and Repast hosts always prepare salt-free breakfasts for me which are exceptional. On those occasions when we were unable to obtain tickets for a football game, our host is often able to get them for us from some of her many friends. We are always made to feel at home." (B. Sacks)

"We always look forward to our visits. Our hosts are kind and gracious and never fail to make us feel wanted. They go out of their way to think of so many little things to do that make us feel we are truly with friends. No hotel could ever match their warm hospitality." (R. Savin)

"Thanks to Rest and Repast for their part in a perfect weekend... proving again that things rarely satisfy man's soulful needs the way good, caring, loving people can." (N. Clark)

B&B Reservation Agencies and Associations

South Carolina

Historic Charleston Bed & Breakfast
43 Legare Street
Charleston, SC 29401
(803) 722-6606, Fax: (803) 853-7266

Office hours: Weekdays 9:30 a.m. - 5:30 p.m.

Geographic area: Reservations can be made for over sixty private homes and carriage houses in Charleston's Historic District as well as other cities throughout the state.

Inspections: Annually.

Deposits: A deposit equal to one night's stay is required to confirm reservations.

Payment: AE, MC, V accepted for full payment.

Guests write: *"Our son had just returned to Charleston after seven months with the Navy in the Middle East. We were looking for a touch of home for Christmas Eve and Christmas Day and found it! Our hosts placed a small, decorated tree in the living room of the carriage house - a lovely touch which was greatly appreciated."* (B. DeCarolis)

"I'm so glad to recommend this service. Our B&B location was very quiet and private." (B. Barnes)

"The girls and I really enjoyed our stay. Everything was so nice. The breakfasts were delicious and we loved having our own little apartment. We especially enjoyed the little garden and fountain. Charleston is truly one of my favorite cities." (A. Fuller)

Virginia

Guesthouses Bed & Breakfast
P.O. Box 5737
Charlottesville, VA 22905
(804) 979-7264

Office hours: Weekdays noon to 5 p.m.

Geographic area: Select from B&Bs located throughout Charlottesville, Albemarle County, and Nelson County. The variety of B&Bs available includes distinctive private homes and guest cottages.

Inspections: Each inspected annually by Guesthouses and certified by the Virginia Health Department.

Deposits: A 25% deposit is required to confirm reservations. Payment: Cash or personal check.

Member of Virginia B&B Association.

Guests write: *"We loved our hostess and her B&B. A great find! Country charm and her warmth made for a great stay. (B. Messerly)*

"We had a wonderful B&B on 1200 acres. Lovely folks! Marvelous solitude. Fabulous breakfast! I will return - recommend highly!" (B. Markesbery)

"The match between host and guest was perfect! My friend who was in a wheelchair found the house perfectly accessible, even more than her own home. She needed an escape for a few days and this was it. She went into the guest room and you should have seen her face brighten and her whole demeanor change for the better." (J. Brown)

"We have been delighted with the accommodations we've arranged through Guesthouses. We have become friends with both families with whom we've stayed and look forward to many continued years of friendship." (J. Santos)

"Guesthouses arranged our first B&B experience. Because of the warmth and hospitality shared us, I am sure it will not be my last. I would not hesitate a moment to recommend our hosts. My traveling companion, who is an experienced B&B person, agrees with me 100%." (M. Cress)

Anniston

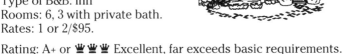

Noble-McCaa-Butler House
1025 Fairmont
Anniston, AL 36201
(205) 236-1791

Type of B&B: Inn
Rooms: 6, 3 with private bath.
Rates: 1 or 2/$95.

Rating: A+ or ♛♛♛ Excellent, far exceeds basic requirements.

Victorian home in the historic district is located 3 miles north of I-20. The entire house with its six guest rooms has been carefully restored to its original Victorian opulence with reproduction wallpapers and fabrics, colors, and period furnishings. Three rooms feature a private bath and the other three rooms offer pedestal sinks and share two and a half baths. Area attractions include Sports Car Museum, Museum of Natural History, and the Women's Army Corp. Full breakfast. Facilities for formal meetings and weddings. Families welcome. Restricted smoking. 1 or 2/$95. AE, MC, V. 10% senior and auto club discounts.

Guests write: *"These are truly excellent hosts and superb innkeepers. We were very pleased with our stay and think this B&B should be a 5-star. I cannot think of a single thing which could have made our stay any more complete." (T. Barnes)*

"Perhaps a stay here is so effective because it is a chance to experience a bit of the elegance and graciousness of the Old South that is popularized in the media but too often neglected in the daily rush of modern times. This inn has provided an environment for our important visiting customers to completely relax and enjoy themselves during their stay in Anniston." (T. Balliett)

Montgomery

Red Bluff Cottage
551 Clay Street
Montgomery, AL 36104
(205) 264-0056

Type of B&B: Small inn.
Rooms: 4 with private bath.
Rates: 1/$48; 2/$55.

Rating: B+ or 👑👑 Good, exceeds basic requirements.

Raised cottage style B&B is located 1 block east of I-65, exit 172, in an area known as Cottage Hill, Montgomery's oldest historic district. The four guest rooms, each with private bath, are at ground level and offer a choice of queen or twin guest beds. The light and airy common rooms are upstairs along with the large front porch with its spacious vista of the Alabama River plain and view of the Alabama State Capitol and downtown. Enjoy the harpsichord in the music room or the collection of good books. Interesting sites nearby include Montgomery's magnificent Shakespeare Festival Theater, Museum of Fine Arts, and the newly expanded zoo. Well-lit off-street parking is available. Full breakfast served. Families welcome. No smoking. 1/$48; 2/$55. Travel agent.

Guests write: *"After visiting the First White House of the Confederacy we mentioned to Anne at Red Bluff Cottage the beautiful white rose we had seen there and that we would like to purchase such a rose plant. Anne contacted the director of the foundation and was told that that particular rose was not available, however, if we would like to get some cuttings we could. We returned to Red Bluff Cottage where Anne had the proper materials to provide a start for the clippings. The hospitality provided was above and beyond even what one comes to expect as southern hospitality. The accommodations are excellent."* (A. James)

Orange Beach

The Original Romar House Bed & Breakfast Inn
23500 Perdido Beach Boulevard
Orange Beach, AL 36561
(205) 981-6156 or (800) 48-ROMAR

Type of B&B: Inn
Rooms: 6 with private bath.
Rates: 1 or 2/$79-100.

Rating: B+ or ♛♛ Good, exceeds basic requirements.

Art Deco style inn built in 1924 is located on the beach side of Highway
182, 4 miles east of Gulf Shores. Period antiques fill the six individually
decorated guest rooms, all with private bath. Stroll along the white, sandy
beach to collect shells, relax in the whirlpool spa or on the deck. Enjoy
the inn's two-seater bicycle for a ride down Perdido Beach Boulevard.
Visit nearby golf courses, nightclubs, seafood restaurants, and local
entertainment. Wine and cheese is served each afternoon in the Purple
Parrot bar. A full breakfast includes "Romar House" grits, homemade
pastries, biscuits, and an egg casserole. Restricted smoking. 1 or 2/$79-
100. MC, V. Travel agent.

Guests write: *"Jackie is a natural who creates a truly comfortable
atmosphere. A rainy period that kept us off the beach gave opportunity to
examine the art deco furnishings and accents that represent the best and
most interesting items from the past." (I. Runkle)*

*"Each room has an original flavor and our four-poster queen-size bed with a
window peeking out to an ocean view was unusually comfortable. The
bathrooms are spotless and modern but retain the historic character of the
inn. The wrap-around porch with deck overlooks the ocean and is
insurpassable in its tranquility and view. And the covered patio area with
cypress swing and Jacuzzi offers extra relaxation. While we knew there was
much to do in the area, we never left the inn except to go to the beach." (L.
Keating)*

*"The house is furnished with old-timey furniture and interesting bric-a-brac
and is situated at the edge of the sandy border along the Gulf beach making
a beach walk and a quick dip in the surf very available." (B. Stone)*

*"On our first morning we were sitting on the deck having a cup of coffee. It
was rather chilly that morning and I had forgotten to bring a jacket. Jackie
loaned me one of hers for the rest of the day. Staying there was like visiting
old friends." (J. Still)*

Anchorage

Arctic Loon B&B
P.O. Box 110333
Anchorage, AK 99511
(907) 345-4935

Type of B&B: B&B home.
Rooms: 3, 1 with private bath.
Rates: 1/$60-70; 2/$75-85.

Rating: A- or ♛♛♛ Excellent, far exceeds basic requirements.

Two-night minimum stay. Contemporary Swedish Long House with bay windows and tongue-in-groove paneling is located 12 miles from the airport and situated high above the city with "million-dollar" panoramic views. Choose from three guest rooms, one with private bath, all decorated with an emphasis on light and open space. One room offers a private entrance, microwave, separate seating area, and a TV with VCR and extensive movie collection. There is a lower level recreation room for guest use with Jacuzzi, sauna, and exercise room. The second-floor music room offers a grand piano. Full breakfast includes fresh fruit, special egg dishes, and regional specialties such as smoked salmon or caribou. 1/$60-70; 2/$75-85. MC, V. 10% senior discount. Travel agent.

Anchorage

Snowline Bed and Breakfast
11101 Snowline Drive
Anchorage, Alaska 99516
(907) 346-1631

Type of B&B: B&B home.
Rooms: 2, 1 with private bath.
Rates: 1 or 2/$50-95.

Rating: A- or ♛♛♛ Excellent, far exceeds basic requirements.

Alpine A-frame home is located in the quiet hillside just 20 minutes from the airport and downtown Anchorage. Two guest rooms are available, one with a king-size bed and shared bath. A second room offers over 500 square feet of living space with a magnificent view, private entrance, queen-size bed and six-person Jacuzzi. Enjoy a panoramic view of Anchorage, Cook Inlet, and Mount McKinley from the living room or sun deck. Chugach State Park, hiking trails, golf course, and the Alaska Zoo are just minutes away. Continental breakfast features homemade pastries and fresh-ground coffee. Families welcome. No smoking. 1 or 2/$50-95. MC, V. Travel agent.

Guests write: *"There was a moose on the beautiful lawn two different nights when we returned to Snowline. Dana and Ed are very pleasant and* informative about the state and city. Breakfasts of homemade goodies were a delicious start for the day." (W. Graham)

"Alaskan hospitality is alive and well at the Snowline B&B. The hosts, Ed and Dana, were friendly and informative. The inn was immaculate and comfortable. A great place to start or finish a trip to Alaska. We did both there." (S. Davison)

"Dana's homemade muffins and sourdough rolls were a wonderful taste treat. Each morning's breakfast was better than the day before. The accommodations were exquisite and had a spectacular view of Anchorage." (J. Evans)

"Very comfortable and attractive. The host's attention to detail and desire to please was evident in every aspect. Mount McKinley presented itself for our viewing pleasure. Wonderful!" (J. Price)

"Our room was enormous and charmingly and comfortably furnished - our own private Jacuzzi and sauna included!" (B. Trueheart)

"They treated me to moose, smoked salmon, homemade muffins, biscuits and lots of coffee and conversation. I took beautiful photos of sunsets and the twinkling lights of Anchorage - all from my room. Ed & Dana had lots of videos and magazines on Anchorage for me to use." (C. Wilde)

Matanuska

Yukon Don's B&B Inn
HC 31, Box 5086
2221 Macabon Circle
Matanuska, AK 99654
(907) 376-7472

Type of B&B: Small inn.
Rooms: 5, 1 with private bath.
Rates: 1/$50; 2/$60; Suite/$70.

Rating: A- or ♛♛♛ Excellent, far exceeds basic requirements.

Historic Alaskan homestead barn with views of the Talkeetna Mountains is now an unique inn located 35 miles north of Anchorage and 4 miles south of Wasilla. Five guest rooms are available, one with private bath. All rooms are spacious, have pleasant decor, and feature a vast collection of Alaskan memorabilia. Enjoy the outdoor hot tub with mountain and lake views or the indoor sauna and exercise room. A large recreation room offers a TV with VCR, pool table and library of books and videos on Alaska. Arrangements can be made for guided tour groups. Continental breakfast. Families welcome. No smoking. 1/$50; 2/$60; Suite/$70. Gold dust, cash, personal checks, or traveler's checks accepted. 10% seniors and business travel discounts.

Phoenix

Westways "Private" Resort Inn
P.O. Box 41624
Phoenix, AZ 85080
(602) 582-3868

Type of B&B: Inn
Rooms: 6, each with private bath.
Rates: 1 or 2/$50-122.

Rating: AA or ♕♕♕ Outstanding.

Contemporary Southwestern Mediterranean style inn has been designed as a mini "private" resort and is located in an executive estate area of Northwest Phoenix, convenient to I-17. Six individually decorated guest rooms are available, each with deluxe private bath, TV, reading area, and fine furnishings. Guests may use the satellite large-screen TV in the leisure room, as well as VCR, table games, stereo, ping-pong table, and a selection of books in the library. Enjoy the diving pool, fitness room, and whirlpool, or borrow ten-speed touring bikes to explore the area. Take advantage of the country club privileges including golf and tennis or just relax in the casual western comfort offered in a private atmosphere. Facilities for meetings, executive retreats, and social functions available. 2/$50-122. AE, MC, V. Senior, auto club, and business travel discounts. Travel agent.

Guests write: *"Westways, and the extraordinary service by the two hosts, has created an ambiance reminiscent of days gone by, when warmth and hospitality were a way of life. An oasis of charm and total escape from stress." (J. Blanco)*

"Heaven forbid you should be like all the other carbon copies. Westways is not for everyone... it's for those who like their vacations to be very special." (D. Kolpin)

"It is always my concern to place my valued clients in a place that I am comfortable in knowing they will get pampered. I have visited this property many times before and have always found it clean and tidy. To me this resort could pass any white glove test." (D. Starkman)

"We have never had the opportunity to experience such hospitality in such a class act atmosphere in our many years of traveling. Our gourmet breakfast daily was more than adequate to carry us through the day until the afternoon in which creative munchies were served. M-mm-good!" (B. Kennedy)

Tucson

The Desert Yankee
1615 North Norton Avenue
Tucson, AZ 85719
(602) 795-8295

Type of B&B: B&B home.
Rooms: 4, each with private bath.
Rates: 1/$65; 2/$75.

Rating: B+ or ♛♛ Good, exceeds basic requirements.

Open September through June. Family residence owned by transplanted Yankees is in a quiet neighborhood two blocks from the University of Arizona, 3 miles from the downtown business district. Four guest rooms each offer a private bath, telephone, and TV. Hosts have an extensive movie collection for guests to enjoy. The home is built around a lovely courtyard with patios, pool, and an abundance of flowers and greenery. Area attractions include Mount Lemon skiing, shopping in Old Mexico, Pima Air Museum, San Xavier Mission, and Desert Museum. Continental breakfast features home-baked pastries. Resident pets. Restricted smoking. 1/$65; 2/$75. Travel agent.

Tucson

Peppertrees Bed & Breakfast
724 East University Boulevard
Tucson, AZ 85719
(602) 622-7167

Type of B&B: B&B home with guest houses.
Rooms: 5, one with shared bath.
Rates: 1/$49-60; 2/$60-65.

Rating: B or ♛♛ Good, exceeds basic requirements.

Victorian home is well-located near the University of Arizona's main entrance. Choose from a guest room in the main house with shared bath or the private guesthouse. Each guesthouse offers two bedrooms, a full bath, living room with TV, dining room, and full kitchen with washer/dryer. This is a convenient location within walking distance to the university, shops, fine restaurants, movies, the Historic District, and concerts. Full breakfast and afternoon tea served daily by experienced hostess who has written a cookbook. Facilities for meetings and small functions. 1/$49-60; 2/$60-65. Travel agent.

Eureka Springs

Singleton House B&B
11 Singleton
Eureka Springs, AR 72632
(501) 253-9111

Type of B&B: Small inn.
Rooms: 4, each with private bath.
Rates: $65-85.

Rating: A or ♛♛♛ Excellent, far exceeds basic requirements.

1890's era Victorian inn is located in the Historic District of this city known as an artist's colony. Each of the four light and airy guest rooms have private baths. The inn is decorated with folk art, antiques, and eclectic treasures. Walk one block down wooded footpath or ride the trolley to shops and cafes and abundance of galleries. Area attractions include Passion Play, Dinner Train, and Bath House. Enjoy a full breakfast on the balcony overlooking woods, wildflower garden, and goldfish pond. $65-85. AE, MC, V. Travel agent.

Hardy

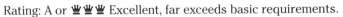

Olde Stonehouse
511 Main Street
Hardy, AR 72542
(501) 856-2983

Type of B&B: Small inn
Rooms: 5, each with private bath.
Rates: 1/$50; 2/$55.

Rating: B+ or ♛♛ Good, exceeds basic requirements.

Native stone home built in the 1920s is in a historical railroad town set on the Spring River. The inn is located just a block from the unique shops of Old Hardy Town and across the street from the river. Choose from five individually decorated rooms, each with private bath, queen-size bed, ceiling fan, air conditioning, and period antiques. Curl up on one of the wicker chairs or large rockers found on the two porches to enjoy a good book or to people watch. Walk to antique and gift shops in Old Hardy Town. Take an easy stroll along the river or visit nearby Mammoth Spring, Grand Gulf State Park, Cherokee Village, country music theaters and Indian cultural museum. Nearby recreation includes canoeing, horseback riding and golf. Full breakfast features homemade granola, strawberry butter, and specialty breads and is served on a lace tablecloth set with Grandma's chinaware and silver. Restricted smoking. 1/$50; 2/$55. MC, V. 10% senior, business, and auto club discount. Travel agent.

Guests write: *"I had a wonderful time. The home is truly lovely, everything was so clean and decorated so lovely, we truly felt at home here. The hostess really went out of her way to leave dessert and coffee for us each night and the food was delicious!" (L. Hall)*

"The breakfast served was wonderful and elegant. We had homebaked bread, German pancakes, cereal, juice, fresh fruit - best I've ever had." (J. Reagan)

"All I can say is that we've been twice and already are talking about when we are going again! They say there is no place like home but this would have to be as close as you can get." (J. Clifton)

"The history and character of the house and furnishings, the delicious food, and the beauty of the Ozarks were only surpassed by the gracious hospitality of our hosts." (S. Payne)

Mountain View

The Inn at Mountain View
P.O. Box 812, Washington Street
Mountain View, AR 72560
(501) 269-4200 or (800) 535-1301

Type of B&B: Inn.
Rooms: Ten, each with private bath.
Rates: 1/$39; 2/$52-85.

Rating: A- or ♥♥♥ Excellent, far exceeds basic requirements.

Rambling 1886 Victorian inn is located a half block from the village square and has been serving up Southern-style hospitality for one-hundred years. Ten guest suites are available, each with private bath, air conditioning, ceiling fan, period antiques, hand-made quilts, and embroidered linens. This town is known as the world capital of folk music and houses the National Folk Center nearby. Other attractions include a variety of local antique and craft shops, Blanchard Springs Caverns in the Ozark National Forest, White River trout fishing, and float trips down the Buffalo River. Full breakfast specialties may include home-made biscuits with sausage gravy or Belgian waffles. Families welcome. No smoking. 1/$39; 2/$52-85. V, AE, MC. Travel agent.

Alameda

Garratt Mansion
900 Union Street
Alameda, CA 94501
(510) 521-4779

Type of B&B: Inn.
Rooms: 6, 3 with private bath.
Rates: 1/$60-100; 2/$70-120.

Rating: A- or ♛♛♛ Excellent, far exceeds basic requirements.

Victorian inn built in the Colonial Revival style was the home of a turn-of-the-century industrialist and is located just 15 miles east of San Francisco. Choose from six distinctive guest rooms, three of which offer a private bath. Enjoy the local examples of fine architecture or travel to nearby San Francisco, Berkeley, or the beach. Full breakfast specialties of the inn include treats such as "Dutch babies" which are low-fat giant popovers filled with fresh fruit as well as fresh squeezed juice and fresh ground coffee. All food is prepared with an accent on health using fresh herbs grown on the property and low-fat or non-fat dishes except the delicious fresh baked chocolate chip cookies served each afternoon! Wedding and meeting facilities available. Families welcome. Smoking outside only. 1/$60-100; 2/$70-120. AE, MC, V. Business traveler discount. Travel agent.

Aptos

Bayview Hotel B&B Inn
8041 Soquel Drive
Aptos, CA 95003
(408) 688-8654

Type of B&B: Country inn with restaurant.
Rooms: 7, each with private bath.
Rates: 1/$75-100; 2/$80-115.

Rating: B or ♛♛ Good, exceeds basic requirements.

Historic Victorian inn built in 1878 is a landmark building located in Aptos Village, less than a mile from the Seacliff exit off Route 1, 35 miles south of San Jose. Choose from seven guest rooms, each offering a private bath and antique furnishings. Area attractions include antique shops, fine restaurants, state beaches, redwood parks, hiking and bicycle trails, golf, and tennis. Buffet-style breakfast includes fresh squeezed juice, seasonal fruit, egg dish, muesli, pastries, and gourmet coffee. Restaurant on premises. No smoking. 1/$75-100; 2/$80-115. MC, V. Travel agent.

Aptos

Mangels House
570 Aptos Creek Road
P.O. Box 302
Aptos, CA 95001
(408) 688-7982

Type of B&B: Inn.
Rooms: 5, 3 with private bath.
Rates: 1 or 2/$89-115.

Rating: B+ or ♕♕ Good, exceeds basic requirements.

Four acres of orchards and woodlands near Monterey Bay's sailing and surfing is the setting for this Southern-style Colonial inn built circa 1880. Five guest rooms are available, three with private bath. This location is ideal as a retreat from city life and is known for the local summer music and theater festivals. Excellent restaurants can be found nearby as well as the North Monterey Bay's forests and beaches. Full breakfast and an evening sherry are offered. Restricted smoking. 1 or 2/$89-115. MC, V. Travel agent.

Guests write: *"We arrived in the rain and were right away offered tea which appeared on a teacart with little tarts fresh out of the oven - plus a most welcome decanter of Dubonnet. The beauty of the place and the warmth of the host and hostess made a cozy evening in the flooding storm." (G. Wheeler)*

"Claus Mangel's soul may grace this home but the hosts are its heart. Because of Mr. Mangel, I was able to give my wife the tranquility of a redwood forest, but the hosts provided the lovely garden to walk through. Mr. Mangel constructed the high ceilings, redwood floor and grand fireplace, but it was the hosts who lit the hearth whenever we returned from an outing. I mentioned my wife's birthday, then magically she found three dozen roses in our room with a card signed by me. Was it my hosts or the Mangel's ghost that pulled that one off?" (C. Accardi)

Arnold

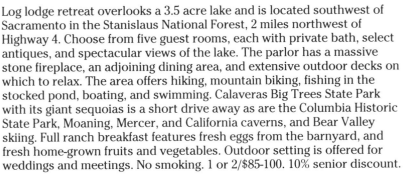

Lodge at Manuel Mill
1573 White Pines Road
Arnold, CA 95223
(209) 795-2622 or (209) 795-3935

Type of B&B: Small lodge.
Rooms: 5, each with private bath.
Rates: 1 or 2/$85-100.

Rating: A- or ♛♛♛ Excellent, far exceeds basic requirements.

Log lodge retreat overlooks a 3.5 acre lake and is located southwest of Sacramento in the Stanislaus National Forest, 2 miles northwest of Highway 4. Choose from five guest rooms, each with private bath, select antiques, and spectacular views of the lake. The parlor has a massive stone fireplace, an adjoining dining area, and extensive outdoor decks on which to relax. The area offers hiking, mountain biking, fishing in the stocked pond, boating, and swimming. Calaveras Big Trees State Park with its giant sequoias is a short drive away as are the Columbia Historic State Park, Moaning, Mercer, and California caverns, and Bear Valley skiing. Full ranch breakfast features fresh eggs from the barnyard, and fresh home-grown fruits and vegetables. Outdoor setting is offered for weddings and meetings. No smoking. 1 or 2/$85-100. 10% senior discount.

Guests write: *"The natural splendor and beauty of the property was breathtaking with its towering green pines as far as the eye could see and running brook next to the lodge. Our guest room was charming with its lace curtains, wood floors and four-poster canopy bed." (J. Horist)*

Baywood Park

Baywood Bed & Breakfast Inn
1370 2nd Street
Baywood Park, CA 93402
(805) 528-8888

Type of B&B: Inn.
Rooms: 15 with private bath.
Rates: 1 or 2/$80-140.

Rating: A or ♛♛♛ Excellent, far exceeds basic requirements.

Newly constructed contemporary inn sits on Morro Bay overlooking the coastal mountains near the San Luis Obispo area of Southern California. Fifteen guest rooms are available. Each offers a private bath, queen-size bed, sitting area, wood-burning fireplace, and kitchenette. Eleven rooms offer a bay view. Visit nearby San Luis Obispo, Hearst Castle, and

Montano De Oro Park. Continental breakfast. Families welcome. Wheelchair access. No smoking. 1 or 2/$80-140.

Guests write: *"Our room, the Appalachian, was beautiful. I rarely drink coffee but I have dreams of theirs and their absolutely wonderful croissants. And best of all there was no TV which "forced" us to go out and enjoy their beautiful surroundings. Everything was great, great, great!"* (B. Kudlo)

"Our unique room was decorated beautifully and was both cozy and clean. We loved the big canopy bed and ocean view. We had dinner delivered both nights so that we could eat at our table by the fireplace. I recommend it to anyone wanting a quiet romantic retreat." (S. Nuttall)

"We especially enjoyed the evening wine and cheese and room tour. Our room was just lovely and very comfortable." (L. Painter)

"All rooms are uniquely decorated. Our favorite is the Manhattan Suite with its cool mauve, gray, and white decor. A few feet out the front door is the bay and the block-long business district is filled with wonderful shops and outstanding restaurants. We can arrive on a Friday night, park our car and not drive again until Sunday when we head for home." (S. Baldwin)

Benicia

Captain Dillingham's Inn
145 East "D" Street
Benicia, CA 94510
(707) 746-7164 or in California
only, (800) 544-2278

Type of B&B: Inn.
Rooms: 9 rooms and 1 suite,
each with private bath.
Rates: 2/$70-125.

Rating: B+ or ♛♛ Good, exceeds basic requirements.

Cape Cod-style inn is located 32 miles northeast of San Francisco off I-80 and surrounded by an English country garden and redwood decks. Choose from nine antique-filled guest rooms and one suite. Each has a private bath, color TV, and beverage cooler. Eight rooms offer Jacuzzi tubs and one features a wood-burning fireplace. Walk one block to marina, restaurants, and specialty shops. Abundant hot-and-cold buffet breakfast served daily and a snack/beverage tray is provided in each room. The grounds are ideal for garden weddings, small meetings and other events. Wheelchair access. 2/$70-125. AE, MC, V. Travel agent.

Berkeley

Elmwood House
2609 College Avenue
Berkeley, CA 94704
(510) 540-5123

Type of B&B: B&B home.
Rooms: 4, 2 with private bath.
Rates: 1/$55-75; 2/$65-85.

Rating: B or ♕♕ Good, exceeds basic requirements.

Redwood home built in 1902 is located near the fashionable Elmwood shopping district and Berkeley campus of the University of California. Choose from four guest rooms, each with private telephone and two with a private bath. Walk to an eclectic collection of ethnic restaurants, specialty shops, and evening entertainment areas. Public transit is available right nearby to San Francisco and all Bay Area attractions. Enjoy nearby golf, tennis, swimming, hiking, and bicycling. Continental breakfast. Facilities for small weddings and meetings. No smoking. 1/$55-75; 2/$65-85.

Big Bear Lake

The Knickerbocker Mansion
869 South Knickerbocker
Big Bear Lake, CA 92315
(714) 866-8221

Type of B&B: Inn.
Rooms: 10, 5 with private bath.
Rates: 1/$75-85; 2/$95-165.

Rating: A or ♕♕♕ Excellent, far exceeds basic requirements.

Turn-of-the-century, four-story log mansion is surrounded by the privacy of a heavily wooded national forest and is located just off Highway 18 in Big Bear Village. Ten rooms are offered in the Rainbow Sun Lodge as well as in the main house. Four rooms offer a private bath. A tree-top honeymoon suite with lake view and private spa tub is available for special occasions. Relax in front of the double native-stone fireplace or on the inn's redwood deck with spa. Area attractions include hiking, horseback riding, all water sports, snow skiing, and mountain biking. Full breakfast. Garden forest setting is ideal for weddings. Families welcome. Restricted smoking. 1/$75-85; 2/$95-165. MC, V. Travel agent.

Bridgeport

The Cain House
11 Main Street
Bridgeport, CA 93517
(619) 932-7040 or (800) 433-CAIN

Type of B&B: Small inn
Rooms: 6, each with private bath.
Rates: 1 or 2/$79-130.

Rating: A or ♛♛♛ Excellent, far exceeds basic requirements.

Historic home built in the 1930's is located off Route 182 in the Eastern
Sierra Mountains near the California/Nevada border. Each of the six guest
rooms with private bath has been restored and features wicker, white
washed pine, oak, and other antique furnishings. Enjoy complimentary
wine and cheese in front of the fireplace in the parlor or watch the beautiful
sunsets over the Eastern Sierra Mountains. Area attractions include fishing,
hunting, and skiing. Yosemite, Bodie Ghost Town, and Mammoth
Mountains are located nearby. A full country breakfast is offered. Families
welcome. No smoking. 1 or 2/$79-130. AE, MC, V. Travel agent.

Carmel

Vagabond House Inn
4th and Dolores
Carmel, CA 93921
(408) 624-7738 or (800) 262-1262

Type of B&B: Large inn.
Rooms: 11, each with private bath.
Rates: 1 or 2/$79-135.

Rating: B or ♛♛ Good, exceeds basic requirements.

Half-timbered English Tudor inn with cottages is situated in the heart of
Carmel Village and has convenient off-street parking for guests. Each of
eleven suites is built around a garden courtyard and offers a private bath,
fireplace, and separate entrance. Several rooms have a theme decor such
as nautical or English hunt scenes. A small central parlor and registration
area offers an interesting collection of British lead soldiers and a large
selection of books. Walk to many unique shops, well-known art galleries,
and fine restaurants. Interesting sites nearby include Carmel Beach, 17
Mile Drive, Pebble Beach, Monterey Bay Aquarium, and Big Sur.
Continental breakfast includes specialty breads and fresh fruit and is
brought to each suite on a large tray. 1 or 2/$79-135. AE, MC, V. Travel
agent.

Davenport

New Davenport B&B Inn
31 Davenport Avenue
Davenport, CA 95017
(408) 425-1818 or 426-4122

Type of B&B: Inn.
Rooms: 12, each with private bath.
Rates: 1 or 2/$55-105.

Rating: B or ♛♛ Good, exceeds basic requirements.

The New Davenport Cash Store and Restaurant is located halfway between San Francisco and Carmel on Coast Highway 1. Twelve guest rooms are available on the second floor of the main building or in the adjacent guest house. Each room offers a private bath and is furnished with antiques, ethnic treasures, collectibles, and local arts and crafts. Several rooms above the Cash Store have ocean views. The store on the main level offers a large variety of folk art, textiles, pottery, and jewelry. Area attractions include a secluded local beach, state redwood parks for hiking and picnics, seasonal whale watching, and elephant seal tours at Nuevo State Reserve. Full breakfast. No smoking. 1 or 2/$55-105. AE, MC, V.

Eureka

Old Town Bed & Breakfast Inn
1521 Third Street
Eureka, CA 95501
(707) 445-3951

Type of B&B: Inn.
Rooms: 5, 3 with private bath.
Rates: 1/$60-95; 2/$75-105.

Rating: B+ or ♛♛ Good, exceeds basic requirements.

Greek Revival Italianate built in 1871 is on a quiet residential street in the heart of Eureka's Old Town, a city located on the Northern California coast, 280 miles north of San Francisco on Highway 101. Choose from five guest rooms, three with private bath. The Maxfield Parrish room features Maxfield Parrish artwork and oak antiques. Gerri's room is quite spacious and features a collection of stuffed animals, king-size bed, and private bath with shower. The decor throughout each room combines whimsy with good fun which is evident by the Teddy Bears on each bed and rubber duckies by the bathtubs. Visit the nearby Redwood National Park, King Range Wilderness, and other Pacific Coast attractions. Full breakfast. No smoking. 1/$60-95; 2/$75-105. MC, V. Business traveler discount. Travel agent.

Guests write: *"Dianne helps Jeff return to his childhood with his favorite breakfast of "Green Eggs and Ham" and Leigh serves it like a character right out of Dr. Seuss. It's one of the high points of our visits." (P. Beardsley)*

"How to put it in a nutshell? We can't get over how the hominess feels like Grandma's. But there's something else - a touch of eccentricity that plays a big part in this B&B. We enjoyed everything from Vincent van Bear to the rose petals in the toilet. If Grandma ever could've cut loose, this is the way she would have lived." (N. Jackson)

"Every day the most delicious truffles would appear on the dresser. Made the whole room smell yummy! Lots of stuffed bears lounging on the bed and a huge stack of country magazines to read. The location is within walking distance to the beach and downtown restaurants. We go for the famous kinetic sculpture race and the contestants pedal by in front of the B&B." (A. Lehman)

"We drove up in our '56 T-Bird. It was raining heavily and the innkeepers were kind enough to garage our car so the leaks yet to be fixed in its restoration wouldn't destroy the interior. We've never had such first-class treatment!" (A. Richards)

"On our last visit they arranged for a guided tour of Old Town Eureka. We saw places that aren't usually available to visitors - or even locals!" (R. Simonds)

Ferndale

Shaw House
703 Main Street, P.O. Box 1125
Ferndale, CA 95536
(707) 786-9958

Type of B&B: Inn
Rooms: 6, 4 with private bath.
Rates: 1 or 2/$65-125.

Rating: A or ♛♛♛ Excellent, far exceeds basic requirements.

Gabled Gothic inn with jutting gables, bay windows, and several balconies was built in 1854. The property is listed on the National Register of Historic Places and is situated on a one-acre landscaped lot in the village. Choose from six guest rooms, four with private baths. All feature flowered wallpaper, quilted bedspreads, and fresh flowers. Relax on a secluded deck overlooking the creek or explore the beautiful gardens. Walk to village antique shops, galleries and restaurants. Area attractions include Avenue of the Giants, Pacific Ocean, Humboldt Bay, redwood forests, and wilderness hikes. Homemade continental breakfast. No smoking. 1 or 2/$65-125. AE, MC, V. Travel agent.

Fort Bragg

Avalon House
561 Stewart
Fort Bragg, CA 95437
(707) 964-5555

Type of B&B: Small inn.
Rooms: 6, each with private bath.
Rates: 1/$70-115; 2/$80-125.

Rating: B+ or ♛♛ Good, exceeds basic requirements.

Restored California craftsman-style home is found on the coast of Mendocino County, 3.5 hours north of San Francisco via Highway 101, 128, and 1. Six guest rooms are available, each with a private bath, posturepedic bed, antique furnishings, individual temperature controls, and thick towels. Walk one block to the Skunk Train station. Nearby activities include hiking, fishing, biking, scenic touring, shopping, and fine dining. Full breakfast includes homemade breads, omelettes, and pancakes. Small wedding facilities available. Families welcome. No smoking. 1/$70-115; 2/$80-125. AE, MC, V. Travel agent.

Fort Bragg

Grey Whale Inn
615 North Main Street
Fort Bragg, CA 95437
(707) 964-0640 or (800) 382-7244

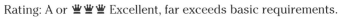

Type of B&B: Inn
Rooms: 14, each with private bath.
Rates: 1/$55-130; 2/$75-150.

Rating: A or ♛♛♛ Excellent, far exceeds basic requirements.

The Grey Whale Inn is a large Colonial Revival structure built in 1915 and is located 160 miles northwest of San Francisco on Highway 1. There are fourteen individually decorated guest rooms. Each offers a private bath and several have ocean views. There is a recreation room on the lower floor with billiards and TV or relax in the main floor parlor with an interesting collection of books. The famous Skunk Train depot is two blocks from the inn. Other area attractions include beaches, restaurants, and specialty shops as well as the nearby redwood forest. Full breakfast includes a special blend of coffee and a sampling of the owner's many freshly baked breakfast breads or coffee cakes. Facilities available for meetings and social functions. 1/$55-130; 2/$75-150 with seasonal discounts available. AE, MC, V. Travel agent.

Guests write: *"The breakfast was perfect, not too hearty - not too light for starting a full-day of business. The buffet style was relaxed and convenient since my day started very early. The staff took very clear and concise phone messages for me, even after 5:00 p.m."* (R. Middleton)

"As career people we need to bring the romance back into our marriage. Our stay at the Grey Whale Inn met our expectations and more! We departed feeling the same way when we returned from our honeymoon." (M. Harmon)

Fort Bragg

Noyo River Lodge
500 Casa del Noyo Drive
Fort Bragg, CA 95437
(707) 964-8045 or (800) 628-1126.

Type of B&B: Inn.
Rooms: 13 with private bath.
Rates: 1 or 2/$75-125.

Rating: B+ or ♛♛ Good, exceeds basic requirements.

Craftsman style lodge sits on two acres overlooking the Noyo Harbor and is located north of San Francisco off Highways 101 and 20 . The main lodge offers seven individually decorated guest rooms with private bath. Special features of some rooms include river views, fireplaces, skylights, and queen-size beds. A newly constructed building nearby offers six new suites, each with private bath, panoramic view of the ocean, private deck, oversized bathtub, and step-down sitting area. At the main lodge there's a multi-level deck with views of ships passing in the harbor. Nearby activities include hiking trails at the state park, charter fishing boats, kayaking, whale watching, and horseback riding on the beach. Continental breakfast and evening wine and cheese served at the main lodge. Facilities for weddings. Families welcome. 1 or 2/$75-125. MC. V. Travel agent.

Guests write: *"The only B&B I've ever felt at home in! We enjoyed sitting by the window in Room #5 watching the boats go by as well as the wildlife activity. The river painted a new scene with every passing moment. We enjoyed feeding the harbor seals fish from the pier outside the lodge and went whale watching on the Tally Hoe."* (D. Fahey)

"What a lovely place for lessons in stress reduction! Everything was perfect down to the last little wonderful details. We'll definitely be back for a longer stay. We'd come back just for the tub, come to think about it!" (L. Ranck)

"We thought England had all the great B&Bs - so glad to find out otherwise." (B. Booth)

"There once was a couple named Ryan, who from work stress thought they were dying. Then they played Rub-a-dub in the big Noyo tub and can now go back home while still smiling!" (K. Ryan)

"Same room, same couple, three years later. It's still just as great as it was then. What a place!" (J. Furco)

Idyllwild

Strawberry Creek Inn
P.O. Box 1818, 26370 Highway 243
Idyllwild, CA 92349
(714) 659-3202

Type of B&B: Inn.
Rooms: 9, each with private bath.
Rates: 1 or 2/$82-125.

Rating: A- or ♛♛♛ Excellent, far exceeds basic requirements.

Strawberry Creek Inn is a mountain inn surrounded by pine and oak forests and is located near the Palm Springs area of Southern California, 26 miles south of I-10. Nine individually decorated guest rooms are available, each with a private bath; four feature fireplaces. A private cottage is also available which can sleep 2-4 people and offers a fireplace, kitchen, and whirlpool tub. Relax in front of the fireplace in the spacious living room and enjoy breakfast in the glassed-in porch. Miles of hiking trails surround the inn offering hikers ample opportunity for enjoying the mountain setting. Nearby attractions include Idyllwild School of Music and Arts as well as quaint shops and restaurants. Full breakfast included. Meeting facilities. No smoking. 1 or 2/$82-125. MC, V.

Laguna Beach

Eiler's Inn
741 South Coast Highway
Laguna Beach CA 92651
(714) 494-3004

Type of B&B: Inn.
Rooms: 11, plus 1 suite, each with private bath.
Rates: 1/$80-165; 2/$85-170.

Rating: B+ or ♛♛ Good, exceeds basic requirements.

Eiler's Inn is located near the beach in the heart of this city which is south of Los Angeles off Highway 1. The New Orleans style architecture features eleven guest rooms and one suite, each with private bath and individual furnishings. Special touches include antiques, unusual linens, fresh flowers, fruit, and candies. Laguna Beach is famous as an art colony and has many galleries to explore. Full gourmet breakfast. Sun tea and coffee are available all day and wine and cheese each evening in the flower-scented brick courtyard with bubbling fountain. Families welcome. 1/$80-165; 2/$85-170. AE, MC, V. Travel agent.

Lake Arrowhead

Saddleback Inn/Arrowhead
P.O. Box 1890
300 South State Highway 173
Lake Arrowhead, CA 92352
(714) 336-3571 or (800) 858-3334

Type of B&B: Inn.
Rooms: 34 rooms, suites, or cottages with private bath.
Rates: 1 or 2/$110-165.

Rating: A- or ♛♛♛ Excellent, far exceeds basic requirements.

Saddleback Inn was built in 1919 and is located in the mountains near routes 173 and 189, 90 miles west of Los Angeles. Thirty-four guest rooms and cottages are spread over several buildings. Each room features private whirlpool bath, fireplace, private phone, TV, heated towel rack, and refrigerator. Several rooms have been decorated around themes reminiscent of the many famous visitors who have frequented the inn such as Charles Lindbergh and Howard Hughes. This is a year-round recreation area which offers water sports, fishing, ice skating, horseback riding, hiking, and skiing. Continental breakfast. Meeting facilities. Wheelchair access. 1 or 2/$110-165. AE, MC, V. Travel agent.

Malibu

Malibu Country Inn
6506 Westward Beach Road
Malibu, CA 90265
(213) 457-9622

Type of B&B: Inn.
Rooms: 16 rooms or suites with private bath.
Rates: 1 or 2/$95-200.

Rating: B or ♛♛ Good, exceeds basic requirements.

Secluded Cape Cod style country inn is situated on three acres of gardens near the Pacific Coast, 30 miles north of Los Angeles. Choose from sixteen guest rooms or suites, each with individual decor, private bath and deck,

TV, phone, fruit basket, fresh flowers, and refrigerator. Take a short walk to a white sand beach or enjoy area attractions including whale-watching, hiking, fine restaurants, J. Paul Getty Museum, and Pepperdine University. Full breakfast and a welcome snack basket included. Families welcome. Facilities available for meetings and social functions. 1 or 2/$95-200. All major credit cards accepted. Travel agent.

Murphys

Dunbar House, 1880
P.O. Box 1375, 271 Jones Street
Murphys, CA 95247
(209) 728-2897

Type of B&B: Inn.
Rooms: 4 with private bath.
Rates: 1/$90; 2/$95.

Rating: A or ♛♛♛ Excellent, far exceeds basic requirements.

Italianate-style home built in 1880 is located southwest of Sacramento, just 8 miles east of Angel's Camp on Highway 4. All four guest rooms offer a private bath and are decorated with antiques, lace, down comforters, and offer wood-burning stoves and central air conditioning. Relax on the wide porches or in front of the fire in the parlor. Calaveras Big Trees State Park offers outdoor activities such as hiking, fishing, and skiing. Explore local wineries, historic towns, and caverns. Full breakfast includes crab cheese delight, fruit kuchen, muffins, and fresh fruit. Restricted smoking. 1/$90; 2/$95. V, MC. Travel agent.

Guests write: *"The atmosphere is warm and comfortable, the breakfasts were superb. I especially enjoyed the view from our windows. My husband and I strolled the garden, sat on the swing under a tree and rocked, and read on the porch. Leisure time like we had here is very precious to us." (L Prinvale)*

"Leaving the cold and fog of the valley behind, we came into sunshine and the warmth of Dunbar House hospitality. The is the perfect place to celebrate 30 years of marriage! If you think B&B stands for bed and breakfast, then you haven't stayed at Dunbar House long enough. We know that B&B stands for Bob and Barbara." (E. Moore)

"My favorite memories will be curling up in the chair by the fire with my book as the rain poured down, the wonderful music playing in the background, and all the yummy smells coming out of the kitchen." (C. Rucker)

"Eating the gourmet breakfasts in the garden is a wonderful start to each day. Also enjoyed reading for an hour in the garden at the end of a busy day of sightseeing - so relaxing!" (P. Schuck)

"Everything from the down comforter to the large claw-foot tub filled with

bubbles was thoroughly enjoyed. The food was downright delicious."
(D. Anderson)

"The porch outside our room is one of my favorite parts of this inn. Sitting out there in the late afternoon with a glass of the local wine and the wonderful appetizers, reading, playing checkers, or just visiting with your spouse is such a relaxing and wonderful treat! We've stayed in more elaborate places, but not many with such a warm comfortable feeling." (P. Schaller)

Napa

Hennessey House Bed & Breakfast Inn
1727 Main Street
Napa, CA 94559
(707) 226-3774, Fax: (707) 226-2975.

Type of B&B: Inn
Rooms: 10, 9 with private bath.
Rates: 1 or 2/$85-150.

Rating: B+ or ♛♛ Good, exceeds basic requirements.

Queen Anne Victorian inn is listed on the National Register of Historic Places and located in California's famous wine country, 50 miles northeast of San Francisco. Choose from ten guest rooms which offer contemporary comfort blended with 1890's style. Nine of the rooms have a private bath and several feature working fireplaces, claw-foot tubs or whirlpool baths. Relax in the parlor with its cozy seating and varied selection of books and games. A guest sauna is available on the back porch and there are rental bicycles for touring the area. Walk to the famous Napa Valley Wine Train. Other area attractions include balloon rides, mud baths, golf, tennis, and winery touring. Full breakfast includes a hot entree and is served in either the guest rooms or a separate dining room. Small wedding and meeting facilities available. Restricted smoking. 1 or 2/$85-150. MC. V. 10% senior discount. Travel agent.

Guests write: *"Breakfasts were superb in variety, quality, well-garnished, and presented and there was attention to personal preferences and dietary needs. Our room was large, well-maintained, and clean. We liked the period furnishings, skylight, fireplace, large Jacuzzi tub, tile floor, twin sinks, and fireplace. The gardens, well-lit staircases and parking areas, sauna, common room, and Heritage House added to the charm and pleasure of our stay and we appreciated the chance to use the bicycles." (B. Dancik)*

"Our room was tastefully decorated. The vanity in the bathroom was an old sideboard transformed into a vanity with two sinks. The location was perfect for visiting the wineries. The hostess was very willing to make a special breakfast dish for me which I had not informed her of until my arrival." (R. Faulkner)

Napa

La Belle Epoque
1386 Calistoga Avenue
Napa, CA 94559
(707) 257-2161

Type of B&B: Inn.
Rooms: 6 with private bath.
Rates: 1 or 2/$95-135.

Rating: A or ♟♟♟ Excellent, far exceeds basic requirements.

Queen Anne Victorian inn built in 1893 is located in the Historic District near the town center, just off Route 29. Choose from six guest rooms, each with private bath and period furnishings. The home is a fine example of Victorian architecture and features multi-gabled dormers, high-hipped roof, decorative carvings, and original stained-glass windows. The inn boasts a wine tasting room and cellar. Area attractions include wine tasting, hot air ballooning, mud and mineral baths, boutiques, gourmet restaurants, and Napa Valley Wine Train. Full breakfast. No smoking. Facilities available for small meetings and social functions. 1 or 2/$95-135. MC, V. 10% business travel and senior discounts. Travel agent.

Guests write: *"Thank you for making our honeymoon just that bit more special. The room was great, the food marvelous, and the wine and appetizers the best yet."* (L. Buehler)

"Breakfasts were delicious and unique. The freshly ground coffee was great! The wine tasting in the evening was a nice way to unwind before dinner. Thank you for the ride to and from the Wine Train and also for loaning us your umbrella. It was the extra special care that made our stay a truly wonderful experience." (L. Bina)

Newport Beach

Portofino Beach Hotel
2306 West Oceanfront
Newport Beach, CA 92663
(714) 673-7030

Type of B&B: Inn.
Rooms: 15 with private bath.
Rates: 1 or 2/$85-235.

Rating: A+ or ♛♛♛ Excellent, far exceeds basic requirements.

Portofino Beach Hotel is on the oceanfront and boardwalk of this fashionable beach town which is located just south of Los Angeles and fifteen minutes from the Orange County Airport. Fifteen guest rooms or suites are available. Each offers telephone, TV, private bath, and individual decor featuring lovely fabrics and antiques. Several rooms include marble baths with Jacuzzis, private sun decks, and fireplaces. Beach chairs and towels are available for a day on the beach. Walk the boardwalk to visit nearby art galleries, bookstores, boutiques, and historical sites. Disneyland is a short thirty minute drive and sailing, golf, and tennis are available nearby. Continental breakfast includes fresh fruit, yogurt, and croissants. Facilities are available for meetings and weddings. 1 or 2/$85-235. AE, MC, V. Travel agent.

Pacific Grove

Gatehouse Inn
225 Central Avenue
Pacific Grove, CA 93950
(408) 649-1881 (reservations only)
or (408) 649-8436

Type of B&B: Small inn.
Rooms: 8, each with private bath.
Rates: 1 or 2/$95-170.

Rating: A- or ♛♛♛ Excellent, far exceeds basic requirements.

Italianate Victorian home built in 1884 has been completely restored and is located off Highway 1 at the Pacific Grove/Pebble Beach exit. Each guest room features reproduction antiques, down comforters, and private bath. Special features of some rooms include a fireplace, stunning ocean view, and claw foot tub. Enjoy afternoon hors d'oeuvres with wine while taking in the ocean view. Walk to Cannery Row or to visit the sea otters at play at Asilomar Beach. Other area attractions include Monterey Bay Aquarium, Pebble Beach Golf Club, Del Monte Forest, and Old Fisherman's Wharf. A full breakfast is offered with fresh baked goods and hot entrees. Garden facilities are available for small meetings or social functions. Wheelchair access. Restricted smoking. 1 or 2/$95-170. AE, MC, V. Travel agent.

Guests write: *"We came here to get away for my sweetie's birthday. What a great choice. The Captain's room was incredible. It was raining but the inn was warm and quite romantic. I highly recommend this place to anyone who can appreciate casual elegance." (M. Scott)*

"We are more relaxed here than at home. The classical music flowing from the dining area to the living room - what a delight. Munchies are available at all hours. It was so cozy to bring the tray to our room with tea and cookies." (A. Mars)

"We have had three vacations in the last nine months and have spent each of them at the Gatehouse Inn. It has become our favorite get-away after busy work seasons. The Wicker Room had the perfect atmosphere for us and the Laura Ashley decor was absolutely beautiful." (C. Bidondo)

Palo Alto

Adella Villa
P.O. Box 4528
Stanford, CA 94309
(415) 321-5195, Fax: (415) 325-5121

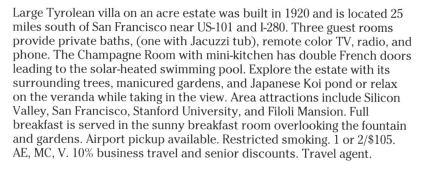

Type of B&B: Private estate.
Rooms: 3 with private bath.
Rates: 1 or 2/$105.

Rating: A+ or ♛♛♛ Excellent, far exceeds basic requirements.

Large Tyrolean villa on an acre estate was built in 1920 and is located 25 miles south of San Francisco near US-101 and I-280. Three guest rooms provide private baths, (one with Jacuzzi tub), remote color TV, radio, and phone. The Champagne Room with mini-kitchen has double French doors leading to the solar-heated swimming pool. Explore the estate with its surrounding trees, manicured gardens, and Japanese Koi pond or relax on the veranda while taking in the view. Area attractions include Silicon Valley, San Francisco, Stanford University, and Filoli Mansion. Full breakfast is served in the sunny breakfast room overlooking the fountain and gardens. Airport pickup available. Restricted smoking. 1 or 2/$105. AE, MC, V. 10% business travel and senior discounts. Travel agent.

Red Bluff

Faulkner House
1029 Jefferson Street
Red Bluff, CA 96080
(916) 529-0520

Type of B&B: Inn.
Rooms: 4, each with private bath.
Rates: 1/$53-78; 2/$55-80.

Rating: B+ or ♕♕ Good, exceeds basic requirements.

Faulkner House is an historic Queen Anne Victorian home built in 1890 and is located one mile off I-5 near downtown. Choose from four antique-filled guest rooms, each with private bath and some featuring carved bedroom sets, wicker accessories, and a brocade "fainting couch". The formal parlor or screened-in porch are great places to relax and meet other guests while enjoying afternoon refreshments. Within walking distance are restaurants, antique and specialty shops, and a historic house tour. Full breakfast includes oranges from the trees in the yard, homemade muffins, and a baked egg dish with meat. Facilities for meetings, weddings, and receptions. No smoking. 1/$53-78; 2/$55-80. Travel agent.

San Diego

The Cottage
3829 Albatross Street
San Diego, CA 92103
(619) 299-1564

Type of B&B: B&B home and cottage.
Rooms: 2 with private bath.
Rates: 1 or 2/$49-75.

Rating: A- or ♕♕♕ Excellent, far exceeds basic requirements.

Redwood cottage built in 1916 is located on a cul-de-sac in the Hillcrest section of the city. The cottage can accommodate three and offers a bath, fully equipped kitchen, pump organ, wood-burning stove, and Victorian style furnishings. A guest room with private bath and separate entrance is also available in the main house. Area attractions include San Diego Zoo, Balboa Park, airport, beaches, and day trips into Mexico. Continental breakfast features freshly baked bread and seasonal fruit. Families welcome. No smoking. 1 or 2/$49-75. MC, V. Two night minimum stay. Travel agent.

Guests write: *"What a delightful cottage! The flower arrangement and garden added an elegance that was most appreciated. My favorite toy is the coffee machine. The breakfasts - they were special!" (M. Evans)*

"I really liked the flowers and the breakfasts, Jonathan and Harry enjoyed the pipe organ and Raya like the couch bunny and the rocks. My husband says this is our best bed and breakfast experience to date." (G. Carr)

"What a delightful way to start the day - a soft knock on the door and a nicely decorated breakfast tray with the yummiest breakfast breads one has ever tasted - muffins, croissants, fresh apple coffee cake, fresh fruit, fresh mint, fresh garden flowers, beautiful dishware, cloth napkins in rings, lace cloths lining the baskets - all served by one who cares!" (M. Oliver)

"Thanks to the Cottage for making the San Diego part of our vacation so comfortable. All the touches in the cottage and those incredible breakfasts, the suggestions of things to do - were terrific." (G. Musselman)

"A memorable four nights in San Diego at the Cottage. Remarkable for a gracious and informative hostess, fresh flowers, luxurious towels, a firm mattress, and last but not least, those decadent breakfasts." (P. Hambly)

"The Cottage has proven to be the best attraction in San Diego not to mention the best bargain! No need to go anywhere else for a sumptuous breakfast." (J. Varner)

San Diego

Heritage Park B&B Inn
2470 Heritage Park Row
San Diego, CA 92110
(619) 299-6832

Type of B&B: Inn.
Rooms: 9, 5 with private bath.
Rates: 1/$80-120; 2/$85-125.

Rating: A- or ♛♛♛ Excellent, far exceeds basic requirements.

Famous Old Town in San Diego is the setting for this Queen Anne Victorian home built in 1889. It's situated in an unusual seven-acre park of historic buildings and has some outstanding architectural features. Choose from nine guest rooms, five with private bath. Each is individually decorated with oriental rugs, handmade quilts, period antiques, and Victorian wallpaper. Attractions nearby include San Diego Zoo, Mission Valley, and the San Diego Harbor cruise. Full breakfast, evening social hour, and classic films available. 1/$80-120; 2/$85-125. MC, V. 10% business travel discount.

San Francisco

Art Center B&B Suites
1902 Filbert near Laguna
San Francisco, CA 94123
(415) 567-1526 or
(800) 821-3877 for reservations
(415) 921-9023 for questions

Type of B&B: Inn.
Rooms: 5 suites with private bath.
Rates: 1 or 2/$85-115.

Rating: B- or ♛♛ Good, exceeds basic requirements.

French Colonial townhouse built circa 1857 is centrally located in the Marina District. The inn gets its name from the owners who especially cater to art lovers and who run a small private gallery and art studio on the premises. Choose from five guest suites, each with private bath and one with whirlpool bath. Each is casually furnished and includes original art work and fully equipped gourmet kitchen or breakfast bar. Within walking distance are Union Street shopping with its boutiques, antique stores, galleries, and varied restaurants. Transportation is available nearby for exploring other parts of this famous city including Fisherman's Wharf which is only 20 minutes away. Prepare your own breakfast at leisure from stocked pantry. Families welcome. No smoking. 1 or 2/$85-115. AE, MC, V. Travel agent.

San Francisco

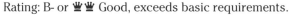

The Chateau Tivoli
1057 Steiner Street
San Francisco, CA 94115
(415) 776-5462 or (800) 228-1647

Type of B&B: Inn.
Rooms: 5 rooms and 2 suites, 5 private baths.
Rates: 1 or 2/$80-200.

Rating: A or ♛♛♛ Excellent, far exceeds basic requirements.

Victorian mansion, circa 1892, has undergone an authentic period restoration and is located in the Alamo Square Historic District. The inn's five guest rooms and two suites offer a step back into San Francisco's romantic golden age of opulence and are furnished with canopy beds, marble baths, balconies, fireplaces, stained glass, and antiques. Five rooms have a private bath. Walk to a variety of restaurants, shopping, theaters, Golden Gate Park, and Alamo Square Park. A continental breakfast is served weekdays and a full champagne breakfast is served on weekends. Meeting facilities available. Restricted smoking. 1 or 2/$80-200. AE, MC, V. Travel agent.

San Francisco

Golden Gate Hotel
775 Bush Street
San Francisco, CA 94108
(415) 392-3702 or (800) 835-1118

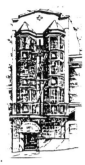

Type of B&B: Small urban B&B hotel
Rooms: 23 rooms, 14 have a private bath.
Rates: 1 or 2/$55-89.

Rating: C+ or ♛ Acceptable, meets basic requirements.

Narrow four-story hotel of Edwardian architecture was built in 1913 and is now a small European-style hotel located two blocks north of Union Square and two blocks down from the top of Nob Hill. Choose from twenty-three guest rooms located throughout four floors with access by elevator. There is quite a variety in room size, prices, and amenities but each offers a bay window and fresh flowers and fourteen have a private bath. The small fireplaced parlor on the main floor is where guests enjoy a continental breakfast of fresh coffee and croissants as well as afternoon tea. Walk to many of the city's famous attractions, restaurants, and shops from this location. The main cable car line stops at the corner giving easy access to Fisherman's Wharf, North Beach, and Ghirardelli Square. Families welcome. Restricted smoking. 1 or 2/$55-89. AE, MC, V. Travel agent.

San Francisco

Jackson Court
2198 Jackson Street
San Francisco, CA 94115
(415) 929-7670

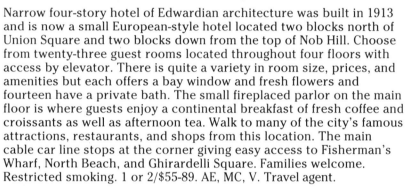

Type of B&B: Inn.
Rooms: 10 with private bath.
Rates: 1 or 2/$95-140.

Rating: AA- or ♛♛♛♛ Outstanding.

Small exclusive townhouse built in 1901 is now a European-style urban inn. Built in 1901, it is located in the Pacific Heights area of the city. Ten individually decorated guest rooms are available. Each offers a private bath, antique furnishings, TV, and telephone. Two rooms feature fireplaces. The Garden Suite on the main floor offers a king-size bed, hand-crafted wood paneling and cabinets, an antique chandelier, and private garden patio with flower beds. Walk to many points of interest within the city or use nearby public transportation. Continental breakfast and afternoon refreshments served daily. $95-140. AE, MC, V.

San Francisco

Monte Cristo
600 Presidio Avenue
San Francisco, CA 94115
(415) 931-1875

Type of B&B: Inn.
Rooms: 14 rooms or suites,
11 with private bath.
Rates: 2/$63-98; Suite/$108.

Rating: B- or ♛♛ Good, exceeds basic requirements.

Built in 1875 as a saloon and hotel, The Monte Cristo has now been restored and is located two blocks from Sacramentos Street's Victorian shops and unique restaurants. Choose from fourteen guest rooms. Each varies in size, decor and amenities but all are comfortably furnished and eleven offer a private bath. Walk to many points of interest in the city including Chinatown, Fisherman's Wharf, Union Square, and Golden Gate Bridge. Convenient transportation is available to downtown and the Financial District. Continental breakfast buffet. 2/$63-98; Suite/$108. AE, MC, V. Travel agent.

San Francisco

Washington Square Inn
1660 Stockton Street
San Francisco, CA 94133
(415) 981-4220 or (800) 388-0220

Type of B&B: Urban inn.
Rooms: 15, 10 with private bath.
Rates: 1 or 2/$85-180.

Rating: B+ or ♛♛ Good, exceeds basic requirements.

Small European-style Victorian inn is located in the historic North Beach district, one block from Telegraph Hill. There are fifteen guest rooms throughout the building which offer a variety in size, decor, and amenities. Each room has a selection of English or French antiques, terry cloth robes, and down comforters. Several rooms which share baths offer an in-room sink and ten rooms or suites have private baths. The elegant parlor area features a fireplace and is an inviting setting for afternoon tea and evening hors d'oeuvres. Walk to many fine restaurants, coffee houses, and bakeries. Cannery shopping is ten minutes away. Take a cable car ride to Union Square, Financial District, or Fisherman's Wharf.

Full breakfast served daily includes famous "Graffeo" coffee and fresh croissants. Families welcome. No smoking. 1 or 2/$85-180. MC, V. 10% senior and business travel discounts.

Guests write: *"I have been a guest here for five days. The staff couldn't have been more cooperative." (A. Law)*

"My mother and I thoroughly enjoyed the warm, efficient service you provided. The continental breakfast, tea hour, and the use of the terry cloth robes were quite nice." (J. Martin)

"The staff at the Washington Square Inn has consistently excellent service. During my recent visit to San Francisco, their patience and assistance helped to make my stay so much more enjoyable. Give them all big raises!" (M. Gould)

"They've restored our faith in customer service and are wonderful. The bottle of wine was perfect." (M. Patterson)

San Jose

The Hensley House
456 North Third Street
San Jose, CA 95112
(408) 298-3537

Type of B&B: Inn.
Rooms: 5 with private bath.
Rates: 1 or 2/$75-125.

Rating: A or ♛♛♛ Excellent, far exceeds basic requirements.

Queen Anne Victorian inn built in 1884 is located downtown in the Hensley Historic District. Choose from five guest rooms, each with private bath and Victorian decor. Relax in the large living room with beamed ceiling, six-foot fireplace, and built-in leaded glass cabinets. Special services for business travelers include fax, personal computer, answering service, access to law library, and conference facilities. Full breakfast. Families welcome. Facilities available for meetings and social functions. 1 or 2/$75-125. AE, MC, V. 10% auto club, business travel, and senior discount.

Guests write: *"Our meeting was a success thanks to the peaceful surroundings, the delightful lunch, and the level of service provided. We especially enjoyed the opportunity to play the piano and burst into song occasionally. I look forward to holding future off-site meetings at the Hensley House." (L. Crane)*

"The whirlpool tub was a luxurious romantic treat in the Judge's Chamber room. After staying at the Hensley House, my husband and I are planning to

purchase a featherbed as our bed was one of the most comfortable beds we have ever slept in." (J. Stroh)

"The accommodations are lovely, the breakfasts tasty, the historical environment gracious. The innkeepers did a wonderful thing in giving me an economy rate while I worked in San Jose for two weeks." (K. Maxson)

"The breakfast was served beautifully on lovely English china and the variety of food each day was excellent. The accoutrements in the room showed that a great deal of thought had been given to the comfort of the traveler. We were also pleased with the wine selection for the afternoon wine and hors d'ouevres. The decor of the house was truly Victorian style including the attire of the innkeeper." (S. Civiletti)

"Another nice thing about the Hensley House stay was the snapshot they took at the end of your stay and mailed to you. It's such a nice remembrance of a very nice visit with them." (L. Maddox)

San Luis Obispo

Garden Street Inn
1212 Garden Street
San Luis Obispo, CA 93401
(805) 545-9802

Type of B&B: Large inn.
Rooms: 13, each with private bath.
Rates: 1 or 2/$80-120; Suites/$140-160.

Rating: A or ♛♛♛ Excellent, far exceeds basic requirements.

Built in 1887, this Victorian Italianate/Queen Anne inn has been recently restored and is located 2 hours south of San Francisco off Highway 101. Choose from nine guest rooms and four suites. Each offers a private bath, king or queen-size beds, armoires, attractive wall coverings, rich fabrics, and antiques. Enjoy the Victorian decor in the McCafery Morning room with its original stained glass windows or sit on one of the outside decks with a good book from the Goldtree Library room. Walk to the 1772 Mission and historic downtown or drive to nearby Hearst Castle, Pismo Beach, Morro Bay, and Cambria. Outdoor activities nearby include tennis, golf, horseback riding, and hiking. A homemade full breakfast includes specialty breads and can be served in the guest room by request. Facilities for small weddings and meetings available. Wheelchair access. Restricted smoking. 1 or 2/$80-120; Suites/$140-160. AE, MC, V. Travel agent.

Santa Barbara

Blue Quail Inn and Cottages
1908 Bath Street
Santa Barbara, CA 93101
(805) 687-2300 or
(800) 549-1622 (in California)
(800) 676-1622 (USA)

Type of B&B: Inn and cottages
Rooms: 9, 7 with private bath.
Rates: 1 or 2/$74-125.

Rating: B or ♛♛ Good, exceeds basic requirements.

California Craftsman bungalow and adjacent cottages are conveniently located near beaches and downtown shopping. Choose from nine guest rooms throughout the main house or cottages. Each has unique decor and features a sitting area, fireplace, antique pieces, and colorful accessories. Seven have a private bath. Walk three blocks to Cottage Hospital and Sansum Clinic. Stroll or borrow bicycles for a ride to the beach, distinctive shops, art galleries, and historic sites. Full breakfast. No smoking. 1 or 2/$74-125. MC, V. Travel agent. Closed Christmas Eve and Christmas Day.

Guests write: *"The charm of the cottages, the brick walkways, and perfectly beautiful gardens, home-baked goodies, friendly faces, all serve to captivate. The warmth just oozes all over the place."* (G. Sugarman)

"The cozy Mockingbird room was perfect for our 5th anniversary! The old-fashioned tub and bed full of soft pillows really lends itself to a night of romance. The wine, hot cider, and special treats in the evening are a nice touch. Riding bikes all around Santa Barbara was fun." (M. Van Ness)

"What fun answering our door to be greeted with smiling faces, balloons, and champagne in recognition of our 1st anniversary. What a thoughtful and personal gesture." (D. LeBarron)

"We loved the balloons, the champagne, soap, the blue hearts that hold the curtains, the bikes, the dogs, the delicious food, the charming staff, and most of all the adorable books - we couldn't put them down." (A. East)

Santa Barbara

Harbor Carriage House
420 West Montecito Street
Santa Barbara, CA 93101
(805) 962-8447 or (800) 594-4633

Type of B&B: Inn.
Rooms: 9 with private bath.
Rates: 1 or 2/$85-175.

Rating: B or ♕♕ Good, exceeds basic requirements.

Harbor Carriage House was built at the turn-of-the-century and is located 3 blocks from the beach and harbor. Choose from nine guest rooms with distinctive decor, private bath, and antique furnishings. Several rooms offer a fireplace, mountain view, and spa tub. Specialty shops and a variety of restaurants are located within walking distance. Within a short drive are interesting historic sites, university, zoo, museums, as well as a wide variety of recreational activities. Full breakfast and early evening refreshment served daily. Wheelchair access. No smoking. 1 or 2/$85-175. MC, V. Travel agent.

Santa Barbara/Summerland

Inn on Summer Hill
2520 Lillie Avenue
Summerland, CA 93067
(805) 969-9998 or (800) 999-8999

Type of B&B: Inn.
Rooms: 16 with private bath.
Rates: 1 or 2/$125-240.

Rating: AA+ or ♕♕♕♕ Outstanding.

New England-style inn in a quiet seaside village is surrounded by rolling foothills and located 2 miles south of Santa Barbara, 90 miles north of Los Angeles. Choose from sixteen guest rooms, each with private bath, canopy bed, fireplace, down comforter, antiques, original art, unique furnishings, and ocean view. A whimsical garden features English country benches, bird houses, and observation deck with spa. Full breakfast and evening refreshments served daily. No smoking. Facilities available for small meetings and social functions. 1 or 2/$125-240. AE, MC, V. 10% business travel and senior discounts offered midweek.

Guests write: *"The decor was really magnificent and the setting superb."* *(B. Reichel)*

"We really enjoyed our stay. Everything was perfect from the decor to the sweets at turn-down time." (W. Chang)

"We loved the classical music, Jacuzzi, robes, spa, hair dryer, down comforter, fireplace, food, and newspaper in the morning." (C. Bocian)

"We cannot say enough for the overall effect of the inn. It was beautiful, clean, and charming. The attention to detail was incredible and not overlooked by us. We loved the canopy bed, Jacuzzi tub, fireplace, balcony and view, outside spa, beautiful grounds, and service was more than excellent. The stereo speakers were nice, too, as were fresh flowers everywhere." (G. Olsen)

Santa Barbara

The Old Yacht Club Inn
and Hitchcock House
431 Corona del Mar
Santa Barbara, CA 93103
(805) 962-1277 or
(800) 549-1676 (in California)
(800) 676-1676 (USA)

Type of B&B: Inn.
Rooms: 9 rooms or suites with private bath.
Rates: 1/$70-130; 2/$75-135.

Rating: B+ or ♛♛ Good, exceeds basic requirements.

Built in 1912, this inn was once headquarters for the yacht club during the 1920's and is located just off US-101, one block from the beach. The inn offers five guest rooms or suites and has been restored and furnished with period pieces, European antiques, Oriental rugs, and fresh flowers. Each room in the Hitchcock House next door has been named after family members and offers a separate entrance, private bath, and sitting area. Guests are welcome to relax on the front porch, in front of the brick fireplace in the parlor, or sunbathe on a large backyard deck. Borrow bicycles to explore the area. Nearby attractions include historic Santa Barbara Mission, picturesque waterfront, fine restaurants, and wine country tours. Swimming, sailing, fishing, tennis, golf, and horseback riding available nearby. Full breakfast. Five course gourmet dinners available Saturday evenings by advance reservation. No smoking. 1/$70-130; 2/$75-135. AE, MC, V. Travel agent.

Santa Barbara

Simpson House Inn
121 East Arrellaga
Santa Barbara, CA 93101
(805) 963-7067

Type of B&B: Inn.
Rooms: 6, with private bath.
Rates: 2/$76-145.

Rating: A or ♛♛♛ Excellent, far exceeds basic requirements.

Victorian inn built in 1874 is secluded on an acre of gardens. Choose from six guest rooms with private bath. Each features antiques, lace, Oriental rugs, goose-down comforters, fresh flowers, and claw-foot tubs. Enjoy a relaxing stroll through the extensive gardens with curving paths, mature oaks, magnolias, and pittosporums. Walk to restaurants, theaters, downtown shops, and museums. Among area attractions are swimming, boating, and bicycling. Full breakfast featuring homemade breads and house specialties is served overlooking the gardens. Afternoon tea, wine and hors d'oeuvres served daily. No smoking. 2/$76-145. MC, V. Travel agent.

Guests write: *"We especially enjoyed our breakfast on the sunroom deck. The scones were light and airy and homemade lemon curd! It was then a joy to lie out on our teak sun loungers to digest and read, to look out over the mountains and beautiful gardens below. There was no need to go anywhere."* (P. Young-Wolff)

"We felt so rested and pampered by the elegant furnishings, romantic gardens and sumptuous food - especially by Gillean's hospitality. The artful hors d'ouevres brought to our room on a silver tray were a wonderful treat." (B. Kendall)

"Staying here is like coming home to the English country house which haunts my dreams. Nestled behind tall Eugenia hedges, surrounded by lawns and gardens, the house itself soothes and comforts world-weary travelers. Sumptuous breakfasts on the balcony with a view of the mountains, wine and cheese in the late afternoon, pleasant chats with the staff - these are memories to savor." (P. Dickson)

California

Santa Cruz

Babbling Brook Inn
1025 Laurel Street
Santa Cruz CA 95060
(408) 427-2437 or (800) 866-1131
FAX: (408) 427-2457

Type of B&B: Inn.
Rooms: 12 with private bath.
Rates: 1 or 2/$85-135.

Rating: A+ or ♛♛♛ Excellent, far exceeds basic requirements.

The Babbling Brook Inn is located south of San Francisco and was built on the foundation of a former 1795 tannery and grist mill. It's name comes from the extensive gardens and waterfalls which surround the inn. Twelve guest rooms with private bath are available. Each is unique in size, amenities, and decor but some special features include French country decor, antiques, fireplaces, skylights, color cable TV, private phone, whirlpool baths, private outside entrances and decks. The Honeymoon Suite features a unique bed used by a local reporatory group in their production of Shakespeare's "Romeo and Juliet". The inn is within walking distance of the beach, wharf, boardwalk, shopping, and tour of historic homes. Full country breakfast includes fresh-baked croissants. Wine and cheese are offered in the evening along with Mrs. King's special cookies. No smoking. 1 or 2/$85-135. AE, MC, V. 10% auto club and business travel discounts. Travel agent.

Guests write: *"We loved the gardens and the Honeymoon suite. The bath tub is great and big enough for two." (J. Sczepanski)*

"We stayed in the Renoir room until the last minute enjoying the view and music of the waterfall." (I. Lusebrink)

"The Countess room was spacious, charming, and lovely. The Talouse Lautrec room on the 2nd night was beautiful. Breakfast here was delicious and staff are so generous and attentive, yet unobtrusive - fantastic!" (S. Nachenberg)

"Our room was the Farmer's Garden room - very quaint and so nice we didn't want to be away from it too much." (G. Metzler)

"We're real homebodys because nothing is usually as comfortable but Babbling Brook is every bit as comfortable plus being enchanting." (C. Unruh)

"Time apart from work and worries, distanced too from a world that hurries. Breakfast treats, cookies, and goodies of the kind that bring one thoughts of

a gentler time. An experience of total pleasure. Lucky us with the memories to treasure." (M. Osborne)

"This is the place where not only dreams are made of but already existing dreams come true. We of course had the Honeymoon Suite and although well-traveled, never had we seen such beauty and warmth incorporated into a room for lovers." (L. Lewis)

Santa Monica

Channel Road Inn
219 West Channel Road
Santa Monica, CA 90402
(213) 459-1920

Type of B&B: Inn.
Rooms: 14 with private bath.
Rates: 1 or 2/$95-210.

Rating: A or ♕♕♕ Excellent, far exceeds basic requirements.

Channel Road Inn, a large Colonial Revival home built in 1910, is located 2 miles north of I-10 in the Los Angeles metropolitan area and is the oldest residence in the surrounding vicinity. Fourteen guest rooms with private baths are available. Each has distinctive period decor and furnishings but all offer an ocean or garden view, fresh cut flowers, and complimentary fresh fruit. Bicycles and picnics are available, and horseback riding as well as tennis are nearby. Area attractions include Getty Museum, pier, beaches, and Will Rogers Park. Continental breakfast served in the mint-green and pink breakfast room features home-baked breads and muffins. Complimentary refreshments are offered each evening. No smoking. Families welcome. 1 or 2/$95-210. MC, V. 10% business travel discount. Travel agent.

Guests write: *"The comfort and warmth provided by the staff are wonderful for someone who's homesick. They patiently answer all my questions, serve a fabulous breakfast, give great directions for driving, and stop to chat when I'm feeling lonely. I'll be coming back here as long as my business keeps bringing me to Los Angeles." (S. Rosenberg)*

"The inn is beautifully decorated in a Victorian manner - lots of wicker furniture and chintz covers. It is all new furniture - not old and musty. Our bedroom was very special and the bed had a wonderful pink and white hand-made quilt and there was an adjoining bathroom." (J. Kennedy)

"It's the little touches that make the Channel Road Inn a special hideaway. The Battenburg lace, the ocean view, the blooming hillside, waking to the smell of fresh coffee, and blueberry coffeecake, and your own key to the front door. I enjoyed reading the thoughts of past guests in the diaries in each room - especially Room #6 - the Honeymoon suite!" (D. Riley)

Seal Beach

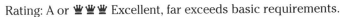

Seal Beach Inn and Gardens
212 5th Street
Seal Beach, CA 90740
(310) 493-2416

Type of B&B: Country inn.
Rooms: 23 rooms or suites with private bath.
Rates: 1 or 2/$98-155.

Rating: A or ♛♛♛ Excellent, far exceeds basic requirements.

Seal Beach Inn and Gardens is located in a seaside village south of Los Angeles and is a complex of French/Mediterranean architecture with a lush garden setting. There are twenty-three distinctive guest rooms or suites. Each offers a private bath and several have full kitchens. Walk one block to the beach or pier. Interesting sites and activities in the area include gondola rides, candlelight dining, seaside strolls, harbor cruises, specialty shops, Disneyland, and Knott's Berry Farm. Hearty buffet breakfast. Facilities available for small meetings. 1 or 2/$98-155. AE, MC, V. 10% senior, auto club, and business travel discounts. Travel agent.

Guests write: *"The gardens are impressive; a dazzling collection of natural beauty. Staying in the villa is like visiting someone's home rather than staying at a hotel. Room rates and service are excellent with regard to level of service and staff responsiveness."* (D. Ishikawa)

"We love the Old World charm with a fantastic breakfast and its nearness to the beach is a great addition to the other attractions." (L. Simons)

"Management and personnel are extremely courteous and helpful. Some rooms are small but very clean. Breakfasts are excellent, location great. All in all a wonderful B&B modestly priced." (J. Harrison)

"This is our 10th visit here. Our compliments on the improvements that have been made since our last stay and the beautiful way that breakfast is being presented now." (R. Wilcox)

Sonoma

Sonoma Hotel
110 West Spain Street
Sonoma, CA 95476
(707) 996-2996

Type of B&B: Country inn with restaurant.
Rooms: 17, 5 with private bath.
Rates: 1 or 2/$62-105.

Rating: B- or ♕♕ Good, exceeds basic requirements.

Historic hotel situated on the city's tree-lined plaza has been completely restored by the present owners who have worked hard at retaining the historic atmosphere of the building. There are seventeen individually decorated guest rooms with pleasant decor, antiques, brass and iron appointments. Several rooms offer private baths with deep claw-foot tubs and herbal bubble bath. Nearby attractions include wineries, hot air balloon rides, art galleries, shops, and historic landmarks. Continental breakfast often includes fresh-baked pastries. Dining available on the premises. Families welcome. 1 or 2/$62-105. AE, MC, V.

Arvada

The Tree House
6650 Simms Street
Arvada, CO 80004
(303) 431-6352

Type of B&B: Inn.
Rooms: 5, each with private bath.
Rates: 1 or 2/$49-$79.

Rating: B+ or ♕♕ Good, exceeds basic requirements.

Chalet style inn is set far back from the road on ten wooded acres and is located only 25 minutes from Denver's Stapleton Airport near the Ward exit off I-70. Each of the five guest rooms offers a private bath and is furnished with brass bed, handmade bedding, and interesting antiques. Four rooms feature a wood-burning fireplace. Several balconies provide a quiet spot for taking in the wooded views. Enjoy a leisurely walk through the forest that surrounds the inn. A large parlor offers a fireplace and comfortable oak and leather furniture. Area attractions include the Rocky Mountains, Denver Mint, Denver Zoo, and Coors Brewery. Full breakfast includes special homemade cinnamon rolls. Families welcome. No smoking. 1 or 2/$49-79. MC. V. Business traveler discount. Travel agent.

Guests write: *"Beautifully decorated and comfortable interior and wooded surroundings. The crowning touch was the gourmet breakfast. As a host of breakfast eaters who feel the day should begin with a good meal, we were all delighted with Amanda's wonderful cooking." (N. Arnold)*

Crested Butte

Alpine Lace Bed & Breakfast
726 Maroon
Crested Butte, CO 81224
(303) 349-9857

Type of B&B: Small inn.
Rooms: 4, 2 with private bath.
Rates: 1 or 2/$35-80.

Rating: B+ or ♛♛ Good, exceeds basic requirements.

Swiss chalet-style inn is surrounded by mountain and valley views and is situated in the National Historic District near Highway 135. Four guest rooms are available. Special features include some with outside balconies, garden or valley views, or a private entrance. The two guest rooms with private baths are slightly larger and have extra amenities. A spacious sunroom on the main floor offers a Jacuzzi tub and guest refrigerator. The main living room has a large stone fireplace and interesting collection of books on Colorado. A mud room along the side of the inn offers accessible storage for skis, bicycles, and hiking equipment. This is a year-round recreation area which offers skiing, ice fishing, snow shoeing, sleigh rides, biking, and horseback riding. Walk to unique shops and restaurants in the village area. Full gourmet breakfast served and beverages are available throughout the day. Facilities available for small social functions. No smoking. 1 or 2/$35-80. MC, V. Travel agent.

Guests write: *"Spending Christmas alone is a bummer unless you're at the Alpine Lace in which case it becomes a memorable high. The genuine warmth here quickly took off the chill for this flatlander. The food was excellent and will be missed immediately when I wake up in Florida upon my return. Also, if Ward can teach me to ski, he can teach anybody anything." (R. Booth)*

"Alpine Lace is our home away from home. The luxurious towels, the flowers on the table, Loree's warmth and friendship, Ward's efficiency and attention to detail, the hot tub soothing our tired muscles, the wonderful

atmosphere of town - these are the things that made our trip a wonderful memory." (S. Sabo)

"We loved our week here and lost all track of time. A really great spot! The shuttle bus to the slopes made life effortless. Every breakfast was better than the one the day before." (D. Killen)

Denver

Castle Marne B&B
1572 Race Street
Denver, CO 80237
(303) 331-0621 or (800) 92-MARNE

Type of B&B: Inn.
Rooms: 9 rooms or suites with private bath.
Rates: 1/$65-145; 2/$75-145.

Rating: A+ or ♛♛♛ Excellent, far exceeds basic requirements.

Historic Victorian mansion built in 1889 is now a luxury urban inn located near the intersection of Routes 40 and 287, 20 blocks east of downtown. Nine guest rooms or suites are available, each with period antiques, family heirlooms, and private bath. Guest suites feature fireplaces and Jacuzzi bath tubs. The original character of the mansion is still evident in its hand-rubbed woods, circular stained-glass peacock window, and ornate fireplaces. Business travelers will appreciate the quiet office setup in the lower level with desk and office equipment ready for use. Full breakfast and afternoon tea served daily. Facilities available for small meetings. No smoking. 1/$65-145; 2/$75-145. AE, MC, V. 10% auto club, business travel, and senior discounts. Travel agent.

Denver

Queen Anne Inn
2147 Tremont Place
Denver, CO 80205
(303) 296-6666

Type of B&B: Inn.
Rooms: 10 with private bath.
Rates: 1/$54-99; 2/$64-109

Rating: A or ♛♛♛ Excellent, far exceeds basic requirements.

Large Queen Anne Victorian home built in 1879 offers the atmosphere and ambiance of Denver's Historic District, yet is located only four blocks from the center of downtown. There are ten guest rooms with private bath available. Each has a unique decor, fresh flowers, original art, and period lighting. The Aspen Room's unusual architectural features are enhanced by an original mural of aspen trees and this central theme is carried out with unique wood lighting fixtures. There are a number of specialty shops, galleries, and restaurants within walking distance. Horse-drawn carriage rides are available for special occasions. Continental breakfast. Group, wedding, and meeting facilities available. 1/$54-99; 2/$64-109. No smoking. AE, MC, V. 10% auto club and business travel discount. Travel agent.

Durango

River House B&B
495 Animas View Drive
Durango, CO 81301
(303) 247-4775

Type of B&B: Inn.
Rooms: 6 with private bath.
Rates: 1/$40-50; 2/$45-65.

Rating: B or ♕♕ Good, exceeds basic requirements.

Casual ranch home north of the city is near the river's edge and located 6 miles from Trimble Hot Springs, 1 mile off County Road 203. There are six guest rooms available, each with private bath. One extra large room is especially geared for families and offers two queen-size beds and ample space for a crib or fold-out bed. There is an unusually large atrium room with interesting collection of Southwestern plants and crafts which provides a pleasant breakfast setting each morning. A large adjacent living room features a fireplace, comfortable television viewing area, and large selection of games. The inn features quilt art, rock pictographs, and works of local artists. Area recreation includes fishing, hiking, tennis, skiing, and golf. Full country breakfast features homemade breads and muffins and a house specialty such as chili-cheese casserole or French toast. Facilities available for meetings and weddings. Families welcome. No smoking. No pets. 1/$40-50; 2/$45-65. MC, V. 10% senior discount. Travel agent.

Guests write: *"We were impressed with the little special things, i.e. the chocolates on the night stand, flowers in our room, the chili-cheese breakfast casserole and unbeatable coffee, the friendliness of the hostess and her knowledge of the Southwest." J. Geitzler)*

Grand Junction

Junction Country Inn
861 Grand Avenue
Grand Junction, CO 81501
(303) 241-2817

Type of B&B: Inn.
Rooms: 3, 1 with private bath.
Rates: 1/$25-35; 2/$30-40.

Rating: B- or ♛♛ Good, exceeds basic requirements.

1907 Victorian two-story inn is located on the corner of Ninth and Grand Avenues in downtown. Choose from three guest rooms, one with private bath. Turn-of-the-century workmanship is evident throughout the theme-decorated rooms, spacious parlors, and dining room. Local attractions include Colorado National Monument, Grand Mesa, Rabbit Valley, Dinosaur Dig, Powderhorn Ski Resort, Kokopellis Trail, and Stocker Stadium. Fruit-filled crepes and yogurt granola parfait are a part of the full breakfast served daily. Two large parlors and the dining room accommodate weddings and meetings. Families welcome. No smoking. 1/$25-35; 2/$30-40. AE, MC, V. 10% senior, business, and auto club discounts. Travel agent.

Redstone

Cleveholm Manor
0058 Redstone Boulevard
Redstone, CO 81623
(303) 963-3463

Type of B&B: Large mansion.
Rooms: 16, 8 with private bath.
Rates: 1 or 2/$78-167.

Rating: A- or ♛♛♛ Excellent, far exceeds basic requirements.

English Manor-style mansion built originally for a wealthy mining baron at the turn-of-the-century sits overlooking the Crystal River and red mountain cliffs and is located south of Grand Junction. Sixteen guest rooms are available which offer a variety in price, decor and amenities. Eight rooms have private baths. Several small rooms which share baths offer fresh, updated decor. Other choices include the suites with period furnishings and decor, private baths, and fireplaces. The main floor has an impressive entry, parlor, and dining rooms whose features include elegant woodwork, stone and marble fireplaces, inlaid floors, gold leaf ceilings, and Persian rugs. The lower level offers a small lounge and bar, television room, and billiards room. Outdoor recreation available nearby includes high country skiing, hiking, bicycling, and fishing. Continental buffet breakfast. Groups up to 100 can be easily accommodated. Families welcome. Restricted smoking. 1 or 2/$78-167. AE, MC, V. Senior and off-season discounts. Travel agent.

Telluride

San Sophia
330 West Pacific Avenue
Telluride, CO 81435
(800) 537-4781

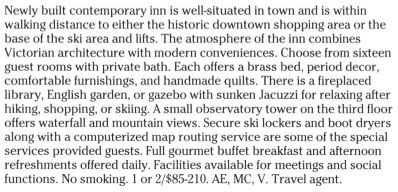

Type of B&B: Inn.
Rooms: 16 with private bath.
Rates: 1 or 2/$85-210.

Rating: AA- or ♕♕♕♕ Outstanding.

Newly built contemporary inn is well-situated in town and is within walking distance to either the historic downtown shopping area or the base of the ski area and lifts. The atmosphere of the inn combines Victorian architecture with modern conveniences. Choose from sixteen guest rooms with private bath. Each offers a brass bed, period decor, comfortable furnishings, and handmade quilts. There is a fireplaced library, English garden, or gazebo with sunken Jacuzzi for relaxing after hiking, shopping, or skiing. A small observatory tower on the third floor offers waterfall and mountain views. Secure ski lockers and boot dryers along with a computerized map routing service are some of the special services provided guests. Full gourmet buffet breakfast and afternoon refreshments offered daily. Facilities available for meetings and social functions. No smoking. 1 or 2/$85-210. AE, MC, V. Travel agent.

Clinton

Captain Dibbell House
21 Commerce Street
Clinton, CT 06413
(203) 669-1646

Type of B&B: Small inn.
Rooms: 4 with private bath.
Rates: 1/$55-75; 2/$65-90.

Rating: B+ or ♛♛ Good, exceeds basic requirements.

Historic Victorian home built in 1866 is conveniently located 2 miles south of I-95 exit 63. There are four guest rooms from which to choose and each offers a private bath. A breakfast room or the parlor with television offer guests a place in which to relax and unwind. A short walk will take you to beaches or the Hammonassett State Park. Other area attractions include Stanton House, Essex Steam Train, Gillette Castle, Goodspeede Opera House, Ivoryton Playhouse, Mystic Seaport, Sundial Herb Garden, and Yale University. Full breakfast specialties may include cheese strata or waffles, fresh fruit, and homebaked muffins. 1/$55-75; 2/$65-90. AE, MC, V. 10% business travel and senior discounts. Closed January. Travel agent.

Colchester

Hayward House Inn
35 Hayward Avenue
Colchester, CT 06415
(203) 537-5772

Type of B&B: Inn
Rooms: 6, each with private bath.
Rates: 1 or 2/$65-125.

Rating: A- or ♛♛♛ Excellent, far exceeds basic requirements.

Historic Georgian Colonial inn and carriage house are located 25 miles east of Hartford on the Town Green. Choose from four guest rooms found in the main house or from two suites in the carriage house, all with private bath. Rooms in the main house feature period furnishings and some offer working fireplaces, Jacuzzis, or king-size beds. The separate carriage house features two suites, each with living room, fully equipped kitchen, and bedrooms; some have cathedral ceilings, exposed beams, and contemporary furnishings. Explore the nearby Connecticut shoreline or visit Goodspeede Opera House, Gillette Castle, Mystic Seaport, and the Mark Twain House. The newly opened Mashantucket-Pequot Indian

Casino is a 20 minute drive. Full breakfast specials may include strawberry crepes, German pancakes or quiche as well as fresh-baked goods. Afternoon tea is brought to the room on a special tea tray. Small wedding and meeting facilities available. Families welcome. Wheelchair access. Restricted smoking. 1 or 2/$65-125. MC. V. Travel agent.

Ivoryton

Copper Beech Inn
46 Main Street
Ivoryton, CT 06442
(203) 767-0330

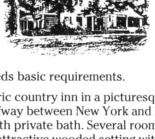

Type of B&B: Inn.
Rooms: 13 with private bath.
Rates: 1 or 2/$100-160.

Rating: B or ♛♛ Good, exceeds basic requirements.

Copper Beach Inn is an historic country inn in a picturesque village setting off Route 9, exit 3, halfway between New York and Boston. Choose from thirteen guest rooms with private bath. Several rooms feature Jacuzzi tubs. The inn has an attractive wooded setting with flower gardens and mature trees whose view can be enjoyed from the Adirondack chairs on the porch. Visitors are attracted to the area's quaint villages, museums, summer stock theaters, and antique shops. Nearby state parks offer outdoor recreation. Complimentary buffet breakfast is served in the restaurant which specializes in Country French cuisine during dinner hours. Facilities for meetings and social functions. 1 or 2/$100-160. AE, MC, V.

Mystic

Adams House
382 Cow Hill Road
Mystic, CT 06355
(203) 572-9551

Type of B&B: B&B home.
Rooms: 6 rooms and 1 cottage, all with private bath.
Rates: 1 or 2/$65-135; Suite/$135.

Rating: B or ♛♛ Good, exceeds basic requirements.

Historic home built in 1790 is located in a quiet residential setting near Mystic Seaport and Aquarium. Choose from six guest rooms in the main house with private baths; two feature fireplaces. The guest cottage offers complete privacy and is a perfect getaway for honeymooners and anniversary couples. The historic atmosphere of the home has been retained with original fireplaces and wide plank wood floors. Interesting area attractions include USS Nautilus Museum, US Coast Guard Academy, submarine base, and sailing. Continental breakfast includes fresh fruit, juice, homebaked breads and jams. No smoking. 1 or 2/$65-135; suite/$135. MC, V.

New London

Queen Anne Inn
265 Williams Street
New London, CT 06320
(800) 347-8818 or (203) 447-2600

Type of B&B: Inn.
Rooms: 10, 8 with private bath.
Rates: 1/$73-150; 2/$78-155.

Rating: A- or ♛♛♛ Excellent, far exceeds basic requirements.

Victorian inn built in 1903 is located off I-95 in a shoreline resort area. Choose from ten guest rooms, eight with private bath. Each room offers antique furnishings, air conditioning, and unique decor. Several rooms feature working fireplaces. A private cable TV and telephone are available in certain rooms upon request. The home's original beauty has been retained and is showcased in its carved alcove, fireplaced foyer, stained-glass windows, and main staircase circular landing. Transportation by bus, train, and ferry is within walking distance. Area attractions include Mystic Seaport and Aquarium, US Coast Guard Academy, Nautilus Submarine Memorial, and Block Island. Full gourmet breakfast and afternoon tea served daily. Facilities for meetings and social functions available. 1/$73-150; 2/$78-155. AE, MC, V. Seasonal senior, auto club, and business travel discounts available.

Guests write: *"Ray's gourmet full breakfasts and teas are both deliciously prepared and graciously served. Our room with brass bed and fireplace was warm and elegant. We were delightfully surprised to return to our room and find champagne chilled and ready to toast our second wedding anniversary. Their note thanking us for celebrating with them really touched us."*
(B. Veronesi)

New Milford

Homestead Inn
5 Elm Street
New Milford, CT 06776
(203) 354-4080

Type of B&B: Inn.
Rooms: 14 with private bath.
Rates: 1/$60-76; 2/$67-86.

Rating: B+ or ♛♛ Good, exceeds basic requirements.

Situated in a picturesque New England village, the Homestead Inn is located north of Danbury in the heart of the Litchfield Hills. Choose from fourteen guest rooms. Each offers a private bath, TV, telephone, and air conditioning. Specialty shops, variety of restaurants, and movie theater are within walking distance from the inn. There is ample recreation nearby including hiking, golfing, and skiing. Local summer theater, concerts, antique shops, museums, and historic sites are special attractions in the area. Hearty continental breakfast. Families welcome. 1/$60-76; 2/$67-86. AE, MC, V. Travel agent.

Guests write: *"Clean, moderately priced, central location to a great area. The owners are friendly but not intrusive. Breakfasts were shared with other couples who were fun to meet. Surprisingly, several couples were married folk from the same area who enjoy a weekend there occasionally to get away from the kids." (S. Brannock)*

"Exceptional hosts. The inn is beautiful and spotless. Nice thick fluffy towels and great water pressure. Candy in the room for our Valentine's Day stay and a bountiful continental breakfast." (D. Schlicher)

"Hosts couldn't have been nicer. They made me feel at home and had suggestions for places to see and have dinner. The continental breakfast was delicious and nicely served." (V. Shindell)

Norfolk

Manor House
P.O. Box 447, Maple Avenue
Norfolk, CT 06058
(203) 542-5690

Type of B&B: Inn
Rooms: 9 with private bath.
Rates: 1 or 2/$85-160.

Rating: A or ♥♥♥ Excellent, far exceeds basic requirements.

The Manor House was built as a Victorian home in 1898 and is set on five acres within the village and located just off Route 44. Choose from nine guest rooms with private bath. Each room differs in size and decor but special features include fireplaces, private balconies, and antique furnishings. Area attractions nearby include Yale Summer School of Music and Art, Tanglewood, Music Mountain, Lime Rock Park, and several theaters and vineyards. Enjoy the area's variety of activities such as skiing, hiking, bicycling, horseback riding, golfing, and water sports. Full breakfast features homemade breads. Facilities available for meetings and social functions. Restricted smoking. 1 or 2/$85-160. AE, MC, V. Travel agent.

Guests write: *"The guest rooms, house, grounds, and general ambiance are absolutely exquisite. The breakfasts served in the beautifully appointed dining room are fabulous. However the Manor's outstanding asset is its proprietors - whether it be directing you to the nearest music festival, suggesting the best antique shops in the area, providing guidance on restaurants, offering you seeds from their lush garden, or donating that warm bowl of popcorn to munch in front of the fireplace."* (A. Phillips)

"Thanks to two wonderful hosts for making us feel as if we're visiting friends in the country. The beautiful home weaves a special magic for all times of the day." (E. Charipper)

"The combination of the warm manner, the fireplace roaring, and the CD player loaded with Schutz, Debussy, George Winston, and John Coltrane was magic! It made for a great, relaxing eighth anniversary celebration." (J. Donner)

"We were so impressed on our first visit we've made it a tradition to go back the same time every year; and have done so for the last five years as well as other visits throughout the year. We look to the Manor House as a sanctuary away from our hectic day-to-day lives and the hosts have always made us feel welcome, at home, and relaxed." (B. McKane)

Ridgefield

West Lane Inn
22 West Lane
Ridgefield, CT 06877
(203) 438-7323

Type of B&B: Inn.
Rooms: 20, each with private bath.
Rates: 1/$90-115; 2/$120-165.

Rating: A or ♛♛♛ Excellent, far exceeds basic requirements.

Victorian inn built in 1848 is set at the end of a broad lawn and surrounded by majestic maples, and located one hour north of New York City and three hours southwest of Boston. Choose from twenty individually decorated rooms, each with private bath, temperature control, and color television. Several rooms feature working fireplaces. There are ample common areas for guest relaxation in front of a fireplace or with a good book. Take long walks on the wooded trails or visit nearby historic sites, museums, art galleries, and antique stores. Area recreation includes swimming, sailing, bowling, skating, and skiing. Continental breakfast is included in the rates but a full breakfast is available. Families welcome. Wheelchair access. 1/$90-115; 2/$120-165. AE, MC, V.

Salisbury

Yesterday's Yankee B&B
Route 44 East
Salisbury, CT 06068
(203) 435-9539

Type of B&B: B&B Home.
Rooms: 3 with shared bath.
Rates: 2/$65-75.

Rating: B+ or ♛♛ Good, exceeds basic requirements.

Cape Cod home built in 1744 has been completely restored and is situated among towering pines of the Berkshire Mountains on Route 44. Choose from three guest rooms. Each is simply but tastefully decorated with braided rugs and down comforters. They are all air conditioned and share a modern bath. Interesting attractions in the area include summer theater, nature centers, Music Mountain, Yale Summer Music Festival, Tanglewood, and Lime Rock car races. Area recreation includes hiking, skiing, golfing, bicycling, canoeing, kayaking, fishing, and swimming. Full breakfast features homemade granola and frittata with Brie. Families welcome. Restricted smoking. 2/$65-75. AE, MC, V. Travel agent.

Dover

Inn at Meeting House Square
305 South Governors Avenue
Dover, DE 19901
(302) 678-1242

Type of B&B: Inn.
Rooms: 4 with private bath.
Rates: 1/$35-50; 2/$42-58.

Rating: B+ or ♛♛ Good, exceeds basic requirements.

The Inn at Meeting House Square was built in 1849 and is situated in the Historic District of Dover. Choose from four guest rooms with private bath. Each is decorated with family antiques and travel memorabilia and offers air conditioning, cable TV, and telephone. There is a cheerful sun porch and small patio area with wrought iron furniture for relaxation. Become a permanent part of the house by signing your name to the original "vitrail." Walk to unique specialty shops and restaurants. Area attractions nearby include the Old State Building, John Dickenson Mansion, Amish community, and a wildlife preserve. Full breakfast includes specialty entrees such as walnut-bread French toast. Families welcome. 1/$35-50; 2/$42-58. AE, MC, V. Travel agent.

New Castle

Janvier-Black House Bed & Breakfast
17 The Strand
New Castle, DE 19720
(302) 328-1339
Fax: (302) 328-9983

Type of B&B: B&B home.
Rooms: 2 with private bath.
Rates: 1 or 2/$85-105.

Rating: A+ or ♛♛♛ Excellent, far exceeds basic requirements.

Federal style riverfront home listed on the National Register of Historic Homes was built in 1825 and is located in a picturesque Colonial village. There are two spacious, air conditioned suites with sitting rooms, private baths, antique furnishings and appointments. Amenities include TV, VCR, classic movie collection, library, private deck, and screened-in porch overlooking the Delaware River. There are several interesting sites nearby including museums that portray life in the Dutch and English Colonial periods. Fine restaurants and shops are within walking distance.

Other nearby attractions include Winterthur, Brandywine River Museum, Longwood Gardens, Hagley Museum, and Fort Delaware. A gourmet continental breakfast featuring Amish-made breads, muffins, and sticky buns is served overlooking the river where ships from all over the world pass by. No smoking. 1 or 2/$85-105.

Wilmington

The Boulevard Bed and Breakfast
1909 Baynard Boulevard
Wilmington, DE 19802
(302) 656-9700

Type of B&B: Inn.
Rooms: 6, 4 with private bath.
Rates: 1/$50-60; 2/$55-70.

Rating: B+ or ♛♛ Good, exceeds basic requirements.

Restored city mansion located in one of the city's tree-lined historic districts, is found one half mile east of I-95 at exit 8. Choose from six guest rooms, four with private bath. Enjoy a walk to the nearby park, downtown district, or take a drive to many cultural and historic sites including Hagley, Winterthur, Delaware Natural History Museum, Longwood Gardens, and Brandywine River Museum. A full breakfast is served in the formal dining room or on the screened-in porch. Small weddings and meeting facilities available. Families welcome. 1/$50-60; 2/$55-70. AE, MC, V.

Guests write: *"Chuck and Judy go well beyond the call of duty. They welcome you into their home as if you were an old friend. We still think about them often and feel the warmth of their hospitality." (D. Hilton)*

"The hostess went out of her way to make us feel comfortable and gave us excellent advice about places to dine as well as numerous directions to wherever we wanted to go. Her breakfasts were delicious too. We were so satisfied that I recommended the B&B to a co-worker of mine who also stayed with them in early June." (R. Glass)

"The Boulevard B&B was the setting for my son's wedding luncheon and the central entrance hall and staircase were used for his wedding pictures. The luncheon was fun for all and the pictures turned out great." (E. Scarfe)

"We had the room on the top floor and just loved it. Whenever we think of true R&R, we think of this home." (T. Kavanagh)

"The Honeymoon suite's whirlpool tub, bed, TV, and heating blanket were great. Accommodations were so wonderful that I could probably use a week straight of that treatment." (L. Sipe)

Washington, DC
(See also Alexandria, VA and Silver Spring, Burtonsville, and Olney, MD)

Amelia Island

Elizabeth Point Lodge
98 South Fletcher Street
Amelia Island, FL 32034
(904) 277-4851

Type of B&B: Inn.
Rooms: 20 with private bath.
Rates: 1/$75-95; 2/$85-105.

Rating: A or ♛♛♛ Excellent, far exceeds basic requirements.

New oceanfront Nantucket-style inn built in a turn-of-the-century manner is found just off Route A1A, 25 miles north of Jacksonville, and fifteen miles off I-95. Twenty guest rooms, each with private bath, have been carefully decorated to emphasize a maritime theme and include oversized tubs and fresh flowers. Enjoy a glass of lemonade and a homemade snack on the main floor's wrap-around porch or visit the deserted beaches nearby. Special children's activities are regularly scheduled and assistance is given in arranging special tours and outings with sailing, fishing charters, golfing, biking, and horseback riding nearby. A full breakfast is served in the oceanfront sunroom and includes special egg dishes and fresh baked goods. Meeting and reception facilities available. Families welcome. Wheelchair access. 1/$75-95; 2/$85-105. AE, MC, V. Senior and auto club discounts. Travel agent.

Amelia Island

Florida House Inn
20 and 22 South Third Street
Amelia Island, FL 32034
(904) 261-3300 or (800) 258-3301

Type of B&B: Inn with restaurant.
Rooms: 12 with private bath.
Rates: 1 or 2/$55-120.

Rating: B or ♛♛ Good, exceeds basic requirements.

In continuous operation since 1857, this Greek Revival country inn with restaurant is located 35 miles north of Jacksonville off I-95. All twelve guest rooms boast private baths, air-conditioning, country oak and pine antiques, and handmade quilts. Some rooms offer fireplaces and whirlpool tubs. Guests are invited to enjoy swimming, golfing, tennis, and antiquing nearby as well as explore twenty miles of beaches, a Civil War fort, Cumberland Island, Big and Little Talbot Island, and state parks. Full country breakfast. Wheelchair access. Restricted smoking. 1 or 2/$55-120. AE, MC, V. 10% senior, business travel, and auto club discounts. Travel agent.

Daytona Beach

Live Oak Inn
448 South Beach Street
Daytona Beach, FL 32114
(904) 252-4667 or (800) 253-4667

Type of B&B: Country inn with restaurant.
Rooms: 16, each with private bath.
Rates: 1/$50-175; 2/$55-180.

Rating: B or ♛♛ Good exceeds basic requirements.

Restored Victorian home is listed on the National Register of Historic Places and offers views of the Halifax Harbor Marina from its location one hour north of Orlando off Route A1A. Choose from sixteen guest rooms with private bath which offer a variety of size, decor, period furnishings, and amenities. Each room's decor theme depicts people or events which helped shape Florida's history and each offers views of Halifax Harbor or the inn's historical garden. Several rooms feature a Jacuzzi or Victorian soaking tub. Nearby attractions include Jackie Robinson Memorial Stadium and Park, St. Augustine, Cape Kennedy Space Center, and Orlando attractions. Explore area beaches, art galleries, museums, and historic sites. Continental plus breakfast includes fresh fruit, pastries, cheese, pate or sausage, and special egg dishes. Facilities available for meetings and weddings. Families welcome. Wheelchair access. Restricted smoking. 1/$50-175; 2/$55-180. AE, MC, V. Travel agent.

Holmes Beach

Harrington House B&B
5626 Gulf Drive
Holmes Beach, FL 34217
(813) 778-5444

Type of B&B: Inn.
Rooms: 7 with private bath.
Rates: 1 or 2/$79-125.

Rating: A or ♛♛♛ Excellent, far exceeds basic requirements.

Unspoiled Anna Maria Island is located south of Tampa on the Gulf. Harrington House sits directly on the beach and offers casual elegance throughout its seven guest rooms. Each room is unique in size, decor, and amenities but all have private baths and air conditioning. Special features include French doors leading out to private balconies with views of the Gulf of Mexico. Moonlight strolls on the beach are a favorite activity here but guests also enjoy gathering around the swimming pool and the high ceilinged living room with fireplace and large collection of interesting books. Disney World is a two hour drive but nearby sites include Ringling Mansion and Museum, Selby Gardens, and Bishop's Planetarium. Full breakfast. No smoking. $79-125. MC, V. Travel agent.

Guests write: *"What can we say to describe our trip here? The welcome was warm and inviting. We loved the room - so cozy and super clean. Breakfast was delicious. We just had a great time. And our only sorrow was it wasn't long enough." (D. Yeager)*

"Our room was lovely and I most appreciated the attention to detail - iced tea on the porch, mints on the dresser, refrigerator in the room, and the little basket with shampoo, etc. in the bath. Those are the things that make it special. Breakfasts were delightful." (K. Goss)

"The setting was wonderful. We want the Sunset Room when we return. Friendliness of staff and guests was like home. Food was wonderful. I appreciated the little touches - decor, accessories, colors, warmth." (C. Cavanagh)

"These folks treat their guests like kings and queens. The service is second to none. The atmosphere is very unique and enjoyable. They create a warm and friendly environment for all." (D. Traudt)

"The room, the ambiance, the staff, breakfasts, the view, the beach - all too nice for words." (T. Ennis)

Key West

Heron House
512 Simonton Street
Key West, FL 33040
(305) 294-9227

Type of B&B: B&B Guesthouse.
Rooms: 18 with private bath.
Rates:1/$55-125; 2/$105-195.

Rating: B or ♛♛ Good, exceeds basic requirements.

Heron House is a historic property built in 1856. It is centrally located near all major tourism attractions in Key West yet located on a quiet residential street off Route 1. There are eighteen guest rooms with private bath available. Each is unique in size, decor, and amenities. Several luxury rooms feature large mirrored walls and unusual wood decorative artwork as well as marble baths. The rooms are located in two buildings that surround a pleasant swimming pool and patio with lush foliage, large pots of tropical plants, and orchids. Nearby attractions include Hemingway House, Mel Fischer's Treasure Museum, snorkeling cruises, tennis, golf, fishing, and hiking. Continental breakfast includes waffles or French toast, bagels and muffins. Wheelchair access. 1/$55-125; 2/$105-195. AE, MC, V. Travel agent.

Key West

The Watson House
525 Simonton Street
Key West, FL 33040
(305) 294-6712 or (800) 621-9405

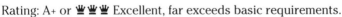

Type of B&B: Guesthouse
Rooms: 3 suites with private bath.
Rates: 1 or 2/$95-360.

Rating: A+ or ♛♛♛ Excellent, far exceeds basic requirements.

Bahamian-style guest house built in 1860 has been fully restored and expanded and is located in the heart of the Historic District. Choose from two guest accommodations in the main house or the Cabana, which is a four-room private apartment. Each is individually furnished and features hardwood floors, paddle fans, wicker and rattan furnishings, floral patterns and textures, private bath, telephone, color cable TV, fully equipped kitchen, and air-conditioning. Private decks overlook a tropical garden setting enhanced by a waterfall, spa, and swimming pool. Walk to many fine restaurants, live theatre, Hemingway House, boating, deep sea fishing, Conch tour trains, and the nightlife of Duval Street. Continental breakfast basket is brought to each suite. 1 or 2/$95-360. AE, MC, V. Travel agent.

Lake Wales

Chalet Suzanne Country Inn & Restaurant
P.O. Drawer AC
Lake Wales, FL 33859
(813) 676-6011 or (800) 288-6011

Type of B&B: Country inn with restaurant.
Rooms: 30 with private bath.
Rates: 1 or 2/$95-185.

Rating: A- or ♛♛♛ Excellent, far exceeds basic requirements.

Chalet Suzanne is an unusual private estate that is now a family-owned and operated European-style inn with restaurant. The inn is listed on the National Register of Historic Places and located in central Florida off US-27. Choose from thirty individually decorated guest rooms with private bath. There is a variety in the size, decor, and amenities of the rooms but each features air conditioning, telephone, and TV. The complex includes a ceramic studio, antique shop, and historic chapel. There are extensive grounds which include a swimming pool and secret garden area where special guests have been invited to sign tiles which are fired in the ceramic studio and used to create a garden wall. Area attractions include Bok Tower Gardens, Cypress Gardens, Disney World, Epcot Center, Sea World, and Busch Gardens. Full breakfast is included in the room rate. Lunch and candlelight dinner available at additional charge. Families welcome. Facilities for meetings and social functions. Guests can fly in as there is a private landing strip on the property. 1 or 2/$95-185. AE, MC, V. 10% business travel discount. Travel agent.

Guests write: *"Our stay at Chalet Suzanne was exceptional (as usual). It's amazing how we can make Lake Wales on our way to everywhere we go in Florida. From the warm welcome greeting on arrival to the excellent service at dinner, to the morning smiles from staffers and the come again waves as we left, we were made to feel this is our Southern home. Although we brought our children, we purposely fed them early so we could enjoy our candlelight romantic dinner alone. The presentation of each course was superb. The melody of flavors and textures and color makes our memories of dinner here linger long after we've left." (D. Thorsen)*

"We think the Chalet Suzanne is fabulous. Since we have flown in 475 times for breakfast, it must be great! The food is superb and the hospitality of the Hinshaws and their staff is simply marvelous." (E. Bowman)

"The Chalet is really out of this world in all respects. The atmosphere, the food, the furniture, the rooms, the classical music, the extremely friendly employees. I was so happy to get to know Mrs. Vita Hinshaw personally and I really was overwhelmed by her warmth, her style, her spirit, her charm, her personality - so I'm sure this is one reason for the aura here. Vita means Life - so there has to be a lot of real life here at this magnificent place." (D. Buck)

Miami

Miami River Inn
118 SW South River Drive
Miami, FL 33130
(305) 325-0045

Type of B&B: Inn.
Rooms: 40, 38 with private bath.
Rates: 1 or 2/$70-110.

Rating: B or ♛♛ Good, exceeds basic requirements.

Four restored Victorian clapboard buildings built between 1906 and 1914 comprise this inn which is located in downtown Miami's Riverview Historic District. There are forty guest rooms available, each with color cable TV and central air conditioning. Thirty-eight rooms offer a private bath. Each room is individually appointed with themes ranging from white wicker to others featuring ornately carved gothic headboards and elaborately swagged drapes. The grounds feature tropical plantings, a swimming pool, spa, and croquet lawn. The inn is a ten minute walk from the heart of downtown, Flagler Street shopping, great restaurants, and cultural centers. Facilities available for meetings and conferences. Continental breakfast. 1 or 2/$70-110. AE, MC, V. Travel agent.

Orlando

Perri House Bed & Breakfast
10417 State Road
Orlando, FL 32836
(407) 876-4830 or (800) 780-4830

Type of B&B: Small inn.
Rooms: 4, each with private bath.
Rates: 1/$50-60; 2/$65-75.

Rating: B or ♛♛ Good, exceeds basic requirements.

Nestled in "Disney's back yard," this 5,400 square foot home is located 3.6 miles North of exit 27 off I-4 on State Road 535 North. Four guest rooms are available, each individually furnished with contemporary decor theme, air conditioning, private bath, private entrance, and brass queen-size bed or four-poster king-size bed. There is a Jacuzzi as well as swimming pool on the property for guest use. Historic downtown Orlando is twenty minutes away by car and DisneyWorld, Sea World, Universal Studios, and Pleasure Island are also nearby. Visit fine area restaurants, golf courses, shopping areas, and water parks. Continental breakfast features fresh fruit, giant muffins, danish, and cereals. Families welcome. Restricted smoking. 1/$50-60; 2/$65-75. AE, MC, V. Family and senior discounts. Travel agent.

Guests write: *"The Perrettis run a wonderful B&B. In addition to charmingly furnished rooms and lovely surroundings, they are extremely warm, friendly, and helpful. They repeatedly asked us if we had any special needs and met each and every one. Breakfast was a potpourri feast of fresh fruit, cereals, juices, and always a special muffin or cake. The house was immaculate. The breakfast area overlooked the yard and pool. There are many birds and the Perrettis are encouraging guests to donate bird feeders as they intend to start a bird sanctuary." (F. Leoussis)*

"The house is modern and each individually decorated room has its own entrance and private bath. At night, you can sit in the jacuzzi by the pool and sip a glass of wine. I particularly liked the fact that Perri House combines the best elements of a first-class hotel (it's completely private and you can come and go as you please) with the hominess and hospitality you expect in a B&B." (K. Monaghan)

Dahlonega

Mountain Top Lodge at Dahlonega
Route 7, Box 150
Dahlonega, GA 30533
(404) 864-5257

Type of B&B: Inn.
Rooms: 13 rooms or suites with private bath.
Rates: 1/$45-105; 2/$65-125.

Rating: A or ♛♛♛ Excellent, far exceeds basic requirements.

Mountain Top Lodge is a secluded rural retreat located 60 miles north of Atlanta. Choose from thirteen guest rooms or suites with private bath. Each is unique in size, decor, and amenities but all are furnished with mountain crafts and antiques. Suites feature sitting rooms and private decks. Two deluxe rooms have gas fireplaces and whirlpool tubs. Enjoy the great room with cathedral ceiling, wood stove, card room loft and library, as well as the large, heated outdoor spa. The inn is surrounded by towering trees and pleasant pastoral scenery. Area attractions include Gold Museum, Amicalola Falls, tennis, fishing, hiking, canoeing, bicycling, and horseback riding. Full breakfast. Facilities available for meetings and social functions. Four bedrooms on lower level have wheelchair access. 1/$45-105; 2/$65-125. AE, MC, V.

Savannah

Ballastone Inn and Townhouse
14 East Oglethorpe Avenue
Savannah, GA 31401
(912) 236-1484 or (800) 822-4553

Type of B&B: Large inn.
Rooms: 24 with private bath.
Rates: 1/$95; 2/$175.

Rating: A+ or ♛♛♛ Excellent, far exceeds basic requirements.

Built in 1853, this restored four-story Federal and Victorian mansion is situated in the center of Savannah's historic district. All of the twenty-four guest rooms feature a private bath, color TV, air conditioning, period antiques, and decor that reflects Savannah's rich past. Visit the area's two historic districts, museum houses, riverfront attractions, historic forts, and the nearby beach. A continental plus breakfast offers specialties such as Southern-style muffins and fruit compote, and is served in guest rooms, the courtyard, or the downstairs parlor. Wheelchair access. 1/$95; 2/$175. AE, MC, V. 10% senior and business discount. Travel agent.

Savannah

Eliza Thompson House
5 West Jones Street
Savannah, GA 31401
(912) 236-3620 or (800) 348-9378

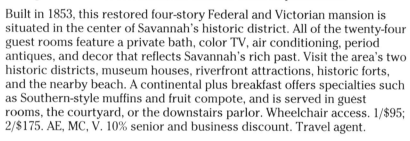

Type of B&B: Inn.
Rooms: 24 with private bath.
Rates: 1/$68-98; 2/$88-108.

Rating: B+ or ♛♛ Good, exceeds basic requirements.

The Eliza Thompson House is a Federal home built in 1847 and located in the heart of Savannah's Historic District. Choose from twenty-four guest rooms, each with private bath, heart pine floors, period furnishings, telephones, and color television. A relaxing parlor is offered as well as an inviting landscaped courtyard with fountains. Area attractions within walking distance include museums, Forsyth Park, and River Street shopping. Continental breakfast includes croissants, muffins, and danish. Afternoon wine and cheese and evening sherry offered. Families welcome. 1/$68-98; 2/$88-108. 10% senior and auto club discounts.

Hilo, Island of Hawaii

Hale Kai-Bjornen
111 Honolii Pali
Hilo, HI 96720
(808) 935-6330

Type of B&B: B&B home.
Rooms: 4 with private bath; guest cottage.
Rates: $75-95.

Rating: AA- or ♛♛♛♛ Outstanding.

Modern home of Scandinavian and Japanese design sits on a bluff facing the ocean and is located 2 miles from downtown Hilo. Choose from four guest rooms (2 kings and 2 queens) with private bath, cable TV, ocean view, and easy access to the bar room, pool, Jacuzzi, patio, and lanais. The guest cottage offers a living room, kitchenette, bedroom with queen-size bed, private bath, cable TV, and faces the ocean. Explore the entire island from this location including nearby Rainbow Falls, Botanical Gardens, Akaka Falls, the volcanos, Waipio Valley, and cities of Hilo and Kona. Full breakfast features dishes such as macadamia nut waffles, Portugese sausage, fruit platters, and Kona coffee. Restricted smoking. Rates $75-95. Three day minimum for the main house and five day minimum reservation for the guest cottage.

Guests write: *"We found our Blue Hawaii as we sipped champagne in Evonne's Jacuzzi and watched the tangerine sunrise on the Pacific Ocean through her swaying coconut and papaya trees. A real second Honeymoon!"* (P. Butler)

"We enjoyed a view of Hilo Harbor that is beautiful and can be seen from the room, pool, or Jacuzzi. The breakfast was as good as I've eaten with island fruits and breads, and macadamia nut waffles, Portugese sausage and Norwegian eggs. The best thing was the friendliness of the hosts who can tell you all the do's and don'ts of the island." (D. McHugh)

"We didn't want to leave! The hosts shared their collections and personal travel experiences with us. Such an interesting and warm couple! They directed us to delicious restaurants for dinner and served delicious full course breakfasts. They treated us as family and kings." (J. Glass)

"The fresh tropical flowers in each room were beautiful. Our room was spotless. I wish I could close my eyes and still hear the sound of the surf like

I could from our patio. Loved the Jacuzzi under the stars after a long day of sightseeing." (D. Talbot)

"Our room was very well done with interesting things about to make you feel close to the host and hostess. We had a view overlooking the bay. Paul directed us to very special places I am sure a tour guide would overlook. He is a native and knew where to send us. The breakfast was always gourmet. Flowers were everywhere and fresh daily." (H. Hagen)

Volcano

Chalet Kilauea at Volcano
P.O. Box 998
Volcano, HI 96785
(808) 967-7786 or (800) 937-7786

Type of B&B: Inn.
Rooms: 4 with shared or private bath.
Rates: 1 or 2/$65-100.

Rating: B or ♛♛ Good, exceeds basic requirements.

Hawaiian chalet has a lush tropical setting outside the village of Volcano. Choose from three guest rooms in the main house which are decorated with Oriental, African, or Victorian themes. The two-level Treehouse suite is adjacent to the main building and offers complete privacy with a bedroom upstairs, a sitting area on the lower level, and private bath. A large parlor with fireplace offers ample comfortable seating among an interesting collection of crafts from around the world. The grounds are spacious and include a hot tub. Volcano National Park is nearby where visitors enjoy hiking, golfing, biking, swimming, birdwatching, and lava viewing. A full two-course gourmet breakfast boasts international and local dishes as well as Kona coffee. Families welcome. Restricted smoking. 1 or 2/$65-100. MC, V. Travel agent.

Volcano

Kilauea Lodge
P.O. Box 116
Volcano, HI 96785
(808) 967-7366

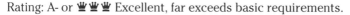

Type of B&B: Lodge.
Rooms: 12 with private bath.
Rates: 1 or 2/$75-100.

Rating: A- or ♛♛♛ Excellent, far exceeds basic requirements.

This 1930's Midwest style lodge is located near Volcano National Park on the Hilo side of the island. Twelve guest rooms all have private bath and six feature fireplaces for the cool mountain evenings. Relax in front of the unique "friendship" fireplace or enjoy the inn's restaurant. Nearby attractions and activities include Volcano National Park, Kilauea Volcano, Botanical Gardens, hiking, golfing, and bird watching. Full breakfast frequently features specials such as pancakes and French toast. Families welcome. Wheelchair access. 1 or 2/$75-100. MC, V.

Guests write: *"Excellent food, hospitality, accommodations in a beautiful surrounding. Would recommend this lodge to anyone and everyone. Can't think of any way in which improvement could be made. Lodge staff also have an excellent first-aid kit available for minor injuries, falls, and scrapes on the lava flows." (E. Murray)*

"Life doesn't get any better than this. We have been home for three months and still feel the same way about the Kilauea Lodge." (F. Harman)

"I almost didn't want to say anything nice about this place because I would like to keep this charming B&B to ourselves. Philip kept wanting to hike around the Volcano while I wanted to return to our cozy room and sip a cocktail by our own fireplace. The staff couldn't have been more courteous, the food was consistently excellent." (A. Rauenhorst)

"Our cottage was beautifully maintained and wonderfully cozy. The staff was exceptionally polite and helpful, and our meals at the lodge were delicious and reasonably priced. Our stay at the lodge will certainly be one of our favorite Honeymoon memories." (J. Lowe)

Kapaa, Island of Kauai

Kay Barker's B&B
P.O. Box 740
Kapaa, Kauai, HI 96746
(808) 822-3073 or (800) 835-4845

Type of B&B: B&B home.
Rooms: 4 with private bath.
Rates: 1/$30-60; 2/$40-70.

Rating: B or ♛♛ Good, exceeds basic requirements.

Kay Barker's B&B is a ranch home set on the slopes of Sleeping Giant Mountain in a quiet residential area. There are four guest rooms in the main house, each with a private bath. A separate cottage offers complete privacy along with a king-size bed, living room, private lanai, and kitchenette. Guests relax and gather together on the lanai or in the living room of the main house which has a comfortable TV viewing area and extensive library. Beach supplies such as boogie boards, ice chests, towels, and beach mats are available as well as a washer and dryer. Popular attractions in the area include Wailua River and the Fern Grotto. Area recreation includes snorkeling, tennis, and hiking. Full breakfast often includes fresh fruit, banana nut muffins, macadamia nut hotcakes, or quiche. Families welcome. 1/$30-60; 2/$40-70. MC, V. Travel agent.

Poipu

Gloria's Spouting Horn B&B
4464 Lawai Beach Road
Poipu, Kauai, HI 96756
(808) 742-6995

Type of B&B: B&B home.
Rooms: 5 with private bath.
Rates: 1/$50-120; 2/$55-125.

Rating: B+ or ♛♛ Good, exceeds basic requirements.

This B&B is located on the ocean at Spouting Horn which offers a marvelous secluded beach and ocean vistas. Each of the five guest quarters offers complete privacy, a private bath, and separate entrance. The decor includes brass beds, antiques and contemporary furnishings, comforters, ceiling fans, cable TV, and small refrigerator. A special honeymoon suite offers a Japanese-style soaking tub and glass doors leading to an exotic fish pond. A hammock is strategically located near the water for those who've dreamed of sleeping under a coconut palm tree on the beach. Whales have been spotted from the private decks off the guest rooms. Popular attractions in the area include Spouting Horn, Waimea Canyon, Hanalei Bay, and Poipu Beach as well as golfing, tennis, and horseback riding. The area offers a good selection of galleries, shops, and restaurants. Tropical continental breakfast features Gloria's own fresh homemade pastries and fresh island fruits and juices. No smoking. 1/$50-120; 2/$55-125. MC, V.

Honolulu, Island of Oahu

Manoa Valley Inn
2001 Vancouver Drive
Honolulu, Oahu, HI 96822
(808) 947-6019

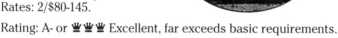

Type of B&B: Inn.
Rooms: 8, 5 with private bath.
Rates: 2/$80-145.

Rating: A- or ♕ ♕ ♕ Excellent, far exceeds basic requirements.

Hawaiian mansion built in 1915 is located in a quiet residential area located near University of Hawaii, and 2 miles from Waikiki Beach. Choose from eight guest rooms, five with private bath. Each room offers an interesting selection of Hawaiian antiques, fresh tropical flowers, and patterned wallpaper. There are a number of common rooms but guests especially enjoy gathering on a spacious porch in the back of the mansion which overlooks a landscaped yard and has been the location for many weddings. Guests from all over the world gather in the main parlor which features a pool table, nickelodeon, antique Victrola, and piano. Walk one block to the University of Hawaii campus and public transportation. Continental breakfast. 2/$80-145. MC, V. Travel agent.

Sun Valley

Idaho Country Inn
134 Latigo Lane
Sun Valley, ID 83340
(208) 726-1019

Type of B&B: Large inn.
Rooms: 10 with private bath.
Rates: 1 or 2/$95-145.

Rating: AA- or ♛♛♛♛ Outstanding.

Contemporary mountain-style inn built of logs and river rock is located high on a hill with panoramic mountain views. Choose from ten guest rooms which offer a private bath, remote control, color TV, refrigerator, and special themes ranging from the "Wagon Days" room to the "Wildflower" room. Many of the pieces of furniture and artwork are created by the host who is also an accomplished fishing guide. There are two parlors with fireplaces, a well-stocked library including books on Idaho, 24 hour beverage service, and well-organized information center. A specially-designed Jacuzzi in the back yard offers views of surrounding mountain peaks. This is a major year-round recreation center offering skiing, ice skating, sleigh rides, trout fishing, and golfing. Generous "Idaho-style" full breakfast. Meeting facilities available. Families welcome. No smoking. 1 or 2/$95-145. AE, MC. V. Travel agent.

Evanston

The Margarita European Inn
1566 Oak Avenue
Evanston, IL 60201
(708) 869-2273 or (708) 869-2283

Type of B&B: Urban inn with restaurant.
Rooms: 34, 5 with private bath.
Rates: 1/$40-50; 2/$45-55.

Rating: C+ or ♛ Acceptable, meets basic requirements.

Originally a private boarding school, this Georgian mansion near Chicago
has been reopened as an inn with a restaurant on the main floor. Choose
from thirty-four guest rooms, five with private bath. Relax in the spacious
parlor which features a molded fireplace and floor-to-ceiling arched
windows. Explore Evanston's fine restaurants, art galleries, theater
companies, cultural arts center, and specialty shops. Nearby Lake
Michigan offers sand beaches, historic walking paths, and biking trails
that are found along Northwestern University's campus. Continental
breakfast. Lunch and dinner available in the restaurant. Facilities for
weddings and small meetings available. 1/$40-50; 2/$45-55. Travel agent.

Galena

The Goldmoor
9001 Sand Hill Road
Galena, IL 61036
(815) 777-3925

Type of B&B: Guesthouse.
Rooms: 5 with private bath.
Rates: 2/$95-205.

Rating: A or ♛ ♛ ♛ Excellent, far exceeds basic requirements.

Grand estate in the country offers quiet seclusion and views of the mighty
Mississippi River. Five guest rooms with private bath are available. One
special honeymoon suite is an extra large room with sitting area, Jacuzzi,
fireplace, and entertainment system with stereo. An atrium spa and sauna
are located on the main level of the inn and there are several private
decks and patios along with extensive landscaped grounds. Romantic
getaway, honeymoon and anniversary packages available. Area
attractions include twenty-five antique shops, General Grant's home, and
Chestnut Mountain Resort Ski Lodge. Full breakfast includes homemade
jams and jellies and fresh baked rolls as well as house specialties. 2/$95-
205. AE, MC, V. Travel agent.

Nauvoo

Mississippi Memories
Box 291, Riverview Heights
Nauvoo, IL 62354
(217) 453-2771

Type of B&B: B&B home.
Rooms: 5, 2 with private bath.
Rates: 1 or 2/$43-63.

Rating: A- or ♛♛♛ Excellent, far exceeds basic requirements.

Mississippi Memories is a spacious brick home nestled in a wooded setting which overlooks the Mississippi River. There are five guest rooms available, two with private bath. Each room differs in size, decor, and amenities but all provide comfortable furnishings and pleasant atmosphere along with fresh fruit, flowers, and air conditioning. A downstairs combination suite of two bedrooms, large private bath, and fireplaced den offer a perfect situation for families or couples traveling together. Two decks overlook the river and guests have been able to view the sunsets, barges drifting by, and local wildlife including Bald Eagles. Popular attractions in the area include historic sites, native crafts, antique shops, and twenty-five restored Mormon homes now open to the public. Full breakfast features homemade treats. 1 or 2/$43-63.

Guests write: *"As a mother of three preschool boys, I am constantly taking care of someone else's needs. Thanks to Marge and Dean at Mississippi Memories, all of my needs were attended to! Above all else, our hosts were incredibly pampering, always anticipating what you might need to make your stay more comfortable. If only I could sneak away right now for one more cup of honey tea served to me by the fireplace."* (E. Johnson)

"The banquet breakfasts were spectacular. We loved the beautiful ornaments, family photographs, and fresh roses at our bedside. And the exotic centerpieces! I liked the one with the peach candles complimented with fresh peaches the best." (E. Gould)

"Our first stay in 1989 was for six nights and we were never bored or at a loss for something to do. We stayed in the Suite, nicer than our own home and roomy and private. We used the library, piano, and in general could stay up as late as we cared to. Breakfasts were excellent and varied. We remember pancakes with Marge's special jellies, Cholesterol Bombs (little wieners baked with brown sugar and bacon) egg and cheese bake, and freshly baked cinnamon rolls." (A. Bertram)

"Seldom have I been in a more hospitable home. Your attention to detail and the personal touch in the food and service was certainly extraordinary." (Fess Parker)

"We had the large country bedroom with equally as large a sitting room library. The view: a sloping hill of green grass leading right down to the edge of the mighty Mississippi." (L. Nokleby)

Rock Island

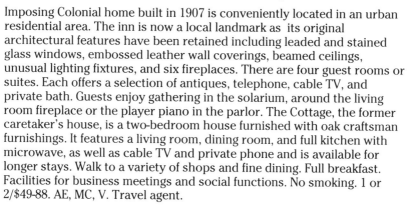

Potter House B&B
1906 7th Avenue
Rock Island, IL 61201
(309) 788-1906 or (800) 747-0339

Type of B&B: Inn.
Rooms: 4 with private bath.
Rates: 1 or 2/$49-88.

Rating: A- or ♛♛♛ Excellent, far exceeds basic requirements.

Imposing Colonial home built in 1907 is conveniently located in an urban residential area. The inn is now a local landmark as its original architectural features have been retained including leaded and stained glass windows, embossed leather wall coverings, beamed ceilings, unusual lighting fixtures, and six fireplaces. There are four guest rooms or suites. Each offers a selection of antiques, telephone, cable TV, and private bath. Guests enjoy gathering in the solarium, around the living room fireplace or the player piano in the parlor. The Cottage, the former caretaker's house, is a two-bedroom house furnished with oak craftsman furnishings. It features a living room, dining room, and full kitchen with microwave, as well as cable TV and private phone and is available for longer stays. Walk to a variety of shops and fine dining. Full breakfast. Facilities for business meetings and social functions. No smoking. 1 or 2/$49-88. AE, MC, V. Travel agent.

Guests write: *"Staying here is a wonderful alternative to motels on my business in Moline. Nancy, the owner, knows that I like breakfast very early and is accommodating." (D. Dawson)*

"We stayed in Mrs. Potter's Suite. It was nicely decorated and had the most comfortable chair and love seat. There were old books as well as current periodicals. A great relaxing weekend of reading in total comfort." (E. McGowan)

Rockford

Victoria's B&B Inn
201 North 6th Street
Rockford, IL 61107
(815) 963-3232

Type of B&B: Inn.
Rooms: 4 with private bath.
Rates: 1 or 2/$69-169.

Rating: A or ♛♛♛ Excellent, far exceeds basic requirements.

Victoria's B&B Inn was built at the turn-of-the-century and is centrally located in the city which is 90 miles west of Chicago off I-90. There are four guest suites with private bath. Each has been decorated with antiques, rich wallpaper and fabrics, and offers a TV and Jacuzzi. The Victorian parlor on the main floor has been the setting for several weddings and it features unusually detailed wallpaper which in itself is a work of art. Popular attractions in the area include Burpee Museum, Tinker Cottage, riverboat rides, and Victorian Village's seventy shops and restaurants. Continental breakfast. Facilities for meetings, receptions and weddings. 1 or 2/$69-169. Weekday special rates and corporate rates as low as $39 per night. MC, V.

Wheaton

The Wheaton Inn
301 West Roosevelt Road
Wheaton, IL 60187
(708) 690-2600 or (708) 690-2623

Type of B&B: Large inn.
Rooms: 16 with private bath.
Rates: 1 or 2/$99-195.

Rating: A or ♛♛♛ Far exceeds basic requirements.

Built in 1987 in a design to reflect Colonial Williamsburg, this urban inn is located 25 miles west of Chicago. Several of the sixteen rooms feature a Jacuzzi tub or gas fireplace. All offer a private bath with European towel warmers and amenities. There are several common rooms including a living room with fireplace, breakfast atrium room with French doors leading onto the patio, and lower-level conference rooms. Explore the historic town of Wheaton or nearby Geneva for shopping and unique restaurants. Nearby attractions include Morton Arboretum, Cantigny War Museum, McCormick Mansion, Wheaton Water Park, or the Billy Graham Center found on the Wheaton College campus. A full breakfast and afternoon refreshments are offered daily. Two meeting rooms available for family reunions, weddings, and business functions. Families welcome. Wheelchair access. 1 or 2/$99-195. AE, MC, V. 10% senior, business and auto club discounts. Travel agent.

Chesterton

Gray Goose Inn
350 Indian Boundary Road
Chesterton, IN 46304
(219) 926-5781

Type of B&B: Inn.
Rooms: 5 with private bath.
Rates: 1/$65-75; 2/$75-85.

Rating: A- or ♛♛♛ Excellent, far exceeds basic requirements.

The Gray Goose Inn is an English Country-style home conveniently located near the intersections of I-94, I-90, and I-80 near the Indiana/Michigan border. The inn is located near shopping malls and restaurants yet has a secluded setting on a lake. Five guest rooms are available, each with private bath. The rooms differ greatly in size, decor, and amenities, but all are comfortably furnished and offer a private telephone. A spacious living room with antiques, fireplace, and collection of artwork is a popular spot where guests gather. The inn offers bicycles for exploring the area as well as boats for an excursion around the small lake. Dunes State and National Lakeshore Parks are located nearby. Full breakfast. Resident dog. 1/$65-75; 2/$75-85. AE, MC, V.

Columbus

Columbus Inn
445 5th Street
Columbus, IN 47201
(812) 378-4289

Type of B&B: Large inn.
Rooms: 34 with private bath.
Rates: 1/$80-90; 2/$95-275.

Rating: A or ♛♛♛ Excellent, far exceeds basic requirements.

Columbus Inn, noted for its Romanesque architecture, is listed on the National Register of Historic Places. Originally built as City Hall, the inn has been completely restored and rivals other examples of fine architecture throughout this city. Thirty-four individually decorated guest rooms are available, each with private bath. The Sparrell Suite is reached by a grand staircase and its main floor serves as an impressive parlor or meeting area with a two-story ceiling, antique furnishings and fine fabrics and upholstered pieces. Columbus is known as the "architectural showplace of America," with more than fifty buildings providing a concentrated and outstanding collection of contemporary architecture. Full breakfast. Facilities for meetings and social gatherings. 1/$80-90; 2/$95-275. AE, D, MC, V. Business travel discount. Travel agent.

Hagerstown

Teetor House
300 West Main Street
Hagerstown, IN 47346
(317) 489-4422

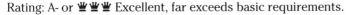

Type of B&B: Inn
Rooms: 4 with private bath.
Rates: 1 or 2/$70-80.

Rating: A- or ♛♛♛ Excellent, far exceeds basic requirements.

Imposing private mansion built in 1936 is situated on a ten acre wooded estate in a small town just 5 miles north of Route 70 in the east/central part of the state. There are four large air-conditioned guest rooms with twin or king sized beds and private bath. Explore this historic home which features carved cherry paneling in the foyer and living room, Steinway concert piano, and in-house museum; or just sit and relax on the pleasant screened-in porch. Popular attractions in the area include fine restaurants, unusual shops, the world's largest antique mall, tennis, golf, and historic tours. Full breakfast. Families welcome. Facilities available for meetings and social functions. Restricted smoking. 2/$70-80.

Guests write: *"Jack did a fine super job both describing the house and telling about one of the great minds of the 20th Century. Hosts were very cordial with prompt attention. Good breakfast was well served. The screened-in porch was especially nice in the evenings."* (C. Tucker-Ladd)

"Exceeded our expectations. The Warmon's add warmth and a unique perspective." (P. Healey)

"The tour was a highlight that impelled us to bring guests for the weekend on our second visit. The house is an expression of the genius and character of Ralph Teetor. The hosts, through their devotion to the house and to the guests, properly memorialize that genius." (H. Hensold)

"We appreciated all the extra touches. The omelette was superb! The tour was fascinating and inspiring. I'd rather stay at a bed and breakfast than any hotel if others are as nice as the Teetor House." (K. Hudson)

Middlebury

Patchwork Quilt Country Inn
11748 County Road #2
Middlebury, IN 46540
(219) 825-2417

Type of B&B: Inn.
Rooms: 9, 6 with private bath.
Rates: 1/$43; 2/$53-95.

Rating: B or ♛♛ Good, exceeds basic requirements.

Historic farmhouse in the heart of the Northern Indiana Amish Country is now a country inn and restaurant located on County Road #2, 1 mile west of SR-13. Choose from nine guest rooms, six with private bath, and each decorated with handmade quilts and distinctive folk art. The most interesting attractions in the area include Amish settlement, Shipshewana flea market, antique auction, Midwest Museum of Art, quilt shops, and Amish back road tours which can be arranged from the inn. Full country breakfast includes fresh eggs, farm-grown fruits, and home baked goods. No smoking. 1/$43; 2/$53-95. MC, V.

Middlebury

Varns Guest House, Inc.
205 South Main Street
Middlebury, IN 46540
(219) 825-9666

Type of B&B: Guesthouse.
Rooms: 5 with private bath.
Rates: 1/$60; 2/$65.

Rating: B+ or ♛♛ Good, exceeds basic requirements.

Varn's Guest House is a modest turn-of-the-century home built in 1898 and located on a tree-lined street in the heart of town. This area is known as Amish country and it is located 5 miles south of the Indiana Toll Road's Middlebury exit. Choose from five guest rooms. They offer a variety of size, decor, and amenities, but each has a private bath, air conditioning, comfortable furnishings, and has been named after relatives and childhood memories. A wrap-around porch is a popular place to watch the activities in this small town but in cold weather guest enjoy gathering around the parlor's brick fireplace. Popular attractions nearby include the giant Shipshewana flea market, Amish communities, and a selection of interesting shops and restaurants with good home-cooked food. Continental plus breakfast includes homemade pastries. No smoking. 1/$60; 2/$65. MC, V.

Guests write: *"Varn's Guest House is a jewel. After more than 200 B&Bs and inns it takes a lot to impress us! Ask for the China Rose Room. It is exquisite. (K. Wellage)*

Newburgh

Phelps Mansion Inn Bed & Breakfast
208 State Street
Newburgh, IN 47630
(812) 853-7766 or (812) 853-3706

Type of B&B: Small inn.
Rooms: 4 with private bath.
Rates: 1/$65; 2/$70.

Rating: A- or ♛♛♛ Excellent, far exceeds basic requirements.

Georgian-style manor home built in 1850 is located twenty miles south of I-64 or 10 miles east of downtown Evansville. The four guest rooms are spacious and feature thirteen-foot ceilings, nine-foot tall windows with original shutters, and wide-plank poplar wood floors. Each has a private bath and either a kitchenette or fireplace. The living room with fireplace, library, and two verandas offers a relaxing area for reading. Walk to the Ohio River nearby or historic downtown area with restaurants, antique and craft shops, art galleries, and an authentic country store. Area attractions include the historic utopian community of New Harmony and Angel Mounds State Park. Continental breakfast. Restricted smoking. 1/$65; 2/$70. AE, MC, V.

Warsaw

White Hill Manor
2513 East Center Street
Warsaw, IN 46580
(219) 269-6933

Type of B&B: Inn.
Rooms: 8 with private bath.
Rates: 1/$68-105; 2/$75-112.

Rating: A+ or ♛♛♛ Excellent, far exceeds basic requirements.

Imposing English Tudor stone mansion is now an inn conveniently located on spacious grounds off Route 30, 40 miles west of Fort Wayne. There are eight guest rooms available. Each has a private bath, quality furnishings, and lovely fabric bedspreads and drapes. Special features of some rooms include four-poster beds, antique claw-foot tub, spa bath, or king-sized brass bed. This is a popular area for lake recreation, Amish settlements, and Shipshewana markets. Guests enjoy local theater and fine dining which are available nearby. Full European breakfast and afternoon tea are included. Facilities available for small weddings and conferences. Restricted smoking. 1/$68-105; 2/$75-112. AE, MC, V.

Amana Colonies/Homestead

Die Heimat Country Inn
Amana Colonies
Homestead, IA 52236
(319) 622-3937

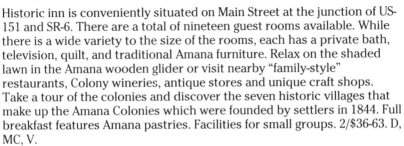

Type of B&B: Inn.
Rooms: 19 with private bath.
Rates: 2/$36-63.

Rating: B or ♛♛ Good, exceeds basic requirements.

Historic inn is conveniently situated on Main Street at the junction of US-151 and SR-6. There are a total of nineteen guest rooms available. While there is a wide variety to the size of the rooms, each has a private bath, television, quilt, and traditional Amana furniture. Relax on the shaded lawn in the Amana wooden glider or visit nearby "family-style" restaurants, Colony wineries, antique stores and unique craft shops. Take a tour of the colonies and discover the seven historic villages that make up the Amana Colonies which were founded by settlers in 1844. Full breakfast features Amana pastries. Facilities for small groups. 2/$36-63. D, MC, V.

Atlantic

Chestnut Charm Bed & Breakfast
1409 Chestnut Street
Atlantic, IA 50022
(712) 243-5652

Type of B&B: Small inn.
Rooms, 5, 3 with private bath.
Rates: 1/$45-65; 2/$55-75.

Rating: B+ or ♛♛ Good, exceeds basic requirements.

Grand Victorian home was built in 1898 and is situated on a large lot in a quiet, residential neighborhood of a small town near exit 54 off of I-80 in the western part of the state. Five guest rooms are available, three with private bath. Each room has been individually decorated and may feature Battenburg lace, Art Deco hand-painted walls, leaded windows, or even a knight in shining armor. There are several parlor areas as well as a sunny porch where breakfast is regularly served. Visitors often come to this area to play golf, visit the nearby state park, or shop at antique stores. Full gourmet breakfast includes several specialties of the house. No smoking. 1/$45-65; 2/$55-75. MC, V.

Dubuque

The Hancock House
1105 Grove Terrace
Dubuque, IA 52001
(319) 557-8989

Type of B&B: Inn.
Rooms: 9 with private bath.
Rates: 1 or 2/$75-150.

Rating: A or ♛♛♛ Excellent, far exceeds basic requirements.

Imposing Queen Anne Victorian mansion is set on the bluffs of this historic town and is located at the intersections of Routes 151, 61, 52, and 20 in the Northeast corner of the state. Nine individually decorated guest rooms are available, each with private bath (two with whirlpool tub). Enjoy a spectacular view of the Mississippi River from this location. Nearby Dubuque offers restored Victorian mansions serving as museums, art galleries, and antique and specialty shops. Don't miss taking a riverboat ride on the Mississippi River. The area's mountains offer hiking, biking, and skiing. Full breakfast. Families welcome. No smoking. 1 or 2/$75-150. MC, V. Travel agent.

Wichita

Inn at the Park
3751 East Douglas
Wichita, KS 67218
(316) 652-0500 or (800) 258-1951

Type of B&B: Inn.
Rooms: 10 rooms and 2 suites, all with private bath.
Rates: 1/$75-125; 2/$85-135.

Rating: AA or ♛♛♛♛ Outstanding.

The Inn at the Park is a mansion built in 1910 that has been completely renovated. In 1989 the entire inn was professionally decorated by a number of well known area designers for use as a Designer's Showcase. There are ten guest rooms with private bath in the mansion and their decor ranges from French Country to Oriental, from Neoclassical to Art Nouveau. A carriage house on the grounds offers two private suites. Amenities include fireplaces, private courtyard, hot tub, cable TV, VCR, and phone. Continental breakfast features fruits, pastries, and often includes quiche or chili rellenos. Special services for business travelers include a conference room, secretarial services, and fax machine. Families welcome. 1/$75-125; 2/$85-135. AE, MC, V. 10% senior, auto club, and business travel discounts. Travel agent.

Guests write: *"They are doing a fine job of providing people with a quality place to spend a night or a Honeymoon. I think that next year we will spend our anniversary at the Inn at the Park." (T. Chamberlain)*

Wichita

Max Paul, An Inn
3910 East Kellogg
Wichita, KS 67218
(316) 689-8101

Type of B&B: Inn and cottages.
Rooms: 14 rooms or suites with private bath.
Rates: 1/$55-95; 2/$65-115.

Rating: A or ♛ ♛ ♛ Excellent, far exceeds basic requirements.

Max Paul is an inn which is comprised of three English Tudor cottages located just west of the intersection of Highways 135 and 54. There are a total of fourteen guest rooms. While the rooms vary in size, decor, and amenities, each offers a private bath, cable TV, European antiques, and a featherbed. Large executive suites feature vaulted ceilings, fireplaces, skylights, and private balconies. There is a spa and exercise room on the premises but guests are also encouraged to walk to the nearby public park for tennis, jogging paths, and children's pool. Airport, downtown shopping centers, and major corporate headquarters are nearby. Continental breakfast. Facilities for business meetings or social functions. 1/$55-95; 2/$65-115. AE, MC, V.

Versailles

Shepherd Place
31 Heritage Road, US-60 Lexington
Versailles, KY 40383
(606) 873-7843

Type of B&B: B&B Home.
Rooms: 2 with private bath.
Rates: 1/$60; 2/$65; 3/$70.

Rating: B or ♛♛ Good, exceeds basic requirements.

Built in 1815, this Federalist-style home is located ten miles from downtown Lexington off of US-60 at Heritage Road. Two spacious guest rooms are available, the Brass bedroom with queen-size bed or the Cherry bedroom with a double bed. Each room offers an additional single bed for a third person. Relax in the parlor or on the old-fashioned porch swing. Explore the grounds and meet the resident ewes, Abigail and Victoria, or stroll down to feed Horace the goose. Visit local Bluegrass area attractions such as Keeneland, Shakertown, Kentucky horse park, or several antique malls. A full breakfast boasts pancakes, raisin toast, and various breakfast meats. No smoking. 1/$60; 2/$65; 3/$70. MC, V.

Versailles

Sills Inn
270 Montgomery Avenue
Versailles, KY 40383
(606) 873-4478 or (800) 526-9801

Type of B&B: Inn.
Rooms: 8 with private bath.
Rates: 2/$55-75.

Rating: A- or ♛♛♛ Excellent, far exceeds basic requirements.

Victorian home built near the turn-of-the-century is located near the historic downtown area of the city. Choose from eight guest rooms, each with private bath. Relax on the wrap-around porch in a wicker rocking chair and enjoy a tune on the old Victrola. There is a fully stocked guest kitchen where you can fix a late night snack before retiring. Area attractions include the Bluegrass Railroad Museum, Keeneland Race Track, Shaker Town, the State Capital, horse farms, and the Kentucky Horse Park. Full breakfast specialties may include eggs Benedict or quiche, cheese grits, and spoon bread. Families welcome. Restricted smoking. 1 or 2/$55-75. AE, MC, V. Travel agent.

New Orleans

Lafitte Guest House
1003 Bourbon Street
New Orleans, LA 70116
(504) 581-2678 or (800) 331-7971

Type of B&B: Inn.
Rooms: 14 with private bath.
Rates: 1 or 2/$69-155.

Rating: A or ♛♛♛ Excellent, far exceeds basic requirements.

Lafitte Guest house is an historic mansion with French architectural influence which is conveniently located in the heart of the French Quarter of the city. Choose from fourteen guest rooms which offer a variety in size, decor, and amenities but each has a selection of period furnishings, rich fabrics and appointments, and a private bath. Several rooms have private balconies with views of the city skyline and French Quarter and these rooms are especially popular during Mardis Gras. Walk to an abundance of world famous restaurants, reknowned nightclubs, specialty shops, museums, and colorful Creole and Spanish cottages. Continental breakfast features fresh pastries. 1 or 2/$69-155. AE, MC, V. Travel agent.

Bangor

Phenix Inn
20 West Market Square
Bangor, ME 04401
(207) 947-3850

Type of B&B: Urban inn.
Rooms: 36 with private bath.
Rates: 1/$42-53; 2/$58-80.

Rating: B+ or ♛♛ Good, exceeds basic requirements.

The Phenix Inn is an urban inn built in 1873 and located off exit 46 of I-95 in the West Market Square area of downtown. Thirty-six guest rooms are available. Each offers mahogany furnishings, individual air conditioning and heating, and private bath. Major office buildings, specialty shops, and restaurants are within walking distance. Continental breakfast. Facilities are available for meetings and social functions. Families welcome. Restricted smoking. 1/$42-53; 2/$58-80. AE, MC, V. 10% senior, auto club, and business travel discounts. Travel agent.

Bar Harbor

The Tides
119 West Street
Bar Harbor, ME 04609
(207) 288-4968

Type of B&B: Inn.
Rooms: 3 with private bath.
Rates: 2/$145-195.

Rating: AA- or ♛♛♛♛ Outstanding.

Classic Greek Revival oceanfront inn is located on historic West Street, just off of Route 3 in the village. Three guest rooms with private baths feature period furnishings and a full ocean view. The impressive foyer leads into gracious living and dining rooms. Take an easy walk downtown to the shops, restaurants, and wharf, or drive to nearby Acadia National Park. A full breakfast and afternoon tea are served daily on a wrap-around veranda with fireplace and ocean views. No smoking. 2/$145-195. MC, V. Travel agent.

Bath

Inn at Bath
969 Washington Street
Bath, ME 04530
(207) 433-4294

Type of B&B: Inn.
Rooms: 5 with private bath.
Rates: 1/$85; 2/$95-120.

Rating: B+ or ♛♛ Good, exceeds basic requirements.

Stately Colonial inn is situated on a main street in Bath which is located forty-five minutes north of Portland off Route 1. Five guest rooms with private bath are offered. There is a variety in the size, decor, and amenities of each room but all are furnished with antiques and offer a pleasing decor. On the main floor is a formal double parlor with fireplaces and a separate dining room where a full breakfast is served. Area attractions include Stelgithern Museum, outlet shops, coastal activities, antique shops, and recreation. No smoking. 1/$85; 2/$95-120. MC. V. Travel agent.

Belfast

Frost House
6 Northport Avenue
Belfast, ME 04915
(207) 338-4159

Type of B&B: Inn.
Rooms: 3, 2 with private bath.
Rates: 1/$50-70; 2/$60-80.

Rating: A or ♛♛♛ Excellent, far exceeds basic requirements.

Victorian turn-of-the-century home is less than a mile off Route 1 on a 1.2 acre lot with gardens. Choose from three guest rooms, two with private bath, which are decorated with period antiques and offer views of the water. The harbor is just blocks away with bay cruises, live theater, concerts, shopping, and dining. Bar Harbor is an hour drive and Camden can be reached in 20 minutes by car. Blueberry pancakes, egg casseroles, Belgian waffles, and fresh muffins are some of the full breakfast specialties. No smoking. 1/$50-70; 2/$60-80. Travel agent.

Boothbay - See also East Boothbay.

Boothbay

Hodgdon Island Inn
P.O. Box 492, Barter's Island Road
Boothbay, ME 04571
(207) 633-7474

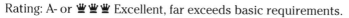

Type of B&B: Inn.
Rooms: 6 with private bath.
Rates: 1 or 2/$50-75.

Rating: A- or ♛♛♛ Excellent, far exceeds basic requirements.

Restored Victorian sea captain's home was built in the 1820's and features water views out of every window. Six guest rooms with private bath are available. A pleasant porch with wicker furniture is a popular place to relax as is the heated swimming pool surrounded by attractive grounds. Area attractions include local clambakes, summer theater, art galleries, fishing, and fall foliage trips. Full breakfast includes homemade granola and muffins. No smoking. 1 or 2/$50-75.

Boothbay Harbor

Anchor Watch B&B Inn
3 Eames Road
Boothbay Harbor, ME 04538
(207) 633-2284

Type of B&B: Inn.
Rooms: 4 with private bath.
Rates: 2/$65-88.

Rating: B+ or ♛♛ Good, exceeds basic requirements.

Shorefront Colonial inn on a quiet scenic lane is 12 miles south of Route 1. Rooms are decorated with country stenciling, quilts, and nautical paintings by local artists. Enjoy tranquil views of islands, lighthouses, lobster boats, and ducks feeding along the shore. Fine restaurants, gift and antique shops, and boating activities are just a five-minute walk away. Afternoon tea is offered and a full breakfast is served in the sunny breakfast nook looking out to sea. Kitchen facilities are available to guests in the winter. No smoking or pets. 2/$65-88. Travel agent. Closed mid-December through mid-January.

Guests write: *"We were very pleased with our recent stay. The decor and cuisine were delightful. Feeding the gulls was an added enjoyment."* (J. Wood)

"The view of Boothbay outer harbor from our own 145-foot pier was fabulous! We especially like the unique spouting whale stencils designed for our room." (E. Miller)

"The breakfasts are outrageously delicious and the variety makes for a pleasant surprise every morning. The B&B's tie-in with the boat tours or the harbor and islands is very convenient." (W. Turcotte)

Boothbay Harbor

Atlantic Ark Inn
64 Atlantic Avenue
Boothbay Harbor, ME 04538
(204) 633-5690

Type of B&B: Small inn.
Rooms: 5, each with private bath.
Rates: 1 or 2/$55-85.

Rating: B+ or ♛♛ Good, exceeds basic requirements.

Small, intimate Victorian inn built in 1875 is found across the harbor on the east side of the village, 11 miles from Route 1. Five guest rooms with private bath are available. Each has been decorated with period antiques, fresh flowers, mahogany poster beds with firm mattresses, and Oriental rugs. Several rooms offer private balconies with harbor views. A separate guest cottage on the property is also available. The front porch is a good spot to view the sunset each evening. Crossing the small foot bridge at the edge of the property leads to the Inner Harbor shops, galleries, and fine restaurants. Full breakfast is served on fine linen and china and features specialties such as English scones, old-fashioned biscuits, cinnamon popovers, and sweet baked goods such as apricot nut bread or strawberry muffins. No smoking. 1 or 2/$55-85. AE, MC, V.

Guests write: *"Waking up in a four-poster bed with the sun shining in through lace curtains is one of our most lasting memories. We truly enjoyed the beautiful front porch where we could watch the fishing boats in the harbor with our morning coffee, or evening cordials. We happened upon the Atlantic Ark the first weekend they opened, and have been back every summer since." (M. Sternberg)*

"It is especially clean, well-managed, and comfortable. The hosts are able to get your day started on the right course by serving a unique and delicious breakfast. Its charm is evident throughout." (H. Craig)

"As we arrived we were greeted and escorted past beautiful petunias to a private chalet overlooking views of a pond to the side and the harbor in

front. Tall glasses of iced-tea adorned with fresh mint from the garden were over-shadowed only by the specially prepared muffins, fresh fruit, and full breakfast served at a private table overlooking the veranda." (M. Caporaso)

Camden

Blue Harbor House
67 Elm Street
Camden, ME 04843
(207) 236-3196 or (800) 248-3196
Fax: (207) 236-6523

Type of B&B: Inn.
Rooms: 10, 8 with private bath.
Rates: 1/$75-140.

Rating: A- or ♛♛♛ Excellent, far exceeds basic requirements.

Classic New England Cape Cod inn built prior to 1835 is 85 miles north of Portland on Route 1. Ten guest rooms, eight with private bath, feature country antiques, quilts, and stenciled walls. Several rooms also offer whirlpool tubs, air-conditioning, and TV. This village is the home of the Windjammer Fleet which offers day sails. Popular activities nearby include hiking, skiing, biking, concerts, theater, art, and craft shops. Full breakfast. Country suppers and picnic lunches are available with advance notice. Indoor sun porch accommodates small meetings and weddings. Families welcome. Restricted smoking. 1/$75-140. MC, V. 10% senior, business traveler, and auto club discounts. Travel agent.

Camden

Hartstone Inn
41 Elm Street
Camden, ME 04843
(207) 236-4259

Type of B&B: Inn.
Rooms: 8 rooms and carriage house with private baths.
Rates: 1/$60-85; 2/$75-90.

Rating: A or ♛♛♛ Excellent, far exceeds basic requirements.

Intimate Victorian inn is located in the heart of the village, a stones throw from the harbor. There are eight guest rooms with comfortable antiques and private baths. Two have fireplaces. There is also a parlor with fireplace and a library with a variety of good books and cable TV. Two efficiency apartments are in the carriage house and available at weekly rates. Shops, galleries, and restaurants are only steps away from the front door. Skiing, golf, swimming, sailing, or kayaking are all nearby. Full breakfast. Candlelight dinners and picnic lunches available by advance reservation. 1/$60-85, 2/$75-90.

Camden

Hawthorne Inn
9 High Street
Camden, ME 04843
(207) 236-8842

Type of B&B: Large inn.
Rooms: 10 with private bath.
Rates: 1/$60-135; 2/$65-140.

Rating: A+ or ♛ ♛ ♛ Excellent, far exceeds basic requirements.

Victorian mansion with turrets and a circular drive was built in 1894 and is located near exit 22 off Route 95. Ten individually decorated guest rooms with private bath are available. Several feature views of the Camden Hills or harbor. The main foyer is graced with a three-story staircase and original stained glass windows. An adjoining carriage house offers townhouse apartments and studio rooms with kitchen and private deck. Concerts and plays take place at the amphitheater just past the back yard. Within walking distance are restaurants, galleries, and specialty shops that line the harbor. Area attractions include Mount Battie and Camden State Park which offer hiking, climbing, skiing, and boating. Full breakfast and afternoon tea served daily. Wedding and meeting facilities available. Families welcome. Restricted smoking. 1/$60-135; 2/$65-140; Apartment:$140-225. MC, V. Travel agent.

Camden

Maine Stay Inn
22 High Street
Camden, ME 04843
(207) 236-9636

Type of B&B: Inn.
Rooms: 8, 2 with private bath.
Rates: 1 or 2/$62-88.

Rating: A or ♛ ♛ ♛ Excellent, far exceeds basic requirements.

Built in 1802 and listed on the National Register of Historic Places, this Colonial inn is located in the center of Camden's historic district, 3 blocks north of the village center and harbor. Eight handsome guest rooms, two with private bath, have brass or oak beds. Two fireplaced parlors and a TV lounge are decorated with Oriental rugs and period furnishings. Stroll through the two-acre wooded glen, walk to the harbor, or hike along miles of well maintained trails in the Camden Hills State Park. Alpine and cross-country skiing, golf, tennis, fishing, sailing, bicycling and ferry service to picturesque islands are available close by. Information is provided for suggested tours and day trips. Tasty egg dishes, French toast, or whole wheat pancakes are frequently part of the full breakfast offered. 1 or 2/$62-88. MC, V. Travel agent.

East Boothbay

Five Gables Inn
Murray Hill Road
East Boothbay, ME 04544
(207) 633-4557

Type of B&B: Large inn.
Rooms: 16 with private bath.
Rates: 1 or 2/$80-120.

Rating: A+ or ♛♛♛ Excellent, far exceeds basic requirements.

Grand hotel with Victorian detailing was built in 1865 and has been completely restored. Sixteen guest rooms with private bath feature reproduction antiques and views of Linekin Bay. Several rooms offer fireplaces and queen-size beds. A wrap-around porch has comfortable seating and bay views. Guests often gather in the parlor in front of the fireplace. Public swimming is available across the street and golf courses are nearby. Popular attractions include a cruise to Cabbage Island for daily lobster bakes or shopping in Boothbay Harbor, Monhegan Island, and Freeport. Full breakfast. Restricted smoking. 1 or 2/$80-120. MC, V. 10% auto club discount. Travel agent.

Freeport

181 Main Street B&B
181 Main Street
Freeport, ME 04032
(207) 865-1226

Type of B&B: Inn.
Rooms: 7 with private bath.
Rates: 1/$60-75; 2/$75-95.

Rating: A or ♛♛♛ Excellent, far exceeds basic requirements.

Cape Cod-style inn built in 1840 is located on US-1 near I-95. Seven guest rooms are available. Each offers a private bath, queen or double bed, handmade quilt, antique furnishings, Oriental rugs, and artwork. Two common rooms on the main floor offer areas for conversing, playing board games, or watching TV. The swimming pool with deck is a popular gathering place during warm weather and there are several Adriondack chairs strategically placed around the lawn for rest and relaxation. Freeport center outlet shops and L.L. Bean are within walking distance from the inn. Bowdoin College, Maine coast, Portland, or Brunswick are a short drive away. Full breakfast includes homemade breads. No smoking. 1/$60-75; 2/$75-95. MC, V.

Freeport/South Freeport

Atlantic Seal B&B
P.O. Box 146
25 Main Street
South Freeport, ME 04078
(207) 865-6112

Type of B&B: Inn.
Rooms: 3, 2 with private bath.
Rates: 1/$50-55; 2/$65-125.

Rating: B+ or ♛♛ Good, exceeds basic requirements.

Seaside Cape Cod home, built circa 1850 offers a harbor view from every room and is located 2.5 miles from Route 1. Three guests rooms feature homemade quilts, down comforters, and fresh flowers. Two rooms have a private bath, one with Jacuzzi tub. The family home is furnished with antique and nautical collections from seafaring hosts. Guests can relax with refreshing beverages in the old-fashioned parlor by the fireplace or on the deck overlooking the harbor. Hosts operate harbor cruises to Eagle Island and offer guest discounts. Visit nearby Freeport with its famous outlet stores and L.L. Bean. Hearty sailor's breakfast often includes lobster omelettes, homemade breads and muffins. Restricted smoking. Resident dog and cat. 1/$50-55; 2/$65-125. Travel agent.

Freeport

Bagley House
R.R. 3, Box 269C
Freeport, ME 04032
(207) 865-6566

Type of B&B: Inn.
Rooms: 5 with private bath.
Rates: 1/$65-80; 2/$80-95.

Rating: A- or ♛♛♛ Excellent, far exceeds basic requirements.

Bagley House is an historic inn built in 1772 and located ten minutes from the center of Freeport on a six acre wooded setting. Choose from five guest rooms with private bath, stenciled rugs, antique furnishings, and handmade quilts. Relax in the living room with fireplace or the library with extensive collection of books, magazines, and games. Popular area attractions include shopping, visiting local museums, state parks, beaches, Audubon nature trails, and the Casco Bay islands. Local recreation includes berry picking and skiing. Full breakfast is served in the country kitchen with brick fireplace, beehive oven, wide pine floors, and handhewn beams. Facilities for meetings and social functions are available. Resident cat and dog. No smoking. 1/$65-80; 2/$80-95. AE, MC, V. Travel agent.

Freeport

Kendall Tavern Bed & Breakfast
213 Main Street
Freeport, ME 04032
(207) 856-1338

Type of B&B: Small inn.
Rooms: 7 with private bath.
Rates: 1/80; 2/$110.

Rating: A or ♛♛♛ Excellent, far exceeds basic requirements.

1850s farmhouse accented with Victorian trim has been completely restored and is situated on three acres at the north end of the village. Choose from seven guest rooms with private bath. While there is a variety in the size, decor, and amenities of the rooms, each is comfortably furnished and freshly decorated. Two parlors with fireplaces grace the main floor and breakfast is served in a pleasant dining room with small tables. Popular activities in the area include shopping at local outlets and L.L. Bean's retail store. Full breakfast specialties include homemade muffins, coffee cakes, pancakes, and waffles. No smoking. 1/$80; 2/$110. MC. V.

Freeport

Porter's Landing Bed & Breakfast
70 South Street
Freeport, ME 04032
(207) 865-4488

Type of B&B: Inn.
Rooms: 3 with private bath.
Rates: 1/$65-80; 2/$75-90.

Rating: A or ♛♛♛ Excellent, far exceeds basic requirements.

Greek Revival home built in 1830 is 1 mile from L.L. Bean on the road that leads to the town harbor. Three guest rooms with private bath are housed in the adjoining renovated Victorian carriage house. Relax in the grand sitting room in front of a working Count Rumford fireplace. Walk along Main Street and explore more than 100 factory outlet stores. Visit nearby Wolf Neck or Winslow Parks and enjoy biking, sailboating, fishing, cross-country skiing, or hiking along the edge of the ocean. A hearty breakfast features Belgian waffles, omelettes, and homemade muffins. No smoking. 1/$65-80; 2/$75-90. MC. V. Travel agent.

Guests write: *"We enjoyed a small but very lovely room with private bath. The common area was warm and attractive with lots of information available on the Freeport area." (T. Lane)*

"I had intended to come up for the cross-country skiing but my husband is deployed in the Persian Gulf. You can be sure upon his return we'll be up for a weekend. After all, he's an L.L. Bean addict and I can't think of a more peaceful and romantic haven to spend time with a long-lost spouse. I can't say enough about Porter's Landing. Upon our arrival, Peter, who had been washing windows, greeted me by name and welcomed me. He ushered us in and Barbara took over and cooled our parched throats with fresh iced tea in the sitting room. The decor was beautiful but comfortable. Our hosts offered us their knowledge about the area and acted on our behalf when making reservations for us locally." (M. Smith)

"The most memorable part of my trip to Maine was my stay at Porter's Landing. Barbara and Peter made us feel welcome the moment we arrived and went out of their way to accommodate us. Their hospitality is second to none." (J. Dodgson)

Freeport

White Cedar Inn
178 Main Street
Freeport, ME 04032
(207) 865-9099

Type of B&B: Inn.
Rooms: 6, 2 with shared bath.
Rates: 1 or 2/$65-90.

Rating: B+ or ♛♛ Good, exceeds basic requirements.

Recently restored Victorian inn was built in 1890 by the famed Arctic explorer Donald McMillan and is located 30 minutes from Portland. Six guest rooms are available, four with private bath. Each room differs in size, decor, and amenities, but all have comfortable furnishings. Common areas for guests include a sunroom, parlor with wood stove, games, and library of books. L.L. Bean's famous retail store is a two block walk from the inn. The area offers an abundance of outdoor recreation including fishing, biking, and skiing. Full breakfast includes blueberry pancakes, French toast, waffles, and a variety of baked goods. No smoking. 1 or 2/$65-90.

Kennebunk

Arundel Meadows Inn
P.O. Box 1129
Kennebunk, ME 04043
(207) 985-3770

Type of B&B: Inn.
Rooms: 7 with private bath.
Rates: 1 or 2/$75-125.

Rating: A- or ♛♛♛ Excellent, far exceeds basic requirements.

Arundel Meadows Inn was built one hundred sixty-five years ago as a farmhouse and is located near exit 3 off I-95. Seven guest rooms are available. Each offers a private bath and individual decor. Three rooms boast working fireplaces and there is a suite especially suited for four traveling together. This area is popular for its diverse specialty shops, restaurants, and art galleries as well as the nearby beaches and interesting New England villages. Full breakfast. 1 or 2/$75-125. MC, V.

Guests write: *"The rooms are wonderfully decorated with antiques and collector's items from all over the world. Afternoon tea is a special time to sit around and chat with the hosts and other guests over a cup of tea and a* plate of warm cookies or some other goodie that Mark has freshly whipped up." (J. Wohlberg)

"The rooms are spotless, beautifully decorated and comfortable with attention to such details as a variety of soaps in the baths and current issues of magazines and other reading materials in the rooms. The breakfasts are so delicious and generous that we often skip lunch. We look forward to our annual visit." (P. Cilea)

"Very enjoyable stay. Staff and host were very helpful and courteous. I would recommend it to anyone." (D. Gagnon)

"Each room is uniquely furnished with a tasteful mix of antique and contemporary furnishings. The warmth of the surroundings is further enhanced by an eclectic collection of paintings. The breakfasts are creative, beautifully presented, and delicious. The blueberry muffins are outstanding!" (E. Greenspan)

"Our richly appointed suite with its large picture window and king-size bed really made us feel like royalty. We'll never forget the taste of those blueberry pancakes with warm syrup. Mark and Murray have anticipated our every need from providing us with a tranquil environment filled with artwork and antiques to even lending us bicycles to use for the beach. These innkeepers leave no stone unturned." (C. Wander)

Kennebunk Beach

Sundial Inn
P.O. Box 1147
48 Beach Avenue
Kennebunk, ME 04043
(207) 967-3850

Type of B&B: Inn.
Rooms: 34 with private bath.
Rates: 1 or 2/$60-145.

Rating: A+ or ♕♕♕ Excellent, far exceeds basic requirements.

Large oceanfront inn offers a quiet setting with beach access. There are thirty-four guest rooms with private bath, cable TV, air conditioning, and turn-of-the-century antique furnishings. Several luxury rooms offer ocean views and whirlpool baths. An attractive living room furnished with Oriental rugs and chintz-covered chairs and sofa offers a pleasant area for conversing or just enjoying the ocean breezes. Popular attractions in the area include shopping at the local art galleries, gift and outlet shops, whale-watching, deep-sea fishing, and hiking at the nearby wildlife refuge and estuary. Continental breakfast features homemade muffins. Wheelchair access. 1 or 2/$60-145. AE, MC, V.

Kennebunkport/Cape Porpoise

Inn at Harbor Head
R.R. 2, Box 1180, Pier Road
Kennebunkport, ME 04046
(207) 967-5564

Type of B&B: Inn.
Rooms: 5 with private bath.
Rates: 1 or 2/$95-175.

Rating: AA or ♛♛♛♛ Outstanding.

Inn at Harbor Head is a century-old saltwater farmhouse located at the harbor's edge on the rocky shore of Cape Porpoise Harbor, 2 miles east of Kennebunkport. Five guest rooms are available. Each is individually furnished and offers queen or king-size bed, a private bath, and view of the lobster boats, islands, and ocean. Explore nearby beaches, tranquil walking paths, and bike routes. Use the inn as a central base for day trips to the New Hampshire mountains, Boston, Salem, or further along the coast to Boothbay Harbor or Camden. Full breakfast is served in a dining room full of crystal, pewter, and original stenciling, and offers varying specialties such as stuffed French toast, eggs Florentine, or homemade roast beef hash with poached eggs and salsa. No smoking. 1 or 2/$95-175. MC, V. Travel agent.

Guests write: *"The Greenery room is wonderfully tranquil and comforting with its walls wrapped in windows and the bed sinking under all those pillows. Joan and David's gourmet breakfasts have turned us into morning people."* (M. Costa)

"Joan is the epitome of a bed and breakfast hostess reaching that rare balance of attention to every detail while maintaining a warm, cozy, friendly, inviting haven for her guests. My soul is restored from the classical guitar, the crystal, silver, starched linens, hammock, and my own bird singing to me from outside the window." (D. Beto)

"The Harbor Suite with its beautiful murals and view is by far the best room in which we've ever stayed and we've been all over the world." (E. Volk)

'The Summer Suite was romantic, done in exquisite taste, the view divine. The breakfasts were more than delicious and they were presented as a work of art." (A. Ferraro)

"The chocolate covered French toast made my daughter Barbra's day." (F. Johnson)

Kennebunkport

Inn on South Street
PO Box 478A
Kennebunkport, ME 04046
(207) 967-5151

Type of B&B: Inn.
Rooms: 3 rooms and 1 suite,
all with private bath.
Rates: 1/$80-135; 2/$90-175.

Rating: A+ or ♛♛♛ Excellent, far exceeds basic requirements.

Inn on South Street is an early nineteenth-century Greek Revival home situated on a quiet side-street 5 miles from I-95 at exit 3. There are four guest rooms. Each offers a private bath, individual decor, fresh flowers, period antique furnishings, brass bed, and a working fireplace. One room is actually a large suite of three rooms with fireplace and Jacuzzi. Walk down tree-lined streets to restaurants, shops, and the beach or drive to nearby golf courses as well as fishing, boating, and hiking areas. Full gourmet breakfast features homemade family specialties such as over-sized German pancakes, herbed cheese souffle, or a light breakfast flan with blueberry sauce. Afternoon refreshments served daily. No smoking. 1/$80-135; 2/$90-175. AE.

Guests write: *"Breakfast is in the tree tops in the 2nd floor kitchen with a view of the Kennebunk River. Featured on the menu were homemade breads and jams, colorful and tasty combinations of fresh fruits and egg dishes served on blue and white china. Elegant, yet unpretentious."* *(J. Chalmers)*

"This inn should be used as an example of how to run an inn properly. All the comforts such as clean, well-appointed rooms were provided but somehow the whole was greater than the sum of its parts. Jack and Eva were delightful hosts not just innkeepers. You felt extremely comfortable yet there was still a degree of elegance that comes only with knowledge and experience. This gives you the feeling of living in Maine, not just being a tourist." (E. DuBose)

Kennebunkport

Kennebunkport Inn
P.O. Box 111, Dock Square
Kennebunkport, ME 04046
(207) 967-2621

Type of B&B: Inn with restaurant.
Rooms: 34 with private bath.
Rates: 1 or 2/$54-165.

Rating: B+ or ♕♕ Good, exceeds basic requirements.

Large sea captain's home situated along the Kennebunk River was built in 1899 and is now an inn with restaurant. There are thirty-four guest rooms available. Each offers a private bath, color TV, and period furnishings. The restaurant lounge with fireplace and swimming pool with patio are popular spots for relaxation in the evening. Antique shops, boutiques, and restaurants are within walking distance from the inn. Local theaters, horseback riding, golf, and fine beaches are within a short drive. Full breakfast is included in the overnight rates. The restaurant serves candlelight dinners. Families welcome. Meeting facilities available. 1 or 2/$54-165. AE, MC, V. 10% senior and business travel discounts. Travel agent.

Kennebunkport

Kilburn House
P.O. Box 1309, Chestnut Street
Kennebunkport, ME 04046
(207) 967-4762

Type of B&B: Guesthouse
Rooms: 5 rooms or suites, 3 with private bath.
Rates: 2/$45-75.

Rating: B- or ♕♕ Good, exceeds basic requirements.

Small Victorian home built in 1890 is situated on a quiet side street one block from the village center. The four guest rooms offer twin or double beds; three have a private bath. A third floor suite offers complete privacy, two bedrooms, separate living room, and private bath. Specialty shops and restaurants are within easy walking distance from the inn and beaches, nightly entertainment, and the L.L. Bean retail store are a short drive. Continental breakfast. No smoking. 2/$45-75. AE, MC, V.

Kennebunkport

Kylemere House 1818
P.O. Box 1333, 6 South Street
Kennebunkport, ME 04046
(207) 967-2780

Type of B&B: Inn.
Rooms: 5, 3 with private bath.
Rates: 1/$60-90; 2/$70-99.

Rating: A+ or ♛ ♛ ♛ Excellent, far exceeds basic requirements.

Historic Federal inn is located on a quiet street a few minutes walk to shops, beaches, and restaurants. Choose from five guest rooms, three with private bath, and all furnished with period antiques and soft colors that enhance the ambience and true New England decor of this seaport inn. Guests enjoy afternoon refreshments in the sitting room or on the porch overlooking the gardens. Nearby sights include Trolley Museum, Monastery, Maritime Museum, and Portland Museum of Art. A variety of outdoor sporting activities available. Full gourmet breakfast. No smoking. 1/$60-90; 2/$70-99. AE, MC, V.

Guests write: *"I forgot my dress shoes and asked her where there was a shoe store close by. She asked what size and brought me several pairs to pick from. At the same time there was a couple staying who were getting married and he forgot his tie. Not to worry. Mary showed him her husband's for him to choose from."* (K. Dubois)

"Breakfasts were superb and unique. Having cocktails for us before our special dinner was a delightful surprise." (G. Spieth)

"Breakfasts were served in their formal dining room which looks out onto the professionally landscaped gardens. The table place settings are different every day on a five day cycle but not to be outdone by the elegant breakfasts with a variety of juices, warmed exotic fruit cocktails, and our favorite puffed pastry filled with eggs, cheese and bacon. During our 2nd visit Maine was in the direct path of Hurricane Bob. We had restaurant reservations but all commercial establishments were boarded up and closed. We were not to be denied though as Mary and Bill very graciously made dinner for all guests and even popped a bottle of champagne in honor of our daughter's 21st birthday. We were very touched." (C. Jonke)

Kennebunkport

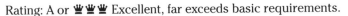

Maine Stay Inn and Cottages
P.O. Box 500-A, 34 Maine Street
Kennebunkport, ME 04046
(207) 967-2117 or (800) 950-2117

Type of B&B: Inn with cottages.
Rooms: 17 rooms or cottages, each with private bath.
Rates: 1/$85-145; 2/$85-180.

Rating: A or ♛♛♛ Excellent, far exceeds basic requirements.

Victorian inn and ten garden cottages built in 1860 is located in the National Historic District just 5 minutes from the village center. The main house offers four guest rooms and two suites, each with private bath. Cottages on the property each offer an efficiency kitchen and wall-to-wall carpeting. Three accommodations have working fireplaces. The inn boasts a suspended stairway, sunburst-crystal glass windows, and a cupola with panoramic view of the town. Relax on the spacious porch or explore the beautiful sandy beaches, picturesque harbor, galleries, antique, and gift shops. Full breakfast features homemade scones, muffins, granola, and specialties such as Serbian eggs, Maine Stay French toast, apple blintz souffle, or apple bread pudding. Afternoon tea is served daily. Small wedding facilities available. Families welcome. 1/$85-145; 2/$85-180. AE, MC, V. Travel agent.

Guests write: *"The bungalow efficiencies at the back of the main building are excellent for a family, particularly if one needs to be able to provide food to children at 3 a.m. because of the time change (from Europe) without annoying other guests. As a vegetarian, I also found the healthy breakfasts a far cry from the usual animal-fats-with-everything level of American cuisine."* (S. Yarnold)

"Even the towels are wonderful - so nice and thick and a pretty color." (M. Newman)

"They know how to make their guests feel comfortable. The accommodations and the pleasant atmosphere provided made us feel right at home." (D. Goegelman)

"The bottle of wine was such a nice gesture. The food, fireplace, and advice on activities in the area were all excellent. We enjoyed the backyard area for reading." (N. Johnson)

"On our 2nd Anniversary we were introduced to another couple at the inn. The four of us have become fast friends and see each other often. Carol and Lindsay have always been helpful in making reservations for evenings out, picnics, and other places of interest." (J. Ellison-Taylor)

Kennebunkport

Welby Inn
Ocean Avenue
Kennebunkport, ME 04046
(207) 967-4655

Type of B&B: Small inn.
Rooms: 7 with private bath.
Rates: 1/$55-75; 2/$65-100.

Rating: A- or ♛♛♛ Excellent, far exceeds basic requirements.

Dutch Colonial home built at the turn-of-the-century is located five minutes from the beach off exit 3 of the Maine Turnpike near Route 35 South. The seven guest rooms each offer a private bath and one room features a working fireplace. There's a large common room on the main floor which displays a collection of botanical watercolors and notecards. Complimentary coffee and tea are available throughout the day. Popular attractions nearby include art galleries, the summer "White House," deep sea fishing, whale watching, and boating. A full breakfast is served from a menu with seven choices of entrees. No smoking. 1/$55-75; 2/$65-100. AE, MC, V.

Naples

Inn at Long Lake
P.O. Box 806
Naples, ME 04055
(207) 693-6226

Type of B&B: Inn.
Rooms: 16 with private bath.
Rates: $1/$61-89; 2/$67-98.

Rating: A or ♛♛♛ Excellent, far exceeds basic requirements.

Renovated Victorian inn built in 1906 sits near Long Lake which is located halfway between Portland and North Conway, New Hampshire. Sixteen bright guest rooms, each with private bath, are decorated in 1900s style and feature wicker furniture, ample comforters and pillows, antiques, and stenciled wooden bath floors. Several nearby lakes provide activities such as water skiing, swimming, boating, and parasailing. Enjoy all four seasons in Maine's picturesque countryside with cross-country skiing, biking, hiking, fishing, and fall foliage. Relax on the inn's veranda or in front of the parlor's fieldstone fireplace. Continental breakfast is served daily. Meeting and wedding facilities available. Families welcome. 1/$61-89; 2/$67-98. AE, MC, V. Auto club, business, and family discounts. Travel agent.

Portland

West End Inn
146 Pine Street
Portland, ME 04102
(207) 772-1377

Type of B&B: Inn.
Rooms: 4 with private bath.
Rates: 1/$70-80; 2/$80-90.

Rating: A+ or ♛♛♛ Excellent, far exceeds basic requirements.

Brick Victorian townhouse built in 1871 is located in the Western Promenade Historic District where there are many fine Victorian homes. Four guest rooms are offered, each with private bath. Take an easy walk to nearby downtown and area attractions such as the Portland Museum of Art, Old Port Exchange, Cumberland County Civic Center, Performing Arts Center, and many fine restaurants. Catch the International Ferry to Nova Scotia nearby. Full breakfast features homemade muffins and a special entree of the day. No smoking. 1/$70-80; 2/$80-90. AE, MC, V.

Rangeley

Northwoods
Main Street, P.O. Box 79
Rangeley, ME 04970
(207) 864-2440

Type of B&B: Inn.
Rooms: 4, each with private bath.
Rates: 1 or 2/$60-75.

Rating: B+ or ♛♛ Good, exceeds basic requirements.

Lakefront colonial inn built in 1912 is located near the intersections of Routes 4 and 16. Four guest rooms each offer a private bath, double, single, or queen-size beds, and eclectic decor ranging from antique to contemporary. A parlor offers comfortable seating, cable TV, and fireplace. This is a picturesque area with surrounding mountains and lakes that offer year-round sports such as boating, fishing, golfing, hunting, skiing, and hiking. A full breakfast includes apple pancakes, farm fresh eggs, waffles, and blueberry muffins. Small wedding and meeting facilities available. No smoking. 1 or 2/$60-75. Auto club discount.

Searsport

Thurston House B&B
P.O. Box 686, 8 Elm Street
Searsport, ME 04974
(207) 548-2213

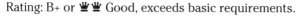

Type of B&B: Inn.
Rooms: 4, 2 with private bath.
Rates: 1/$40; 2/$45-60.

Rating: B+ or ♛♛ Good, exceeds basic requirements.

Colonial home built in 1831 is located on a quiet side street of the village opposite Penobscot Marine Museum and just off US-1. Four guest rooms are available with pleasant decor and selected antique furnishings. Two rooms offer a private bath. Walk to local restaurants, galleries, specialty shops, and beach park. Popular local attractions include state parks and forts, ocean cruises, and day trips to Blue Hill, Castine, Bar Harbor, and Camden. Indulge in a "forget-about-lunch" full breakfast. No smoking. 1/$40; 2/$45-60. 10% senior, military, and veteran discounts. Travel agent.

Southwest Harbor

The Lambs Ear Inn
P.O. Box 30, Clark Point Road
Southwest Harbor, ME 04679
(207) 244-9828

Type of B&B: Inn.
Rooms: 6 with private bath.
Rates: 1 or 2/$65-110.

Rating: A- or ♛♛♛ Excellent, far exceeds basic requirements.

Classic Maine Colonial inn built in 1857 is situated in the village located 1 block from Highway 102 at the intersection of Clark Point Road and Herrick. Choose from six guest rooms, each with private bath and most offering ocean views. View the harbor from the porch and open deck. Visit nearby restaurants, antique and art galleries, the ferry to Swans Island, Oceanarium, and Acadia National Park. Full breakfast includes a variety of chef's specials of the day. Wheelchair access. No smoking. 2/$65-110. MC, V. Travel agent.

Southwest Harbor

Two Seasons
P.O. Box 829
Southwest Harbor, ME 04679
(207) 244-9627

Type of B&B: Inn.
Rooms: 3 with private bath.
Rates: 2/$50-70.

Rating: B or ♥♥ Good, exceeds basic requirements.

Colonial home on Mt. Desert Island is located on a quiet residential street and is surrounded by the Acadia National Park. Three guest rooms offer a private bath and views of the harbor. A common room on the main floor has a fireplace along with games, TV and VCR. Nearby activities include hiking, golf, swimming, canoeing, bicycling and sailing. Continental breakfast is served on the pleasant sunporch which overlooks the harbor. No smoking. 2/$50-70.

Spruce Head

Craignair Inn
Clark Island Road
Spruce Head, ME 04859
(207) 594-7644

Type of B&B: Inn with restaurant.
Rooms: 22, 8 with private bath.
Rates: 1/$40-44; 2/$60-65.

Rating: B+ or ♥♥ Good, exceeds basic requirements.

Waterfront country inn is surrounded by natural beauty and located 8 miles from Route 1 in Thomaston. There are twenty-two guest rooms in the main house or annex. Each is furnished with homemade quilts, hooked rugs, and colorful wallpaper; eight offer a private bath. A comfortable porch overlooks the water and there are attractive gardens whose paths lead to the coastline's tidal pools, clam flats, meadows, and offshore islands. Within a short drive are Rockland, Camden, antique shops, art galleries, museums, tennis, golf, sailing, and festivals. Full breakfast. There's a restaurant on the premises as well as facilities for meetings and social functions. Families welcome. 1/$40-44; 2/$60-65. AE, MC, V. Open March through December.

Guests write: *"The hospitality shown led to a lasting friendship. Terry, upon my 1st visit, invited me to go antiquing with her and gave me the use of her car for my independent excursions. If I missed meals, I was made to feel welcome to take my meals with her family."* (B. Sajdak)

"The setting is beautiful and not crowded - right on the ocean. The food and service was excellent and moderately priced. The innkeepers have always made our stays fun." (J. Dacey)

Sullivan Harbor

Island View Inn
Route 1, Box 24
Sullivan Harbor, ME 04689
(207) 422-3031

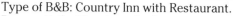

Type of B&B: Country Inn with Restaurant.
Rooms: 7, 5 with private bath.
Rates: 1 or 2/$40-70.

Rating: A or ♛♛♛ Excellent, far exceeds basic requirements.

Quiet waterfront property was built as a turn-of-the-century summer cottage and is located just off Route 1, fifteen minutes from Ellsworth and thirty minutes from Bar Harbor. Seven guest rooms feature original furniture and detailed restoration work; five offer a private bath. The spacious common room on the main floor has a fireplace and pleasant water views. Right outside the back door is a private beach and picturesque views of Frenchman's Bay and the mountains of Mt. Desert Island. Full breakfast often features a selection of eggs, pancakes, breakfast meats, and freshly baked muffins. Dinner is available in the restaurant. Facilities for small weddings and meetings. Restricted smoking. 2/$40-70. MC, V. Open Memorial Day through mid-October.

Annapolis

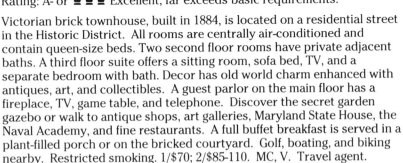

Prince George Inn Bed & Breakfast
232 Prince George Street
Annapolis, MD 21401
(301) 263-6418

Type of B&B: Inn.
Rooms: 3 with private bath.
Rates: 1/$70; 2/$85-110.

Rating: A- or ♛♛♛ Excellent, far exceeds basic requirements.

Victorian brick townhouse, built in 1884, is located on a residential street in the Historic District. All rooms are centrally air-conditioned and contain queen-size beds. Two second floor rooms have private adjacent baths. A third floor suite offers a sitting room, sofa bed, TV, and a separate bedroom with bath. Decor has old world charm enhanced with antiques, art, and collectibles. A guest parlor on the main floor has a fireplace, TV, game table, and telephone. Discover the secret garden gazebo or walk to antique shops, art galleries, Maryland State House, the Naval Academy, and fine restaurants. A full buffet breakfast is served in a plant-filled porch or on the bricked courtyard. Golf, boating, and biking nearby. Restricted smoking. 1/$70; 2/$85-110. MC, V. Travel agent.

Baltimore/Stevenson

Gramercy Bed & Breakfast
1400 Greenspring Valley Road
Stevenson, MD 21153-0119
(410) 486-2405

Type of B&B: Small inn.
Rooms: 8, 4 with private bath.
Rates: 1/$40; 2/$100-125.

Rating: A+ or ♛♛♛ Excellent, far exceeds basic requirements.

English Tudor estate situated on 45 wooded acres in Green Spring Valley is located northwest of Baltimore near exit 21 off Route 695 Beltway. A total of eight guest rooms are available. Four rooms offer single beds and share baths. Four other rooms are larger and offer a working fireplace and private bath. All rooms feature fine antiques and are enhanced by the distinguished architecture of the building. The spacious grounds include a swimming pool, tennis court, woodland trails, and herb gardens. This location is near Baltimore's Inner Harbor, Topiary Gardens, and Cloisters Children Museum. A full breakfast features house specialties such as mushroom omelettes, French toast, and raspberry pancakes. Meeting and wedding facilities available. Families welcome. 1/$40; 2/$100-125. MC, V. Travel agent.

Burtonsville

Upstream at Water's Gift
3604 Dustin Road
P.O. Box 240
Burtonsville, MD 20866
(301) 421-9562 or 421-9163

Type of B&B: Guesthouse.
Rooms: 2 with private bath.
Rates: 1 or 2/$75-125.

Rating: A+ or ♛♛♛ Excellent, far exceeds basic requirements.

Country home situated on a fifty-three acre Colonial horse farm is surrounded by several thousand acres of secluded woods and located halfway between Baltimore and Washington, D.C. The guesthouse offers two rooms, each with air conditioning and a private bath. The Great room features a large fireplace, cathedral ceilings and unusual antique pine paneling. An expansive glass wall provides a spectacular view of the rolling landscape and horse pastures. Enjoy the many outdoor activities available such as hiking and mountain biking. Full gourmet breakfast. Facilities available for meetings, weddings and social functions. Restricted smoking. 1 or 2/$75-125. Travel agent.

Frederick/Cascade

Bluebird on the Mountain
14700 Eyler Avenue
Cascade, MD 21719
(301) 241-4161

Type of B&B: Inn.
Rooms: 4 suites with private bath.
Rates: 1/$60-85; 2/$85-105.

Rating: A- or ♛♛♛ Excellent, far exceeds basic requirements.

Colonial mansion is located in the peaceful Catoctin Mountains off Route 15 at Thurmont, just ninety minutes from Baltimore and an hour from Washington, D.C. There are four luxurious suites with private baths. Special rooms offer Jacuzzi tubs big enough for two as well as private fireplaces. Relax on the large, old-fashioned wicker porches, or visit Catoctin and Cunningham Falls parks, Gettysburg and Antietam battlefields, and the Appalachian Trail. Apple orchards, golf, and skiing nearby. Gourmet continental breakfast featuring homebaked breads and muffins is served in the guest room or downstairs. Resident cats. 1/$60-85; 2/$85-105. MC, V.

Hagerstown

Beaver Creek House B&B
20432 Beaver Creek Road
Hagerstown, MD 21740
(301) 797-4764

Type of B&B: Inn.
Rooms: 5, 3 with private bath.
Rates: 1/$65; 2/$75.

Rating: A or ♛♛♛ Excellent, far exceeds basic requirements.

Beaver Creek House is a restored farmhouse built at the turn-of-the-century and located 4 miles east of Hagerstown in historic Beaver Creek. Five guest rooms are available with air conditioning, antique furnishings, and family memorabilia. A Honeymoon Suite is available for special occasions. Hosts have an extensive collection of Civil War books and tapes on the Antietam battlefield. A common room on the main floor offers an area for watching TV or reading. Explore the country garden and attractive courtyard with fountain. Popular local attractions include antique shops, Civil War battlefields, Appalachian Trail hiking, skiing, golf, and trout fishing. Full breakfast features homemade muffins, biscuits, and rolls, as well as hearty serving of eggs, sausage, and pancakes. Afternoon tea is served in the parlor. No smoking.

Olney

The Thoroughbred Bed & Breakfast
16410 Batchellors Forest Road
Olney, MD 20832
(301) 774-7649 or 774-7571

Type of B&B: Country estate.
Rooms: 13, 7 with private bath.
Rate: 1 or 2/$65-125.

Rating: B+ or ♛♛ Good, exceeds basic requirements.

Country estate situated on 175 acres is located 12 miles from Washington, D.C. on a site where champion race horses have been bred and raised for years. The main house has five guest rooms, three with private bath. The farm house annex has four rooms with shared baths and a newly built cottage offers four guest rooms with private bath, fireplace, and double whirlpool tub. Popular activities here include swimming in the pool, relaxing in the hot tub, and playing billiards. Full breakfast offered with egg dishes, waffles or pancakes, and homemade muffins. 1 or 2/$65-125. MC, V. Travel agent.

Guests write: *"We thoroughly enjoyed our stay including the marvelous food, conversation (especially golf and horses), and the lovely surroundings." (S. Pierce)*

"My husband wants to return to play the golf course. The quiet serenity of this beautiful B&B was wonderful as was the hospitality of our hostess and her gourmet culinary skills." (H. VanSant)

"Thoroughbreds cross the fields, time to relax around the pool, complete comfort in our room, and memorable mornings enjoying breakfast made this an exceptional experience." (A. Miller)

St. Michaels/Oxford

1876 House
110 North Morris Street
Oxford, MD 21654
(301) 226-5496

Type of B&B: Inn.
Rooms: 3, 1 with private bath.
Rates: 1 or 2/$81-92.

Rating: B or ♛♛ Good, exceeds basic requirements.

Historic Victorian home built in 1876 is 11 miles south of Easton on Route 333. There are two guest rooms with shared bath and a master suite with queen-sized, four-poster bed, private bath, and dressing room. The home is furnished in Queen Anne decor and Oriental rugs with ten-foot ceilings and wide-plank pine floors. Walk to village boutiques, fine restaurants, and antique shops. Recreation available in the area includes swimming, golf, tennis, bicycling, fishing, boating, and hunting. Continental breakfast served in formal dining room. 1 or 2/$81-92.

St. Michaels

Parsonage Inn
210 North Talbot Street
St. Michaels, MD 21663
(301) 745-5519

Type of B&B: Inn.
Rooms: 7 with private bath.
Rates: 1 or 2/$72-108.

Rating: A or ♛♛♛ Excellent, far exceeds basic requirements.

Brick Victorian home built in 1883 is situated in the heart of this small coastal village on Maryland's Eastern Shore. Choose from seven guest rooms with king or queen-size bed, private bath, ceiling fans, Queen Anne-style furnishings, and Laura Ashley linens. Three rooms have working fireplaces. Popular gathering spots include the library with collection of good books, upstairs deck for sunbathing, and quiet parlor with fireplace. Bicycles are available for exploring the village. Walk to great seafood restaurants, antique and gift shops, the historic harbor, and Maritime Museum. Continental breakfast. Families welcome. Restricted smoking. 1 or 2/$72-108 + 8% tax. MC, V.

Silver Spring

Varborg
2620 Briggs Chaney Road
Silver Spring, MD 20905
(301) 384-2842

Type of B&B: B&B home.
Rooms: 3 with shared bath.
Rates: 1/$30; 2/$50.

Rating: B or ♛♛ Good, exceeds basic requirements.

Colonial home in a residential area just west of Route 29 offers a convenient location midway between Baltimore and Washington D.C. yet with lovely views of the countryside. Three comfortable guest rooms share a bath. Guests use Varborg as a convenient base for day trips by car or subway to Gettysburg, Baltimore, Annapolis, or Washington, D.C. Tennis, swimming, and hiking are available nearby. Continental breakfast. No smoking. 1/$30; 2/$50.

Guests write: *"They are excellent hosts and I enjoyed my stay when I came for collaborative work with the Applied Physics Lab and Johns Hopkins University. I have used their home for a number of years. They are nice people looking to the comfort and happiness of their guests. The place is nice and quiet and well-kept." (D. Venkatesan)*

"Their welcome and the freedom of their house beats hotels anytime - as do their rates! The perfect antidote to lonely business trips." (M. Pinnock)

"I feel that the highlight of my stays are the interesting and stimulating discussions we have on a large variety of subjects. Any slack time goes by quickly with Pat and Bob." (A. Kelln)

"Bob and Pat have a broad knowledge of D.C. and Baltimore and are able to provide excellent detailed maps and directions. Their home is conveniently located between the two areas. Their knowledge of fine restaurants was a plus. They helped us find interesting ones that a tourist would not find without help. These are very special people." (A. Vieweg)

"The room was large and clean and Bob and Pat even invited me to dinner. They made their lovely home available for my use (not just my room). The area is rural, even though close to Washington, D.C. Perhaps the best of all is that the cost is about a third of the cost of a typical hotel room." (J.D. Menietti)

Snow Hill

River House Inn
201 East Market Street
Snow Hill, MD 21863
(410) 632-2722

Type of B&B: Small inn.
Rooms: 7 with private bath.
Rates: 1 or 2/$65-95.

Rating: A or ♛ ♛ ♛ Excellent, far exceeds basic requirements.

Historic riverfront Victorian country home built in 1860 is situated on two acres of rolling lawn on Maryland's Eastern Shore about fifteen miles southwest of Ocean City on Route 394. Seven guest rooms are available. Each of four rooms in the main house has a private bath and air conditioning and several feature a marble fireplace and wrap-around porch. A newly renovated carriage house built in 1835 provides three additional rooms. There are several common areas throughout the inn including a two spacious parlors with fireplaces, living room, and elegant dining room for group meals. Porches with ceiling fans overlook the back lawn, gardens and the riverfront. Popular activities in the area include walking the village's picturesque streets and exploring the Pocomoke River which offers canoeing and fishing. Assateague and Chincoteague are nearby as are Ocean City beaches. Guests have their choice of full breakfast from a variety of entrees and afternoon refreshments are served daily. Box lunches and dinners can be prepared by advance arrangement. Small wedding and meeting facilities available. Restricted smoking. 1 or 2/$65-95. V, MC. 10% family, senior, and auto club discount. Travel agent.

Guests write: *"We had a lovely time here. Everything was perfect including their attention to our two-year-old." (D. Pankratz)*

"Our host family was very hospitable. The breakfasts were delicious. The house and grounds are lovely and well-kept. We were within walking distance of canoe rentals and enjoyed canoeing on the Pocomoke River. They provided us with a pass to enjoy Assateague Island and the ocean beaches there. We look forward to a return visit." (J. Nieberding)

"We gathered our closest friends together for a wedding on their property and it was beautiful! They took care of so many details and made each of our guests feel at home. I cannot think of another inn at which such an event could be carried out with such ease." (J. Christodoulon)

"What makes the River House Inn so special, besides its lovely decor, large comfortable rooms, and quiet location, is the Knudson's. They love people and running their inn. Their rare enthusiasm for life makes their inn a pearl indeed." (S. Jones)

Westminster

Westminster Inn
5 South Center Street
Westminster, MD 21157
(301) 857-4445 or 876-2893

Type of B&B: Inn with restaurant.
Rooms: 13 with private bath.
Rates: 1 or 2/$105-155.

Rating: A or ♛♛♛ Excellent, far exceeds basic requirements.

Brick Victorian inn with tower and "gingerbread" porches is thirty minutes northwest of Baltimore, sixty minutes from Washington, D.C., thirty minutes from historic Gettysburg. Thirteen guest rooms are available, each with queen-size bed, private bath, and Jacuzzi. Athletic club offers indoor swimming, running track, basketball, and racquetball. Historic Union Mills Homestead, Carroll County Farm Museum, vineyards, and antique shops are nearby. Continental breakfast buffet features homemade pastries and jams. Fine dining restaurant offers contemporary American cuisine and there is also a pub which offers light fare and entertainment. 1 or 2/$105-155. AE, MC, V. 10% auto club and business travel discounts offered as well as special mid-week packages which include dinner. Travel Agent.

Andover

Andover Inn
Chapel Avenue
Andover, MA 01810
(508) 475-5903

Type of B&B: B&B Inn.
Rooms: 33, 23 with private bath.
Rates: 1/$62-95; 2/$80-113.

Rating: B+ or ♛♛ Good, exceeds basic requirements.

Neo-Georgian-style brick inn is located on the campus of Phillips Academy in Andover just 5 miles north of Route 93. Thirty-three air-conditioned guest rooms are available, twenty-three with private bath. The inn's limousine service accommodates any business, airport, or wedding needs and for nights on the town. Stroll the Academy campus and visit the art or archaeology museums nearby. The North Andover Textile Museum and the National Park in Lowell are within 20 minutes from the inn. Continental breakfast served in the dining room includes smoked salmon and the chef's daily special. Wedding and meeting facilities available. Families welcome. 1/$62-95; 2/$80-113.

Attleboro

The Colonel Blackinton Inn
203 North Main Street
Attleboro, MA 02703
(508) 222-6022

Type of B&B: Inn.
Rooms: 16, 11 with private bath.
Rates: 1/$42-68; 2/$52-72.

Rating: B+ or ♛♛ Good, exceeds basic requirements.

Colonial Blackinton Inn is a Greek Revival structure built in 1850 and located just south of I-95, exit 5. Sixteen guest rooms are available, eleven have a private bath. A guest parlor on the main floor offers a fireplace, comfortable TV viewing area, and sunny porch. Nearby recreation includes golf, tennis, and fishing. Full breakfast and afternoon tea offered in special tea room. Remodeled carriage house is available for social functions. Wheelchair access. 1/$42-68; 2/$52-72. AE, MC, V. 10% business travel discount.

Guests write: *"In the past 3 or 4 years my job has me staying in hotels and inns four nights a week and I must say that this fine B&B is the best. The warmth and friendliness made me feel quite at home except more pampered. From the peach pancakes to the Victorian sitting room, this B&B rates a top shelf rating. The large common room with comfy couches and fireplace is right out of a magazine." (J. Walsh)*

Boston

Emma James House
47 Ocean Street
Boston, MA 02124
(617) 288-8867 or 282-5350

Type of B&B: Inn.
Rooms: 6, 2 with private bath.
Rates: 1/$40-60; 2/$50-70.

Rating: B or ♛♛ Good, exceeds basic requirements.

Victorian home built in 1894 is located off I-93, 4 miles south of downtown Boston. Choose from six guest rooms, two with private bath. The main floor has two parlors including an oak-paneled sitting room with comfortable TV area. Original architectural features of the home are still evident in its stained glass, woodwork, and carved fireplace mantels. Subway transportation nearby whisks guests to area attractions including JFK Presidential Library, Bayside Expo Center, University of Massachusetts harbor campus, universities, and hospitals. Continental plus breakfast. Facilities available for meetings and social functions. Families welcome. No Smoking. 1/$40-60; 2/$50-70. 10% auto club, business travel, and senior discounts. Travel agent.

Guests write: *"We stayed here while recovering from eye surgery. Vicki and Boo showed genuine concern for our comfort and safety with extra pillows to prop up the patient and a cooler to keep special medicines cold. Mike led us on a short cut to the hospital. We reveled in their warm concern. Piping hot muffins awaiting us each morning and waffles with real maple syrup. What a delightful way to start the day. Exquisite stained-glass windows in the hall and living rooms laid rich colors over the 1890 intricately carved woodwork. A treat for the eyes." (H. Petraske)*

Boston

Newbury Guest House
261 Newbury Street
Boston, MA 02116
(617) 437-7666

Type of B&B: Urban inn.
Rooms: 15 with private bath.
Rates: 1 or 2/$70-150.

Rating: B or ♛♛ Good, exceeds basic requirements.

Nineteenth-century brick brownstone was completely renovated in 1991 and is located in the heart of the Back Bay area of Boston. Fifteen guest rooms are located on three different floors of this walkup brownstone. Each offers a private bath, period furniture, accent rugs on hardwood floors, telephone, and individual heat and air conditioning. A small parlor on the main floor offers a comfortable area for watching TV. The inn is located in one of Boston's best known areas for specialty shops, restaurants, and art galleries. Walk to the Charles River nearby which offers jogging or biking trails. Many of Boston's famous landmarks are nearby including the Museum of Fine Arts, Museum of Science, Freedom Trail, Fenway Park, and Harvard University. Continental breakfast. Families welcome. Wheelchair access. Limited off-street parking available in the back of the building. 1/$70-150; add $10 for each additional person. AE, MC, V. Travel agent.

Cambridge

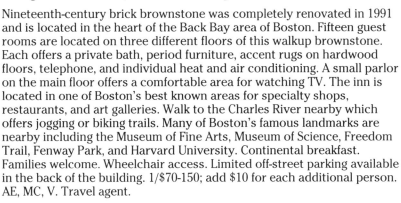

Cambridge House B&B
2218 Massachusetts Avenue
Cambridge, MA 02140
(617) 491-6300 or (800) 232-9989

Type of B&B: Inn.
Rooms: 12 with shared or private bath.
Rates: 1/$59-119; 2/$79-149.

Rating: A or ♛♛♛ Excellent, far exceeds basic requirements.

Historic Colonial Revival home built in 1892 is located near Harvard Square and only three minutes from the subway to downtown Boston. Choose from twelve guest rooms with private or shared bath. One spacious room on the second floor offers a full private bath, working fireplace, telephone, color TV, and elegant furnishings. Two other rooms have private half baths and eight rooms offer convenient sinks in the rooms. This location is near all major colleges and hospitals and is easily accessible to Routes 2 and 93 or Turnpike. Full breakfast. No smoking. 1/$59-119; 2/$79-149. AE, MC, V. Travel agent.

Chatham

The Cranberry Inn at Chatham
359 Main Street
Chatham, MA 02633
(508) 945-9232 or (800) 332-4667

Type of B&B: Inn.
Rooms: 14 with private bath.
Rates: 2/$90-160.

Rating: A+ or ♕♕♕ Excellent, far exceeds basic requirements.

Cranberry Inn is an historic landmark located in the quaint seaside Cape Cod village at exit 11 off Route 6. Completely restored, the inn offers fourteen guest rooms appointed with antiques, reproductions, and four-poster or canopy beds. All rooms include a private bath, air-conditioning, telephone, and TV. Some rooms feature fireplaces and private decks. Golf, tennis, beaches, shops, and excellent restaurants are just steps away. The landscaped grounds offer ample off-street parking. Home-baked continental breakfast is served daily. Facilities for small group meetings and social functions available. Restricted smoking. 2/$90-160. AE, MC, V. Travel agent.

Guests write: *"We love the charm, the clean feel, the homey feel of it. Peggy makes a wonderful country breakfast and Richard cannot do enough to please everyone. On our anniversary we went to the inn. It was our 25th. My daughter called and asked could they do a little something as a surprise from the kids. We had wine, cheese, fruit, flowers, and our reservations waiting for us at our favorite eating place."* (R. Bruno)

"The beautifully decorated rooms are a great source of decorating ideas. Peggy is quick to share sources and provide directions to out-of-the-way shops on the Cape. We even got hints on what to order that's especially good at local restaurants." (R. Grudzeen)

"On several occasions we found a chilled bottle of our favorite wine awaiting our arrival. During one visit I was called back to work overnight. They arranged to get me to the airport and when I returned arranged a surprise cocktail party to celebrate my wife's birthday." (D. Ernest)

Chatham

The Old Harbor Inn
22 Old Harbor Road
Chatham, MA 02633
(508) 945-4434 or (800) 942-4434

Type of B&B: Inn.
Rooms: 7 with private bath.
Rates: 1/$85-145; 2/$95-155.

Rating: A+ or ♛♛♛ Excellent, far exceeds basic requirements.

Classic Colonial Cape Cod-style inn built in 1936 is located in a residential area, one house in from Main Street. Choose from seven guest rooms decorated in English Country style with private bath, queen, king-size or twin beds, antique and wicker furnishings, and designer linens. A fireplaced gathering room offers a quiet spot to read, relax, play the baby grand piano or converse. Walk to beaches, gift and antiques shops, art galleries, museums, wildlife sanctuary, restaurants, golf, tennis, and boating. Continental buffet breakfast includes home-baked muffins and scones and is served in the sunroom or on the outside deck overlooking flower gardens. 1/$85-145; 2/$95-155. AE, MC, V.

Concord

Hawthorne Inn
462 Lexington Road
Concord, MA 01742
(508) 369-5610

Type of B&B: Inn.
Rooms: 7 with private bath.
Rates: 1/$75-85; 2/$110-125.

Rating: B+ or ♛♛ Good, exceeds basic requirements.

Ralph Waldo Emerson, the Alcotts, and Nathaniel Hawthorne once owned the land this 1870 Colonial inn sits on. Choose from seven guest rooms, each with private bath, and individual decor. Each room features a selection of antique furnishings, handmade quilts, and wood floors graced with Oriental and rag rugs. Popular attractions in this area steeped in history include Wayside, Walden Pond, Great Meadows Wildlife Sanctuary. Many guests have enjoyed canoeing and quiet picnics in the area. Continental breakfast. Families welcome. Restricted smoking. 1/$75-85; 2/$110-125. Travel agent.

Guests write: *"I'm happy to report that the law of diminishing returns has spared Marilyn and Gregory Burch's charming Hawthorne Inn. I returned recently and the place (and therefore I) was undiminished. The nurturing and enriching ambience of the inn with its books, art, distinctive beds, masterful quilts, location, location, location, and appetizing aromas nudges me into planning yet another stay." (D. Dasch)*

Dennis

Isaiah Hall B&B Inn
152 Whig Street
Dennis, MA 02638
(508) 385-9928 or (800) 736-0160

Type of B&B: Inn.
Rooms: 11, 10 with private bath.
Rates: 1/$44-84; 2/$50-94.

Rating: A or ♛ ♛ ♛ Excellent, far exceeds basic requirements.

Isaiah Hall is a Greek Revival farmhouse built in 1857 and located 10 miles north of Hyannis. There are eleven guest rooms in the main inn or the adjacent restored barn. Ten offer a private bath. Each room features fine antiques, Oriental rugs, and handmade quilts. There are several common rooms offering private areas for reading, playing board games, or conversing with other guests. Within walking distance can be found the Museum of Fine Arts, Playhouse, and Cinema. Bicycle trails and golf courses are nearby. Continental plus breakfast. Resident cat. Limited wheelchair access. Restricted smoking. 1/$44-84; 2/$50-94. AE, MC, V. Travel agent. Open April 1 through October 20.

Guests write: *"Breakfasts are always fun at the Isaiah Hall Inn - good food, especially the cranberry muffins, and good conversation with Marie and the other guests. Marie's good spirits and enthusiasm are very much what makes the inn a special place to stay. The inn is lovely with common rooms that are warm and inviting. The guest rooms are spacious and always immaculate. Our favorite room is #10, overlooking the flower gardens in the back of the house." (L. Garavalia)*

"We have never experienced anything but clean rooms with everything in working order. Every room we have stayed in has had good lighting for reading at night and windows to open to savor the Cape breezes. We have stayed in both the main house and the attached renovated barn. We've had a hard time deciding which we enjoy the most, but have over time found we like the barn. Furnishings are country casual with a mix of antiques. The innkeepers are there when you need them but don't force themselves upon you." (T. Stapleton)

"The historic house is homey, beautiful and furnished with authentic antiques. However, the one thing that makes Isaiah Hall Inn different from

any other inn we have visited and brings us back year after year is the warm hospitality of the host and hostess. They make their guests feel at home. The comforts, cleanliness, and amenities we pay for but this sincere interest and caring is priceless." (A. Coveney)

Dennisport

Rose Petal B&B
152 Sea Street
P.O. Box 974
Dennisport, MA 02639
(508) 398-8470

Type of B&B: Inn.
Rooms: 4 with shared baths.
Rates: 1 or 2/$40-55.

Rating: B or ♛♛ Good, exceeds basic requirements.

Quaint New England-style farmhouse built in 1872 is located 7 miles east of Hyannis on Cape Cod. There are four second-floor guest rooms with shared baths. A pleasant parlor on the main floor offers a piano, selection of reading material, and comfortable area for watching TV. Warm-water beaches of Nantucket Sound are nearby as are several antique shops, theaters, museums, and restaurants. Recreation available in the area includes golf, fishing, boating, and bicycle trails. The ferries to Nantucket and Martha's Vineyard are a short drive away. Full breakfast includes home-baked goods. Families welcome. Restricted smoking. 1 or 2/$40-55.

Guests write: *"This home is lovely. We found the accommodations tastefully decorated and meticulously clean and very comfortable. Breakfast was always a treat. A hearty breakfast that gave us a great start to the day." (D. Ewing)*

"Genuine friendliness but non-intrusive - a tough balance to strike and done with graciousness and topped with some of the most delicate buttery pastry we've ever had." (K. McLeod)

"Perfect. Every detail was appreciated. Breakfast was tasty and the right way to start our day. The map and guides Gayle gave us were extremely useful. We also like having the bathrobes and fan. Everything was very comfortable and homey." (B. Polk)

"We were made to feel at home almost immediately. Nothing was missing: comfortable bed, nice bath, conveniences. Breakfast was a welcome day's beginning; ample and tastefully done." (J. Bulkley)

"They were extremely helpful in pointing us in the right direction and making suggestions. Always a smile and friendly conversations each

morning. The accommodations were very charming and like Old New England. The rooms and bathrooms were immaculate. Breakfast was delicious. Such a wide variety of foods offered each morning which we really looked forward to. They really won my husband over with the Eggs Benedict. He is sure to return just for that." (L. Grimm)

East Orleans

Ship's Knees Inn
186 Beach Road, P.O. Box 756
East Orleans, MA 02643
(508) 255-1312

Type of B&B: Inn.
Rooms: 22 rooms, 5 with private bath; efficiency and 2 cottages.
Rates: 1 or 2/$45-100.

Rating: B or ♛♛ Good, exceeds basic requirements.

160-year-old sea captain's home has been restored and is located a short walk from Cape Cod's Nauset Beach. Twenty-two guest rooms are available; five with private bath. All rooms offer a selection of antique furnishings and several have ocean views, beamed ceilings, quilts, and old four-poster beds. Two housekeeping cottages on the water are available for weekly rentals. The landscaped grounds feature a tennis court and swimming pool with golf and horseback riding available nearby. Continental breakfast offers muffins, baked breads, and jams. 1 or 2/$45-100. Travel agent.

East Sandwich

Wingscorton Farm Inn
11 Wing Boulevard
East Sandwich, MA 02537
(508) 888-0534

Type of B&B: Inn.
Rooms: 7 with private bath.
Rates: 1/$95; 2/$115-150.

Rating: B+ or ♛♛ Good, exceeds basic requirements.

Colonial landmark built in 1758 is situated on seven landscaped acres off Route 6A on Cape Cod. Seven guest rooms each offer a private bath, working fireplace, and restored antique furnishings. An historic carriage house on the property features completely modern decor and amenities with fireplace, full kitchen, private sun-deck, and brick patio. There is a private ocean beach within a short walk and other area attractions include golf, whale watching, antique shops, and outdoor recreation nearby. Full breakfast includes eggs, breakfast meats, and vegetables from the inn's own livestock and gardens. Resident dogs and cats. Families welcome. 1/$95; 2/$115-150. AE, MC, V. Travel agent.

Eastham

Over Look Inn
3085 County Road
P.O. Box 771
Eastham, MA 02642
1-800-356-1121 or (508) 255-1886

Type of B&B: Inn.
Rooms: 10 with private bath.
Rates: 1 or 2/$65-110.

Rating: A or ♛♛♛ Excellent, far exceeds basic requirements.

Overlook Inn is a Victorian mansion built in 1869 and located across from Cape Cod National Seashore in the heart of Eastham's historic district. Ten guest rooms offer a private bath, brass bed, antique and wicker furniture, and lace curtains. There are several common areas which include a Victorian parlor, Hemingway room with billiard table, and library with good selection of books. Popular attractions in the area include beaches, nature trails, historic homes, Audubon Wildlife Sanctuary, bicycle paths, specialty shops, galleries, and restaurants. Scottish hospitality and a full breakfast are offered daily as well as afternoon tea. Facilities available for small meetings. Restricted smoking. 1 or 2/$65-110. AE, MC, V. Travel agent.

Essex

George Fuller House
148 Main Street
Essex, MA 01929
(508) 768-7766

Type of B&B: Inn.
Rooms: 5 with private bath.
Rates: 1 or 2/$70-83.

Rating: A- or ♛♛♛ Excellent, far exceeds basic requirements.

George Fuller House was built in 1830 and is located 30 miles north of Boston on Cape Ann. There are five guestrooms. Each offers a private bath, television, telephone, country decor, antique furnishings, braided rugs, comfortable rockers, and a brass or canopy bed. Two rooms have working fireplaces. The inn's original architectural features have been retained and include folding Indian shutters, fireplaces, Colonial paneling and woodwork. There are over fifty antique shops to visit in Essex as well as the Shipbuilding Museum. The inn offers a mid-week sailing package on board a thirty-foot cruising sailboat. Full breakfast may include Grand Marnier French toast or Belgian waffles. 1 or 2/$70-83. AE, MC, V. Travel agent.

Guests write: *"Cindy and Bob were friendly and helpful hosts. The room had everything - private bath, a phone, a fireplace, TV. We had the best breakfast ever. The food was 4-star. We had pears in cream, Belgian waffles with yogurt and orange sauce, apple strudel, coffee, juice, and seconds on anything we wanted. After this I'm afraid other B&Bs might be a let down!" (J. Saggerer)*

"The Andrew Suite we relished is The Best. From the canopy bed to the blazing fireplace, we couldn't have dreamt of a nicer inn. The breakfast is without equal in our experience. If George Fuller was awarded only three crowns, what does a four or five crown inn have that they don't? I would like to visit one of them because I think it would be hard to beat our favorite." (J. Donaher)

"I travel 50% of the time throughout the Eastern U.S. As a business traveler I try to stay in B&B whenever I can. The George Fuller House has provided the best stay I have had anywhere. What really makes a noticeable difference at places to stay are the innkeepers. All three mornings I had to leave by 6:30 a.m. for meetings. Each morning I woke to a full gourmet breakfast at 6:00 a.m.!' (E. Rosenwinkel)

"Only minutes after our late morning arrival we were sitting on the porch deep in good conversation with another guest over hot coffee and a delicious cranberry coffee cake just out of Cindy's oven." (T. Cromwell)

Falmouth

Palmer House Inn
81 Palmer Avenue
Falmouth, MA 02450
(508) 548-1230

Type of B&B: Inn.
Rooms: 8 with private bath.
Rates: 1/$60-110; 2/$70-120.

Rating: A- or ♛♛♛ Excellent, far exceeds basic requirements.

Falmouth's Historic District is the setting for this Victorian inn built in 1901. Choose from eight guest rooms with private bath and antique furnishings. Popular attractions in the area include beaches, parks, and the nearby ferry to Martha's Vineyard and Nantucket. Breakfast entrees include such gourmet specialties as Pain Perdue with orange cream or Finnish pancake with strawberry soup. 1/$60-110; 2/$70-120. AE, MC, V.

Guests write: *"We enjoyed our 15th wedding anniversary here. The room and the inn are lovely. Both breakfasts were very good and very filling. The tips on touring Martha's Vineyard worked out fine and the convenience of purchasing ferry tickets at the inn made the difference between making or missing the boat as we were the last to board!"* (R. Swisher)

"The house is charming and beautifully furnished. I just love all the pink in Cousin Elizabeth's Room, the picture above the bed, the fragrant soaps, the potpourri, the gorgeous lace curtains." (J. Myrth)

"The Palmer House was one of the most comfortable and charming B&Bs that we have visited. We were on our honeymoon and they made just the right amount of fuss. The breakfasts were definitely in the top 10. We will do our best to make another trip up to the Cape so get the bed ready in Grandmother's Room and heat up the chocolate stuffed French toast!" (G. Gottlieb)

"We slept like babies. When the room is decorated like that out of a magazine, you can't help noticing the time and care given. The Tower Room will always be special to us." (C. O'Neil)

"My Mom and I thoroughly enjoyed our Thanksgiving weekend at the inn. We think we're spoiled now and no other B&B will do!" (M. Myer)

"Coming home from traveling around all day and finding tea and cookies on the porch was a great touch." (A. Zonin)

Falmouth

Village Green Inn
40 West Main Street
Falmouth, MA 02540
(508) 548-5621

Type of B&B: Inn.
Rooms: 5 with private bath.
Rates: 1/$60-90; 2/$70-100.

Rating: A or ♛♛♛ Excellent, far exceeds basic requirements.

The Village Green Inn is a combination Victorian/Colonial structure built in 1804 and located on the village green, 15 miles south of Cape Cod Canal. Four guest rooms and one suite each offer a private bath and working fireplace. Popular area attractions include beaches, museums, plantations, and Woods Hole Oceanographic Institute and Aquarium. Full breakfast includes homemade specialties such as blueberry-almond bread or nutmeg muffins. No smoking. 1/$60-90; 2/$70-100.

Great Barrington

Round Hill Farm Non-Smokers' B&B
17 Round Hill Road
Great Barrington MA 01230
(413) 528-3366

Type of B&B: Inn.
Rooms: 5 rooms share 3 baths.
Rates: 1/$65-75; 2/$75-85.

Rating: B+ or ♛♛ Good, exceeds basic requirements.

Classic 19th-Century hilltop farm on 300 acres in western Massachusetts boasts panoramic views of the Berkshire Hills. The farm house offers five guest rooms in summer (two in winter), which share three baths, a private entrance, wrap-around porches, and comfortable parlor. Guests are invited to fish or swim in the trout stream. Hiking, bicycling, and cross-country skiing are available right out the front door. Popular attractions in the area include downhill skiing at nearby Catamount or Butternut Basin, Tanglewood, Norman Rockwell Museum, Berkshire Theatre, and Hancock Shaker Village. Full breakfast is served at guest's convenience. Horses can be boarded overnight in the barn. Non-smokers only. 1/$65-75; 2/$75-85. AE, MC, V. Travel agent.

Guests write: *"Retiring from Tanglewood at 11 p.m., up the gravel road, stars blazing. Front door opens, we're the last ones in. Fall asleep in a flash with down pillows, extra plump under our heads. Awakened by soft rain; time to walk around the property with trails marked. Then back to have quiet conversation with Thomas as he turns eggs-over-easy. Hooray, blueberry yogurt today! Short drive to pick up the Sunday paper. Negotiate with the porch cat for a wicker chair. Observe wisely that the pace of our lives should be the rhythm of days at Round Hill Farm. Thank heavens our son will be back at music camp this summer so we'll return to have our souls tended!"* (A. Davol)

"We have been guests at Round Hill Farm for so many years that we now feel like family and would never consider staying anywhere else. Having breakfast with Peg and Tom's homemade coffee cakes and yogurt, we find that we can pick up the conversation almost where we left off the previous year. The non-smoking policy we feel is certainly a plus." (J. Dow)

"Round Hill Farm must be unique among B&Bs for the quality and quantity of the books (in every room). The farm somehow manages to be in deep rural surroundings of great beauty and still be a short simple drive to town." (J. Caulkins)

"We have enjoyed our encounters in this oasis: art and science in the service of what matters. The experience was the antithesis of hotel life: we were taken into the daily life of the hosts and the locality." (S. Vernon)

Great Barrington

Round Hill Farm's "Uttermost Barn"
for Non-Smokers
17 Round Hill Road
Great Barrington MA 01230
(413) 528-3366

Type of B&B: Inn.
Rooms: Apartment and suite with private baths.
Rates: 1/$55-140; 2/$65-150.

Rating: AA or ♛ ♛ ♛ ♛ Outstanding.

From its stern exterior, the "Uttermost Barn" looks very much like the 19th-century dairy barn it was constructed to be. But the hayloft has been completely transformed into a hidden jewel; it is now a "cow palace" with three air conditioned guest rooms. Two of the rooms are suites, one with a full modern kitchen. The Box Room is available for additional persons renting either suite. Oriental rugs carpet the oak stairs and floors throughout the rooms which boast many museum-quality antiques, English fabrics, and interesting architectural features such as the barrel-vaulted ceiling, decorative columns, skylights, and abundant windows. Individually prepared breakfasts are served in the main house at guest's convenience. No smoking. 1/$55-140; 2/$65-150. AE, MC, V. Travel agent.

Guests write: *"My husband and I love coming each summer. He enjoys Thomas' perfect eggs and I especially look forward to the fresh-daily, homemade yogurt and the special coffee pot he uses when he makes me my very own pot of decaf coffee. The Uttermost Barn is perfection right down to the antiques, down comforters, door knobs, light switches, and bathroom fixtures. It is a dream house topped off with a lovely porch from which you can observe and appreciate the bucolic countryside."* (J. Prokop)

"The bathroom in the Barn apartment is a sybaritic masterpiece - like bathing at Topkapi. The whole barn apartment is light, bright and beautiful. A glorious place to sit toasty warm and watch the snow fall." (A. Anastos)

"What can be more heavenly than viewing the sun sparkling on rolling green hills from a private porch filled with white wicker furniture as music plays from an old phonograph - except lying on a fluffy bed staring up at a sky full of stars!" (J. Sussman)

Great Barrington

Windflower Inn
SR 65, Box 25, Route 23
Great Barrington, MA 01230
(413) 528-2720

Type of B&B: Country inn.
Rooms: 13 with private bath.
Rates: 2/$160-190.

Rating: A- or ♕♕♕ Excellent, far exceeds basic requirements.

Built in 1862, this Colonial country inn is located in the Berkshire Hills area. All thirteen guest rooms are individually furnished and offer a private bath. Several have working fireplaces. Two living rooms on the main floor offer several areas for conversing, playing board games or the piano, or reading. Area attractions include Tanglewood, Jacobs Pillow, Berkshire Theater, museums, and antique shops. Recreation nearby includes skiing and hiking. Rates include a full breakfast and dinner featuring seasonal berries, herbs, and vegetables from the garden. Small meeting facilities available. Families welcome. Wheelchair access. Restricted smoking. 2/$160-190.

Harwich/West Harwich

Cape Cod Sunny Pines B&B Inn
77 Main Street, P.O. Box 667
West Harwich, MA 02671
(508) 432-9628 or (800) 356-9628

Type of B&B: Inn.
Rooms: 8 suites, all with private bath.
Rates: 2/$75-115.

Rating: B- or ♕♕ Good, exceeds basic requirements.

Irish hospitality is offered in this Victorian home located 3 miles south of Route 6 at Exit 9, just 1 1/2 hours drive from Providence or Boston. Choose from six suites in the inn or two suites in the cottage nestled in the pines, all with private bath, air conditioning, television, and refrigerators. There is an outdoor spa on the wrap-around "gingerbread" porch overlooking the swimming pool and picnic gardens. The lower level features the authentically reproduced "Claddagh Tavern," an on-site Irish pub. Popular attractions in the area include day trips to nearby Islands, Plymouth or Provincetown. Walk to Nantucket Sound Beach, area restaurants, hiking and biking trails. Gourmet Irish breakfast is served by candlelight on bone china and crystal. 2/$75-115. AE, MC, V. Travel agent.

Harwichport

Captain's Quarters
85 Bank Street
Harwichport, MA 02646
(800) 992-6550

Type of B&B: Small inn.
Rooms: 5 with private bath.
Rates: 1/$60-100; 2/$65-105.

Rating: B+ or ♛♛ Good, exceeds basic requirements.

1850 Victorian home with turret and gingerbread trim was remodeled in 1980 and is situated on an acre of shady lawn at the elbow of Cape Cod. Five guest rooms offer private bath, brass beds, reading chairs, lace curtains, and other period details. The cottage offers a full kitchen and second floor sleeping area. A wrap-around porch has white wicker chairs and hanging flower baskets. Walk to the village or beach from this location. Area attractions include whale watching, the National Seashore, and island cruises. Continental breakfast features home-baked breads. Restricted smoking. 1/$60-100; 2/$65-105. AE, MC, V.

Harwichport

Dunscroft By-The-Sea B&B Inn & Cottage
24 Pilgrim Road
Harwichport, MA 02646
(800) 432-4345 or (508) 432-0810

Type of B&B: Large inn and cottage.
Rooms: 9 with private bath.
Rates: 1/$75-120; 2/$85-150.

Rating: B+ or ♛♛ Good, exceeds basic requirements.

Gambrel roofed Colonial inn was built in 1920 and is located on Cape Cod. Nine guest rooms with private bath are available. Popular attractions in the area include Plymouth Rock, Plymouth Plantation, National Seashore, Kennedy Memorial, sand dunes, beaches, nature trails, fishing, and sailing. Full breakfast. Facilities for small meetings available. Restricted smoking. 1/$70-120; 2/$85-150. AE, MC, V. Travel agent.

Hyannis

Sea Breeze Inn by the Beach
397 Sea Street
Hyannis, MA 02601
(508) 771-7213, or 771-2549

Type of B&B: Inn.
Rooms: 14 with private bath.
Rates: 1 or 2/$45-85.

Rating: B or ♛♛ Good, exceeds basic requirements.

Historic Victorian inn is in a secluded setting a short walk from the Sea Street Beach. Fourteen guest rooms each offer a private bath, TV, and radio. Several feature ocean views. Popular area attractions include the Kennedy family Compound, summer theater, nightclubs, whale watching, boating, golfing, and shopping at local galleries and specialty shops. Continental breakfast. 1 or 2/$45-85. AE, MC, V.

Marblehead

Harbor Light Inn
58 Washington Street
Marblehead, MA 01945
(617) 631-2186

Type of B&B: Inn.
Rooms: 12 rooms or suites with private bath.
Rates: 1 or 2/$80-175.

Rating: A+ or ♛♛♛ Excellent, far exceeds basic requirements.

Federal Colonial inn built in the Eighteenth-century is located fifteen minutes north of Boston off Route 114 East. The inn offers twelve guest rooms or suites each with distinctive decor, private bath, chandeliers, brasswork, hand carvings, antique furnishings, artwork, and fireplaces. A small parlor with fireplace on the main floor offers a relaxing room for conversing with other guests. A private rooftop walk offers views of ships in the harbor. It's only a short walk from the inn to the village's antique shops, restaurants, and galleries and guests often use the inn as a convenient base when exploring nearby Boston. Continental breakfast. Facilities for meetings and retreats. Restricted smoking. 1 or 2/$80-175. AE, MC, V.

Marblehead

Spray Cliff on the Ocean
25 Spray Avenue
Marblehead, MA 01945
(508) 744-8924 or (800) 625-1530

Type of B&B: Small inn.
Rooms: 5 with private bath.
Rates: 1 or 2/$100-200.

Rating: B or ♛♛ Good, exceeds basic requirements.

Large Old-English Tudor style home sits on a bluff above the Atlantic Ocean and is located north of Boston. Five guest rooms each offer a private bath, selected antiques, wicker furniture, fresh flowers, ocean views, and a fireplace. A guest parlor on the main floor offers a fireplace, stereo, and full kitchen. There is a small path to the backyard which drops off to a rocky bluff with dramatic ocean views. Walk to Preston Beach from this location. The village of Marblehead is a five minute drive. Area attractions include historic Salem and sites in Boston. Continental self-service breakfast. Families welcome. 1 or 2/$100-150; Suite/$200. AE, MC, V. Travel agent.

Martha's Vineyard, Edgartown

Colonial Inn of Martha's Vineyard
P.O. Box 68, 38 North Water Street
Edgartown, MA 02539
(508) 627-4711

Type of B&B: Inn.
Rooms: 42 with private bath.
Rates: 1/$75-170; 2/$85-170.

Rating: A- or ♛♛♛ Excellent, far exceeds basic requirements.

Large Colonial inn built in 1911 is located in the historic district of downtown Edgartown and overlooks the harbor. The forty-two guest rooms are light and airy and offer private bath, cable TV, telephone, and air-conditioning. On the premises are two restaurants, eight shops, and a beauty salon. Walk to a historical village, variety of restaurants, unique shops, swimming, boating, fishing, windsurfing, and museums. Continental breakfast is served with fresh baked muffins. Facilities for small meetings available. Families welcome. Wheelchair access. 1/$75-170; 2/$85-170. AE, MC, V. Travel agent.

Guests write: *"The rooms were beautifully decorated with white pine furniture and plush carpeting. The rooms were modern but maintained that feeling of a stately sea captains home, just perfect for the island!" (R. Lewis)*

"With four children ages 1-8, a vacation trip can easily turn into an adventure, sometimes a nightmare. The staff at the Colonial Inn made our stay a real treat. Our room had a beautiful view of the harbor, the location is downtown, the breakfast muffins and fresh fruit eaten on wicker porch furniture on the deck was right out of travel brochure accounts. In fact, the Colonial Inn was everything it claimed to be. It's "Bid Deals for Big Wheels" rate (super discount with bike rentals included) saved us money on the room and bike transport on the ferry." (J. Rok)

Martha's Vineyard, Edgartown

Daggett House
P.O. Box 1333, 59 North Water Street
Edgartown, MA 02539
(508) 627-4600

Type of B&B: Country inn with restaurant.
Rooms: 26 with private bath.
Rates: 1/$65-85; 2/$75-165; Suites/$150-500.

Rating: B or ♛♛ Good exceeds basic requirements.

Shingled Colonial inn constructed in 1660 has been in operation for over 240 years. Each guest room or suite features a private bath and modern day comforts that blend with Early American decor. Discover the secret stairway, walk along the harbor front lawn, or relax in the old breakfast room in front of the antique paneled fireplace. Within walking distance of the inn is a theater, churches, and museums. A short drive will take you to Gay Head Cliffs, gingerbread cottages, beaches, wildlife sanctuaries, and water activities. Continental breakfast. Outdoor terraces can be tented for weddings and meetings. Families welcome. 1/$65-85; 2/$75-165; Suites/$150-500. AE, MC, V. Travel agent.

Martha's Vineyard, Oak Bluffs

Oak House
Seaview Avenue, P.O. Box 299-BB
Oak Bluffs, MA 02557
(508) 693-4187

Type of B&B: Inn.
Rooms: 10 rooms or suites with private bath.
Rates: 1 or 2/$110-220.

Rating: A or ♛♛♛ Excellent, far exceeds basic requirements.

Romantic Victorian inn on the beach offers ten guest rooms or suites, each featuring private bath and Victorian furnishings. Most rooms have balconies and water views. This Victorian seaside resort includes miles of bicycle paths and beaches. Walk to Oak Bluffs landing and the village from the inn. Continental breakfast. Facilities available for small meetings and social functions. 1 or 2/$110-220 with off-season discounts. MC, V. Open mid-May through mid-October.

Martha's Vineyard, Vineyard Haven

Hanover House
P.O. Box 2107
10 Edgartown Road
Vineyard Haven, MA 02568
(508) 693-1066

Type of B&B: Inn.
Rooms: 16 with private bath.
Rates: 1 or 2/$50-153.

Rating: B+ or ♛♛ Good exceeds basic requirements.

Walk to the ferry from this renovated inn built in 1930. Sixteen guest rooms each offer a private bath, cable TV, and individually controlled air conditioning and heating. Many rooms have sundecks and housekeeping units are available with full kitchens. The village of Vineyard Haven offers quaint shops and restaurants. Shuttle buses are nearby to take guests to Oak Bluffs and Edgartown. Nearby beaches provide swimming, sailing, fishing, and windsurfing. Fresh baked muffins round out a hearty continental breakfast served on an enclosed sunporch. Wedding facilities available. Families welcome. 1 or 2/$50-153. AE, MC, V. Senior and military discounts. Travel agent.

Nantucket

Easton House
17 North Water Street, P.O. Box 1033
Nantucket MA 02554
(508) 228-2759

Type of B&B: Inn.
Rooms: 10, 8 with private bath.
Rates: 1/$30-60; 2/$55-125.

Rating: B or ♛♛ Good, exceeds basic requirements.

Colonial inn built in 1812 is located in the center of the Historic District near in-town beaches, shops, restaurants, and museums. Choose from ten guest rooms which feature canopy beds, Oriental rugs, and antiques; eight offer a private bath. Relax in the fireplaced sitting room with cable TV, or enjoy the private backyard with country gardens, lawn chairs, and bike racks. Popular surf beaches are a fifteen-minute bicycle ride from the inn. Continental breakfast features home-baked goods. 1/$30-60; 2/$55-125. Travel agent. Open April-December.

Nantucket

The Four Chimneys
38 Orange Street
Nantucket, MA 02554
(508) 228-1912

Type of B&B: Inn.
Rooms: 10 with private bath.
Rate: 2/$115-175.

Rating: A or ♛♛♛ Excellent, far exceeds basic requirements.

Greek Revival sea captain's home built in 1835 is a short walk from cobblestoned Main Street. Choose from ten guest rooms with private baths that have been authentically restored and furnished with period antiques, oriental rugs, and canopy beds. A suite on the third floor features pine and country furnishings and a harbor view. Many of the area attractions are a short walk away including shops, art galleries, golf, windsurfing, fishing, tennis, fine restaurants, and beaches. Continental breakfast can be served in guest rooms or on the porch furnished in white wicker. A large double parlor with twin fireplaces and porches easily accommodates weddings. Resident dog. 2/$115-175.

Nantucket

Ten Lyon Street Inn
10 Lyon Street
Nantucket, MA 02554
(508) 228-5040

Type of B&B: Inn.
Rooms: 7 with private bath.
Rates: 2/$65-150.

Rating: A or ♛♛♛ Excellent, far exceeds basic requirements.

Colonial inn built in 1849 has been completely renovated and is located in the center of town on a quiet side street near the harbor. Choose from seven guest rooms with double or queen-size beds and private baths. Each room offers quality antique furnishings, linens, down comforters and pillows, and interesting prints. Walk to historic sites, beaches, water sports such as sailing and windsurfing, fine restaurants, or rent bicycles to tour the island. Continental breakfast. 1 or 2/$65-150. MC, V.

Princeton

Harrington Farm
178 Westminster Road
Princeton, MA 01541
(508) 464-5600

Type of B&B: Country inn with restaurant.
Rooms: 8, 2 with private bath.
Rates: 1/$58; 2/$68-100.

Rating: B or ♛♛ Good, exceeds basic requirements.

Historic Colonial farmhouse is now a country inn located north of Worcester off Route 190 near the western slope of Wachusett Mountain ski area. Choose from eight guest rooms which feature original antique farm furniture and Colonial period stenciling; two offer a private bath. A small parlor on the main floor offers board games, and VCR movies as well as an intimate restaurant. Popular activities here include a quiet walk around the farm, bicycling, hiking, skiing, and exploring an Audubon Society reservation nearby. Full breakfast. Dinner is served by request in the inn's restaurant. Families welcome. No smoking. Facilities available for small weddings or group meetings. 1/$58; 2/$68-100. MC, V.

Rockport

Yankee Clipper Inn
96 Granite Street
Rockport, MA 01966
(508) 546-3407 or 546-3408

Type of B&B: Country Inn
Rooms: 27 with private bath.
Rates: 1/$60-175; 2/$98-204.

Rating: A- or ♛♛♛ Excellent, far exceeds basic requirements.

Impressive oceanfront Victorian mansion is located 45 minutes north of Boston near the northeast end of Route 128. There are twenty-seven guest rooms in the mansion or two smaller inns on adjacent properties. Each room differs in size, decor, and amenities but special features found in some rooms include ocean views, canopy beds, glass-enclosed porches, and 19th-century furnishings. The landscaped grounds invite exploration and feature a heated salt water swimming pool and paths that end at the rocky water's edge. Each of the three buildings offers a parlor with television lounge. The mansion's living room features floor to ceiling bookcases and original wall murals. Full breakfast. Candlelight dinner available at the restaurant. The lower level offers an attractive function room with large windows. Families welcome. Restricted smoking. 1/$69-175; 2/$98-204. AE, MC, V. Travel agent.

Salem

The Salem Inn
7 Summer Street
Salem, MA 01970
(508) 741-0680

Type of B&B: Large urban inn.
Rooms: 21 with private bath.
Rates: 1 or 2/$90-125.

Rating: B or ♛♛ Good, exceeds basic requirements.

Federalist-style inn built in 1834 is located in the heart of the historic seaport town of Salem which is located about 45 minutes north of Boston off Route 1A. Period furnishings fill the twenty-one guest rooms which feature private bath, color TV, and air conditioning. Several rooms have working fireplaces. Two-room apartments with full kitchens are especially suitable for families. There is a parlor on the main floor as well as a gift shop with crafts from local artists. The city of Salem is rich with Early American history. Area attractions at Boston, Marblehead, Gloucester,

Concord, and Rockport are within a short drive. Continental breakfast is included in the room rate and there is a restaurant on-site. Families welcome. 1 or 2/$90-125. AE, MC, V. 10% business discount. Travel agent.

Sandwich

Bay Beach B&B
1-3 Bay Beach Lane
Sandwich, MA 02563
(508) 888-8813

Type of B&B: Small inn.
Rooms: 3 suites with private bath.
Rates: 1 or 2/$100-150.

Rating: AA- or ♛♛♛♛ Outstanding.

New oceanfront contemporary inn overlooks the beach and Cape Cod Bay. Choose from three spacious guest suites with ocean views, private balconies, contemporary wicker furnishings, and ceiling fans. The Honeymoon suite features a whirlpool bath and each room offers a private bath, cable color TV, phone, refrigerator, and air-conditioning. Visit nearby museums, historic sites, and fine restaurants within walking distance. Full breakfast. No smoking. 1 or 2/$100-150. Travel agent.

Sandwich

Captain Ezra Nye House
152 Main Street
Sandwich, MA 02563
(800) 388-2278 or (508) 888-6142

Type of B&B: Small inn.
Rooms: 9, 7 with private bath.
Rates: 1 or 2/$50-75.

Rating: B+ or ♛♛ Good, exceeds basic requirements.

Historic clapboard Federal-style home is located in the heart of Sandwich near Route 6, exit 2. Nine guest rooms offer hand-stenciled walls, original artwork, and furnishings collected from around the world including Oriental rugs, spindle beds, sleigh beds, and claw-foot tubs. Seven of the rooms offer a private bath. A small den offers a fine library of books and comfortable seating for watching TV. Area attractions include Sandwich Glass Museum, Heritage Plantation, Thornton Burgess Museum, Doll Museum, Shawme Lake, and Hoxie House, the oldest house on Cape Cod. Full breakfast. No smoking. 1 or 2/$50-75. AE, MC, V. Travel agent.

Sandwich

Isaiah Jones Homestead
168 Main Street
Sandwich, MA 02563
(508) 888-9115

Type of B&B: Inn.
Rooms: 4 with private bath.
Rates: 1/$55-109; 2/$65-119.

Rating: A or ♛♛♛ Excellent, far exceeds basic requirements.

Historic home built in 1849 is now an inn conveniently located in the village of Sandwich, one mile off Route 6. There are four guest rooms available. Each offers a private bath, sitting area, and antique furnishings. A special Honeymoon suite features a whirlpool tub. The main floor has a gift shop with interesting craft items and clothing for sale. The formal parlor features an original fireplace and deep window seats. Popular area attractions include Sandwich Glass Museum, Thornton Burgess Museum, Yesterday Doll Museum, tennis, and fishing. Continental breakfast served by candlelight in a formal dining room features homemade breads and muffins. A daily afternoon tea is also offered. Facilities available for social functions. No smoking. 1/$55-109; 2/$65-119. AE, MC, V. Travel agent.

Stockbridge/South Lee

Merrell Tavern Inn
Route 102, Main Street
South Lee, MA 01260
(413) 243-1794

Type of B&B: Inn.
Rooms: 9 with private bath.
Rates: 1/$55-115; 2/$65-135.

Rating: A- or ♛♛♛ Excellent, far exceeds basic requirements.

Historic Federal home built in 1800 as a stagecoach inn and listed on the National Register of Historic Places, is in a small village 3 miles from exit 2 on I-90. Nine guest rooms are available, each with private bath, antique furnishings, and period decor. Some feature fireplaces or canopy beds. Relax in the parlor, sit by the fire in the tavern room, or stroll on the grounds, which extend to the banks of the Housatonic River. The gardens feature the original stone walls of the inn's barns and livery stables. Area attractions include Norman Rockwell Museum, Tanglewood Music Festival, golf, tennis, fishing, hiking, and skiing. Full breakfast. Families welcome. Restricted smoking. 1/$55-115; 2/$65-135. MC, V.

Sturbridge

Colonel Ebenezer Crafts Inn
Fiske Hill
Sturbridge, MA 01566
(508) 347-3313

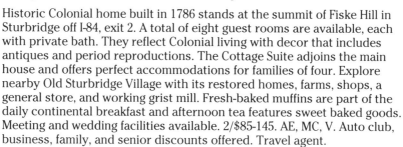

Type of B&B: Inn.
Rooms: 8 with private bath.
Rates: 2/$85-145.

Rating: B+ or ♕♕ Good, exceeds basic requirements.

Historic Colonial home built in 1786 stands at the summit of Fiske Hill in Sturbridge off I-84, exit 2. A total of eight guest rooms are available, each with private bath. They reflect Colonial living with decor that includes antiques and period reproductions. The Cottage Suite adjoins the main house and offers perfect accommodations for families of four. Explore nearby Old Sturbridge Village with its restored homes, farms, shops, a general store, and working grist mill. Fresh-baked muffins are part of the daily continental breakfast and afternoon tea features sweet baked goods. Meeting and wedding facilities available. 2/$85-145. AE, MC, V. Auto club, business, family, and senior discounts offered. Travel agent.

Sturbridge

Sturbridge Country Inn
530 Main Street, P.O. Box 60
Sturbridge, MA 01566
(508) 347-5503

Type of B&B: Inn.
Rooms: 9 with private bath.
Rates: 1 or 2/$69-149.

Rating: A- or ♕♕♕ Excellent, far exceeds basic requirements.

Historic Greek Revival Victorian home is now an inn located 1 mile west of Turnpike exit 9 on Route 20. There are nine guest rooms. Each offers a private bath and selection of antique or reproduction furnishings as well as a fireplace and whirlpool bathtub. Popular area attractions include Old Sturbridge Village, tennis, fishing, hiking, and skiing. Continental breakfast. 1 or 2/$69-149. AE, MC, V. Travel agent.

West Harwich

Lion's Head Inn
P.O. Box 444
West Harwich, MA 02671
(800) 321-3155

Type of B&B: Inn.
Rooms: 6 with private bath.
Rates: 1/$50-95; 2/$55-125.

Rating: A- or ♛♛♛ Excellent, far exceeds basic requirements.

Historic sea captain's home built in the early 1800s has been fully restored and is located near Route 6, exit 9. Choose from six guest rooms in the main house which each offer a private bath and pleasant decor. The original pine floors, fireplace, and root cellar of the home have been preserved intact and are enhanced by a selection of period antiques. Two private guest cottages on the property offer accommodations especially suited for families. A large glassed-in addition overlooks the swimming pool and patio area. Popular area attractions include bicycle paths, fishing, whale watching, golf, shopping, antiquing, theaters, and fine dining. Full breakfast. Families welcome. Facilities available for meetings and social functions. 1/$50-95; 2/$55-125. MC, V. Travel agent.

West Yarmouth

The Manor House
57 Maine Avenue
West Yarmouth, MA 02673
(508) 771-9211

Type of B&B: Inn.
Rooms: 6 with private bath.
Rates: 1 or 2/$50-65.

Rating: B or ♛♛ Good, exceeds basic requirements.

Built in the 1920's, this Dutch Colonial home has views of Lewis Bay and is located 3 miles from exit 7 off Route 6. Choose from six guest rooms with private bath and pleasant decor. A small sitting room serves as the breakfast area and offers comfortable seating while viewing TV. Within walking distance of the inn are beaches, a boat launch area, antique shops, and restaurants. The island ferries to Nantucket and Martha's Vineyard are a short drive away. Continental breakfast features homemade muffins. Facilities available for small meetings and social functions. 1 or 2/$50-65. MC. V.

Yarmouthport

The Colonial House Inn
Route 6A, 277 Main Street
Yarmouthport, MA 02675
(508) 362-4348 or (800) 999-3416

Type of B&B: Inn with restaurant.
Rooms: 21 with private bath.
Rate: 1/$45-80; 2/$60-95.

Rating: B+ or ♕♕ Good, exceeds basic requirements.

Victorian inn with restaurant was originally constructed in the 18th-century and is located less than two miles from Route 6, midway between exits 7 and 8. Each of the twenty-one guest rooms is air-conditioned, offers a private bath, is decorated with antiques, and has its own view of the grounds and surrounding historic homes. An indoor heated swimming pool is on the premises. Local area attractions include nature trails, antique shops, beaches, and theaters. Continental breakfast. Meeting facilities are available for up to 150 people. Families welcome. Wheel chair access. 1/$45-80; 2/$60-95. Rates include breakfast and dinner. AE, MC, V. 10% auto club, business travel, family, and senior discounts. Travel agent.

Guests write: *"We had the two most beautiful rooms one could ask for. Ours had a canopy bed and complete bathroom with claw-foot tub. My parent's had a fireplace ready to use. We will never forget the warm reception." (M. de Prada)*

Yarmouthport

Wedgewood Inn
83 Main Street
Yarmouthport, MA 02675
(508) 362-5157 or 362-9178

Type of B&B: Small inn.
Rooms: 6 with private bath.
Rates: 1 or 2/$90-145.

Rating: A or ♛♛♛ Excellent, far exceeds basic requirements.

Greek Revival inn built in 1812 and refurbished in 1983 is located on
Cape Cod and surrounded by majestic elms and original stone walls.
Each of the six guest rooms offers a private bath, pencil post bed,
vintage quilt, period wallpaper, and fresh flowers. Some rooms also
feature working fireplaces and suite accommodations. Popular
attractions in the area include beaches, nature and bike trails, whale
watching, and visiting antique shops, art galleries, and museums.
Belgian waffles and home-baked goods are a part of the full breakfast
offered in an elegant dining room. Small function rooms available for
meetings and weddings. Restricted smoking. 1 or 2/$90-145. AE, MC, V.
Travel agent.

Bay City

Stonehedge Inn Bed & Breakfast
924 Center Avenue (M-25)
Bay City, MI 48708
(517) 894-4342

Type of B&B: Inn.
Rooms: 7 with shared bath.
Rates: 1 or 2/$68-85.

Rating: B- or ♛♛ Good, exceeds basic requirements.

English Tudor mansion boasts many of its original architectural details and is located near Bay City downtown area which is about two hours north of Detroit near the junctions of Routes 10 and 75. Seven guest rooms on the second or third floor are furnished with antiques and reproductions, decorated in soft colors, and share several baths. Nine fireplaces grace the inn as well as original stained-glass windows, open foyer and staircase, and speaking tubes. Popular attractions in the area include swimming, boating, fishing, golfing, and nature trails. Continental buffet breakfast includes homemade muffins and breads. Facilities available for small weddings and meetings. Restricted smoking. 1 or 2/$65-85. AE, MC, V. 10% senior, business, and auto club member discount. Travel agent.

Fennville

Hidden Pond Bed & Breakfast
5975 128th Avenue
Fennville, MI 49408
(616) 561-2491

Type of B&B: B&B home.
Rooms: 2 with private bath.
Rates: 2/$80-110.

Rating: B+ or ♛♛ Good, exceeds basic requirements.

Hidden Pond combines modern amenities with a secluded rural atmosphere on twenty-eight acres of private, wooded grounds, 40 miles southwest of Grand Rapids. Two guest rooms are available, each with private bath. There is a large common room with comfortable seating for conversing with other guests, playing board games, or reading. Bird watching and hiking on the property have proven popular with guests but golf, tennis, skiing, hiking, bicycling, and water sports are nearby. Full breakfast is served on an enclosed porch overlooking a wildlife pond. 2/$80-110.

Harbor Springs

Main Street Bed & Breakfast
403 East Main Street (Route 119)
Harbor Springs, MI 49740
(616) 526-7782

Type of B&B: Small inn.
Rooms: 4 with private bath.
Rates: 1 or 2/$60-90.

Rating: B+ or ♛♛ Good, exceeds basic requirements.

Victorian inn built in the late 1800s is situated in a resort community of Northern Michigan that is filled with historic homes and located on State Route 119 near US-31. Four guest rooms each offer a private bath and are decorated with country themes. The enclosed wrap-around porch features views of Main Street and Traverse Bay. The gathering room offers comfortable seating for viewing TV. Walk one block to unique shops, restaurants, and the sandy city beaches of one of the protected deep water harbors on the Great Lakes. Popular attractions in the area include the scenic drive to Mackinaw City and Island, downhill skiing at Boyne Highlands and Nubs Nob. Full breakfast specialties include pancakes and waffles. Families welcome. No smoking. 1 or 2/$60-90. MC, V. Travel agent.

South Haven

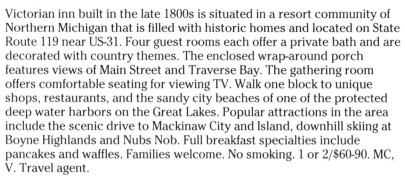

Yelton Manor
140 North Shore Drive
South Haven, MI 49090
(616) 637-5220

Type of B&B: Inn.
Rooms: 11 with private bath.
Rates: 1 or 2/$90-150.

Rating: A+ or ♛♛♛ Excellent, far exceeds basic requirements.

Large Victorian mansion is located near the Lake Michigan shoreline a half-mile west of I-196. Eleven spacious guest rooms each offer a private bath and distinctive decor with a selection of antique furnishings, fresh wallpaper, interesting pictures, and collectibles. Several rooms feature a working fireplace, views of the lake, and Jacuzzi tub. The inn has several common rooms including a fully enclosed porch and parlor with fireplace. A spacious meeting room with fireplace offers comfortable seating and conference equipment. Brownies are a specialty here as well the freshly popped popcorn each evening. Full breakfast. No smoking. 1 or 2/$90-150. AE, MC, V.

Guests write: *"Our children gave us this week-end for R&R. We will always be thankful to them for introducing us to the charm and warmth of Yelton Manor. The food was delicious and prepared and served in such a homey way - we loved it! The Rose room was beautifully decorated and quiet."* *(C. Vander Horst)*

"We wanted a place to escape the hustle bustle at home never realizing how relaxed we'd get here! We found all the childhood treasures to make us feel pampered especially Marge's brownies and the books, sitting spots, chocolates, popcorn - just outstanding!" (J. Maslowsky)

"Delicious food, homey and spotless surrounding and warm sharing, and fun personality. The visit for our family was unforgettable!" (C. Bowling)

Yelton Manor exceeded our expectations: the manor, the Jasmine room, the breakfasts. The aura of the home enveloped us with friendliness and charm." (L. Bertsche)

Union Pier

Pine Garth Inn
15790 Lakeshore Road
Union Pier, MI 49129
(616) 469-1642

Type of B&B: Inn.
Rooms: 7 with private bath
plus five housekeeping cottages.
Rates: 1 or 2/$70-130; cottages/$140-225.

Rating: A+ or ♛ ♛ ♛ Excellent, far exceeds basic requirements.

Restored summer estate and nearby cottages overlook Lake Michigan and are located 90 miles from Chicago. Each of the inn's seven guest rooms feature antique furnishings, whirlpool tub, fireplaces, and a lake view. Five country cottages, each with two bedrooms offer a complete bath, private deck and hot tub, fully equipped kitchen, TV with VCR, and wood-burning fireplace. The inn has a private beach, beautiful lake views, and a pleasant Great Room with fireplace where breakfast is served and guests gather for evening refreshments. Full breakfast is included in the rates for the guest rooms in the main inn only. Families are welcome in the cottages. Restricted smoking. 1 or 2/$70-130; Cottages/$140-225. AE, MC, V. Business travel discount. Travel agent.

Pelican Rapids

Prairie View Estate
Route 2, Box 443
Pelican Rapids, MN 56572
(218) 836-4321

Type of B&B: Small inn.
Rooms: 3, 1 with private bath.
Rates: 1 or 2/$30-45.

Rating: B or ♛♛ Good, exceeds basic requirements.

Scandinavian farmhouse built in the 1920s has a rural setting one mile from town and is located 45 miles southeast of Fargo or 200 miles northwest of Minneapolis. Three guest rooms on the second floor are decorated with family heirlooms; one offers a private bath. The main floor offers three common rooms including an enclosed sun porch and living room with TV. Area lakes offer hunting, fishing, and swimming. Seasonal events include the Water Carnival, We Fest, Steam Thresher's Reunion, and Turkey Days. Choice of continental or full breakfast with specialties such as oven French toast or oven souffles served with fresh fruit plates and a wide variety of home-baked breads. Families welcome. No smoking. 1 or 2/$30-45. MC, V.

Long Beach

Red Creek Colonial Inn
7416 Red Creek Road
Long Beach, MS 39560
(601) 452-3080 (for information)
or (800) 729-9670 (for reservations)

Type: Inn.
Rooms: 6, 5 with private bath.
Rates: 1/$34-54; 2/$44-64.

Rating: B or ♛♛ Good, exceeds basic requirements.

Historic Southern/French Colonial-style inn with graceful columns enjoys a quiet rural setting on eleven acres just south of I-10, exit 28. Choose from six guest rooms. Five offer a private bath and there is a special bunk room for children. A spacious guest room on the main floor features antique furnishings and fireplace. The inn boasts an original art collection and a 64-foot front porch. Popular attractions in the area are the nearby beaches for swimming and boating. Continental breakfast. 1/$34-54; 2/$44-64. 10% senior and auto club discounts. Travel agent.

Independence

Woodstock Inn
1212 West Lexington
Independence, MO 64050
(816) 833-2233

Type of B&B: Inn.
Rooms: 11 with private bath.
Rates: 1/$40-60; 2/$45-65.

Rating: B+ or ♛♛ Good, exceeds basic requirements.

Modified Colonial inn situated in the Historic District is located 3 miles north of I-70 or 3 miles east of I-435. Choose from eleven guest rooms, each with private bath, air conditioning, and telephone. Area attractions include Truman Home, Mormon visitor's center, RLDS Temple, Worlds of Fun theme park and sports stadiums. Full breakfast features hot cereals, an egg dish, and pastries. Families welcome. Wheelchair access. No smoking. 1/$40-60; 2/$45-65. MC, V. 10% seasonal senior discount.

Kimmswick

Kimmswick Korner Inn
P.O. Box 117
Front & Market Streets
Kimmswick, MO 63053
(314) 467-1027

Type of B&B: Small inn.
Rooms: 2 share one bath.
Rates: 1 or 2/$55-60.

Rating: B or ♛♛ Good exceeds basic requirements.

Kimmswick Korner Inn is the top floor of an historic storefront building in the quaint downtown area of Kimmswick located twenty minutes south of St. Louis. Two guest rooms are offered on the second floor and they share a large bath. Each room has a distinctive decor with antique furnishings, papered walls, wood floors with area rugs, and designer linens. A Victorian parlor offers comfortable seating and a collection of reading material. Specialty shops and restaurants with homemade cooking line the streets of this small town and Mastadon State Park is one mile away. Continental breakfast includes the inn's special jellies and jams, homemade breads, fresh fruit, and fresh-ground coffee. No smoking. 1 or 2/$55-60. MC, V.

Helena

Upcountry Inn
2245 Head Lane
Helena, MT 59601
(406) 442-1909

Type of B&B: Country inn with restaurant.
Rooms: 5, 1 with private bath.
Rates: 1/$40; 2/$50.

Rating: B or ♛♛ Good, exceeds basic requirements.

Upcountry Inn is located 2 miles west of Helena off US-12. Quilts, stencils, iron beds, and wicker chairs fill the five guest rooms and add to the inn's home-style hospitality. One room offers a private bath. The dining hall and great room are decorated country-estate style with wood, wool, and leather. Area attractions include Spring Meadow Lake State Recreation Area, historic Helena, Green Meadow Golf Course, and the Archie Bray Pottery Studio. Enjoy a full breakfast by the fire. Afternoon tea and dining in the Red Fox Restaurant are available by advance reservation. Facilities for weddings and meetings available. Families welcome. Wheelchair access. No smoking. 1/$40; 2/$50. MC.

Three Forks

Sacajawea Inn
5 North Main Street
Three Forks, MT 59752
(406) 285-6934

Type of B&B: Inn with restaurant.
Rooms: 33 with private bath.
Rates: 1/$40-65; 2/$50-85.

Rating: Unrated as restoration work not completed at press time.

Mid-19th-century Western lodge has been in operation as an inn since 1910 and is located 50 miles east of Butte and 28 miles west of Bozeman off I-90. The inn has been totally renovated in 1992 and offers thirty-three guest rooms with private bath. The large lobby with polished wood beams, high ceilings, and original light fixtures has served as a gathering place for outdoorsmen visiting Yellowstone National Park and summer-long guests from the East for over eighty years. Popular attractions in the area include Yellowstone Park, Gallatin Valley, Lewis and Clark Caverns, Madison Buffalo Jump State Monument, Three Forks Museum, and Museum of the Rockies. Area recreation includes hunting, fishing, skiing, horseback riding, biking, and hiking. Continental breakfast includes home-baked pastries. Small meeting facilities available in the restaurant's dining room. Families welcome. Restricted smoking. 1/$40-65; 2/$50-85. AE, MC, V. 10% senior, business, and auto club member discount. Travel agent.

Ashland

Glynn House "Victorian" Inn
43 Highland Street
Ashland, NH 03217
(603) 968-3775

Type of B&B: Small inn.
Rooms: 4 with private bath.
Rates: 1/$60; 2/$65-75.

Rating: A or ♛♛♛ Excellent, far exceeds basic requirements.

Queen Anne Victorian home built in 1890 is situated in a quaint village setting just off of I-93 at exit 24. Four guest rooms with private bath feature period furniture and unique interior design. A wrap-around porch with comfortable seating has gingerbread accents. Several restaurants and specialty shops are nearby and Squam Lake and the White Mountains offer year-round recreation including fishing, cycling, golfing, and tennis. Full breakfast includes the house specialty of strudel. Restricted smoking. 1/$60; 2/$65-75. MC, V. Senior discount. Travel agent.

Bartlett

Country Inn at Bartlett
P.O. Box 327, Route 302
Bartlett, NH 03812
(603) 374-2353

Type of B&B: Country inn.
Rooms: 17 with shared or private baths.
Rates: 1/$36-48; 2/$64-84.

Rating: C+ or ♛ Acceptable, meets basic requirements.

Historic Victorian Inn built in 1885 is located in the White Mountain region of the state. Set in a tall stand of pines and surrounded by National Forest, this inn is a quiet haven for hikers, skiers, and all who love to be outdoors. Choose from seventeen guest rooms, six in the main inn, or eleven guest rooms in the cottages with some offering private bath. Relax on the front porch in one of the rockers or by the fire in the large living room. Cross-country skiing and an outdoor hot tub are available. This household of active hikers offers hiking tips to guests. Full country breakfast. Restricted smoking. 1/$36-48; 2/$64-84. AE, MC, V. Travel agent.

Guests write: *"This inn is the kind of place I could move to. Honest people, environmentally minded community, no lines at the post office, infinite opportunities for outdoor activities. These are the type of things which make life enjoyable and exciting and the inn provided for me a wonderful place to experience this community." (J. Hoffman)*

"We had a charming room on the first floor with a working fireplace whose ample supply of wood was replenished at our request. Breakfast was served in courses; beginning with fresh fruit, plenty of fresh hot coffee, followed by delicious home-baked lemon poppy seed muffins and a full cooked-to-order breakfast." (W. McGrath)

"We very much appreciated being able to return post-hill climb for a hot tub and pre-journey snack." (C. Muskat)

"We just enjoyed our 7th stay at the country inn. It's always delightful, especially the people and food." (P. Curda)

Center Harbor

Savards Bed & Breakfast
S.R. 62, Box 549
Center Harbor, NH 03226
(603) 253-6151

Type of B&B: Private home.
Rooms: 2 with private bath.
Rates: 1/$55; 2/$60.

Rating: C+ or ♛ Acceptable, meets basic requirements.

Ranch-style home is located near the center of the state, north of Laconia off Route 3. Two guest rooms are available, each with private bath. Area recreation includes swimming, boating, golfing, and skiing. Continental breakfast. Families welcome. Restricted smoking. 1/$55; 2/$60. 10% senior, business, and auto club discount. Travel agent.

Franconia

The Franconia Inn
Easton Valley Road
Franconia, NH 03580
(603) 823-5542 or (800) 4RE-LAXX

Type of B&B: Country inn
Rooms: 34, 4 with shared bath.
Rates: 1/$60-80; 2/$75-95.

Rating: B+ or ♛♛ Exceeds basic requirements.

Traditional New England white clapboard structure is situated on 107 acres and located in the northwestern side of the state off I-93 near Littleton. There are thirty-four guest rooms, most with private bath. Ten rooms have an extra bed for a third guest. Two suites are especially suited for families. The Honeymoon suite includes a Jacuzzi tub and queen-size bed. An oak-paneled library and large living room offer beautiful views of the mountains. Two porches offer comfortable seating and views of the surrounding countryside. The Rathskeller Lounge on the lower level has a hot tub and game room with movies available. Year-round recreation includes riding, tennis, swimming, trout fishing, hiking, skiing, and sledding. Area attractions include the Robert Frost home, Franconia State Park, and Maple Sugar Museum. Full breakfast and dinner are available at the restaurant at an additional cost. Facilities for weddings and functions available. Families welcome. 1/$60-80; 2/$75-95. AE, MC, V. Travel agent.

"We can suggest nothing to improve. Everything and everyone was very nice and pleasant." (R. Stavnitsky)

"This year we are going to stay in the same room on the 1st floor next to the library. This place has fantastic food, plenty to do and the people are just great." (A. Greenberg)

"Our return stay (the 3rd or 4th time) was just as enjoyable as the previous visits. It is heartwarming to return and recognize members of the staff and have them recognize you - acknowledging your previous visits! It is like a homecoming of sorts and certainly increased our desire to continue our treks to Franconia Inn." (J. Wright)

Freedom

Freedom House Bed 'n' Breakfast
1 Maple Street, Box 478
Freedom, NH 03836
(603) 539-4815

Type of B&B: B&B home.
Rooms: 6 with shared baths.
Rates: 1/$40; 2/$60.

Rating: B- or ♛♛ Good, exceeds basic requirements.

Historic Victorian home is situated in a quaint village located 9 miles east of Route 16 and 2 miles east of Route 153. Choose from six guest rooms with shared baths that are furnished with antiques and handmade furnishings. Within walking distance of the inn is a lake, country store, and library. Popular area attractions include Loon Lake, Lake Ossipee, White Mountain range, Conway's factory outlets, and Wolfeboro. Hosts speak French and Spanish. Full breakfast. Families welcome. No smoking. 1/$40; 2/$60. MC, V.

Gorham

Gorham House Inn
55 Main Street
P.O. Box 267
Gorham, NH 03581
(603) 466-2271

Type of B&B: Inn.
Rooms: 4 with shared bath.
Rates: 1/$38; 2/$54

Rating: C or ♛ Acceptable, meets basic requirements.

Victorian inn built in 1891 is located on the town common at the junction of Routes 2 and 16, the northern gateway to the White Mountains. Choose from four guest rooms with shared baths. An elegant fireplaced parlor offers a relaxing area in which to unwind, socialize, or enjoy the entertainment center. Area attractions include Mount Washington auto road and train, ski areas, golf, hiking, and fishing. Full breakfast. Families welcome. 1/$38; 2/$54.

Hampstead/Manchester

Stillmeadow Bed & Breakfast at Hampstead
P.O. Box 565
545 Main Street
Hampstead, NH 03841
(603) 329-8381

Type of B&B: Inn.
Rooms: 5 with private bath.
Rate: 1/$50; 2/$60-90.

Rating: A or ♛♛♛ Excellent, far exceeds basic requirements.

1850 Greek Renaissance Colonial home is located on Main Street (Route 121) near the junction of Route 111. Five guest rooms or suites are available, each with private bath. A large suite offers queen-size bed and sitting room with trundle bed. Another suite is ideal for families with crib, changing table, and stairs leading to a playroom - all child-proof. Children will also enjoy the fenced-in play yard. The home is adjacent to the Hampstead Croquet Association's twin grass courts. Other area attractions include the Robert Frost Farm, America's Stonehenge, Rockingham Park Race Track, and Kingston State Park. Continental breakfast is served mid-week and full breakfast on weekends. Small meeting facilities available. Families welcome. No smoking. 1/$50; 2/$60-90. AE.

Guests write: *"Our stay at the Stillmeadow was the only peaceful and pleasant time in our lengthy moving-in process. We can wholeheartedly recommend their hospitality to future visitors."* (P. Broadwater)

"You can't go too many places where someone would even loan you their own makeup. They sure helped me get off to a good start. They've done such a lovely job here that we felt right at home." R. Snyder)

"They played a part in our big reunion weekend and smaller clan gathering. It had been four years since we had all been together. All week long one or another of us would say how we have to get together at a place like Stillmeadow more often. It was perfect." (D. Rozeboom)

Hampton

Curtis Field House
735 Exeter Road
Hampton, NH 03842
(603) 929-0082

Type of B&B: B&B home.
Rooms: 3, 2 with private bath.
Rates: 1 or 2/$65.

Rating: B+ or ♛♛ Good, exceeds basic requirements.

Historic Cape Cod home has been completely restored and is situated on five country acres on Route 101-C, just over the Exeter line. Choose from three spacious guest rooms. Each is air conditioned and furnished with antiques and reproductions crafted by a descendant of Darby Field; two have a private bath. Popular area attractions include the Atlantic coast, golf, tennis, boating, skiing, swimming, hiking, and bicycling. This is a convenient location near Phillips Exeter Academy and Strawbery Banke. Full breakfast. Restricted smoking. 1 or 2/$65. MC, V.

Hampton

Inn at Elmwood Corners
252 Winnacunnet Road
Hampton, NH 03842
(603) 929-0443

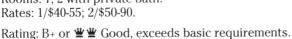

Type of B&B: Inn.
Rooms: 7, 2 with private bath.
Rates: 1/$40-55; 2/$50-90.

Rating: B+ or ♕♕ Good, exceeds basic requirements.

Colonial home built in 1870 by a sea captain has retained much of its original charm and is located near the ocean, 3.5 miles east of I-95, exit 2. Choose from seven guest rooms, including two studio apartments with private bath, air conditioning, and kitchenette. Each room is decorated with a theme in mind and features hand-quilted bedspreads, wall hangings, and varied collections of baskets, dolls, needlework, or antique teddy bears. Area attractions include Hampton Beach, playhouse, whale watching, bicycling, factory outlets, skiing, tennis, fishing, and hiking. Full breakfast may feature home-made sausage, poached trout, or eggs benedict. Families welcome. Restricted smoking. 1/$40-55; 2/$50-90. MC, V.

Hampton

The Victoria Inn
430 High Street
Hampton, NH 03842
(603) 929-1437

Type of B&B: Small inn.
Rooms: 6, 2 with private bath.
Rates: 1/$70; 2/$90.

Rating: A- or ♕♕♕ Excellent, far exceeds basic requirements.

Recently renovated Victorian home was originally built as a carriage house and is located on the coast, 20 minutes south of Portsmouth. Six guest rooms are available, two with private bath. Area attractions include Hampton Beach, Hampton Playhouse, Seabrook Race Track, White Mountains, and Hampton Casino. Boston is a forty-five minute drive. Full breakfast is included in the rates with brunch and dinner available by advance reservation. Facilities available for small functions. Restricted smoking. 1/$70; 2/$90. MC, V. 10% senior, business, and auto club discount.

Hopkinton

Windyledge Bed & Breakfast
Hatfield Road, RFD #3
Hopkinton, NH 03229
(603) 746-4054

Type of B&B: B&B home.
Rooms: 3, 1 with private bath.
Rates: 1/$45-65; 2/$55-75.

Rating: A or ♛♛♛ Excellent, far exceeds basic requirements.

Colonial home overlooks the White Mountains and is located eleven miles west of Concord off Route 202/9. Three guest rooms are available, one with private bath. Special features of the rooms include pencil-post bed, hand-stenciled walls, hand-made antique furnishings, and Oriental rugs. The sitting room has a fireplace, piano, and comfortable seating for viewing TV. Popular spots for relaxation include the deck and swimming pool. Area attractions include antique shops, New England College, St. Paul's school, country fairs, concerts, boating, fishing, golfing, skiing, canoeing, and biking. Rooms for small functions available. Families welcome. Full gourmet breakfast features house specialties such as apricot glazed French toast, sour cream souffle, and honey and spice blueberry pancakes. No smoking. 1/$45-65; 2/$55-75. MC, V. Senior, family, business, and auto club discounts. Travel agent.

Guests write: *"When my husband announced that he had found a place for us to stay outside of Concord for only fifty-five dollars per night for the two of us, plus breakfast, I was understandably leery. How nice could this place be? Happily my fears were groundless. The Windyledge B&B would have been a bargain and a treat at twice the price. We were served breakfasts that were simply wonderful ranging from fruit-filled pancakes to vegetable frittatas. The Vogts have set up a wonderful, cozy family room which not only has a video library of immense proportions but also comes with a nice fire in the winter and glass of wine. A truly memorable stay." (K. Berky)*

"Windyledge was a cinch to find and what a haven on a blustery, frigid night! The warmth of their welcome was only equal to the warmth and charm of the home - super. Also, those blueberry-spice pancakes are destined for fame." (R. Willcox)

"After a five-hour drive and our arrival at Windyledge, Dick and Susan greeted us with warmth and friendliness and most importantly a much needed cold beer to unwind and relax. Our stay was like a visit with friends." (E. Botz)

"Susan thought of every detail to make our room beautiful and cozy from the white eyelet bedding on the four-poster bed to the fresh flowers on the antique dressing table." (B. Whyte)

Jackson

Inn at Jackson
P.O. Box H
Jackson, NH 03846
(603) 383-4321

Type of B&B: Inn.
Rooms: 9 with private bath.
Rate: 1/$44-86; 2/$61-86.

Rating: B+ or ♛♛ Good, exceeds basic requirements.

Victorian inn built in 1910 is located near the village's covered bridge on Route 16A in the White Mountain National Forest. Choose from nine guest rooms, each with private bath. Enjoy panoramic views of the village or Presidential Mountain Range. Among area attractions are cross-country skiing from the inn's front door, outlet shops, and hiking. Full breakfast is served in the fireside dining room or on the glassed-in porch. Families welcome. 1/$44-86; 2/$61-86. AE, MC, V. Travel agent.

Jackson

Nestlenook Farm on the River
P.O. Box Q
Jackson, NH 03846
(603) 383-9443

Type of B&B: Inn.
Rooms: 7 rooms or suites with private bath.
Rates: 1/$85-216.

Rating: AA or ♛♛♛♛ Outstanding.

Riverfront estate on 65 acres was built in 1780 and is reached through a covered bridge which sets the scene for escaping into a Victorian past. The inn is located 3 hours from Boston off Route 16. Choose from seven guest rooms or suites, each with private bath and oversized Jacuzzi, fine antique furnishings, and original paintings. Special features of the inn include horse-drawn Austrian sleigh rides, ice skating, cross-country skiing on groomed trails, heated pool, gazebo, and a gingerbread chapel. Full family-style breakfast. No smoking. 2/$85-216.

Lincoln

Red Sleigh Inn B&B
Pollard Road, P.O. Box 562
Lincoln, NH 03251
(603) 745-8517

Type of B&B: Inn.
Rooms: 8, 2 with private bath.
Rates: 1/$30-35; 2/$50-75.

Rating: B or ♛♛ Good, exceeds basic requirements.

Historic New England farmhouse built in the late 1800s is located just off I-93 and scenic Kancamangus Highway. There are eight guest rooms with antiques and panoramic views of the surrounding mountains; two have a private bath. Common areas include a sunporch, library with fieldstone fireplace, and barbecue area. Popular attractions in the area include four ski areas, hiking, bicycling, performing arts center, outlets, golf, and tennis. Hearty full country breakfast. 1/$30-35; 2/$50-75. MC, V. 10% senior discount. Travel agent.

North Conway

Buttonwood Inn
P.O. Box 1817, Mt. Surprise Road
North Conway, NH 03860
(603) 356-2625
or 1-800-258-2625 (U.S. and Canada)

Type of B&B: Inn.
Rooms: 9, 3 with private bath.
Rates: 1/$40-55; 2/$50-100.

Rating: A or ♛♛♛ Excellent, far exceeds basic requirements.

New England Cape Cod inn is situated in a quiet, secluded mountain setting two miles north of North Conway. Nine guest rooms are available which are furnished with antiques; three offer a private bath. A comfortable ski lounge or TV room is popular with guests after a busy day of skiing or hiking and there is an outdoor swimming pool. This area offers year-round recreation including cross-country skiing out the back door on groomed trails. Full breakfast. Resident dog and cat. 1/$40-55; 2/$50-100. AE, MC, V. Travel agent.

North Conway

Cranmore Mountain Lodge
Kearsarge Road
P.O. Box 1194
North Conway, NH 03860
(603) 356-2044 or (800) 356-3596

Type of B&B: Inn.
Rooms: 16, 5 with private bath.
Rates: 1 or 2/$59-99.

Rating: B+ or ♛♛ Good, exceeds basic requirements.

New England farmhouse inn built in 1865 is located in Mt. Washington Valley, less than 2 miles northeast of town off Route 16. The lodge has sixteen guest rooms, five with private bath. Stay in either the main house or the renovated barn, which has spacious rooms ideal for families and groups with private bath, cable TV, and fireplaced recreation room. Abundant area recreation includes hiking, bicycling, rock climbing, kayaking, cross-country and downhill skiing, golf, and fishing. Enjoy the on-site swimming pool, Jacuzzi, tennis, volleyball, tobogganing, ice skating, and the farm animals on the property. Full breakfast. Families welcome. 1 or 2/$59-99. AE, MC, V. 10% auto club discount.

North Conway/Intervale

Old Field House
P.O. Box 1, Route 16A
Intervale, NH 03845
(603) 356-5478

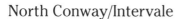

Type of B&B: Motor lodge.
Rooms: 17 with private bath.
Rates: 1 or 2/$59-109.

Rating: A- or ♛♛♛ Excellent, far exceeds basic requirements.

Colonial-style motor inn with a stone facade is located 3 miles north of North Conway on Route 16A. Choose from seventeen guest rooms, each with private bath, air conditioning, phone, and TV. Sit in front of the fireplace in the living room, relax with a book, or listen to soothing music. On the premises are clay tennis courts, an outdoor heated swimming pool, shuffleboard, and cross-country skiing. Area attractions include alpine ski resorts, hiking, mountaineering, fishing, canoeing, and factory outlets. Continental breakfast. Families welcome. 1 or 2/$59-109. AE, MC, V. 10% auto club and business travel discounts. Travel agent.

North Conway

Victorian Harvest Inn
Locust Lane
North Conway, NH 03860
(603) 356-3548

Type of B&B: Inn.
Rooms: 6, 4 with private bath.
Rates: 1/$55; 2/$65-75.

Rating: A or ♛♛♛ Excellent, far exceeds basic requirements.

Restored multi-gabled Victorian inn is found one-half mile south of North Conway off Route 16 tucked away on a quiet side street. Each of the six guest rooms, four with private bath, have ample sitting room, air-conditioning, and antique furnishings. Swim in the Victorian decorated pool, relax on the enclosed porch or large deck, or play the new piano in the library-sitting room. Enjoy the all-season recreation nearby including downhill and cross-country skiing, ice skating, kayaking, canoeing, hiking, swimming, and viewing the magnificent autumn leaves. Full country breakfast. Facilities available for social occasions. No smoking. 1/$55; 2/$65-75. AE, MC, V. 10% auto club discount. Travel agent.

Guests write: *"As always, we thoroughly enjoyed ourselves when visiting the inn. Their warmth and hospitality are wonderful as are the delicious meals and the acceptance as family. The music was great - like everything else."* *(I. McDonald)*

"Since I discovered the Victorian Harvest Inn in the Autumn of 1988, I have had the pleasure of staying there nine times. It's elegant yet comfortable, and the atmosphere is always warm and welcoming. The innkeepers, Bob and Linda, have a flair for making people feel special. The breakfasts were exceptional. They are quite talented in the kitchen." (V. Hagstrom)

North Woodstock

Woodstock Inn
80 Main Street
North Woodstock, NH 03262
(603) 745-3951 or (800) 321-3985

Type of B&B: Country inn with restaurant.
Rooms: 17, 11 with private bath.
Rates: 1/$40; 2/$89.

Rating: B or ♕♕ Good, exceeds basic requirements.

Century old Victorian inn is nestled in the middle of the White Mountains.
Seventeen guest rooms are available in the main house or the inn; eleven
offer a private bath. All rooms feature air conditioning, color TV, and
telephone, with some offering separate sitting areas and porches
overlooking the Pemigewasset River. The Cascade swimming area is a
short walk from the inn and additional recreation nearby includes hiking
and skiing. Popular attractions in the area include Old Man of the
Mountain, Kancamagus Highway, Lost River, Fantasy Farm, Mount
Washington Cog Railway, the Whales Tale Water Slide. Full breakfast is
served in the restored railroad station restaurant which also serves lunch
and dinner. Facilities available for large functions. Families welcome.
1/$40; 2/$89. AE, MC, V.

Wakefield

The Wakefield Inn
R.R. 1, Box 2185
Mountain Laurel Road
Wakefield, NH 03872
(603) 522-8272 or (800) 245-0841

Type of B&B: Inn.
Rooms: 6 with private bath.
Rates: 1/$50; 2/$65.

Rating: B+ or ♕♕ Good, exceeds basic requirements.

Historic country inn built in 1815 as a stagecoach stop is situated in the
Historic District, a half mile east of Route 16. A spiral staircase leads up to
six second floor guest rooms. Each offers a private bath, small-print
wallpaper, handmade quilts, and plants. Popular attractions in the area
include lake recreation, White Mountains for hiking and skiing, antique
shops, and factory outlets. Full breakfast is served and dinner is available
upon request and served in dining room which features the inn's original
three-sided fireplace. 1/$50; 2/$65. MC, V.

Guests write: *"The Wakefield Inn has become a part of any visit we make to New England. We've stayed there on four separate trips and have always felt warmly welcomed - and saddened when it's time to leave. Spending our last two nights in a regular motel was a real contrast - no friendly proprietress to treat us like old friends, no pretty quilts, no conversation at night in the living room, and certainly no slabs of bread crammed with nuts and blueberries."* (D. Perry)

"The rooms are homey with country-style furnishings, private bathrooms, and handmade quilts. Everything was immaculate, comfortable, and spacious. Upon our arrival, our hostess brought to our room a freshly brewed pot of coffee and homemade pasties." (R. Grossman)

Wentworth

Hilltop Acres
East Side and Buffalo Road
Wentworth, NH 03282
(603) 764-5896 or (718) 261-2919

Type of B&B: Inn.
Rooms: 4 with private bath
and two cottages.
Rates: 1 or 2/$60-75.

Rating: C or ♛ Acceptable, meets basic requirements.

Colonial inn and cottages built in 1806 are located at the foot of the White Mountains, approximately 20 minutes from I-93, exit 26. There are five guest rooms with private bath and double brass or twin beds in the main inn. Each has scenic views, plants, a selection of books, and ceiling fans. Two housekeeping cottages especially suited for families are available May through mid-November and include full kitchen unit, separate bedroom, fireplace, and screen-in porch. A pine-paneled recreation room offers games, a large collection of books, and cable TV. Wentworth has three swimming holes, several hiking trails, and fishing streams. Area attractions include Polar Caves, Ruggles Mine, Morse Museum, and Franconia Notch. Continental breakfast includes an assortment of muffins, pastries, and breads. Families welcome. Room/$60; Cottage/$75. MC, V. Travel agent.

Guests write: *"Hilltop Acres is at once a great amalgam of old-fashioned decor, style and elegance with truly modern, luxurious facilities, conveniences, and services. In all the cozy bedrooms there are big, comfortable old-fashioned brass rail beds. On the walls are pictures and maps tracing New England tradition and history. Upbeat friendliness and wonderful services provided by Ms. Kauk, the proprietress, complement the great setting."* (L. Warshaw)

"For those of us enmeshed in the 9-5 syndrome, my recent stay at Hilltop has become a memorable experience. It was a reminder that the simple things in life oftentimes are the most wonderful. The inn isn't Ritzy but rather luxuriates comfort in a simple way - comfy bed, cozy fireplace, wonderful breakfast room which basks in the morning sunlight. Our discovery of a brook meandering through the woods behind the inn was a delightful surprise and added to the serenity of our visit which was much too brief. We look forward to another refreshing dip in the local swimming hole - another unexpected treat. I didn't know those types of places still existed."
(R. Doukas)

"They've done a splendid job of decorating with a modest Victorian touch that allows a visitor to enjoy the uniqueness of the accommodations while feeling completely at home. The downstairs paneled living room was thoughtfully designed for easy mingling and it succeeds wonderfully. After a long country walk, the jazz concert on the lawn made our stay even more memorable." (R. Jorgensen)

Wentworth Village

Wentworth Inn & Art Gallery
Ellsworth Hill Road off Route 25
Wentworth Village, NH 03282
Information: (603) 764-9923
Reservations: (800) 542-2331

Type of B&B: Inn.
Rooms: 6, 3 with private bath.
Rates: 1 or 2/$60-80.

Rating: B- or ♛♛ Good, exceeds basic requirements.

Historic Colonial inn in a quiet, rural setting is located at the base of the White Mountains, 30 minutes from I-91 and twenty minutes from I-93. The inn houses an art gallery in addition to B&B accommodations. There are six guest rooms on the second floor; three with private bath. A small parlor offers comfortable seating for viewing TV. There is year-round recreation in the area including skiing, hiking, and biking. Full breakfast. Restricted smoking. 1 or 2/$60-80. AE, MC, V. Travel agent.

Bay Head

Conover's Bay Head Inn
646 Main Avenue
Bay Head, NJ 08742
(201) 892-4664

Type of B&B: Inn.
Rooms: 12 with private bath.
Rates: 1/$60-130; 2/$70-165.

Rating: A or ♛♛♛ Excellent, far exceeds basic requirements.

Shingle-style inn built in 1912 as a summer cottage, is located in a small town at the seashore. Choose from twelve guest rooms, each offering private bath, air conditioning, and featuring dramatic color-coordinated decor including matching spreads and ruffled pillows. Enjoy the views of the ocean, the bay, and the marina from one of the expansive porches or large windows. Area attractions include ocean and bay recreation, quaint shops, golf, tennis, fishing, and hiking. Full breakfast includes fresh-baked goods and is served in the dining room, front porch, or on the manicured front lawn. No smoking. 1/$60-130; 2/$70-165. AE, MC, V. 10% business travel discount.

Cape May

Carroll Villa B&B Hotel
19 Jackson Street
Cape May, NJ 08204
(609) 884-9619

Type of B&B: Historic hotel with restaurant.
Rooms: 21 with private bath.
Rates: 1 or 2/$50-110.

Rating: B+ or ♛♛ Good, exceeds basic requirements.

Historic Victorian hotel built in 1881 is a half block from the beach in the center of the town's Historic District. Twenty-one guest rooms are available, all with private bath. Each room is individually decorated with antique furnishings, Victorian period wallpaper, lace curtains, and overhead fans. Some rooms offer air-conditioning. Common areas include a wicker-filled living room, garden terrace, and cupola with panoramic views. Walk to the Victorian Mall, lighthouse, bird sanctuaries, and picturesque village shops. Full breakfast. Families welcome. Facilities available for social functions and meetings. 2/$50-110. MC, V.

Cape May

Columns by the Sea
1513 Beach Drive
Cape May, NJ 08204
(609) 884-2228

Type of B&B: Inn.
Rooms: 11 with private bath.
Rates: 1/$95-145; 2/$105-155.

Rating: A+ or ♕♕♕ Excellent, far exceeds basic requirements.

Oceanfront Italianate Colonial Revival mansion was built in 1905. There are eleven guest rooms, each with private bath, Victorian furnishings and collectibles, hardwood floors, and Oriental rugs. There are several common areas including a first floor wicker TV room, and third floor library. A large front porch has ocean views and wicker furnishings. Bicycles are available to explore the historic village with its interesting shops and sites. Popular attractions in the area include Cold Spring Village, fishing, boating, swimming, antique shopping, and bird watching. Hosts speak German. Full gourmet breakfast and complimentary afternoon tea served daily. No smoking. 1/$95-145; 2/$105-155.

Cape May

Mason Cottage
625 Columbia Avenue
Cape May, NJ 08204
(609) 884-3358

Type of B&B: Inn.
Rooms: 5, 4 with private bath.
Rates: 1 or 2/$75-135.

Rating: A- or ♕♕♕ Excellent, far exceeds basic requirements.

Victorian seaside home with lofty ceilings, sweeping veranda, and full length windows was built in 1871 and is located two hours from Philadelphia at the end of the Garden State Parkway. Choose from five antique-furnished guest rooms, four with private bath. The veranda offers an ocean view. Popular attractions in the area include Lewes Ferry, village shopping, golf, tennis, fishing, boating, swimming, hiking, and bicycling. Continental plus breakfast. 2/$75-135. MC, V. 5% senior discount.

Guests write: *"We have been going to the Mason Cottage every June since 1985. Being one block from the ocean and a couple of blocks from some of the best restaurants make this one of our favorite places. Dave and Joan and the staff always go out of the way to make our stay comfortable and they always have suggestions for something different to do." (E. Ross)*

"When our daughter was married in Cape May last summer we reserved the Mason Cottage for ourselves, family, and friends. The Mason's gracious hospitality is unsurpassed! In the midst of all the wedding preparations, the Mason Cottage was a haven to which we could return, rock on the porch, feel the ocean breezes, enjoy the aroma of flowers and be pampered. Being from the Midwest, we especially enjoyed the location near the ocean and in the center of the Victorian district. One of our favorite activities was strolling the lanes of the Victorian homes in the neighborhood during the day and night." (J. Colson)

Cape May

Queen Victoria
102 Ocean Street
Cape May, NJ 08204
(609) 884-8702

Type of B&B: Inn.
Rooms: 24 with private or shared bath.
Rate: 1 or 2/$55-225.

Rating: A+ or ♕♕♕ Excellent, far exceeds basic requirements.

Three restored Victorian seaside villas comprise the Queen Victoria which is located one block from the ocean in the center of the Historic District. There are twenty-four guest rooms which feature hand-made quilts, ceiling fans, and private or shared baths. Each room offers individual decor and several have fireplaces, whirlpool tubs, and air conditioning. Use the inn's bicycles to tour historic sites, antique shops, and the town center. Area attractions include restaurants, specialty shops, tennis, fishing, boating, swimming, and biking. Hosts speak French. Full breakfast. Facilities available for small weddings and meetings. 1 or 2/$55-225. MC, V.

Guests write: *"Congratulations to them for such good work in restoration, livability, and comfort. As we know, old houses can be greedy entities - but the owner's wills have prevailed here." (H.B. Crisman)*

" Our suite oozed charm. We had a sitting room which stepped into a bedroom which took us back to the Victorian days. We have stayed in many B&Bs and this Queen Victoria has topped them all. This was our first Christmas in thirty-nine years away from our children and family. Joan and Dane and all of their guests made Christmas 1991 one to remember and we would do it again." (N. Martin)

"The first thing we noticed was that the grass and walks were extremely well-manicured. We liked the location within walking distance to so many things and the ocean. I could not believe it when they emptied the wastebaskets twice a day and turned down the bed with chocolates on each pillow. We could get really spoiled at the Queen Victoria." (R. Mylod)

"We particularly appreciated the restaurant information they provided including menus, food critic's reports, and guest's comments." (R. McGuinnes)

"We were very impressed with the booklet of information they provided for each guest. One other extra they provided that we really enjoyed was the free use of their bicycles for touring the city. Theirs was the 7th B&B we have reviewed but while we enjoyed all of them, the Queen Victoria had the most to offer and left us with the most pleasant memories of hospitality." (K. Sasdelli)

Cape May

White Dove Cottage
619 Hughes Street
Cape May, NJ 08204
(800) 321-DOVE

Type of B&B: Guesthouse.
Rooms: 6 with private bath.
Rates: 1 or 2/$75-125.

Rating: B+ or ♛♛ Good, exceeds basic requirements.

Historic Victorian home originally built as a summer cottage is located two blocks from the beach on a quiet side street in town. Choose from six guest rooms or suites which offer a private bath, European antiques, family heirlooms, period wallpapers, prints, and handmade quilts. Popular attractions in the area include beaches, fishing, tennis, hiking, theaters, concerts, and historic home tours. Full breakfast is served at the grand banquet table set with lace, fine china, and heirloom crystal. No smoking. 1 or 2/$75-125.

Chatham

Parrot Mill Inn
47 Main Street
Chatham, NJ 07928
(201) 635-7722

Type of B&B: Inn.
Rooms: 11 with private bath.
Rates: 1 or 2/$95.

Rating: B or ♛♛ Good, exceeds basic requirements.

Large Gambrel-roofed home built around 1780, is located three miles from Route 78. Choose from eleven guest rooms, each with private bath. Relax before the fireplace in the keeping room. Area attractions include New York City, museums, shopping, hiking, and bicycling. Continental breakfast. Families welcome. 1 or 2/$95. AE, MC, V.

Guests write: *"The Parrot Mill Inn was a home away from home for five weeks during our relocation from South Carolina. Our stay was a vacation for Betsy and her staff were so warm, friendly, and helpful. The room was delightful and her breakfasts most enjoyable. Thanks to them our move has been much easier than we would have thought possible." (L. Spieth)*

Flemington/Clinton

Leigh Way
66 Leigh Street
Clinton, NJ 08809
(908) 735-4311 or 735-6846

Type of B&B: Inn.
Rooms: 5, 2 with private bath.
Rates: 1/$55-65; 2/$65-75.

Rating: A or ♛♛♛ Excellent, far exceeds basic requirements.

Second Empire Victorian home with mansard roof was built in the mid-1800s and is located in the heart of the village, ten minutes north of Flemington. Five guest rooms have been recently redecorated with a mix of antique and contemporary furnishings; two offer a private bath. A living room or old-fashioned porch offers comfortable seating for conversing or reading. Popular attractions in the area include the downtown shopping area, Clinton Historic Museum, Arts Center, Spruce Run, and Round Valley Reservoirs for fishing, hiking, and swimming. Continental breakfast features fresh fruits and home-baked breads and muffins. Space for small functions available. No smoking. 1/$55-65; 2/$65-75. AE, MC, V. Travel agent.

Spring Lake

Sea Crest By the Sea
19 Tuttle Avenue
Spring Lake, NJ 07762
(908) 449-9031

Type of B&B: Inn.
Rooms: 12 with private bath.
Rates: 1 or 2 $80-140.

Rating: A+ or ♕♕♕ Excellent, far exceeds basic requirements.

Thirty-five room Victorian mansion is located 5 miles east of the Garden State Parkway at exit 98; one half block from the ocean. Choose from twelve individually decorated guest rooms, all with private bath. Two offer fireplaces. Play croquet in the yard or borrow a bicycle to explore the town with its charming Victorian homes, lovely beaches, restaurants, antique shops, and boutiques. Golf, tennis, sailing, Garden State Art Center, and Monmouth race tracks are also nearby. Extended continental breakfast features scones, fruit tarts, carrot cake, and homebaked bread. Restricted smoking. 1 or 2 $80-140. MC, V. Travel agent.

Albuquerque

Casa De Suenos Bed & Breakfast Inn
310 Rio Grande Boulevard S.W.
Albuquerque, NM 87104
(505) 247-4560 or (800) CHAT W/US

Type of B&B: Large inn complex.
Rooms: 12 with private bath.
Rates: 1/$66-125; 2/$66-250.

Rating: B+ or ♛♛ Good, exceeds basic requirements.

Casa De Suenos is a Southwestern garden compound built in 1930 with a main house and small "casitas" or cottages. Originally built as an artist's colony, the inn is located one block from Old Town shops and restaurants. Each of the twelve guest rooms offers a private bath and eclectic blend of Southwestern decor and furnishings with European antiques, American Indian rugs, thick down comforters, and original art. There are two large common rooms as well as several patios and secluded garden areas. From the inn it's a short walk to museums, galleries, restaurants, nature park, and historic sites. Popular attractions include wineries, the world's largest aerial tram, ancient ruins, and archaeological sites. Full breakfast includes a hot entree and home-baked goods. Function rooms are available. Restricted smoking. Wheelchair access. 1/$66-125; 2/$66-250. AE, MC, V. Travel agent.

Guests write: *"The casitas are so comfortable and complete, with sitting room and garden, that we consider Casa de Suenos our home in New Mexico. Each suite we visit becomes our favorite: La Miradora for the elegance with its Chinese silk rug and antique furniture or the Taos suite with its built-in adobe headboard and pueblo-like atmosphere. The birdsongs in the garden and the gas lamps at night make this a magical world of its own." (J. Cassidy)*

Continental Divide

Stauder's Navajo Lodge
Navajo Lodge - Coolidge
Continental Divide, NM 87312-9701
(505) 862-7553

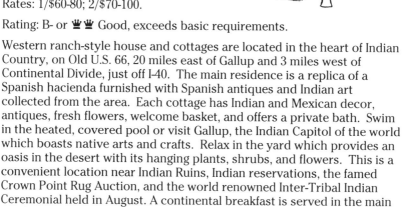

Type of B&B: Cottages.
Rooms: 2 cottages, each with private bath.
Rates: 1/$60-80; 2/$70-100.

Rating: B- or ♛♛ Good, exceeds basic requirements.

Western ranch-style house and cottages are located in the heart of Indian Country, on Old U.S. 66, 20 miles east of Gallup and 3 miles west of Continental Divide, just off I-40. The main residence is a replica of a Spanish hacienda furnished with Spanish antiques and Indian art collected from the area. Each cottage has Indian and Mexican decor, antiques, fresh flowers, welcome basket, and offers a private bath. Swim in the heated, covered pool or visit Gallup, the Indian Capitol of the world which boasts native arts and crafts. Relax in the yard which provides an oasis in the desert with its hanging plants, shrubs, and flowers. This is a convenient location near Indian Ruins, Indian reservations, the famed Crown Point Rug Auction, and the world renowned Inter-Tribal Indian Ceremonial held in August. A continental breakfast is served in the main residence in the Great Room with a breathtaking view of the Red Rocks. Picnic baskets can be prepared upon request. No smoking. 1/$60-80; 2/$70-100.

Guests write: *"We recently had a return visit to Stauder Lodge. It felt like coming home. They are warm, gracious hosts. We were appreciative of the many extra touches, the welcome basket of wine and cheese, the snacks of cookies that were left in the room. Bobbie is an excellent cook. Knowing of our interest in Indian jewelry they sent us to wonderful shops in the area."* *(A. Goldberg)*

Corrales

Corrales Inn Bed & Breakfast
58 Perea Road
Corrales, NM 87048
(505) 897-4422

Type of B&B: Small inn.

Rooms: 6 with private bath.

Rates: 1/$55-65; 2/$65-75.

Rating: A- or ♛♛♛ Excellent, far exceeds basic requirements.

Newly built Territorial adobe-style inn is located in a quaint village about
thirty minutes north of Albuquerque. There are six guest rooms. Each
offers a private bath, individual temperature controls, dressing area, and
decor themes such as Oriental, Hot Air Balloons, Victorian, and
Southwestern. A large common room features comfortable seating and a
library which houses 2,000 books. There is a small, secluded courtyard
with hot tub, fountain, and shade trees. There are a number of small
restaurants in the village as well as interesting shops with handmade
crafts and original art. The nearby Bosque Trail is a popular nine-mile
hiking trail along the Rio Grande. Full breakfast. Rooms for small
functions or seminars available. Families welcome. Wheelchair access.
Restricted smoking. 1/$55-65; 2/$65-75. MC, V.

Guests write: *"Nestled off the main street of Corrales away from the city
bustle, the warm hospitality and planning of the owners and the tastefully,
peaceful rooms created a stay of true Southwest pleasure. There is easy
access to areas of interest to visitors and a peak experience at breakfast!"*
(L. Dunne)

*"I enjoyed the hot tub on the cool moonlit night - it was so relaxing. It was
truly a gift to have the good fortune to stay at this B&B." (G. Yee)*

Hernandez

Casa del Rio
P.O. Box 66
Hernandez, NM 87532
(505) 753-2035 or 753-6049

Type of B&B: Small ranch.
Rooms: 2 with private bath.
Rates: 1 or 2/$70-90.

Rating: B+ or ♛♛ Good, exceeds basic requirements.

Casa del Rio is a small Southwestern ranch with adobe structures. Hernandez is not on most maps but it is located equi-distant from Sante Fe or Toas off of Highways 84/285. A small, newly-built adobe cottage on the property offers complete privacy with views of the cliffs above the Rio Chama from the secluded patio. The cottage features a king-size bed, kiva fireplace, locally made crafts, and a private, modern bath with handmade Mexican tile. A second room is available in the main house and also offers a private bath. The ranch breeds Arabian horses and raises sheep for wool. Popular attractions in the area include Indian Pueblos, Anazi ruins, a ghost ranch, white-water rafting, hiking, and biking. A full breakfast is served in the main house with varied entrees such as stuffed French toast served with pure maple syrup and fresh strawberries. Picnic and patio suppers available with advance notice. Restricted smoking. 1 or 2/$70-90. MC, V. Travel agent.

Los Ojos

Casa de Martinez
P.O. Box 96
Los Ojos, NM 87551
(505) 588-7858

Type of B&B: Inn.
Rooms: 7, 3 with private bath.
Rates: 2/$55-75.

Rating: B or ♛♛ Good, exceeds basic requirements.

Historic Spanish adobe inn built in 1861 has been in the same family for several generations and is located in a rural area 13 miles south of Chama on old US-84 in the small community of Los Brazos. Choose from seven guest rooms decorated with antique furniture and local crafts; three offer a private bath. One large first-floor guest suite offers a private bath and fireplace. The inn is hosted by the great-granddaughter of early settlers in the area and has views towards the famous Brazos waterfall named El Chorro. Popular attractions in the area include fishing, hunting, cross-country skiing, and train rides over the Rocky Mountains. Full breakfast is served. Families welcome. The newest addition to the inn is a small conference room and gift shop. Wheelchair access. No smoking. 2/$55-75. 10% senior discount. Travel agent. Open February through October.

Guests write: *"Clorinda's special breakfast meals are worth the drive to Casa de Martinez. She and her husband are both interesting to talk to as well as informative about the area."* (D. Crone)

"We enjoy the romantic atmosphere on our annual winter get-away." (J. Ghahate)

"This is a great and pleasant place with wonderful hospitality." (B. Cherin)

"I enjoyed my stay very much since it was such a warm and cozy atmosphere. I will be back." (S. Gonzales)

Sante Fe

Alexander's Inn
529 East Palace Avenue
Santa Fe, NM 87501
(505) 986-1431

Type of B&B: Small inn.
Rooms: 5, 3 with private bath.
Rates: 1/$65; 2/$115.

Rating: A- or ♛♛♛ Excellent, far exceeds basic requirements.

Renovated Victorian home built in 1903 is located on the east side of the city. Five guest rooms with four-poster beds are available. Three offer a private bath and one room on the main level has a fireplace. Canyon Road and the downtown Plaza with museums, galleries, opera, and symphony are not far from the inn. Within a short drive are pueblos, cliff dwellings, national parks, and skiing. Continental breakfast includes homemade bread, granola, fresh fruit, and muffins. Afternoon refreshments include sweets, cheeses, chips, and salsa. Space is available for garden weddings. 1/$65; 2/$115. MC, V. Travel agent.

Guests write: *"We stayed at Alexander's while visiting our son who lives in Santa Fe. I was cooking the Christmas turkey at my son's new sparsely furnished home and noticed that he lacked basic cooking materials like a turkey pan and rack. Mary Jo at Alexander's immediately offered a pan and a rack from her own cupboard. Christmas breakfast at Alexander's was a warm comaraderie topped off with cleverly handcrafted gifts for each guest made by the owner. The spirit of Christmas lives all year long at this unique Santa Fe B&B." (J. Harrison)*

"I have fond memories of leisurely breakfast on the sun-dappled terrace under tall trees and with flowers everywhere, fresh morning air and bird voices. Our hostess not only ran the place with great efficiency, but saw to the comfort of her guests with unobtrusive, loving care." (M. Stoll)

"The pleasure of waking up to the smell of home-baked muffins and fresh brewed Frangelica and cream coffee was enough to delight our sense and start our day off right." (E. Fuller)

"Other hotels and B&Bs were at least 20% more expensive and none that I saw were as inviting or comfortably and tastefully furnished as Alexander's Inn. Carolyn and Mary Jo are very meticulous about housekeeping there." (L. Downing)

Santa Fe

Inn on the Alameda
303 East Alameda
Santa Fe, NM 87501
(800) 289-2122

Type of B&B: Large urban inn.
Rooms: 42 with private bath.
Rates: 1/$125-135; 2/$250-260.

Rating: A+ or ♥♥♥ Excellent, far exceeds basic requirements.

Large adobe and Spanish-Colonial inn is located 5 miles north of I-25, exit 289 in downtown. The inn has forty-two guest rooms, each with private bath, fireplace, TV, and phone. Relax in the ground floor main lounge with fireplace, seating, and cocktail service. Area attractions include Southwest Center for the Arts, Native American and Spanish cultural sites, desert wilderness, tennis, fishing, hiking, and skiing. Continental breakfast is served in the "country kitchen" with a choice of pastries, cheeses, and seasonal fruits. Families welcome. Wheelchair access. 1/$125-135; 2/$250-260. AE, MC. V. 10% senior, auto club, business travel, and family discounts. Travel agent.

Santa Fe

Pueblo Bonito Bed & Breakfast Inn
138 West Manhattan
Santa Fe, NM 87501
(505) 984-8001

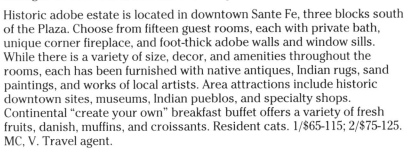

Type of B&B: Inn.
Rooms: 15 with private bath.
Rates: 1/$65-115; 2/$75-125.

Rating: B or ♛♛ Good, exceeds basic requirements.

Historic adobe estate is located in downtown Sante Fe, three blocks south of the Plaza. Choose from fifteen guest rooms, each with private bath, unique corner fireplace, and foot-thick adobe walls and window sills. While there is a variety of size, decor, and amenities throughout the rooms, each has been furnished with native antiques, Indian rugs, sand paintings, and works of local artists. Area attractions include historic downtown sites, museums, Indian pueblos, and specialty shops. Continental "create your own" breakfast buffet offers a variety of fresh fruits, danish, muffins, and croissants. Resident cats. 1/$65-115; 2/$75-125. MC, V. Travel agent.

Taos

Casa Europa Inn and Gallery
157 Upper Ranchitos Road
Taos, NM 87571
(505) 758-9798

Type of B&B: Small inn.
Rooms: 6 with private bath.
Rates: 1/$60; 2/$70-95.

Rating: A+ or ♛♛♛ Excellent, far exceeds basic requirements.

Historic Southwestern adobe has been completely restored with modern European finishing and has a rural setting outside the city. There are six guest rooms that vary in size, decor, and amenities but all have a selection of interesting antiques and a private bath. Several offer a fireplace or wood stove and full-size Jacuzzi. There are several common areas throughout the inn offering quiet places for reading, conversing with other guests, or viewing the traditional or contemporary crafts and paintings of native American artists. A ski area is nearby as are Indian pueblos and white-water rafting. Full breakfast and afternoon refreshments served daily. Families welcome. Restricted smoking. 1/$60; 2/$70-95. MC, V.

Barneveld

Sugarbush Bed & Breakfast
RR 1, Box 227, Old Poland Road
Barneveld, NY 13304
(315) 896-6860

Type of B&B: Inn.
Rooms: 5, 2 with private bath.
Rates: 1/$40; 2/$55-80.

Rating: B- or ♛♛ Good exceeds basic requirements.

Historic Colonial home is nestled among old maple trees and located twelve miles north of Utica off Route 12. There are five guest rooms on the first or second floor; two offer a private bath. The rooms differ greatly in size and amenities, but all have a pleasant decor, comfortable chairs, and fresh flowers. A large guest suite on the first floor offers a private bath, bedroom and sitting room. There are several common rooms including a living room with comfortable seating, fireplace, and views of the countryside. Area attractions include Adirondack Park with skiing and water sports. Full breakfast includes eggs, bacon, and waffles topped with New York state maple syrup. Afternoon refreshments are offered and additional meals are available upon request. Families welcome. Restricted smoking. 1/$40; 2/$55; Suite/$80. MC, V. Senior, family, business, and auto club discounts. Travel agent.

Bellport

The Great South Bay Inn
160 South Country Road
Bellport, NY 11713
(516) 286-8588

Type of B&B: Inn.
Rooms: 6, 2 with private bath.
Rates: 1/$50; 2/$70-120.

Rating: B or ♛♛ Good, exceeds basic requirements.

Restored, late 19th-century Cape Cod inn is located on Long Island's South Shore. It is in close proximity to the Hamptons and 8 miles southeast of exit 64 of the Long Island Expressway. Each of the six guest rooms are furnished in period antiques and feature the original wainscotting. Two offer a private bath. Stroll Bellport's historic shopping district and view the old historic homes or dine at a variety of fine restaurants. A town ferry is available to take you across to the village's private beach on Fire Island. Homemade scones, cereals, and breads are featured in the continental breakfast and lunch is available. The garden accommodates small weddings and gatherings. Families welcome. Restricted smoking. 1/$50 2/$70-120. Senior discount. Travel agent.

Canandaigua

J.P. Morgan House
2920 Smith Road
Canandaigua, NY 14424
(716) 394-9232

Type of B&B: Small inn.
Rooms: 7, 5 with private bath.
Rates: 1/$60; 2/$85-175.

Rating: A- or ♛♛♛ Excellent, far exceeds basic requirements.

Stone mansion built in 1810 sits at the top of a hill in a rural setting in the Finger Lakes area of northern New York. Seven guest rooms are available. Each has distinctive decor such as French Country, Victorian, or the Farmer's Daughter's room, and all offer air conditioning. There are several common rooms throughout the inn as well as a pleasant patio overlooking the countryside. The property has forty-six acres of fields and woods to explore as well as a tennis court. Popular attractions in the area include lake recreation, wagon rides, skiing, wineries, antique shops, and outdoor theaters as well as Sonnenberg Gardens, Bristol Mountain, Granger Homestead, and the Radio Museum. Full gourmet breakfast is served by candlelight and an afternoon tea is offered daily. Dinner is available by advance reservation. No smoking. 1/$60; 2/$85-175. MC, V. 10% business discount. Travel agent.

Clarence

Asa Ransom House
10529 Main Street
Clarence, NY 14031
(716) 759-2315

Type of B&B: Country inn
Rooms: 9 with private bath.
Rates: 1/$75-105; 2/$85-135.

Rating: A or ♛♛♛ Excellent, far exceeds basic requirements.

Historic Colonial country inn is located in a small village eighteen miles northeast of Buffalo off NY-5 or exit 48A off I-90. Four guest rooms with private bath in the original building are on the second floor and are individually decorated with period furnishings and accessories. Five newly built rooms in the attached annex offer private baths, fireplaces, and one wheelchair accessible room. Each room has an interesting collection of old radio shows on tapes. There's a small parlor and gift shop available near the restaurant which serves dinner Sunday through Thursday. This area is popular for its abundance of antique shops and is an easy drive from Buffalo or Niagara Falls. Full gourmet breakfast features egg souffle or crepes and fine country dinners are available in the restaurant. Air conditioned function rooms available for weddings or meetings. No smoking. 1/$75-105; 2/$85-135. MC, V. Travel agent.

Cooperstown

Angelholm
14 Elm Street, Box 705
Cooperstown, NY 13326
(607) 547-2483

Type of B&B: B&B home.
Rooms: 4 with shared or private bath.
Rates: 1/$50; 2/$65-90.

Rating: A or ♛♛♛ Excellent, far exceeds basic requirements.

Historic Colonial house built in 1815 is situated in town on a quiet side street and located 25 miles south of Route 90, 17 miles north of Route 88. There are four guest rooms with private or shared bath, collection of antique furniture, period wallpaper, fine linens, and interesting artwork. A side porch with comfortable furniture overlooks the garden and the living room offers a fireplace. Stroll along the streets of Cooperstown with it's many historic homes, parks, museums, and shops. Area attractions include Baseball Hall of Fame (only a four minute walk away), Farmer's Museum, Fenimore House Museum, and many outdoor activities. Full breakfast is served in the formal dining room. Resident dog. Families welcome. 1/$50; 2/$65-90. MC, V.

Cooperstown

The Inn at Cooperstown
16 Chestnut Street - A
Cooperstown, NY 13326
(607) 547-5756

Type of B&B: Historic hotel.
Rooms: 17 with private bath.
Rates: 1/$68-78; 2/$78-88.

Rating: B or ♛♛ Good, exceeds basic requirements.

Built in 1874 as the annex to the Hotel Fenimore, this Second Empire inn is situated in Cooperstown's Historic District. The Inn was designed by Henry Hardenberg, noted architect of the Dakota Apartments and the Plaza Hotel in New York City. Seventeen guest rooms are available on the second or third floor of the inn. Each has a private bath and comfortable reading chair. Relax in a rocking chair on the veranda or in front of the fireplace in the parlor. Walk to the many nearby shops and restaurants. Area attractions include Baseball Hall of Fame and Museum, Fenimore House Museum, The Farmers' Museum, Glimmerglass Opera House, golf, tennis, and fishing. Continental breakfast. Wheelchair access. 1/$68-78; 2/$78-88. AE, MC, V. Travel agent.

Corning

Rosewood Inn
134 East First Street
Corning, NY 14830
(607) 962-3253

Type of B&B: Inn.
Rooms: 6 with private bath.
Rates: 1/$73-89; 2/$83-99.

Rating: B+ or ♛♛ Good, exceeds basic requirements.

English Tudor-style home built in 1855 and restored in 1980 to reflect a Victorian splendor, is one block south of Route 17 as it goes through the city. Each of the six rooms are named for famous individuals and offer pleasant decor combining fine antiques, wallpapers, and draperies. All rooms have a private bath. A sitting room furnished with antique Cooper rockers invites conversation and television viewing. Local attractions include the Corning Glass Center and Rockwell Museum as well as the restored Market Street. Full breakfast is served in a candlelit Victorian dining room. Families welcome. Restricted smoking. 1/$73-89; 2/$83-99. MC, V.

Croton on Hudson

Alexander Hamilton House
49 Van Wyck Street
Croton on Hudson, NY 10520
(914) 271-6737

Type of B&B: Inn.
Rooms: 9, 3 with private bath.
Rates: 1/$50-60; 2/$60-250.

Rating: A or ♛♛♛ Excellent, far exceeds basic requirements.

Historic Victorian home built in 1889 is located four blocks east of Route 9 and offers sweeping views of the valley and river below. Choose from nine individually decorated and air conditioned guest rooms, three with private bath. The Aaron Burr suite features a private bath, queen-size bed, and fireplaced sitting room with sofabed. A separate apartment offers private entrance, bath, and full kitchen. The newly opened Penthouse Bridal Chamber features king bed, skylights, private bath with Jacuzzi, and fireplace. Guests are invited to use the inground swimming pool and outdoor patio with gas grill. Area attractions include Van Cortlandt Manor, Teatown Reservation, West Point, and easy train access to New York City sights. Full breakfast. Families welcome. No smoking. 1/$50-60; 2/$60-85; Suite/$125. Bridal Chamber/$250. AE, MC, V. Travel agent.

DeBruce

DeBruce Country Inn on the Willowemoc
DeBruce Road, Route 286A
DeBruce, NY 12758
(914) 439-3900

Type of B&B: Country inn with restaurant.
Rooms: 15 with private bath.
Rate: 1/$85-100; 2/$140-170.

Rating: B or ♛♛ Good, exceeds basic requirements.

Historic country inn on the banks of the Willowemoc is situated in the Catskill Forest Preserve near exit 96 off Route 17, two hours from New York City. There are fifteen guest rooms on the second and third floor of the inn. Each has a private bath, original yellow pine woodwork and molding, brass bed, and hand-made bedspread. There is a large selection of contemporary art exhibited throughout the inn and an exercise room, sauna, and swimming pool are offered in addition to a full bar and wine cellar. Several wooded trails are on the property as well as a stocked trout pond. Area attractions include Catskill Forest Preserve, state parks, covered bridges, museums, antique shops, and outdoor recreation. Fresh home-made specialties are included in the full breakfast and dinner menus and both are included in the rates. Space for large functions is available. Families welcome. 1/$85-100; 2/$140-170.

Guests write: *"The hosts are artists in the fine art of hospitality. The food is equally impressive. Imagine this - the sensitivity and nuances of the finest New York City restaurant in the middle of the Catskill Mountains!" (A. Carr)*

"We celebrated our 40th birthdays along with four other couples at DeBruce Country Inn. The owners were very accommodating to our wishes and made us feel welcome and at home. The food was excellent and it was the perfect setting for our get-together." (R. Flachs)

"On an inspection of the property for prospective clients, I was most impressed. The rooms are cheery and bright and tastefully decorated." (M. Cole)

"We have fond memories of a great inn, friendly innkeepers, and without a doubt the best meals ever. Our fondest remembrance is from our first visit and the lovely trout that our daughter caught on the inn's property. Ron served it for breakfast the next morning." (J. Burson)

"Marilyn and Ron value the friendship and company of their guest and you feel this from your very first visit. Ron is a superb cook and the menu is always a unique treat." (J. Spinella)

Dolgeville

Adrianna's Bed & Breakfast
44 Stewart Street
Dolgeville, NY 13329
(315) 429-3249

Type of B&B: B&B home.
Rooms: 3 share 2 baths.
Rates: 1/$45; 2/$55-58.

Rating: B+ or ♛♛ Good, exceeds basic requirements.

Modern raised ranch home is located 6 miles north of exit 29-A off I-90 on the New York Thruway. There are three air conditioned guest rooms that share two baths and have been decorated with comfort in mind. Relax in the swimming pool or visit the local golf course. A living room on the main floor offers a fireplace, TV, and comfortable seating. Nearby attractions include Saratoga Raceway and Performing Arts Center, Herkimer Diamond Mines, Herkimer Home, Daniel Green Slipper Outlet, Erie Canal in Little Falls, and the Lyndon Lyon Greenhouses which specialize in violets. Full traditional breakfast served. Families welcome. Restricted smoking. Resident cat. 1/$45; 2/$55-58.

Guests write: *"The accommodations are very comfortable and spacious. Adrianna serves a terrific breakfast and is an informed and hospitable hostess."* (G. Romanic)

"Our trip to Dolgeville was for my Dad's funeral. The funeral director suggested Adrianna's. She didn't know us from Adam but she made us feel like her home was ours and we almost felt like family when we left. The decor was very tastefully done throughout. The food was wonderful and the setting and service just beautiful. In each of the bedrooms was a tastefully selected library that made me want to stay for a month to read, read, read." (B. Luft)

"At no place we have been - motels, hotels, B&Bs - have we received hospitality, cordiality and accommodations akin to Adrianna's B&B. Hers is tops on our list." (F. Belford)

"Our brief stay was more than a wonderful night's rest followed by a delectable breakfast, it was an experience in friendship. Never before have we met a stranger who immediately by her friendliness and warmth, was transformed into a charming friend." (G. McCloskey)

"This is our favorite stop-over when we drive East. It's like a friend's house and we always look forward to an elegant breakfast before we drive on." (M. Pendergast)

"This was my best night's sleep in weeks. Adrianna is a wonderfully talented hostess." (B. Campbell)

Gilbertsville

Leatherstocking Trails
Box 40, Route 51
Gilbertsville, NY 13776
(607) 783-2757

Type of B&B: Small inn.
Rooms: 6, 2 with private bath.
Rates: 1/$38-54; 2/$58-65.

Rating: B or ♛♛ Good, exceeds basic requirements.

English Colonial home situated on six acres of wooded land and gardens is located thirty minutes north of Oneonta. There are six guest rooms on the second floor. Two offer a private bath and the master suite also features a fireplace. Popular attractions in the area are the Baseball Hall of Fame in nearby Cooperstown, Gilbert Lake State Park, Hartwick, theaters, antiques stores, and Glimmerglass Opera. Continental breakfast includes home-baked breads. A formal dining room and porch area can accommodate small functions. Families welcome. No smoking. 1/$38-54; 2/$58-65.

Hammondsport

The Blushing Rosé Bed & Breakfast Inn
11 William Street
Hammondsport, NY 14840
(607) 569-3402 or 569-3483

Type of B&B: Small inn.
Rooms: 4 with private bath.
Rates: 1/$65-75; 2/$75-85.

Rating: A- or ♛♛♛ Excellent, far exceeds basic requirements.

Small Victorian-Italianate home built in 1835 is located at the southern tip of Keuka Lake in the Finger Lakes region, about twenty-five miles west of Corning. There are four guest rooms on the second floor. Each offers a private bath, air conditioning, and individual decor with special touches such as handmade quilts, stenciled walls, lace canopy beds, and white wicker furnishings. There is a beverage and snack center near the guest rooms with small refrigerator. Popular attractions in the area include Curtiss Museum, Corning Glass Museum, Watkins Glen auto racing as well as lake activities. Full breakfast specialties include baked French toast, lemon poppy seed waffles, and strawberry bread. No smoking. 1/$65-75; 2/$75-85. Senior, business, and auto club discounts. Travel agent.

Lake Placid

Highland House Inn
3 Highland Place
Lake Placid, NY 12946
(518) 523-2377

Type of B&B: Inn.
Rooms: 7 with private bath.
Rates: 1/$45-60; 2/$50-95; Cottage/$75-95.

Rating: B or ♛♛ Good, exceeds basic requirements.

Historic Colonial inn with cottage is located on a side street overlooking Main Street and the village below. There are seven guest rooms in the main inn. Each has a private bath and unique Adirondack-style decor. The common room on the first floor is a happy gathering place for guests at breakfast time and in the evenings. A separate cottage provides complete privacy for a couple or family and includes a fireplace, full kitchen, TV, VCR, stereo, and deck with a view. Take a five minute walk to Main Street and the Olympic Center or enjoy other area attractions such as Whiteface Mountain, skiing, golf, tennis, fishing, and hiking. Full breakfast includes the house specialty of blueberry pancakes. Families welcome. 1/$45-60; 2/$50-65; Cottage/$75-95. MC, V.

Lake Placid

Interlaken Inn
15 Interlaken Avenue
Lake Placid, NY 12946
(518) 523-3180

Type of B&B: Country inn
Rooms: 12 with private bath.
Rates: 1/$80; 2/$100-150.

Rating: B+ or ♛♛ Good, exceeds basic requirements.

Victorian inn with restaurant is near the village off I-87 and Route 73. Choose from twelve guest rooms with private bath. There is a wide variety in the size, decor and amenities of each room but special features in some rooms include tin ceilings, claw-foot tubs, antiques, and flowers. Enjoy afternoon tea in the parlor and take advantage of the small but well-stocked bar on the premises. Area attractions include Olympic Village and surrounding ski areas. Full breakfast and dinner featuring country fare are served in a Victorian dining room and included in the overnight rates. Resident dogs. 1/$80; 2/$100-150. AE, MC, V. Travel agent.

Lisle

Dorchester Farm
RD 1, Box 6, Keibel Road
Lisle, NY 13797
(607) 692-4511

Type of B&B: B&B home.
Rooms: 4, 2 with private bath.
Rates: 1 or 2/$50-75.

Rating: A- or ♛♛♛ Excellent, far exceeds basic requirements.

Pre-Civil War Colonial home is located 20 miles north of Binghamton near exit 8 off Route 81. Four guest rooms are available, two with private bath. Enjoy the area's antique shops, swimming, sailing, windsurfing, or just relax on the Victorian porch overlooking the five-mile-long lake. Visit nearby Binghamton, Ithaca, and Cortland. Breakfast includes fresh fruit, omelets, Belgian waffles, sweet rolls, and blueberry muffins and is served in the antique-filled dining room with lake view. Restricted smoking. 1 or 2/$50-75. MC, V.

Guests write: *"I have to say that this was one of the most unique and beautiful B&Bs I have been to. I could spend all day looking at her great antique collections of kitchenware, Teddy Bears, and furniture. The suite with its magnificent view of the lake was breathtaking and I felt very at* home with my favorite Crabtree and Evelyn amenities which were so specially arranged in the bathroom." (M. Vorhies)

"This was our first B&B experience. Any in the future will have a hard time measuring up to the charm and hospitality here." (L. Harwood)

"Everything was super. The house is beautiful, food delicious, gracious hosts. I was completely fascinated by the home." (E. Stiering)

"This is a 150 year old farmhouse that has been restored and is absolutely wonderful in every respect. But more important than the decor (which is extraordinary), the full delicious homemade breakfast and the lovely touches, is the warmth and entertaining side of the hosts." (J. Watson)

"We arrived at Dorchester at night greeted by a blazing fire. The next morning, we woke with a view of mist rising over the lake below our window. The feather-bed mattress and Laura Ashley quality linens almost made it impossible to get out of bed. Before exploring the gigantic turn-of-the-century barn and swinging in the chair above the lake, we feasted on a glorious breakfast of homemade muffins and breads, eggs, sausage, and a hot apple crisp to die for (I still dream about this apple crisp)." (H. Else)

New York City

The 412 House
412 East 84th Street
New York, NY 10028
(212) 744-6157 or (914) 294-6567

Type of B&B: Brownstone home.
Rooms: 2 with private bath.
Rates: 1/$110; 2/$125.

Rating: B+ or ♛♛ Good, exceeds basic requirements.

Victorian townhouse built in 1880 is in the Upper East side located between 1st and York Avenues near the Mayor's Mansion and Gracie Square Park. Guest accommodations are in a second-floor, private wing of the house that has a private entrance, two bedrooms with private bath, fully equipped kitchenette, air conditioning, cable TV/VCR and private telephone with answering machine. While hosts are available on-site, the guest quarters are designed to be private and self-sufficient. This location is convenient to the Metropolitan Museum of Art, Guggenheim, Museum of the City of New York, Cooper-Hewitt, numerous sidewalk cafes, bistros, public transportation, and parking garages. Self-service continental breakfast is provided in the guest kitchenette. Families welcome. No smoking or pets. 1/$110; 2/$125 with three day minimum reservations. Travel agent.

Guests write: *"Staying in this chic East side brownstone was an original New York experience, not to mention the cost savings from noisy mid-town hotels! We felt like native New Yorkers with our own separate entrance, kitchenette, and private telephone number. I particularly enjoyed the proximity to safe and nice places to walk as I try to walk four miles a day."* (P. Light)

Port Jervis

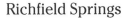

Educators Bed and Breakfast
23 Hudson Street
Port Jervis, NY 12771
(914) 856-5543

Type of B&B: B&B home.
Rooms: 2 with shared bath.
Rates: 1/$35; 2/$45.

Rating: C or ♛ Acceptable, meets basic requirements.

Small Victorian home is located in a residential area of town one block east of Route 97. There are two guest rooms available. Each has a double bed and they share one bath. The home has retained much of its original woodwork, doors and locksets and the hosts have an interesting collection of family heirlooms, Victorian antiques, and unusual items collected from all over the world. Popular attractions in the area include white-water rafting, canoeing, swimming, antiquing, golf, tennis, and fishing. Full breakfast. Families welcome. 1/$35; 2/$45. 10% business travel discount.

Richfield Springs

Country Spread Bed & Breakfast
23 Prospect Street
Richfield Springs, NY 13439
(315) 858-1870

Type of B&B: B&B home.
Rooms: One guest suite sleeps 5 with private bath.
Rates: 1/$40-45; 2/$50-65.

Rating: A or ♛♛♛ Excellent, far exceeds basic requirements.

Built in 1893, this Victorian home is located directly on Route 28, 14 miles south of I-90 near Cooperstown. A suite of two rooms with private bath are offered and feature a country decor. Enjoy the quiet, small-town atmosphere here or take an easy trip to neighboring Cooperstown to see the National Baseball Hall of Fame, historical museums, summer theater, and opera. Nearby lakes offer boating, fishing, and swimming. A hearty breakfast includes homemade spreads and local maple syrup to top off fresh pancakes and muffins, and guests are provided with a "care package" of goodies to eat, including a jar of "country spread" jam. Families welcome. No smoking. 1/$40-45; 2/$50-65. MC, V. Family discount.

Guests write: *"This spotless country home was fully supplied with everything we could possibly need or want. Our breakfasts were not only delicious and filling, but also beautifully presented with linens and lace. Finally, as we were preparing to return to Nebraska on Amtrak, they sent us off with a goody bag of cookies and sandwiches - a wonderful ending to a wonderful stay!" (R. Smith)*

"We found the Watson's home to be immaculately clean and furnished in quaint country charm. They offer help regarding directions, restaurants, local things to do, and especially the Baseball Hall of Fame. At the end of our day, they greeted us in their TV room and invited the four of us for strawberry shortcake and a few innings of the All-Star Baseball game. They are terrific people including their handsome, well-behaved young sons." (J. Downey)

"Country Spread is utterly charming, warm, and immaculate. We were so impressed with the decor and the special little kindnesses of the Watsons." (G. Hutchens)

"We wanted to visit the Baseball Hall of Fame in Cooperstown and were happy to find out that Bruce works there and was able to make suggestions as what not to miss. We've been to many B&Bs and I have to say this is one of the most beautifully decorated. Curtains, bedspreads, rugs, towels, everything is color coordinated. There is a little refrigerator in the bathroom where soft drinks, fruit, cheese and crackers were left for an afternoon snack. We've already made reservations to return." (E. Skiff)

"The decor reflects creativity and love, and the thoughtful extras - fresh robes for post-shower comfort, a basket of freshly-picked apples outside the bedroom door, and white glove cleanliness - are punctuated by miniature decorations which tickle an art lover's heart." (G. Schneider)

Rochester

Dartmouth House B&B
215 Dartmouth Street
Rochester, NY 14607
(716) 271-7872 or 473-0778

Type of B&B: B&B home.
Rooms: 4, 2 with private bath.
Rates: 1/$45-70; 2/$55-80.

Rating: B+ or ♛♛ Good, exceeds basic requirements.

Spacious English Tudor built in 1905 is located in a quiet, city
neighborhood near I-490. Choose from four guest rooms, two with
private bath, and two offering semi-private bath. The decor is enhanced
by the massive fireplace, family antiques, window seats, Oriental rugs,
leaded glass windows, and beamed ceilings. Downtown Rochester is only
one mile away. Walk to museums, antique shops, and restaurants or take
an easy, three block walk to the George Eastman International Museum of
Photography. Full gourmet breakfast by candlelight. No smoking. No pets.
1/$45-70; 2/$55-80. Travel agent.

Guests write: *"I feel like I'm coming home at Dartmouth House. Having to
make a business trip to Rochester is now like having a home to go back to
at the end of a long day. It beats cold, impersonal hotel rooms anytime. The
bedrooms are spacious and comfortable. Each one has its own personality. I
especially appreciate the large rooms so that I can spread out and work
when I need to. Everything you could possibly need has been thought of from
the hair dryers in each bathroom to the little baskets with shampoo, sewing
kits, etc. Each room has a few snacks in a jar and cans of soda for each
guest. I haven't had anyone make such a fuss of me since I left my parent's
home over 30 years ago." (C. Woodford)*

Saratoga Springs

Westchester House
102 Lincoln Avenue
Saratoga Springs, NY 12866
(518) 587-7613

Type of B&B: Inn.
Rooms: 7, with private bath.
Rates: 1 or 2/$70-200.

Rating: A- or ♛♛♛ Excellent, far exceeds basic requirements.

Queen Anne Victorian home built in 1885 is in a residential area located 4 miles north of exit 13N, off Route I-87. There are seven guest rooms available, each with private bath. The inn features hand-crafted chestnut moldings and a whimsical roofline complete with cupola and balcony as well as old-fashioned gardens. Overall, they've done a fine job in combining Old World ambiance with up-to-date comforts. Popular attractions in the area include Saratoga Race Track, Performing Arts Center, dance museum, golf, tennis, fishing, hiking, and skiing. Continental breakfast. Facilities for meetings and social functions. No smoking. 1 or 2/$70-200. AE, MC, V. 10% senior and business travel discounts. Travel agent.

Guests write: *"The house and its furnishings brought us back to an era of elegance and craftsmanship. The hospitality and personal attention helped to turn an ordinary business trip into an experience that we will forever treasure." (S. Bearse)*

"We both enjoyed all of the little extras and amenities such as the sherry in the front parlor, the fresh flowers in almost every room, and the time in making calls for our dinner reservations." (P. Smyth)

"The restoration and interior environment of the house is one of the most aesthetically well-done places of its kind that we have encountered thus far with our B&B experience." (J. Thomas)

Utica

The Iris Stonehouse
16 Derbyshire Place
Utica, NY 13501
(315) 732-6720 or (800) 446-1456

Type of B&B: B&B home.
Rooms: 3, 1 with private bath.
Rates: 1/$35-50; 2/$45-60.

Rating: A or ♛ ♛ ♛ Excellent, far exceeds basic requirements.

Set in the city, close to area attractions, this 1932 stone Tudor home is on the local Register of Historic Homes and is 3 miles south of I-90 at exit 31. Leaded glass windows add charm to the eclectic decor of the three guest rooms with private or shared baths and central air. A guest-sitting room offers a comfortable area for relaxing, playing games, or watching TV. Area attractions include Munson-Williams-Proctor Art Institute, Children's Museum, Oneida County Historic Society, Utica Zoo, and F.X. Matt Brewery tour. In nearby Cooperstown and Rome, visitors can see the Baseball Hall of Fame, Farmer's Museum, Erie Canal Village and Fort Richey Game Farm. A full breakfast is served. No smoking. No pets. 1/$35-50; 2/$45-60. MC, V. 10% auto club, family, and senior discounts. Travel agent.

Waterville

Bed & Breakfast of Waterville
211 White Street
Waterville, NY 13480
(315) 841-8295

Type of B&B: B&B home.
Rooms: 3, 1 with private bath.
Rates: 1/$35-45; 2/$40-50.

Rating: B or ♛ ♛ Good, exceeds basic requirements.

Historic Victorian home built in 1871 is located in the village of Waterville which is about thirty minutes south of Utica off Route 8. There are three guest rooms available. One large room on the ground floor offers a private bath. Two additional rooms on the second floor share a bath. Area attractions include antique shops, historic sites, Hamilton College, Colgate University, and Cooperstown Baseball Hall of Fame. Full breakfast specialties include German pancakes, Belgian waffles, and omelettes. Families welcome. No smoking. 1/$35-45; 2/$40-50; 3/$55-65. MC, V. Travel agent.

Guests write: *"They shared their hospitality with us and the conversations were a real pleasure."* (G. Yoder)

"This house is absolutely lovely. They gave us a warm welcome and hospitality despite the lateness of the hour when we arrived. We loved the all-cotton sheets too." (L. Pascale)

Westhampton Beach

Seafield House
2 Seafield Lane, P.O. Box 648
Westhampton Beach, NY 11978
(516) 288-1559

Type of B&B: Inn.
Rooms: 2 suites with private bath.
Rates: 2/$100-195.

Rating: B+ or ♛♛ Good, exceeds basic requirements.

Historic Victorian home built in 1880 is situated in town near shops and restaurants and located 3 miles south of Route 27, exit 63, or ninety minutes from Manhattan. There are two spacious guest suites with private bath, and sitting room, antiques and family treasures. Enjoy the warmth from the 1907 Modern Glenwood pot belly stove or the fireplace in the parlor. An enclosed porch overlooks the tennis courts and swimming pool on the property. The beach as well as the shops on Main Street are just a short walk away as are local attractions such as historic homes, antique shops, golf, fishing, swimming, hiking, and bicycling. Full breakfast features home made goodies. No smoking. 2/$100-195.

Asheville

Richmond Hill Inn
87 Richmond Hill Drive
Asheville, NC 28806
(704) 252-7313 or (800) 545-9238

Type of B&B: Country inn.
Rooms: 21 with private bath.
Rates: 2/$95-200.

Rating: A+ or ♛♛♛ Excellent, far exceeds basic requirements.

Victorian country inn with restaurant was built in 1889 and sits majestically atop a hill overlooking the city which is three miles away. There are 12 guest rooms in the mansion and 9 rooms in charming cottages situated around a croquet courtyard. Each of the 21 guest rooms feature private baths and many have fireplaces. Special appointments include Victorian furniture, Oriental rugs, and draped canopy beds. Savor American and nouvelle cuisine in the gourmet restaurant. Play croquet or visit the nearby Biltmore Estate, Blue Ridge Parkway, and downtown Asheville. Full breakfast may feature omelettes or egg dishes, as well as fresh baked muffins and breads. Facilities are available for weddings, social events, and small business conferences. Restricted smoking. 2/$95-200. AE, MC, V. Travel agent.

Guests write: *"We spent two weeks in the mountains of Virginia, North Carolina, and Tennessee. We did not stay exclusively in B&B inns but Richmond Hill Inn was by far the nicest of the B&Bs we visited and superior to any motel or the condo we visited. They truly deserve 1st class status."* (F. Forehand)

"Richmond Hill Inn is a treasure and certainly worthy of comment. Clean and neat goes without saying, but how many forget the setting which is so essential to doing business. The art of their magirics was supreme and the staff congratulated. Only love can describe the way in which the finest cuisine here is served." (L. Brain)

"Everything is so well done. Our dinner was excellent and the gown I left behind was in the mail to me before I even called to enquire about it." (M. Rogers)

"The food was outstanding. This renovation of a Victorian mansion was remarkably well planned. The insulation in the walls provided great quiet." (R. Lee)

"This was our first stay in the new cottages. They are terrific! These folks do an absolutely first-rate job. Thanks to all the crew who keep the rooms and grounds so clean." (R. Spuller)

Asheville

The Wright Inn
235 Pearson Drive
Asheville, NC 28801
(704) 251-0789 or
(800) 552-5724 ext. 235

Type of B&B: Large inn.
Rooms: 9 with private bath.
Rates: 2/$75-110; Carriage house/$175.

Rating: A or ♕♕♕ Excellent, far exceeds basic requirements.

Historic Queen Anne home is situated in a neighborhood of stately Victorian homes in Asheville located seven blocks off I-240. There are nine guest rooms. Each has a private bath, turn-of-the-century decor, cable TV, and telephone; two have fireplaces. The Carriage House is a separate building on the grounds which is especially suited for families or small groups traveling together. It offers three bedrooms, full kitchen, bath, living room, and dining room. Popular attractions in this area include Blue Ridge Parkway, Biltmore House and Gardens, Smoky Mountain National Park, Thomas Wolfe Home, and Cherokee Indian reservation. Full breakfast is served in a formal dining room and is not included in carriage house rates. No smoking. 1 or 2/$75-110; Carriage house/$175. MC, V. Travel agent.

Banner Elk

Archers Inn
Route 2, Box 56A
Banner Elk, NC 28604
(704) 898-9004

Type of B&B: Inn.
Rooms: 14 with private bath.
Rates: 1 or 2/$45-125.

Rating: B+ or ♕♕ Good, exceeds basic requirements.

Recently built inn of post-and-beam construction is located on Highway 184 high up on Beech Mountain. Choose from fourteen guest rooms in the main lodge or annex. There is a wide variety in the size, decor, and amenities of each room but all have a private bath, stone fireplace, and deck or porch. Some rooms have a small refrigerator, cable TV, and microwave, and one room has an outdoor hot tub. A common room in the main lodge has a massive stone fireplace, comfortable couches, and views of the mountains. Popular attractions in the area include

Grandfather Mountain, ski resorts, golf, tennis, hiking, and horseback riding. Full breakfast. Families welcome. 1 or 2/$45-125. MC, V. Travel agent.

Beaufort

Captains' Quarters of Beaufort, Inc.
315 Ann Street
Beaufort, NC 28516
(919) 728-7711

Type of B&B: B&B home.
Rooms: 3 with private bath.
Rates: 1/$50-80; 2/$60-100.

Rating: A or ♛♛♛ Excellent, far exceeds basic requirements.

Historic turn-of-the-century Victorian home has been completely restored and is situated one block from the waterfront in the heart of the Historic District. There are three guest rooms on the second floor. Each has a private bath, family heirlooms, and antique furnishings. Take part in the inn's tradition to "toast the sunset" on the veranda or by the parlor fireplace and celebrate the day with wines and fresh fruit juices. Explore the nearby Outer Banks or walk to Maritime Museum, Old Burying Grounds, shops, and restaurants. Airport transportation is available. Continental plus breakfast includes fresh fruits and homemade breads featuring Ms. Ruby's "Riz" biscuits. Restricted smoking. 1/$50-80; 2/$60-100. MC, V. Travel agent.

Belhaven

River Forest Manor Inn and Marina
600 East Main Street
Belhaven, NC 27810
(919) 943-2151

Type of B&B: Country inn with restaurant.
Rooms: 9 with private bath.
Rates: 1 or 2/$48-75.

Rating: B- or ♛♛ Good, exceeds basic requirements.

Historic riverfront mansion built in 1900 is located on the Pungo River just east of Route 264. There are nine guest rooms throughout the inn and each has a private bath and selection of Victorian antique furnishings. The mansion has retained all of its original architectural treasures including leaded glass doors, Ionic columns, elaborately carved oak fireplaces, ornate plaster ceilings, leaded and stained-glass, and crystal chandeliers. Tennis courts, swimming pool, hot tub, and boat marina are on the premises as well as a restaurant. Guests who arrive by boat can borrow golf carts equipped to run on regular city streets. Continental breakfast. Dinner and smorgasbord available in the restaurant. Facilities available for meetings and social functions. 1 or 2/$48-75. MC, V.

Brevard

The Inn at Brevard
410 East Main Street
Brevard, NC 28712
(704) 884-2105

Type of B&B: Country inn
Rooms: 15, 13 with private bath.
Rates: 1/$55-65; 2/$59-99.

Rating: B- or ♕♕ Good, exceeds basic requirements.

Elegant Victorian home built in 1885 is located near the Pisgah National Forest about one hour south of Asheville off Route 280. There are fifteen guest rooms located in the main house or adjacent lodge; two have a shared bath. Popular attractions in this area include touring the nearby Blue Ridge Parkway, Brevard Music Center, Biltmore House in Asheville, and outdoor recreation such as fishing, hiking, golfing, and horseback riding. Full breakfast served year-round. Dinner available in-season. Facilities for meetings and functions provided. Families welcome. Restricted smoking. 1/$55-65; 2/$59-75; Suite/$99. MC, V.

Clyde

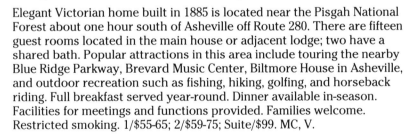

Windsong: A Mountain Inn
120 Ferguson Ridge
Clyde, NC 28721
(704) 627-6111

Type of B&B: Inn.
Rooms: 4 with private bath.
Rates: 1/$81-85; 2/$90-95.

Rating: AA or ♕♕♕♕ Outstanding.

Contemporary log inn situated in a rural mountain setting is 4.5 miles off I-40 exit 24, and 36 miles west of Asheville. Choose from four spacious guest rooms, each with quality furnishings, private bath, Jacuzzi, high beamed ceiling, light pine log walls, Mexican tile floors, and a delightful decor scheme. There is an extensive videocassette library, piano, billiard table, swimming pool, and tennis court for guest's enjoyment. Hosts raise llamas on the property. Among area attractions are Great Smoky Mountain National Park, Appalachian Trail, Cherokee Indian Reservation, Biltmore House, Blue Ridge Parkway, hiking, skiing, and white-water rafting. Full breakfast. Facilities available for small group meetings. No smoking. 1/$81-85; 2/$90-95. MC, V. Travel agent.

Durham

Arrowhead Inn
106 Mason Road
Durham, NC 27712
(919) 477-8430

Type of B&B: Inn.
Rooms: 8, 6 with private bath.
Rates: 1/$60-135; 2/$65-135.

Rating: A or ♛♛♛ Excellent, far exceeds basic requirements.

Stately manor home built in 1775 sits on a hill with commanding views and is located on Route 501, 7 miles north of I-85 at Durham. There are seven air-conditioned guest rooms or cottages plus accommodations in a restored cabin. All rooms are decorated with period furnishings and six offer a private bath. Stroll the acreage with mature trees and gardens which is often the site of weddings. The inn has several common rooms with fireplaces where guests enjoy gathering in the morning and evening hours. Popular attractions in the area include nearby historic Hillsborough, museums, Duke and North Carolina universities, or the world-famous Research Triangle Park. Full country breakfast includes fruit, meat, eggs, and home baked breads. Families welcome. Restricted smoking. 1/$60-135; 2/$65-135. AE, MC, V. Travel agent.

Edenton

The Lords Proprietors' Inn
300 North Broad Street
Edenton, NC 27932
(919) 482-3641

Type of B&B: Inn.
Rooms: 20 with private bath.
Rates: 1/$53; 2/$90.

Rating: A or ♛♛♛ Excellent, far exceeds basic requirements.

The Lord's Proprietors' Inn is comprised of four restored buildings including one historic tobacco barn and they are situated on an acre of grounds in town. Twenty spacious guest rooms are available throughout the buildings. Each offers a private bath, cable TV, VCR, and telephone. Common areas include three spacious parlors with period furnishings and a front porch with rocking chairs. Popular attractions in the area include Hope Plantation, Somerset Place, and Merchants Millpond State Park. Full breakfast. Dinner served November through March as a part of special Winter Weekend programs. Families welcome. Facilities available for meetings. Wheelchair access. Restricted smoking. 1/$53; 2/$90. Travel agent.

Flat Rock

The Woodfield Inn
Box 98
Flat Rock, NC 28731
(704) 693-6016 or (800) 533-6016

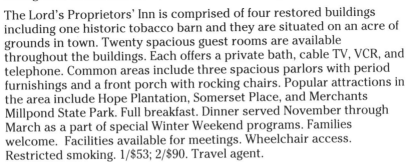

Type of B&B: Inn.
Rooms: 20, 12 with private bath.
Rates: 1 or 2/$45-100.

Rating: B or ♛♛ Good, exceeds basic requirements.

Historic antebellum inn situated on twenty-five acres was built in 1850 and has been in continuous operation for 140 years. There are twenty guest rooms available. Each is decorated in the Victorian period with antique furnishings and hand-crafted coverlets. Most rooms offer a private bath and several have fireplaces. There are several common rooms on the property including a wine room, restaurant dining rooms, a parlor filled with antiques and collectibles and a secret room where Confederate soldiers hid valuables during the Civil War. Area attractions include Flat Rock Playhouse, Carl Sandburg estate, Kenmure golf course, and Flat Rock historic sites. Continental breakfast. Function facilities include the gazebo and pavilion. Families welcome. 1 or 2/$45-100. MC, V. Senior, family, business, and auto club discounts. Travel agent.

Hendersonville

Claddagh Inn at Hendersonville
755 North Main Street
Hendersonville, NC 28792
(704) 697-7778 or (800) 225-4700

Type of B&B: Inn.
Rooms: 14 with private bath.
Rates: 1/$32-59; 2/$49-79.

Rating: B or ♛♛ Good, exceeds basic requirements.

Historic inn with Classical Revival architecture was built in 1898 and is now listed on the National Register of Historic Places. The inn is situated right in town and located about 25 minutes south of Asheville on Route 26. Choose from fourteen guest rooms. There is a wide variety in the size, decor, and amenities in the rooms but each has a private bath, telephone, and TV and several rooms have working fireplaces. Popular attractions in the area include Smoky Mountains, Pisgah National Forest, Blue Ridge Parkway, Biltmore Estate, and Carl Sandburg's home. Seven golf courses are nearby as well as tennis, fishing, hiking, and swimming. Full country breakfast. Facilities for social functions and meetings; fax machine for business travelers. 1/$32-59; 2/$49-79. AE, MC, V. Travel agent.

Kill Devil Hills

Ye Olde Cherokee Inn
500 North Virginia Dare Trail
Kill Devil Hills, NC 27948
(919) 441-6127

Type of B&B: Inn.
Rooms: 6 with private bath.
Rates: 1 or 2/$55-80.

Rating: C or ♛ Acceptable, meets basic requirements.

Ye Olde Cherokee Inn is a traditional beach house located 500 feet from the water on Highway 12 in the Nags Head area. Six guest rooms are available, each with private bath, soft cypress interior, white ruffled curtains, and ceiling fan. Relax on the wrap around porch or in the sitting the sitting room. Popular attractions in the area include Wright Brothers Memorial, Fort Raleigh, Cape Hatteras National Seashore, and seashore activities. Continental breakfast buffet. 1 or 2/$55-80. AE, MC, V. Senior discount. Travel agent.

Guests write: *"Lovely home! We've never had room service at a B&B before." (S. Hallinan)*

"This inn is neat, extremely clean and thoroughly enjoyable." (P. Elliott)

"My son felt it was just like Grandma's home." (W. Brooks)

"We had a very enjoyable stay as it was quite comfortable. It was pleasant to wake to the smell of delicious brewing coffee - like being at home." (L. Kulick)

"The inn was rustic and one block from the ocean so you could smell the sea air. I loved my room - feminine with lots of pillows. The night I arrived there was a storm. The next day I wanted to go for a walk on the beach. Phyllis lent me a rainproof jacket and boots which I lived in. I was able to go out and have a great time." (J. Dail)

New Bern

Harmony House Inn
215 Pollock Street
New Bern, NC 28560
(919) 636-3810

Type of B&B: Large inn.
Rooms: 9 with private bath.
Rates: 1/$49-55; 2/$75-80.

Rating: A- or ♛♛♛ Excellent, far exceeds basic requirements.

Historic Greek Revival inn built in 1850 is located two hours north of Wilmington in a town steeped in history. There are nine guest rooms with private baths available. Each features antique furnishings and hand-crafted furniture by local artisans. Popular attractions in the area include Tryon Palace, Trent and Neuse Rivers, antique and specialty shops, and museums. Full breakfast includes a hot entree and homemade granola. Families welcome. Restricted smoking. 1/$49-55; 2/$75-80. AE, MC, V. Travel agent.

Waynesville

Grandview Lodge
809 Valley View Circle Road
Waynesville, NC 28786
(704) 456-5212 or 255-7826

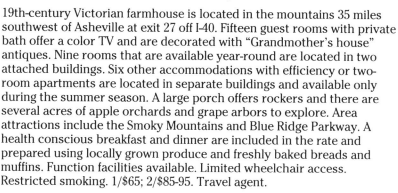

Type of B&B: Country inn with restaurant.
Rooms: 15 with private bath.
Rates: 1/$65; 2/$85-95 MAP.

Rating: B- or ♕♕ Good, exceeds basic requirements.

19th-century Victorian farmhouse is located in the mountains 35 miles southwest of Asheville at exit 27 off I-40. Fifteen guest rooms with private bath offer a color TV and are decorated with "Grandmother's house" antiques. Nine rooms that are available year-round are located in two attached buildings. Six other accommodations with efficiency or two-room apartments are located in separate buildings and available only during the summer season. A large porch offers rockers and there are several acres of apple orchards and grape arbors to explore. Area attractions include the Smoky Mountains and Blue Ridge Parkway. A health conscious breakfast and dinner are included in the rate and prepared using locally grown produce and freshly baked breads and muffins. Function facilities available. Limited wheelchair access. Restricted smoking. 1/$65; 2/$85-95. Travel agent.

Waynesville

Swag Country Inn
Route 2, Box 280-A
Waynesville, NC 28786
(704) 926-0430

Type of B&B: Country inn with restaurant.
Rooms: 12 with private bath.
Rates: 1/$108-188; 2/$118-198.

Rating: A or ♕♕♕ Excellent, far exceeds basic requirements.

Historic hand-hewn log lodge is two hundred years old and has a breathtaking setting at 5,000 feet in the mountains and is located 10 miles off I-40, exit 20. Choose from twelve guest rooms with unique decor, antique furnishings, patchwork quilts, local crafts, ceilings fans, and fireplaces. Several common rooms provide quiet havens for reading, conversing with other guests, or enjoying a blazing fire. Popular attractions here are hiking, fishing, bird watching, and games of croquet, badminton, horseshoes, and racquetball. Full breakfast, lunch and dinner are included in the rates. 1/$108-188; 2/$118-198. AE, MC, V. Open Memorial Day through October.

Guests write: *"I'm not sure I would have survived this year without my Swag Fix. As always my stay was absolutely delightful. Their ability to make everyone comfortable and feel completely at ease is to be commended." (M. Barron)*

"Ed and I enjoyed a wonderful long weekend at the Swag. The accommodations were grand and the site breathtaking. The food was delicious and their smiles wrapped it all beautifully." (L. James)

"The inn provided the perfect combination of rest and relaxation that we were both hoping for. They are to be commended for the accommodations, food, and hospitality. I would also like to commend them for the way the family has developed the Swag. As a native of North Carolina mountains and an architect, I have great admiration for someone who can fit a man-made structure into such a powerful landscape as this property."
(C. Winstead)

"We were placed in the cabin and it was a delight to have the extra space. Erine had her first horseback ride, saw a deer, chased lots of butterflies and salamanders, walked in the river, and learned a little about birds and plants." (E. Smith)

Wilmington

Catherine's Inn on Orange
410 Orange Street
Wilmington, NC 28401
(800) 476-0723

Type of B&B: Small inn.
Rooms: 4 with private bath.
Rates: 1/$55; 2/$60.

Rating: A- or ♛♛♛ Excellent, far exceeds basic requirements.

HIstoric home built in 1875 is situated in a quiet residential area of the city. Four spacious guest rooms on the second floor offer a private bath, selected antiques, fireplace, telephone and have central air-conditioning. Two common rooms on the main floor offer comfortable seating, antique furnishings, and pleasing decor. A landscaped garden and patio area in the back yard overlook a small swimming pool. Full breakfast. Function space for small weddings or meetings is available. 1/$55; 2/$60. AE, MC, V. Business travel and auto club discounts.

Luverne

Volden Farm B&B
R.R. 2, Box 50
Luverne, ND 58056
(701) 769-2275

Type of B&B: B&B home.
Rooms: 2 rooms share one bath.
Rate: 1/$40; 2/$50-60.

Rating: B+ or ♛♛ Good, exceeds basic requirements.

Wood farmhouse with a Scandinavian atmosphere is located 33 miles northwest of exit 71 off I-94. Choose from two guest rooms which share a private guest bath in the main house or the newly renovated "Law Office" which is a private cottage a few yards from the main house. The rooms have a comfortable country decor and feature a lace-canopied or metal bed. There are several common areas in the house which offer private areas for reading, sitting in front of a fireplace, playing a game of pool, or conversing with other guests. The farm has several acres inviting exploration and a small playhouse and swing set are available to delight children. Full breakfast specialties include Swedish pancakes or Danish Ableskiver with fresh farm produce. Families welcome. No smoking. 1/$40; 2/$50-60.

Guests write: *"Joanne's attention to detail was great. She thought of everything (even a light over the bathtub to read by). I travel a great deal and this is one of the nicest places I have stayed in." (M. Scholz)*

Dayton/West Milton

Locust Lane Farm Bed & Breakfast
5590 Kessler Cowlesville Road
West Milton, OH 45383
(513) 698-4743

Type of B&B: Farm B&B.
Rooms: 3, 1 with private bath.
Rates: 1/$40; 2/$45-50.

Rating: A- or ♛♛♛Excellent, far exceeds basic requirements.

Traditional Cape Cod home in a rural setting is twenty minutes north of Dayton near exit 69 off I-75, or 7 miles southwest of Troy. Of three guest rooms available, one has a queen-size bed and private bath. The other two rooms offer a double bed and shared bath. There are two relaxing common rooms on the first floor including the library with an interesting collection of books and dolls. Popular attractions in this area include antique shopping, visiting a nearby nature center, golfing, and canoeing. Full breakfast is served on the screened porch in summer. Families welcome. 1/$40; 2/$45-50. No smoking.

Painesville

Rider's Inn Bed'n Breakfast
792 Mentor Avenue
Painesville, OH 44077
(216) 942-2742

Type of B&B: Country inn with restaurant and pub.
Rooms: 9 with private bath.

Rates: 1 or 2/$65-90.

Rating: B+ or ♛♛ Good, exceeds basic requirements.

Historic Colonial country inn built in 1812 is located 1 mile west of this college town on Route 20. Choose from nine guest rooms, each with private bath, queen-size bed, and antique furnishings that are all for sale. Three rooms are available in the private guesthouse on the premises. Area attractions include Lake Erie College, Fairport Harbor, Grand River Winery, Indian Museum, golf, tennis, horseback riding, watersports, and Amish Country tours. Continental breakfast-in-bed service available. A full-service restaurant and separate English pub offer additional meals and a Sunday brunch. A second floor common room offers facilities for functions and meetings. Families welcome. 1 or 2/$65-90. AE, MC, V.

Piqua

The Pickwinn B&B Guesthouse
707 North Downing Street
Piqua, OH 45356
(513) 773-6137 or 773-8877

Type of B&B: Guesthouse.
Rooms: 4, 1 with private bath.
Rates: 1/$40-50; 2/$50-60.

Rating: A- or ♛♛♛ Excellent, far exceeds basic requirements.

Spacious brick home situated on a tree-lined street of family homes was built in 1880 and is located 1.5 miles west of I-75, exit 82. There are four comfortable second-floor guest rooms furnished with English countryside antiques, twin, double, or queen-size beds, and TV. One offers a private bath. Relax in the downstairs sitting room or on the large front porch with wicker chairs and swing. Area attractions include the Johnston Farm and Indian Museum, Stillwater Prairie, and Big Woods Reserve. Full country breakfast often includes eggs, meat, toast, and pastries. Families welcome. Restricted smoking. 1/$40-50; 2/$50-60. Open March through October.

Tiffin

Zelkova Inn
2348 South County Road 19
Tiffin, OH 44883
(419) 447-4043

Type of B&B: Inn.
Rooms: 4, 2 with private bath.
Rates: 1 or 2/$70-95.

Rating: A- or ♛♛♛ Excellent, far exceeds basic requirements.

Country French inn nestled in the woods on thirty-five acres is located 14 miles south of I-80 at exit 6. Four guest rooms are available, two with private bath. French doors, mahogany woodwork, and botanical prints grace the 18th-century decor. The spacious living room contains a baby grand piano and the library is available for quiet reading, card playing, or watching a videotaped movie. Visit nearby Lake Erie and Ceder Point. Historic downtown Tiffin is only minutes away with the circa 1928 Ritz Theater, Heidelberg College, Tiffin University, as well as antique, craft, and specialty shops. Full breakfast. Gourmet dinner available by advance reservation. Meeting facilities are available for small weddings and social functions. Families welcome. Restricted smoking. 1 or 2/$70-95. MC, V. Business travel discount. Travel agent.

Ashland

Hersey House
451 North Main Street
Ashland, OR 97520
(503) 482-4563

Type of B&B: Inn.
Rooms: 4 with private bath.
Rate: 1 or 2/$70-100.

Rating: A or ♛♛♛ Excellent, far exceeds basic requirements.

Historic Victorian inn built in 1904 is located in the Rogue Valley off I-5. Choose from four guest rooms, each with private bath, antique furnishings, and individual decor. A comfortable parlor provides a place to read, relax, play the piano, and socialize with other guests each evening. Area attractions include Shakespearean Festival, Britt Music Festival, Crater Lake, winery tours, white-water rafting, horseback riding, fishing, hiking, and hot air balloon rides. Full breakfast features specialties such as gingerbread pancakes with lemon curd sauce, Blueberry blintzes, Danish omelette, and baked pear; all prepared with locally grown produce and Oregon made products. No smoking. 1 or 2/$70-100. Travel agent.

Ashland

The Morical House
668 North Main Street
Ashland, OR 97520
(503) 482-2254

Type of B&B: Inn.
Rooms: 5 with private bath.
Rate: 1/$55-80; 2/$65-100.

Rating: A or ♛♛♛ Excellent, far exceeds basic requirements.

Victorian farmhouse built in 1884 is located 1 mile from downtown, 1.5 miles southwest of I-5, exit 19. Choose from five guest rooms, each with private bath, period furniture, handmade comforters, family heirlooms, air conditioning, and mountain views. Relax in the parlor with books or games, stroll through the acre of grounds, try out the putting green, and join other guests for afternoon refreshments each day. Area attractions include Shakespearean Festival, Britt Music Festival, Rogue River recreation, art galleries, tennis, hiking, golf, and skiing. Full breakfast features Morical House fresh fruit "smoothies" and daily main course specialties such as cheese and mushroom omelettes, French toast, or pancakes. All breads, muffins, and coffee cakes are baked "from scratch." 1/$55-80; 2/$65-100. MC, V.

Ashland

Mt. Ashland Inn
550 Mt. Ashland Road
Ashland, OR 97520
(503) 482-8707

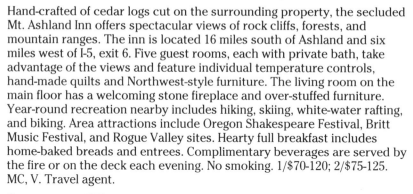

Type of B&B: Small mountain inn.
Rooms: 5 with private bath.
Rate: 1/$70-120; 2/$75-125

Rating: A or ♛♛♛ Excellent, far exceeds basic requirements.

Hand-crafted of cedar logs cut on the surrounding property, the secluded Mt. Ashland Inn offers spectacular views of rock cliffs, forests, and mountain ranges. The inn is located 16 miles south of Ashland and six miles west of I-5, exit 6. Five guest rooms, each with private bath, take advantage of the views and feature individual temperature controls, hand-made quilts and Northwest-style furniture. The living room on the main floor has a welcoming stone fireplace and over-stuffed furniture. Year-round recreation nearby includes hiking, skiing, white-water rafting, and biking. Area attractions include Oregon Shakespeare Festival, Britt Music Festival, and Rogue Valley sites. Hearty full breakfast includes home-baked breads and entrees. Complimentary beverages are served by the fire or on the deck each evening. No smoking. 1/$70-120; 2/$75-125. MC, V. Travel agent.

Guests write: *"What you can't imagine, you must see for yourself, are the special saddle-notchings in the corners, the chamfered beams that extend through the exterior wall, the log arches, magnificent stone fireplace. Impressive, too, are the handsome madrone and black oak headboards, the hand-carved mountain scenes on each guest room door, and decorative deck railing. Beautiful antiques and Oriental rugs add a richness to this quietly elegant inn. Each bedroom is a work of art with colorful handmade quilts and matching curtains." (N. Bringhurst)*

"We love the mountains around and all the beautiful hand-craftsmanship of Jerry and Elaine. The breakfasts are always wonderful and although we have stayed at the inn more than twenty times, they are always new! The location of the inn is spectacular - unbelievable views and crisp mountain air all around. A great place for meditation, reading, and getting away from the swarm of city life." (J. Bent)

Cloverdale

Sandlake Country Inn
8505 Galloway Road
Cloverdale, OR 97112
(503) 965-6745

Type of B&B: Small inn.
Rooms: 4 with private bath & cottage.
Rates: 1/$60-95; 2/$65-100.

Rating: A- or ♛♛♛ Excellent, far exceeds basic requirements.

Two-story farmhouse built in 1894 is nestled on 1.5 acres just off the Three Capes Scenic Loop, 16 miles south of Tillamook. Four guest rooms in the main house offer fresh flowers, antique furnishings, and collectibles. A Honeymoon suite with four rooms on the second floor features a deck overlooking the garden, private dining room with refrigerator and claw-foot tub. The small, modest looking cottage is a treasure inside with a private bedroom, luxury bath with whirlpool tub for two, living room with black marble fireplace, and full kitchen. Popular attractions in the area include Netarts Bay, Cape Lookout State Park, Tillamook cheese factory, and beaches. Full breakfast with home-baked goods. Special gourmet picnic baskets are available at an additional cost for those arriving late at night, or for day trips in the area. No smoking. Cabin is wheelchair accessible. 1/$60-95; 2/$65-100. MC, V. Travel agent.

Guests write: " *Sandlake Country Inn is a peaceful retreat. My husband always said he would never set foot in a B&B but he took us back four times last year. The privacy, personal attention, and food have made it a place we will return to at least once a year.*" (E. Doyle)

"*It's the last morning of our stay at Sandlake. I've lit a fire and am curled up on the sofa reflecting on the past few days. This has been a special time for us because it is the beginning time for dreaming, setting goals, and time for us alone. I don't think we could have found a more perfect place to do that and more.*" (J. Marcotte)

"*From the moment we arrived and saw the heart cookie inscribed with our names and "eleven" for our 11th anniversary, we knew we chose the right place to celebrate. The beautiful room, the relaxing tub, the quilt, and luscious breakfasts all combined to create a perfect weekend.*" (J. Edbert)

"*Last summer my husband and I made a tour of the B&Bs on the Oregon coast, only to discover that our initial judgement had been correct. The Sandlake Country Inn is by far the best. It is secluded, yet within easy driving* distance of many points of interest and forms of entertainment. But the innkeeper, a superb hostess, and her gourmet breakfasts, are what keep us going back for more." (D. Grier)

"To be doted on and pampered like that yet still have privacy was wonderful! It was so quiet and restful there my husband and I could really focus on the specialness of our marriage relationship." (K. Hopfer)

Depoe Bay

Channel House Bed & Breakfast Inn
35 Ellingson Street, P.O. Box 56
Depoe Bay, OR 97341
(503) 765-2140

Type of B&B: Large inn.
Rooms: 9 with private bath.
Rates: 1 or 2/$52-150.

Rating: A- or ♛♛♛ Excellent, far exceeds basic requirements.

Oceanfront inn built high on the rocky shore of the rugged Oregon coastline is one block west of the south end of the Depoe Bay bridge. There are nine guest rooms or suites, each with private bath. Special features of the deluxe rooms include private balcony, whirlpool baths, and ocean views. Walk to the town's center that has a good selection of seaside shops and restaurants. Area attractions include the beach, whale watching, and charter fishing. A full breakfast with pancakes, waffles, or omelettes is served in the nautical dining room or in the guest room. Families welcome. No smoking. 1 or 2/$52-150. MC, V. Travel agent.

Guests write: *"There was genuinely warm and friendly hospitality here, lovely food presentation, comfortable beds, and clean accommodations. Loved the soothing sound of the surf and sea. Incomparable setting and the binoculars in the room was a nice touch." (P. Lovell)*

"The whirlpool was great and a unique experience for us to be right on the water." (K. Delich)

Elmira

McGillivray's Log Home B&B
88680 Evers Road
Elmira, OR 97437
(503) 935-3564

Type of B&B: B&B home.
Rooms: 2 with private bath.
Rate: 1/$45-55; 2/$55-65.

Rating: A- or ♥♥♥ Excellent, far exceeds basic requirements.

Log home built from scratch is just 14 miles west of Eugene yet has a secluded, tranquil setting among fir and pine trees. Two large guest rooms are available, each with private bath and air conditioning. A spacious loft room is especially suitable for families or couples traveling together. A pleasant parlor on the first floor features comfortable seating for TV viewing and a piano. Popular activities in this area include biking and hiking quiet country roads or swimming and fishing nearby. Full old-fashioned breakfast is usually prepared on the antique wood-burning cookstove. Families welcome. Wheelchair access. No smoking. 1/$45-55; 2/$55-65. MC, V.

Guests write: *"We enjoyed this home, the fresh grape juice, the blackberries and cream, the pancakes and grape syrup, the eggs in bacon cups, the zucchini bread, jam, and butters, and especially the dried pears given us for our packs. They tasted wonderful along the roadways." (H. Gordon)*

"The Mcgillivray's home cannot be accurately described as simply rustic. Artfully hand-crafted is more like it. From the massive log beams down to intricate wooden door latches, it is evident that much love, care and considerable skill went into this wonderful home. Our loft room was spacious with its soaring cathedral ceiling and outdoor balcony - enough space in this room for our family group of five with space leftover." (L. Stafford)

"When my hands got cold in my early morning run, Evelyn gave me a choice of three pairs of her own gloves that I could borrow. Her loveliest and most generous gestures, however, revolved around her hospitality to my daughter and my four-year-old grandson. Not only did she make my family feel right at home but she decorated the table a la Halloween and gave a delighted little boy a pumpkin to take home with him. No motel was ever like this!" (S. Olds)

"I must tell you all about this log cabin. It was marvelous! In the morning we had a wonderful breakfast. Fresh raspberries from the garden with cream. Grape juice from their grapes. Buttermilk pancakes made on a cast-iron stove, scrambled eggs and ham, butter molded into maple leaves and homemade peach jam." (P. Schoenstein)

Eugene

The Lyon and the Lambe Inn
988 Lawrence at Tenth
Eugene, OR 97401
(503) 683-3160

Type of B&B: Inn.
Rooms: 4 with private bath.
Rate: 1/$55-70; 2/$60-75.

Rating: A- or ♛♛♛ Excellent, far exceeds basic requirements.

Newly constructed inn is located 1.5 miles west of I-5 at exit 194-B. Four spacious guest rooms are offered, each with private bath. Relax in the first floor fireplaced living room and library or soak in the large whirlpool bath located in the special tub room on the second floor which features heated towel bar and stereo music. Area attractions include Hult Center for Performing Arts, Fairgrounds and Convention Center, University of Oregon, and local vineyards. Full gourmet breakfast features specialties such as Symphony Salmon, Kaiserschmarrn, or Eggs Florentine along with home-made bread, muffins, or croissants. 1/$55-70; 2/$60-75. V, MC. Travel agent.

Junction City

Black Bart Bed & Breakfast
94125 Love Lake Road
Junction City, OR 97448
(503) 998-1904

Type of B&B: B&B home.
Rooms: 3, 2 with private bath.
Rates: 1/$50; 2/$50-60.

Rating: A- or ♛♛♛ Excellent, far exceeds basic requirements.

Historic farmhouse built in the 1880's is located less than two miles east of Highway 99 or 12 miles northeast of I-5 at exit 195 northbound. Three guest rooms feature new decor, air conditioning, and Early-American furnishings. One room on the second floor offers a king-sized canopy bed and private bath. There are several common rooms including an old-fashioned parlor, sunporch, and breakfast room with gift shop items and a wall of windows overlooking the flower beds. Local attractions in the area include Junction City Museum, Lochmead Dairy tours, winery tours, country bike rides, jogging, boating, and antique shopping. Full breakfast specialties feature Danish Aebleskivers, Bohemian Liwanzen, strawberry pancakes, or bear muffins. No smoking. 1/$50; 2/$50-60. MC, V.

Lincoln City

Palmer House Bed & Breakfast
646 North West Inlet
Lincoln City, OR 97367
(503) 994-7932

Type of B&B: Small inn.
Rooms: 3 with private bath.
Rates: 1 or 2/$75-95.

Rating: A or ♛♛♛ Excellent, far exceeds basic requirements.

Architecturally designed to maximize the ocean view, this home built in 1950 has been recently renovated and is located in a quiet, residential area one block west of Highway 101 across from the beach access. Three guest rooms offer private bath, queen-size beds, telephone, TV, and designer linens. Each has a casual elegance with light colors and a good deal of privacy. Guests enjoy gathering on the outdoor deck and in the living room with fireplace and floor-to-ceiling windows framing the ocean view. The beach is a short walk from the inn. A three-course, full breakfast includes homemade sausages, breads, jams, and healthy dessert course such as marinated fruit-filled meringue with creme anglaise. No smoking. 1 or 2/$75-95. MC, V.

Newport

Ocean House Bed & Breakfast
4920 North West Woody Way
Newport, OR 97365
(503) 265-6158 or 265-7779

Type of B&B: Small inn.
Rooms: 4 with private bath.
Rates: 1/$58-90; 2/$63-95.

Rating: B+ or ♛♛ Good, exceeds basic requirements.

Large Country French-style home built in 1941 sits on a bluff overlooking the ocean and Agate Beach below and is located 2.5 hours south of Portland. There are four guest rooms available, each with an ocean view and private bath. A living room on the main floor has comfortable built-in seating, fireplace, TV area, and large windows with an ocean view. The inn boasts a lovely garden with flowers and native shrubs and there is a short, steep path down to the beach for fishing, clamming, surfing, and sunning. Popular area attractions include lighthouses to explore, Marine Science Center, Bay Front Aquarium, restaurants, and art galleries. Full breakfast includes fresh fruit and hot entree and coffee is always ready for early morning risers. No smoking, children, or pets. Wheelchair access. 1/$58-90; 2/$63-95. MC, V.

Adamstown/Lancaster County

Adamstown Inn
62 West Main Street
P.O. Box 938
Adamstown, PA 19501
(215) 484-0800 or (800) 594-4808

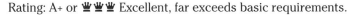

Type of B&B: Inn.
Rooms: 4 with private bath.
Rates: 1 or 2/$65-95.

Rating: A+ or ♛♛♛ Excellent, far exceeds basic requirements.

Two-and-a-half-story brick Victorian home built in 1925 is located in a small town in the heart of Pennsylvania Dutch Country off exit 21 of the Turnpike. Choose from four guest rooms, all with private baths. Each room features family heirlooms, handmade quilts, lace curtains, fruit, and fresh flowers. The inn boasts leaded-glass windows and doors, chestnut woodwork, and Oriental rugs. This town is known as the "Antique Capital of America" and offers an abundance of antique shops. Other attractions include factory outlets, Amish tours, Maple Grove Speedway, and fine restaurants. Continental plus breakfast. Facilities available for weddings. Restricted smoking. 1 or 2/$65-95. MC, V. 10% business travel.

Guests write: *"The innkeepers were very cordial and welcoming. They go out of their way to see to your comfort and enjoyment. It's a tastefully done Victorian home, comfortable and easy to live in, not a museum but a home with a great location in the heart of antique territory. Breakfast is a multi-course feast all homebaked and fresh. A wonderful experience. We've been there three times and will keep going."* (W. Butti)

"This location is so close to Reading and the outlets and Amish Country nearby is so pleasant and quaint. They do everything possible to make your visit very comfortable: welcome drink and lovely breakfast including coffee at your door early in the morning. It has lovely Victorian decor, comfortable beds, and a relaxing Jacuzzi. Who could ask for more?" (P. Mallon)

"The master bedroom is huge with absolutely gorgeous decor. It has a lovely sitting area with comfortable upholstered chairs for reading or relaxing as well as beautiful antique table and chairs. The adjoining bathroom must be seen to be believed. Both rooms are like pictures in magazines. There is a deliciously inviting two-person Jacuzzi and a separate shower. We loved it!" (P. Holmes)

Allentown

Coachaus
107-111 North Eighth Street
Allentown, PA 18101
(215) 821-4854 or
(800) 762-8680.

Type of B&B: Large urban inn.
Rooms: 24 with private bath.
Rates: 1/$64-115; 2/$74-125.

Rating: A- or ♛♛♛ Excellent, far exceeds basic requirements.

Victorian European-style urban hotel has been restored and is located in downtown Allentown, 1.5 miles south of US-22 and 3.5 miles from I-78. There are twenty-four guest rooms and while there is a wide variety in the size, decor, and amenities offered, each room has a private bath, cable TV, telephone, and air conditioning. Walk to fine dining, boutiques, antique shops, Old Allentown Historic District, and the Liberty Bell Shrine from the inn. Recreation nearby includes Dorney Amusement Park, skiing, hiking, white-water rafting, and biking. Full breakfast and evening refreshments offered daily. Families welcome. 1/$64-115; 2/$74-125. AE, MC, V. Family, weekly, and monthly rates available. Travel agent.

Allentown/Fogelsville

Glasbern
R.D. 1, Box 250
Fogelsville, PA 18051
(215) 285-4723

Type of B&B: Inn with restaurant.
Rooms: 23 with private bath.
Rates: 1/$80-95; 2/$95-200.

Rating: AA or ♛♛♛♛ Outstanding.

This original 1800's Pennsylvania barn has been refurbished into an inn with exposed timber, cathedral ceilings, and many windows. It is situated on one-hundred acres near Allentown, 2 miles northwest of the intersection of Routes I-78 and 100. Choose from twenty-three guest rooms with a mix of contemporary and antique furnishings, private bath, phone, TV, VCR and radio. Sixteen rooms have whirlpool baths, several also have a fireplace or wood-burning stove. Popular activities in the area include bicycling, parks, wildlife sanctuaries, wineries, antique markets, and covered bridge tours. Tennis, fishing, hiking, and skiing are nearby. Full breakfast. Country French dining is available in the restaurant

Tuesday through Saturday. Facilities available for meetings and social functions. Wheelchair access. 1/$80-95; 2/$95-200. AE, MC, V.

Guests write: *"Glasbern has a very enjoyable and relaxed atmosphere, the food is excellent, and hospitality superb. We had our small wedding in front of the fireplace in November 1991 and dinner afterwards. The day could not have been more beautiful." (A. Xander)*

"We thoroughly enjoyed our stay at Glasbern. The service was excellent, atmosphere and decor of the rooms and lodge was outstanding. It was just what we needed after having a baby three months before." (D. Butler)

"They made our 34th Anniversary so special! Everything is already excellent and no improvement is necessary." (C. Kampmeyer)

Allentown/Bethlehem

Wydnor Hall
Old Philadelphia Pike
Bethlehem, PA 18015
(215) 867-6851

Type of B&B: Inn.
Rooms: 4, 2 with private bath.
Rates: 1/$80; 2/$95.

Rating: A or ♛♛♛ Excellent, far exceeds basic requirements.

Restored late-Georgian Manor house is located three miles south of Bethlehem on the historic Old Philadelphia Pike. Each of the four guest rooms has been furnished in the style of an English Country home with antiques and beautiful quilts. Two of the rooms offer a private bath. Sip afternoon tea in the living room with inviting sofas and chairs. Area attractions include historic sites in Bethlehem, Lehigh, Moravian, and Lafayette Colleges, Bach Festival Musikfest, and Celtic Classic. Full breakfast offers a choice from a varied menu. A morning coffee tray is delivered to guest rooms and afternoon tea is served daily. Restricted smoking. 1/$80; 2/$95. AE. Business travel discount. Travel agent.

Guests write: *"Our weekend stay at Wydnor Hall was similar to being the guest at a very grand and well-staffed home. The quality of the surroundings, the service, and the food was superb. From the coffee tray in the morning with newspaper, through the superb breakfast and afternoon tea (and wine), the comfort of the service and surroundings is on a par with a fine European hotel." (P. Kuyper)*

Bethlehem/Easton

Lafayette Inn
525 West Monroe Street
Easton, PA 18042
(215) 253-4500

Type of B&B: Large inn.
Rooms: 18 with private bath.
Rates: 1/$80-100; 2/$90-110.

Rating: A or ♛♛♛ Excellent, far exceeds basic requirements.

Historic Victorian inn nestled in the Lehigh Valley is situated two blocks from Lafayette College in a town that is located ninety minutes from New York City, Philadelphia, or the Pocono Mountains. There are eighteen guest rooms available with private bath, custom decor, remote TV, and climate control system. Several rooms have kitchenettes. Nearby attractions include historic Easton, Bethlehem, New Hope, Bucks County, and Delaware River water sports such as canoeing and rafting. Continental breakfast includes homemade breads and muffins. Catered luncheons, dinner, and full breakfast are available at an additional cost. Several catering service and function rooms are available for meetings, dinner parties, and social occasions. Families welcome. Restricted smoking. 1/$80-100; 2/$90-110. AE, MC, V. 10% senior and business discount.

Guests write: *"Upon entering, strong antiques and soft colors set the tone of the environment for total comfort and elegance. What a winning combination! Perhaps most importantly, I can honestly say that I've never slept better thanks to the quality of the mattresses. The rating I would give them is heavenly. The continental breakfast was most elaborate. We sampled an assortment of homemade breads, English muffins, and Chambard jellies. (M. Rizzotto)*

"We've stayed in cold, impersonal hotels, cutsie B&B's, and a lot in-between. May I tell you what they've done is a miracle. They've managed to blend efficiency, great taste, and fine manners in just the right amounts." (S. Miller)

"Having George Burns as a guest at this inn was the highlight of our stay. What a great flip-flop of clientele the Lafayette Inn boasts - all the celebrities at the State Theatre sharing the beautiful inn with all us stuffy corporate guys! They have the feel of a modern hotel - fax, copies, catering - yet such Old World charm." (R. Gilmore)

Brackney

Linger Longer at Quaker Lake
RD 1, Box 44
Brackney, PA 18812
(717) 663-2844

Type of B&B: B&B home.
Rooms: 3, 1 with private bath.
Rates: 1/$70; 2/$75.

Rating: B- or ♛♛ Good, exceeds basic requirements.

Turn-of-the-century lakeside Cape Cod home is located 12 miles south of I-81 at Binghamton, New York. There are three guest rooms furnished with brass beds, interesting paintings, and prints; one offers a private bath. This is a popular year-round recreation area with fishing, hiking, and skiing. Area attractions include Salt Springs State Park, and antique and pottery shops. The innkeeper's Thistledown Pottery studio is on the premises as well as a hot tub. Continental breakfast. No smoking. 1/$70; 2/$75. MC, V. Travel agent.

Cook Forest

Clarion River Lodge
River Road
Cook Forest, PA 16217
(800) 648-6743

Type of B&B: Country inn.
Rooms: 20 with private bath.
Rates: 1 or 2/$72-104.

Rating: B+ or ♛♛ Good, exceeds basic requirements.

Contemporary inn constructed of stone and timber is a naturally secluded retreat 15 miles north of exit 13 off of I-80. Twenty guest rooms are available which offer private bath, TV, air-conditioning, and refrigerator. Relax in front of the massive eight-foot fireplace and take in the rustic beauty of the inn's cherry and butternut paneling, log beams, cathedral ceilings, and native stone architecture. Nearby recreational activities include snowmobiling, canoeing, horseback riding, hiking, and inner-tubing. Continental breakfast. Meeting and banquet facilities available. Full service restaurant on premises. 1 or 2/$72-104. AE, MC, V. 10% senior and auto club discounts. Travel agent.

Elizabethtown

West Ridge Guest House
1285 West Ridge Road
Elizabethtown, PA 17022
(717) 367-7783

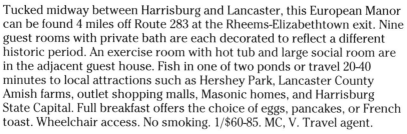

Type of B&B: Inn.
Rooms: 9 with private bath.
Rates: 1 or 2/$60-85

Rating: A+ or ♛♛♛ Excellent, far exceeds basic requirements.

Tucked midway between Harrisburg and Lancaster, this European Manor can be found 4 miles off Route 283 at the Rheems-Elizabethtown exit. Nine guest rooms with private bath are each decorated to reflect a different historic period. An exercise room with hot tub and large social room are in the adjacent guest house. Fish in one of two ponds or travel 20-40 minutes to local attractions such as Hershey Park, Lancaster County Amish farms, outlet shopping malls, Masonic homes, and Harrisburg State Capital. Full breakfast offers the choice of eggs, pancakes, or French toast. Wheelchair access. No smoking. 1/$60-85. MC, V. Travel agent.

Guests write: *"Being a disabled veteran, I appreciated the ample access to the guest house and spacious parking. I had a large room, luxurious bathroom, all linens were changed every day, snacks and newspapers were available outside the bedroom door. The exercise room and hot tub were just across the hall and you can get full value in the breakfast alone. I stay in the Ritz Hotel in London, the George V Hotel in Paris, and the Waldorf in New York, but I always request accommodation at West Ridge Guest House in this area and I plan on accommodating and entertaining my guests here."* (R. Roberts)

Elizabethville

Inn at Elizabethville
30 West Main Street
Elizabethville, PA 17023
(717) 362-3476

Type of B&B: Inn.
Rooms: 7 with private bath.
Rates: 1/$55; 2/$60.

Rating: B or ♛♛ Good, exceeds basic requirements.

Small Victorian inn located in the heart of the state is one block west of the intersection of Routes 225 and 209. Built in 1883, the inn offers seven guest rooms with private bath and is decorated in Mission Oak and Arts & Crafts styles. Guests are welcome to use the dining, living, and conference rooms, as well as the kitchen, porch, and sun parlor. Area attractions include the Millersburg Ferry, an 18-hole golf course, Appalachian Trail hiking, hunting, fishing, and country auctions. Continental breakfast features organic granolas, yogurt, and bagels. Small meeting facilities available. Families welcome. No smoking. 1/$55; 2/$60. Business travel and long-term discounts available. MC, V. Travel agent.

Franklin

Quo Vadis Bed & Breakfast
"Whither Goest Thou?"
1501 Liberty Street
Franklin, PA 16323
(814) 432-4208

Type of B&B: Small inn.
Rooms: 6 with private bath.
Rates: 1 or 2/$48-70 plus tax.

Rating: B or ♛♛ Good, exceeds basic requirements.

1867 Queen-Anne Victorian home accented with terra cotta is located near the junction of Routes 8, 62, and 322, midway between Chambersburg and Gettysburg. Six guest rooms each offer a private bath, high ceilings, detailed woodwork, quilts, embroidery, and lacework, as well as furniture that has been acquired by four generations of the same family. Area attractions include the Historic District with Victorian homes, DeBence Antique Museum, antique malls, Drake Well Museum and Park with its 2.5 hour train trips, and outdoor recreation. Continental breakfast includes fresh fruit, home-baked goods, croissants, and varied specialties on weekends. No smoking. 1 or 2/$48-70 plus tax. AE, MC, V. Travel agent.

Gettysburg/Hanover

Beechmont Inn
315 Broadway
Hanover, PA 17331
(800) 553-7009

Type of B&B: Inn.
Rooms: 7 with private bath.
Rates: 1 or 2/$70-125.

Rating: A+ or ♥♥♥ Excellent, far exceeds basic requirements.

Historic Georgian home built in 1834 is located 13 miles east of Gettysburg on Route 194. There are seven guest rooms or suites with private bath available. Special features of some rooms include fireplace, whirlpool, and private balcony. Popular attractions in the area include Gettysburg National Park, Codorus State Park, antique shops in New Oxford, and the Pennsylvania Dutch countryside. Golf, tennis, fishing, boating, hiking, and canoeing are nearby. Full breakfast might include homemade granola and shirred egg in a bread basket. Restricted smoking. 1 or 2/$70-125. MC, V.

Guests write: *"This is a proven value for the money with superb accommodations and all the amenities. I wish most B&Bs had these wonderful attributes. It was the perfect answer for a long awaited romantic evening together and to think it was hidden here in Hanover!"* (C. Lutzkanin)

"It is beautifully decorated. I especially love the landscaped courtyard in back. Having breakfast outdoors early in the morning was a real treat." (B. Jamison)

"Well, I have no romance to report (my sweetie at home will be happy about that)! I am a working girl used to so many boring hotels and nights on the road. A travel agent locally suggested I stay here and I am certainly in their debt. I just came in from a relaxing evening on the porch petting the tabby cat and enjoying the night air. Sure can't find that at a Holiday Inn!" (D. Huber)

"Three things brought us to the Beechmont Inn: our 3rd Wedding Anniversary, the desire for a little romance and pampering, and Gettysburg National Park. What a weekend we had! As we sat by the fire sipping champagne and nibbling on the goodies in that basket waiting for us we thought it can't get any better than this. But it did get better! - at breakfast - absolutely wonderful." (J. Tanner)

Gettysburg

Dobbin House Tavern Gettystown Inn
89 Steinwehr Avenue
Gettysburg, PA 17325
(717) 334-2100

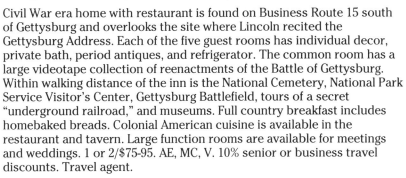

Type of B&B: Country inn with restaurant.
Rooms: 5 with private bath.
Rates: 1 or 2/$75-95.

Rating: B or ♛♛ Good, exceeds basic requirements.

Civil War era home with restaurant is found on Business Route 15 south of Gettysburg and overlooks the site where Lincoln recited the Gettysburg Address. Each of the five guest rooms has individual decor, private bath, period antiques, and refrigerator. The common room has a large videotape collection of reenactments of the Battle of Gettysburg. Within walking distance of the inn is the National Cemetery, National Park Service Visitor's Center, Gettysburg Battlefield, tours of a secret "underground railroad," and museums. Full country breakfast includes homebaked breads. Colonial American cuisine is available in the restaurant and tavern. Large function rooms are available for meetings and weddings. 1 or 2/$75-95. AE, MC, V. 10% senior or business travel discounts. Travel agent.

Guests write: *"The dining room was unique. It was filled with romantic tables with a dinner-in-bed effect complete with the four-posters dressed with hand-knitted canopies. After dinner, we returned to a room that was romantic, warm, and full of old country charm. There were lace doilies, silver brushes, an antique writing desk and bureau, and small, special soaps and creams in the bathroom. Finally, breakfast was scrumptious! Fresh fruit and juice, muffins and breads, bacon, homemade waffles and cheese-filled omelettes." (K. De Lorenzo*

Gettysburg

Old Appleford Inn
218 Carlisle Street
Gettysburg, PA 17325
(717) 337-1711 or
1-800-TREADWAY
Fax: (717) 334-6228

Type of B&B: Inn.
Rooms: 12 with private bath.
Rates: 1/$78-98; 2/$83-93.

Rating: A+ or ♛♛♛ Excellent, far exceeds basic requirements.

Historic Victorian inn built in 1867 is located less than three blocks north of Lincoln Square on Route 15 in a quiet residential neighborhood. There are twelve guest rooms available, each with a private bath. Common areas include a sunroom, fireplaced library, and large parlor with baby grand piano. Gettysburg College is right next to the inn and nearby can be found the battlefield, mountains, antique shops, skiing, hiking, tennis, fishing, and golf. Full breakfast. Facilities are available for meetings and social functions. No smoking. 1/$78-98; 2/$83-93; $10 each additional person. AE, MC, V. Travel agent.

Gettysburg

The Tannery Bed & Breakfast
449 Baltimore Street
Gettysburg, PA 17325
(717) 334-2454

Type of B&B: Small inn.
Rooms: 5 with private bath.
Rates: 1/$50; 2/$65-85.

Rating: B+ or ♛♛ Good, exceeds basic requirements.

Historic Gothic inn rich with Civil War history is located four blocks south of the center of town. Five large guest rooms each feature a private bath and traditional furnishings. A large activity room offers games and a collection of books on the Civil War. Afternoon refreshments are often served on the spacious front porch. The Gettysburg tour buses are headquartered one block from the inn and well-known landmarks are within walking distance as well as shops and restaurants. Continental breakfast. Restricted smoking. 1/$50; 2/$65-85. MC, V.

Harrisburg/New Cumberland

Farm Fortune
204 Limekiln Road
New Cumberland, PA 17070
(717) 774-2683

Type of B&B: Small inn.
Rooms: 4, 2 with private bath.
Rates: 1/$47-56; 2/$55-64.

Rating: A or ♛♛♛ Excellent, far exceeds basic requirements.

Limestone farmhouse built in the 1700's is situated on a hill overlooking the Yellow Breeches Creek just off Route 83 at exit 18-A. Each of the four guest rooms offer a double or twin bed, antique furnishings, and comfortable seating with good lighting. Two rooms offer a private bath and large porch area. Popular activities here are trout fishing on the property, sitting on the porch or terrace, and birdwatching while enjoying the scenic view. An antique store called the "Honeycomb Shop" is on the premises. Area attractions include historic homes, museums, antique shops, ski areas, and hiking. Gettysburg, York, and Lancaster County are a short drive away. Full breakfast. Function rooms are available for small meetings and weddings. 1/$47-56; 2/$55-64. AE, MC, V. Travel agent.

Hershey

Pinehurst Inn B&B
50 Northeast Drive
Hershey, PA 17033
(717) 533-2603 or
(800) 743-9140

Type of B&B: Inn.
Rooms: 14, 1 with private bath.
Rates: 1 or 2/$42-54.

Rating: C+ or ♛ Meets basic requirements.

Historic brick inn on the north side of Hershey is located on Route 743, 6 miles south of I-81. There are fourteen air-conditioned guest rooms. The size, decor, and amenities of each room differs but one room offers a private bath. Popular attractions in the area include nearby Hershey Park and Museum, Rose Garden, Chocolate World, sports arena and stadium, theater, and outdoor recreation. Full breakfast features an egg dish or pancakes and hot, fresh muffins. Resident cat. Families welcome. Wheelchair access. No smoking. 1 or 2/$42-54. MC, V.

Kennett Square

Meadow Spring Farm
201 East Street Road
Kennett Square, PA 19348
(215) 444-3903

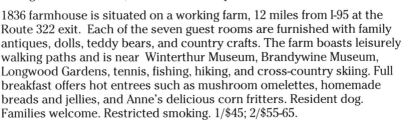

Type of B&B: B&B home.
Rooms: 7, 4 with private bath.
Rates: 1/$45; 2/$55-65.

Rating: B or ♛♛ Good, exceeds basic requirements.

1836 farmhouse is situated on a working farm, 12 miles from I-95 at the Route 322 exit. Each of the seven guest rooms are furnished with family antiques, dolls, teddy bears, and country crafts. The farm boasts leisurely walking paths and is near Winterthur Museum, Brandywine Museum, Longwood Gardens, tennis, fishing, hiking, and cross-country skiing. Full breakfast offers hot entrees such as mushroom omelettes, homemade breads and jellies, and Anne's delicious corn fritters. Resident dog. Families welcome. Restricted smoking. 1/$45; 2/$55-65.

Kennett Square

Scarlett House
503 West State Street
Kennett Square, PA 19348
(215) 444-9592

Type of B&B: Small inn.
Rooms: 4, 2 with private bath.
Rates: 1 or 2/$65-75; Suite/$90.

Rating: A or ♛♛♛ Excellent, far exceeds basic requirements.

American Foursquare Victorian home has been completely restored and is located in the heart of Chester County off Route 1 South. There are four guest rooms with authentic period decor and furnishings; two offer a private bath. Two parlors on the main floor offer several comfortable nooks for fireside reading and conversing. Area attractions include Longwood Gardens, Brandywine River Museum, Chadds Ford Winery, Hagley Museum, Brandywine Battlefield, and Chadds Ford. The Brandywine River area offers canoeing, tubing, biking, hiking, and hot air ballooning. Shoppers come from all around to visit the antique and outlet shops in the area. Continental breakfast includes homebaked breads, scones, muffins, and fresh squeezed juice. Small function rooms available. No smoking. 1 or 2/$65-75; Suite/$90. Business travel discount.

Lancaster/Wrightsville

1854 House
810 Grand Manor Drive
Wrightsville, PA 17368
(717) 252-4643 or
(800) 722-6395

Type of B&B: B&B home.
Rooms: 3 with private bath.
Rates: 1 or 2/$60-70.

Rating: B+ or ♛♛ Good, exceeds basic requirements.

Historic brick Manor home has been completely restored and is located midway between York and Lancaster, one mile north of Route 30 at the Wrightsville exit. There are three guest rooms with private bath, family antiques of mahogany or oak, and views of pond and pasture. Two rooms offer a whirlpool tub. Stroll the farmland, relax on the large porch, or swim in the spring-fed pond. The York Street Ride, held in late May or early June is a gigantic auto convention of pre-1939 customized street rods. The Train Collector's Association holds their annual meeting in York during April and October. The area has many antique shops, historic sites, and attractions such as the York Interstate Fair. Hershey, Gettysburg, and Reading are an hour away. Full breakfast. Restricted smoking. 1 or 2/$60-70. MC, V.

Lancaster/Willow Street

Apple Bin Inn
2835 Willow Street Pike
Willow Street, PA 17584
(717) 464-5881 or 1-800-338-4296

Type of B&B: Inn.
Rooms: 4; 2 with private bath.
Rate: 1/$45-65; 2/$50-70.

Rating: A- or ♛♛♛ Excellent, far exceeds basic requirements.

Historic home built in 1865 is in a residential setting located four miles south of Lancaster. There are four guest rooms which feature Country and Colonial reproductions, air-conditioning, cable TV, and stuffed wing chairs; two offer a private bath. Popular attractions in the area include the Amish countryside, outlets, restaurants, historic sites, tennis, and golf. Full breakfast may include house specialties such as German Apple Pancakes, French toast with pecan sauce, or breakfast casseroles. Home canned fruits are offered throughout the year. Picnic lunches can be packed with advance notice. No smoking. 1/$45-65; 2/$50-70. AE, MC, V.

Lancaster

Gardens of Eden
1894 Eden Road
Lancaster, PA 17601
(717) 393-5179

Type of B&B: B&B home.
Rooms: 4, 2 with private bath.
Rates: 1/$55; 2/$75-95.

Rating: B+ or ♛♛ Good, exceeds basic requirements.

Victorian home built in 1850 overlooks the Conestoga River and is located three miles northeast of Lancaster. Antiques and family mementos fill the four guest rooms, two of which offer a private bath. The adjoining guest house on the property features a walk-in fireplace, dining area, bedroom, and private bath. The innkeeper has a floral workshop in the basement of the house where local artist's works are displayed. The gardens and terraced grounds feature a variety of herbs, perennials and wild flowers. Area attractions include Lancaster County's Amish communities, shops, restaurants, and outlets. A continental breakfast includes homemade muffins and fresh fruit. Facilities for small weddings and meetings available. No smoking. 1/$55; 2/$75-95. MC, V. Travel agent.

Guests write: *"Their hospitality all the way from the herbal tea and strawberries upon our arrival to the interesting wild flower tour before departing was unsurpassed."* (R. Carlson)

"This was our very first B&B which we both had apprehension about but it turned into a genuinely warm and rich experience. Their hospitality made this a memorable weekend. We particularly love the Master Suite." (L. Silverman)

Lancaster/Manheim

Herr Farmhouse Inn
2256 Huber Drive
Manheim, PA 17545
(717) 653-9852

Type of B&B: Inn.
Rooms: 4, 2 with private bath.
Rates: 1 or 2/$70-95.

Rating: A or ♛♛♛ Excellent, far exceeds basic requirements.

Historic Colonial farmhouse built in 1738 has a country setting on eleven
acres near the junctions of Routes 230 and 283. There are four fireplaced
guest rooms or suites. Two feature a private bath and canopy bed. Five
common rooms on the first floor offer fireplaced dining room, kitchen
with walk-in fireplace, sunroom with wicker furniture, and library.
Popular attractions in the area include Amish farms, antique shops, flea
and farmer's markets, tennis, fishing, and golf. Continental breakfast is
served in the country kitchen with a walk-in fireplace. Restricted smoking.
1 or 2/$70-95. MC, V.

Lancaster

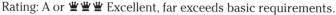

The King's Cottage
1049 East King Street
Lancaster, PA 17602
(717) 397-1017 or (800) 747-8717

Type of B&B: Inn.
Rooms: 7 with private bath.
Rates: 1 or 2/$75-115.

Rating: A+ or ♛♛♛ Excellent, far exceeds basic requirements.

Spanish Colonial mansion built in 1913 is located near the Greenfield
Road exit off Route 30. Seven guest rooms with private bath feature king
or queen-size beds, comfortable sitting area, and antique and
reproduction furniture. The inn's special architectural features including
a sweeping staircase, art deco and marble fireplaces, and hardwood
floors, are enhanced with Oriental rugs, crystal chandelier, and fine
Chippendale reproductions. Full gourmet breakfast, afternoon tea, and

evening refreshments served daily. No smoking. Facilities available for meetings and social functions. 1 or 2/$75-115. MC, V. 10% business travel and auto club discounts. Travel agent.

Guests write: *"We enjoyed a cozy room, creative and tasty breakfast, and very informative hostesses. A pleasant stay overall." (F. Raymond)*

"We thoroughly enjoyed our stay at King's Cottage. The rooms were lovely and the hosts gracious. Karen was very helpful in planning our excursions." (L. Hunter)

Lancaster/Strasburg

Limestone Inn B&B
33 East Main Street
Strasburg, PA 17579
(717) 687-8392

Type of B&B: Inn.
Rooms: 5 with private bath.
Rates: 1 or 2/$75-95

Rating: A or ♛♛♛ Excellent, far exceeds basic requirements.

Historic Georgian-style home built circa 1786 is located 9 miles southeast of Lancaster, 3 miles south of Route 30 on 896. The home has been completely restored and is now listed on the National Register of Historic Places. There are five guest rooms with private bath. The master suite features a private bath, corner fireplace, queen-size spindle bed, original random plank floors, and antique furnishings. Area attractions include Amish country, buggy rides, Pennsylvania Railroad Museum, antique shops and outlets, miniature golf, tennis, fishing, cross-country skiing, hiking, and bicycling. Full breakfast. Resident dogs. Restricted smoking. 1 or 2/$75-95. AE.

Lancaster/Ephrata

The Smithton Inn
900 West Main Street
Ephrata, PA 17522
(717) 733-6094

Type of B&B: Inn.
Rooms: 7 rooms, 1 suite, all with private bath.
Rates: 1/$55-105; 2/$65-115; Suite/$140-170.

Rating: A+ or ♕♕♕ Excellent, far exceeds basic requirements.

Stone inn that first opened in 1763 stands in the historic part of the village on Highway 322, 2.5 miles west of access Highway 222. The inn's seven guest rooms and one suite offer private baths, canopy and four-poster beds with Pennsylvania Dutch quilts, working fireplaces, and comfortable sitting areas. All rooms have a refrigerator, phone jack, chamber music, night shirts, fresh flowers, and optional candle lighting. Lancaster County's Old Order Amish and Mennonite people, still farming with horses and living the life of our ancestors, make this area a fascinating place. Attractions include farm tours, historic sites, handcrafts, daily auctions, farm markets, and the largest antique market in the East. Full breakfast with all-you-can-eat waffles, pastries, and fruit. Families welcome. Wheelchair access. No smoking. 1/$55-105; 2/$65-115; Suite/$140-170. AE, MC, V.

Lancaster/Lititz

Swiss Woods Bed & Breakfast
500 Blantz Road
Lititz, PA 17543
(717) 627-3358 or (800) 594-8018

Type of B&B: Inn.
Rooms: 7 with private bath.
Rates: 1/$60-95; 2/$70-115.

Rating: A+ or ♕♕♕ Excellent, far exceeds basic requirements.

A quiet, wooded area is the setting for this Swiss-style inn located in the heart of Amish country, 10 miles north of Lancaster. Seven guest rooms with private bath are available. One large suite features two rooms, queen-size bed, and Jacuzzi. A spacious common room on the first floor overlooks the meadow, gardens, lake, and woods and has attractive French Country furnishings. Popular attractions in the area include Hershey Park and Chocolate Factory, golf, tennis, fishing, boating, swimming, hiking, canoeing, and bicycling. Full breakfast often includes Swiss breads and pastries, as well as freshly baked quiches, casseroles, or souffles. Families welcome. No smoking. 1/$60-95; 2/$70-115.

Lancaster/Bird In Hand

The Village Inn of Bird-in-Hand
Box 253
2695 Old Philadelphia Pike
Bird-in-Hand, PA 17505
(717) 293-8369

Type of B&B: Inn.
Rooms: 11 with private bath.
Rates: 1 or 2/$74-139.

Rating: A or ♛♛♛ Excellent, far exceeds basic requirements.

Mid-nineteenth century Victorian inn is 7 miles east of Lancaster on Route 340. Each of the eleven guest rooms has its own private bath and down-filled bedding. Four of the rooms are suites, some with king-sized beds, whirlpool baths, and one with a working wood stove. Enjoy a complimentary tour of the Dutch Country or visit the adjacent farmer's market, country store, family restaurant, bakery, and number of quilt and craft shops. Just a few minutes away are Lancaster County attractions including museums, outlet shops, golf courses, and farmlands. Continental breakfast and light evening snacks served daily. Families welcome. Restricted smoking. 1 or 2/$74-139. AE, MC, V.

Lewisburg

Inn on Fiddler's Tract
R.D. 2, Box 573A
Buffalo Road
Route 192 West
Lewisburg, PA 17837
1-800-326-9659

Type of B&B: Country inn.
Rooms: 5 with private bath.
Rates: 1/$65; 2/$75-95.

Rating: A+ or ♛♛♛ Excellent, far exceeds basic requirements.

Historic German limestone country inn built in 1810 has been completely restored and is situated on thirty-three rolling acres 2 miles west of Route 15. There are five guest rooms with private bath and individual decor.

Popular activities and attractions in the area include downtown Lewisburg, Bucknell University, cross-country skiing and hiking, caverns, and state parks. A gourmet continental breakfast is served mid-week. Full breakfast specialties served on weekends include New Orleans stuffed French toast with bourbon whipped cream or Mickey Mouse waffles. Private dining available by advance reservation. Facilities available for meetings and social functions. Resident dog. Restricted smoking. 1/$65; 2/$75-95. AE, MC, V. Travel agent.

Guests write: *"This was a hectic year for us since our first child was born and we weren't expecting to get away for our 7th Wedding Anniversary. We were able to make this inn our getaway and it was superb. A dinner out, some champagne before bed, and an invigorating after-breakfast hot-tubbing. It's been a very special break for us."* (A. Cooper)

"Pure elegance is the term for a stay at the inn. My 41st birthday gift will be remembered as a pampered, personalized, and cherished evening from my loving husband." (L. Moran)

"We were treated to a delicious breakfast as pleasing to look at as it was to eat. The decor is elegant and comfortable. The care in which they have considered guest's needs is gracious." (M. Jureckson)

"The room was well furnished with comfortable beds and the first floor is very relaxing. Breakfasts are top notch and the dinners are the match of the finest restaurants with much better atmosphere." (R. Ashman)

"This visit to the inn brings Marge and I full circle to our first year of a wonderful marriage. It was the perfect touch to celebrating our anniversary as well as starting the next year on the right foot. Our only regret is having to check out." (J. Price)

Milford

Black Walnut B&B Inn
R.D. 2, Box 9285
Milford, PA 18337
(717) 296-6322 or
(800) 866-9870

Type of B&B: Inn.
Rooms: 12, 8 with private bath.
Rates: 1 or 2/$53-85.

Rating: B- or ♛♛ Good, exceeds basic requirements.

160-acre estate with Tudor-style mansion is located 2 miles southeast of I-84 exit 10. There are twelve guest rooms available with antique furnishings and brass beds; eight offer a private bath. Popular activities at the inn include swimming in the small lake and paddleboat rides. There are several common areas including a front porch with wicker furniture, and dining area that overlooks the pond. Area attractions include fishing, swimming, rafting, canoeing, skiing, golf, horseback riding, and hiking. Full buffet breakfast is served overlooking the lake. A wrap-around deck is available for group get-togethers. Resident dogs. No smoking. 1 or 2/$53-85. AE, MC, V.

Montgomeryville/North Wales

Joseph Ambler Inn
1005 Horsham Road
North Wales, PA 19454
(215) 362-7500

Type of B&B: Country inn.
Rooms: 28 with private bath.
Rates: 1/$85; 2/$140.

Rating: B+ or ♛♛ Good, exceeds basic requirements.

Colonial country inn situated on a twelve-acre estate of rolling countryside is 40 miles from Philadelphia near the intersection of Routes 202 and 309. Twenty-eight guest rooms are available in the main inn or the converted barn. Each room provides a private bath, antique furniture, four-poster bed, and Oriental rugs. Enjoy a stroll on the grounds or relax in three living rooms, one with massive, walk-in fireplace. Area attractions include Valley Forge, Peddler's Village, Skippack, picturesque New Hope, and historic sites of Philadelphia. Full breakfast. A restaurant on the premises offers dining. Families welcome. Facilities available for meetings and social functions. 1/$85; 2/$140. AE, MC, V. Auto club discount.

Montrose

The Montrose House
26 South Main Street
Montrose, PA 18801
(717) 278-1124

Type of B&B: Country inn.
Rooms: 12, 8 with private bath.
Rates: 1/$35-55; 2/$42-60.

Rating: C+ or ♛ Acceptable, meets basic requirements.

Set in the heart of the Endless Mountains, this Colonial country inn is located 10 miles west of I-81 at exit 67. Twelve guest rooms, eight with private bath, offer air-conditioning and color TV. Enjoy the area's downhill or cross-country skiing, auctions, antique shops, back-road exploring, and hiking. Full country breakfast served. 200-seat banquet room accommodates large groups and weddings. Families welcome. 1/$35-55; 2/$42-60. AE, MC, V. Travel agent.

Mount Pocono

Farmhouse Bed 'n' Breakfast
HCR 1, Box 6B
Mount Pocono, PA 18344
(717) 839-0796

Type of B&B: Inn on a farm.
Rooms: 2 suites and 1 cottage, all with private bath.
Rates: 1 or 2/$75-95.

Rating: B or ♛♛ Good, exceeds basic requirements.

Historic farmhouse built in 1850 has been completely restored and is situated in a quiet wooded setting on six acres located 2 miles south of Mt. Pocono in Paradise Valley. The main inn offers two guest suites which feature private bath, fireplace, and living room. The original icehouse on the property has been renovated into a private cottage that offers a fireplace and balcony. Popular activities at the inn are quiet walks through the grounds and gardens, and watching the wildlife from the parlor with large windows. Recreation and attractions in the area include skiing, golf, hiking, fishing, antique shopping, and fine restaurants. Full breakfast is served in unlimited quantities and includes fresh baked sourdough breads or muffins and an entree specialty such as blueberry stuffed French toast. No smoking. 1 or 2/$75-95. MC, V. Travel agent.

Guests write: *"This was our very first stop at a B&B and it won't be our last! Our accommodations were very comfortable, clean, and hospitality was outstanding. We both enjoyed good food in a relaxed setting." (M. Caley)*

"It doesn't get much better than this! Each visit is better than the last. The bottle of champagne tucked away in the refrigerator was a delightful surprise and a great way to celebrate Valentine's Day. We always enjoy Jack's gourmet breakfasts and Donna's homemade bedtime treats. The warm friendly hospitality provided at the farmhouse is the reason we keep coming back." (L. Adalbert)

"We came to have a weekend alone in the country and to relax. We couldn't have asked for a better setting. We enjoyed the privacy and the coziness of our evenings by the fire. The teas, coffee, and bedtime snacks were especially nice. A snowy winter evening sitting in front of a crackling fire sipping herbal teas and munching on chocolate chip cookies. It was perfect!" (C. Kratz)

New Hope/Doylestown

Inn at Fordhook Farm
105 New Britain Road
Doylestown, PA 18901
(215) 345-1766

Type of B&B: Inn.
Rooms: 5, 3 with private bath
plus carriage house.
Rates: 1 or 2/$93-126.

Rating: A or ♔♔♔ Excellent, far exceeds basic requirements.

Colonial home built of fieldstone in the 1760's is set on sixty acres and located 12 miles from New Hope, one hour from Philadelphia. There are five guest rooms furnished with antiques and family mementos; three with private bath. A separate carriage house on the property offers complete privacy with two bedrooms, bath, and living area. The first Burpee seed catalogs were written in this house and the grandchildren of W. Atlee Burpee have retained the quiet elegance of the home and gardens. A living room on the main floor features a fireplace, high ceilings, and tall mirrors. Popular activities in the area include fishing, hiking, and tennis. Full breakfast and afternoon tea served daily. Facilities available for meetings and social functions. No smoking. 1 or 2/$93-126. AE, MC, V. 10% auto club and business travel discounts.

New Hope

Wedgwood Collection of Historic Inns
111 West Bridge Street
New Hope, PA 18938
(215) 862-2570

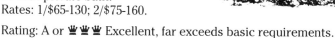

Type of B&B: Inn.
Rooms: 18 rooms and suites,
16 with private bath.
Rates: 1/$65-130; 2/$75-160.

Rating: A or ♛♛♛ Excellent, far exceeds basic requirements.

The Wedgwood Inn is comprised of three 19th-century homes located near the village center. Choose from eighteen guest rooms and suites. Each room features hardwood floors, antiques, Wedgwood pottery, original art, handmade quilts, and fresh flowers. Relax in three parlors with fireplace, books, and games, or sit outside on the veranda, porte-cochere, and gazebo. Hosts speak Spanish, French, Dutch, and Hebrew and offer seminars for prospective innkeepers. Hearty continental breakfast. Function rooms are available for meetings and social events. No smoking. 1/$65-130; 2/$75-160. 10% business travel discount. Travel agent.

Guests write: *"The rooms were warmly decorated in soft pastels and the added touch of Carl's most delicious homemade liqueur at our night table added the right ending to a perfect day. It was wonderful slipping into the robes that were provided. Upon waking in the morning, one could smell the aroma of the homemade muffins that were served along with a beautiful display of fresh fruits along with yogurt and a delicious raspberry granola that made a absolute perfect topping." (T. Katz)*

"I spent the weekend with a life-long friend at the Wedgwood Inn to celebrate her 40th birthday. We spent a lot of time talking about our lives both personal and professional. On Sunday we took time to talk with Carl about my dream of becoming an innkeeper. He was supportive and truly helpful and even sent me additional information. What a pleasure to find someone who is not sterile and negative about their vocation." (B. Blyshak)

"Normally I don't have to do business on vacation; but when that call came for me and I was out and about, the staff thought fast and helped me close a million-dollar deal! If they didn't have a fax machine and if I wasn't carrying my beeper, it would have fallen through. When Carl noticed I was wearing a beeper and asked for my pager number upon arrival I thought it was a little strange - why would an innkeeper want my pager number? As it turned out, he had great insight. He'd make a great stockbroker! I'll be back with my beeper - often." (J. Carsover)

Philadelphia

Thomas Bond House
129 South 2nd Street
Philadelphia, PA 19106
(215) 923-8523 or
(800) 845-BOND

Type of B&B: Inn.
Rooms: 12 with private bath.
Rates: 1 or 2/$80-150.

Rating: A+ or ♛♛♛ Excellent, far exceeds basic requirements.

Brick Federal inn built in the 1700's is located one mile off I-95 in the Independence National Historic Park and was the former residence of an early Philadelphia physician. There are twelve distinctive guest rooms with private bath, period furnishings, TV, and telephone. Two rooms offer queen-size beds, sofa beds, working fireplaces, and whirlpool baths. Reproduction furniture, maps, and accessories are offered in the Key and Quill gift shop located in the inn. Continental breakfast is served weekdays and a full breakfast on weekends. Facilities are available for meetings and social functions. 1 or 2/$80-150. AE, MC, V. 10% business travel discount. Travel agent.

Pocono/Canadensis

Brookview Manor
Route 447, RR #1, Box 365
Canadensis, PA 18325
(717) 595-2451

Type of B&B: Small inn.
Rooms: 8, 6 with private bath.
Rates: 1/$55-125; 2/$65-135.

Rating: B- or ♛♛ Good, exceeds basic requirements.

Edwardian Manor home is nestled on four acres in the heart of the Pocono Mountains, 15 miles north of Stroudsburg and I-80. Eight guest rooms feature panoramic views of woods, mountains, and a stream; six have a private bath. Popular activities at the inn include sitting in the glider on the large wrap-around porch, hiking the wooded trails, fishing in the stocked stream, relaxing on the sunporch with views of the brook and surrounding landscape, and playing lawn games. Area attractions include skiing, golfing, boating, and shopping at antique and outlet stores. Full breakfast includes fresh fruit, choice of juice, homemade muffins and specialties such as French toast L'Orange served with pure maple syrup and Auntie Lucille's frittata stuffed with cheese, eggs, broccoli, and artichoke hearts. Small function rooms available. Restricted smoking. 1/$55-125; 2/$65-135. AE, MC, V. Travel agent.

Guests write: *"This was my first stay at a B&B and I'm sold! We hope to come again next year. We greatly appreciated the early check-in and late check-out, help in making dinner reservations, and getting suggestions on things to do." (P. Ness)*

"I have enjoyed many pleasant visits to the Brookview. The new innkeepers have kept up the warmth and hospitality of the inn. The private waterfalls are a must-see." (B. Sulth)

"The walk from the property on a well-marked trail to a waterfall at the back was very enjoyable. We also enjoyed the wonderful breakfast in the beautiful, bright breakfast room." (J. Shepard)

"My husband and I were so impressed with the atmosphere, the aesthetics of this cozy inn lodged in the woods that we knew on our walk to their falls that we had made the right choice. We were so impressed that we have given weekend certificates as shower, wedding, and Christmas gifts to our friends and family. We're thrilled to say that everyone has loved it as much as us and that they, too, have been using these weekend getaway certificates as gifts to their friends and relatives." (K. Coar)

Sayre

Paetzell Haus Bed & Breakfast
211 West Lockhart Street
Sayre, PA 18840
(717) 888-4748

Type of B&B: Guesthouse.
Rooms: 5, 2 with private bath.
Rates: 1 or 2/$35-45.

Rating: C or ♛ Acceptable, meets basic requirements.

Historic Victorian home located midway between Corning and Binghamton, New York is located off Route 17 in the center of Sayre, one block from the Robert Packer Hospital and Guthrie Clinic. There are five guest rooms which feature counted cross-stitch name plates on doors, and double or twin beds; two offer a private bath. Popular attractions in the area include the Finger Lakes, Corning Glass factory, Mark Twain drama, museums, hunting, fishing, and tennis. Full Pennsylvania Dutch breakfast includes sausage, scrapple, buckwheat cakes, and shoo-fly pie. No smoking. Two resident cats. 1 or 2/$35-45. 10% senior discount. Travel agent.

Slippery Rock

Applebutter Inn
152 Applewood Lane
Slippery Rock, PA 16057
(412) 794-1844

Type of B&B: Inn.
Rooms: 11 with private bath.
Rates: 1/$55-81; 2/$69-115.

Rating: A+ or ♛♛♛ Excellent, far exceeds basic requirements.

Federal Colonial inn built in 1844 is nestled in the rolling green meadows of rural Western Pennsylvania, 3 miles southeast of I-79 exit 30. Choose from eleven guest rooms, each with unique decor, antique furnishings, and private bath. Special features of the inn include 12-inch brick walls on a hand-cut stone foundation, exposed brick fireplaces, and original chestnut and poplar floors. The main floor offers a relaxing sitting room and parlor with fireplace. Area recreation includes golf, bicycling, jogging, and country walks. Cafe on the premises serves lunch on Tuesday-Sunday. Full breakfast. Families welcome. No smoking. 1/$55-81; 2/$69-115. MC, V. Travel agent.

Guests write: *"Exceptionally clean, neat and tidy! Breakfast was served hot and hearty. I love the decorating." (C. Sampson)*

"On a cold February night I've never felt such comfort and warmth. It's a true feeling of being brought back to the ambiance of the 1800's but with the 1990's standard of excellence." (C. Kohnfelder)

"All the kind people at Applebutter Inn and Schoolhouse cafe made our anniversary a very special one. Tell them to come out with their own cookbook and I will be the first to buy it even if it cost $50." (L. Herrod)

"The atmosphere was so elegant, but still cozy. The breakfast was delicious - there was no room for improvements. From the moment we arrived until departure we were thrilled." (E. Cratty)

Smethport

Blackberry Inn Bed & Breakfast
820 West Main Street
Smethport, PA 16749-1039
(814) 887-7777

Type of B&B: Small inn.
Rooms: 5 rooms share 2 full baths.
Rates: 1/$38-43; 2/$42-47.

Rating: B+ or ♛♛ Good, exceeds basic requirements.

Victorian home with gingerbread detailing was built in 1890 and is situated in a small town located northeast of the Allegheny National Forest off Route 6 and PA-59. Five guest rooms share two full baths and offer twin, king, full, or queen-size beds. A Victorian parlor on the main floor is a popular area to read, converse, view TV, play table games, and work on a jigsaw puzzle. Two spacious porches look out onto mountain scenes. Area attractions include Allegheny Mountains and National Forest, Kinzua Bridge State Park and Dam, and Allegheny Reservoir plus America's first Christmas Store. Full breakfast includes fruit, juice, homebaked muffins or breads, and a hot entree. Families welcome. No smoking. 1/$38-43; 2/$42-47.

Stroudsburg

Country Roots
203 Keller Drive
Stroudsburg, PA 18360
(717) 992-5557

Type of B&B: B&B home.
Rooms: 1 with private bath.
Rates: 1 or 2/$50-75.

Rating: C+ or ♛ Acceptable, meets basic requirements.

Country Roots is a gambrel-style log cabin guest house located four miles south of Stroudsburg near I-80 and PA-33. It features a private bath, large cathedral room with sitting area, double bed and daybed, and library with TV, tapes, and games. There are large gardens to explore on-site along with an herb shop and garden tours. The Pocono Mountain region nearby offers skiing, fishing, golf, tennis, and hunting. Continental breakfast includes homemade muffins, jams, and jellies. Restricted smoking. 1 or 2/$50-75; $15/extra person. Business travel discount. Travel agent.

Thorndale

Pheasant Hollow Farm B&B
South Bailey Road, P.O. Box 356
Thorndale, PA 19372
(215) 384-4694

Type of B&B: B&B home.
Rooms: 2 with shared bath.
Rates: 1/$50-60; 2/$65-75.

Rating: B+ or ♕♕ Good, exceeds basic requirements.

Historic post and beam constructed country home on several acres is 1 mile from Business Route 30 and convenient to Pennsylvania Turnpike exit 23. Choose from two fireplaced guest rooms with poster beds which share a bath. Explore the property which offers a restored spring house, pond, stream, gardens, and woods, or relax and have breakfast in the solarium. Area attractions include Longwood Gardens, Brandywine River Museum, Hagley Museum, Winterthur, and Valley Forge. Full breakfast. Families welcome. No smoking. Wheelchair access. 1/$50-60; 2/$65-75. Travel agent.

Wilkes-Barre/Dallas

Ponda-Rowland Bed & Breakfast
R.R. 1, Box 349
Dallas, PA 18612-9604
(717) 639-3245 anytime
or (800) 950-9130 (12-4 p.m.)

Type of B&B: Inn on a working farm.
Rooms: 3 with private bath.
Rates: 1 or 2/$50-60.

Rating: B+ or ♕♕ Good, exceeds basic requirements.

Mid-nineteenth-century plank frame home with beamed ceilings has a rural setting and is located 10 miles northwest of Wilkes-Barre off Route 309. Three guest rooms with private bath have been furnished with American Colonial antiques and country accents. Guests are invited to relax on the enclosed front porch or sit in front of the fire in the Great Room. Popular activities in the area include fishing at the family trout fishing park just up the road, local rail tours, Pocono Downs, canoeing, swimming, skiing, and tobogganing. Hay rides are offered on-site with advance notice as well as visits with the farm's animals. A master timberframe craftsman has a shop on the premises. A hearty breakfast is served by the fire in the Great Room. Families welcome. Restricted smoking. 1 or 2/$50-60. MC, V. Travel agent.

Guests write: *"We were pleased with the accommodations, the area, touring the workshop, the genuine feeling of relaxation, and how much the Rowlands made us feel at home." (E. Strollo)*

"Mr. Rowland gave us all a ride up on top of the hill to see their geese, pigs, sheep, and rabbits. It was fall and being on top of a hill, the view was beautiful. It is fun staying here because we are treated like family, having the use of the property to swing, walk, play ball, swim, and watch TV." (M. Pilger)

"Any American antique furniture collector would be in awe of all the Rowland's furnishings, from the pewter to the antique tools in the converted dairy barn which is now a wood-working shop. Everything was clean and the antique furnishings made one feel like you were stepping back in time visiting a country farm." (V. Wright)

"Our room was clean and decorated in lovely antique fashion. The bed was especially comfortable and the sheets were the softest we have ever slept on. Our breakfast was delicious and plentiful consisting of fresh fruits, orange juice, blueberry and corn pancakes, and delicious fresh-brewed coffee. After breakfast we took a walk around the 130 acres and enjoyed ourselves as we encountered snow geese and numerous birds." (S. Buzzoro)

York

Briarwold Bed and Breakfast
RD 24, Box 469
York, PA 17406
(717) 252-4619

Type of B&B: B&B home.
Rooms: 3 share 2 baths.
Rates: 1 or 2/$60.

Rating: B+ or ♛♛ Good, exceeds basic requirements.

Set in the rolling hills of York Country, this brick Colonial dating back to 1830 is 7 miles east of York on Route 462 (Market Street), just one half mile past the Village of Hallem. Choose from three guest rooms which share two baths. Visit nearby Gettysburg Battlefield or ski Round Top. A full country breakfast is served. 1 or 2/$60. 10% senior discount.

York/Brogue

The Miller House
Route 1, Box 742
Brogue, PA 17309
(717) 927-9646
Fax: (717) 927-6538

Type of B&B: B&B home.
Rooms: 3 with shared bath.
Rates: $75/room or $200 for house.

Rating: B or ♛♛ Good, exceeds basic requirements.

Historic Colonial home built in 1850 is located in a small village southeast of York on Route 74. Three guest rooms with private bath are available. Popular attractions in the area include historic sites, Amish settlements, canoeing, hiking, and antique shopping. Full breakfast includes fresh fruit, meat, eggs, and souffle or casserole. Lunch and dinner are available by advance reservation. Facilities for functions is available in the Grist Mill. Families welcome. Restricted smoking. $75/room; $200/house. MC, V. 10% family and business travel discount.

Guests write: *"The Marino's let us roam their peach and apple orchard. We really had a great time in the old Miller's house by the creek. We highly recommend this B&B for a quiet, private getaway in the country." (M. Banks)*

"This is a winter wonderland. The proprietors, Ed and Sharon Marino, are both generous and accommodating. It's such a pleasure to stay at the Miller House." (A. Rutter)

"We were wined and dined and enjoyed the interaction with hosts and their family. We have grown comfortable with the house on Otter Creek and will return as often as we can." (A. Becker)

Puerto Rico

Ceiba Country Inn
Carr # 977 KM 1.2
Ceiba, Puerto Rico 00735
(809) 885-0471
Fax: (809) 885-0471

Type of B&B: Large inn.
Rooms: 9 with private bath.
Rates: 1/$45; 2/$55.

Rating: Unrated at the time this book went to press.

Tropical architecture graces this fifteen-year-old countryside inn located on the east coast of Puerto Rico, thirty-five miles southwest of San Juan. There are nine guest rooms washed in white walls with colorful pillows, curtains, and bedspreads. Guests enjoy the palm trees and sea breezes as well as the surrounding ocean views and rolling hills. Visit nearby Luquino Beach, Seven Seas Beach, El Yunque Rain Forest, and the five marinas that are within twenty miles. Continental breakfast includes homebaked nut breads and a selection of tropical fruit. Function rooms available for small meetings. Families welcome. 1/$45; 2/$55. AE, MC, V. Travel agent.

Newport

Admiral Fitzroy Inn
398 Thames Street
Newport, RI 02840
(401) 848-8018, 848-8019 or
(800) 343-2863.

Type of B&B: Large inn.
Rooms: 18 with private bath.
Rates: 1 or 2/$65-150.

Rating: A- or ♛♛♛ Excellent, far exceeds basic requirements.

Admiral Fitzroy Inn is listed on the National Register of Historic Places and located in the heart of Newport's waterfront district, 1.5 hours from Boston. Choose from eighteen guest rooms with private bath and unique hand-painted walls. The inn's roof-deck offers views of the harbor. The narrow streets of this old seaport town boast examples of Victorian architecture, Colonial houses, and summer cottage mansions along with Fort Adams, restaurants, art galleries, and shops. A full breakfast includes muffins, hot entrees, fresh fruit, croissants and is served in the breakfast room or taken up to guest rooms. Complimentary beverages are served each evening. Meeting facilities available. Families welcome. Wheelchair access. 1 or 2/$65-150 with off-season discounts. AE, MC, V. Travel agent.

Newport

Melville House
39 Clarke Street
Newport, RI 02840
(401) 847-0640

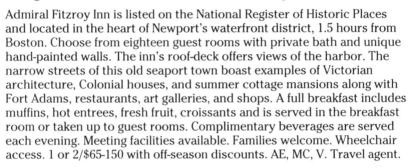

Type of B&B: Inn.
Rooms: 7, 5 with private bath.
Rates: 1 or 2/$40-95.

Rating: B+ or ♛♛ Good, exceeds basic requirements.

Historic Colonial home built in 1750 is located in Newport's Historic District and offers off-street parking behind the inn. Choose from seven guest rooms with antique furnishings; five have a private bath. Walk to Newport's interesting boutiques and restaurants from the inn as well as the Brick Market, Touro Synagogue, and Trinity Church. Popular attractions in the area include beaches, mansion tours, sailing, Cliff Walk, and 10-mile Ocean Drive. Continental breakfast includes homemade muffins and bread, granola, and yogurt. Complimentary evening beverages are offered. 1 or 2/$40-95. AE, MC, V.

Guests write: *"We continue to visit Newport several times a year. We always stay at Melville House because the hospitality here adds as much as any Newport sight or event to the pleasure of a weekend getaway. Friends and relatives often join us and Rita and Sam, the innkeepers, make newcomers feel as welcome as us old-timers. On learning that my husband is a student of architecture and historic preservation, Sam had him climbing up into the rafters and down into the original basement to see how his house is put together. When we arrived for a weekend's anniversary celebration, we discovered our lovely room decorated with balloons."* (B. Ismael)

"The accommodations are comfortable with a quiet elegance. Much is done to ensure a guest's comfort with excellent reading materials and extra pillows and blankets. In addition, the house itself is like a mini-museum with lots of beautiful paintings and antiques. Breakfast is a treat. Homemade muffins and delicious coffee, granola, and yogurt. All this is served on exquisite china." (A. Calkins)

"A group of us (seven couples) wanted a place to gather where we could feel free to use the house during our reunion and not bother anyone. Rita and Sam were the perfect hosts and Melville House the perfect place." (P. Willey)

Providence

The Old Court Bed & Breakfast
144 Benefit Street
Providence, RI 02903
(401) 751-2002 or 351-0747.

Type of B&B: Large inn.
Rooms: 11 with private bath.
Rates: 1/$95-110; 2/$110-140.

Rating: B or ♛♛ Good, exceeds basic requirements.

Italianate brick home built in 1863 overlooks the Capitol and downtown Providence and is located on historic Benefit Street. Choose from eleven guest rooms with private bath and modified Victorian beds that are both unique and comfortable. Some rooms offer wet bars and all have been decorated to reflect the Victorian period. The common room features nineteenth-century decor with ornate Italian mantelpieces, plaster moldings, and twelve-foot ceilings. Walk to downtown in three minutes or to the nearby campuses of Brown University, Rhode Island School of Design or the city's East Side with its interesting architecture and shops including Benefit Street's collection of Colonial and Victorian houses. Continental breakfast includes homemade breads. A fax machine and private telephones for guest rooms are available along with function rooms for weddings and meetings. 1/$95-110; 2/$110-140. AE, MC, V. 10% business discount. Travel agent.

Westerly/Charlestown

Inn the Meadow
1045 Shannock Road
Charlestown, RI 02813
(401) 789-1473

Type of B&B: Small inn.
Rooms: 4 with shared bath.
Rates: 1/$32-40; 2/$40-50.

Rating: C+ or ♛ Acceptable, meets basic requirements.

Garrison-style home is situated in a secluded country setting located 9 miles from the University of Rhode Island or 30 miles south of Providence off Route 1 South. Four guest rooms feature twin, queen, or king-size beds, hand stenciled walls, and share baths. One room with queen-size bed features a private deck overlooking the garden below. Popular activities here include exploring the five acres of surrounding countryside, visiting the stained-glass workshop at the inn, and sitting by the fireplace in the evening. Six of Rhode Island's beaches are just minutes away offering swimming, surfing, and sailing. Visit nearby bird-watching sites, hiking trails, biking roads, and ponds for canoeing. Area attractions include Theatre-by-the-Sea, Westerly Center for the Arts, Mystic Seaport, Marine Life Aquarium, and Groton submarine base. Full breakfast. No smoking. 1/$32-40; 2/$40-50. MC, V. Travel agent.

Guests write: *"Some of the small touches that are memorable are the books and novels available to peruse, the basket in the bathroom containing extra toothbrushes, razors, soap, and other toiletries one sometimes forgets to pack, and variety of menus from different local restaurants. Breakfast was a tempting array of treats each day with so many delicious choices very prettily presented." (M. Rafael-Flynn)*

"For this (current) visit, there were additions to the old hat collection on the dining room wall, new details in the bedroom, seasonal treats on the breakfast menu, and lots of suggestions for restaurants and activities in the area. When hosts bother to remove the extra seating and tables from the breakfast room to make the lone winter weekend guests feel comfortable, you know the place is well run." (E. Greenfield)

"Taking the immaculate neatness and the cozy creature comforts as a given, I would like to stress that this place is good for your mood, for your peace of mind. Quiet nature, off the beaten path, with well-kept grounds big enough to be by yourself or in company. Nothing phony!" (H. Taussig)

Westerly

Shelter Harbor Inn
10 Wagner Road
Westerly, RI 02891
(401) 322-8883

Type of B&B: Country inn.
Rooms: 24 with private bath.
Rates: 1/$54-96; 2/$64-106.

Rating: B or ♛♛ Good, exceeds basic requirements.

Historic Colonial country inn with restaurant located just off Routes 1 and 78, was built in 1810 and has a rural setting surrounded by fields, stone walls, and gardens. Ten guest rooms with private bath are available in the main house and several feature fireplaces. Families and business travelers will appreciate the fourteen guest rooms with private bath located in the large, converted barn and guest house. Popular activities at this inn include sunning on the private beach, paddle tennis games, and a large hot tub. Area attractions include golf, tennis, swimming, bicycling, Mystic Seaport, Marinelife Aquarium, and ferry to Block Island. Full breakfast is served daily and included in the rates. Other meals are available at the restaurant. Families welcome. Facilities available for meetings and social functions. 1/$54-96; 2/$64-106. AE, MC, V. 10% auto club and senior discounts. Travel agent.

Beaufort

Bay Street Inn
601 Bay Street
Beaufort, SC 29902
(803) 524-7720

Type of B&B: Inn.
Rooms: 6 with private bath.
Rates: 1/$65-75; 2/$70-80.

Rating: B+ or ♛♛ Good, exceeds basic requirements.

Historic planters mansion built in 1852 is located on the river within the historic district and has been recently used as a movie location. Six guest rooms are offered, each with bath, fireplace, antiques, and river views. Area attractions include fine restaurants, historic tours, beaches, golf, and tennis. Borrow bicycles to explore the area. Full breakfast is served daily along with complimentary fruit basket upon arrival and evening chocolates. 1/$65-75; 2/$70-80. MC, V. 10% business travel and military officer discounts. Travel agent.

Beaufort

The Rhett House Inn
1009 Craven Street
Beaufort, SC 29902
(803) 524-9030

Type of B&B: Inn with restaurant.
Rooms: 10 with private bath.
Rates: 1/$70-110; 2/$80-120.

Rating: A+ or ♛♛♛ Excellent, far exceeds basic requirements.

Historic antebellum plantation built in 1820 is located in the historic downtown area one block from the Intracoastal Waterway. Each of the eight guest rooms with private bath offers period antique furnishings, fresh flowers, homespun quilts and several rooms have working fireplaces. The inn has a billiards room and large veranda for evening entertainment or quiet relaxation. Within walking distance of the inn is the recently restored waterfront area, fine restaurants, and specialty shops. Area attractions include beaches, fishing, sailing, wind-surfing, golf, tennis, hunting, and horseback riding. A full breakfast is included in the rates and gourmet dining is available in the restaurant. No smoking. 1/$70-110; 2/$80-120. MC, V. Travel agent.

Gatlinburg

Butcher House in the Mountains
1520 Garrett Lane
Route 2, Box 750
Gatlinburg, TN 37738
(615) 436-9457

Type of B&B: B&B inn.
Rooms: 5, 4 with private bath.
Rates: 1/$65; 2/$65-90.

Rating: A+ or ♛♛♛ Excellent, far exceeds basic requirements.

Swiss chalet nestled high in the Smoky Mountains is located 2,800 feet (3 miles) from Gatlinburg near the entrance to Smoky Mountain National Park. Choose from five guest rooms, four with private bath. Relax in one of several spacious living rooms with fireplaces. There is a full, stocked kitchen with small dining area just for guests. The chalet's deck offers an outstanding view of mountains and the valley below. Area attractions include Dollywood, Ober Gatlinburg, outlet malls, horseback riding, white-water rafting, golf, fishing, and tennis. Full breakfast is served on fine china with lace table linens and crystal glasses. Restricted smoking. 1/$65; 2/$65-90. MC, V. Auto club discounts.

"Guests write: *"I have never enjoyed a B&B as much as Butcher House and we have stayed in many in Europe and in the States. The food was absolutely fantastic and the hospitality the best."* (B. Gaines)

"The rooms were beautiful and the food was delicious. We had plenty of privacy but we were close enough to downtown to enjoy the tourist attractions." (M. Barfield)

"Everything about Butcher House was marvelous from the congenial host couple and exquisitely decorated rooms to the gourmet food. High up in the Smoky Mountains, this is what a B&B should be. Take some time before exploring Gatlinburg and environs and do what we did - sit in the old-fashioned porch swing, breath that clean mountain air, and feast your eyes on the view." (A. Wagner)

Greenville

Hilltop House Bed & Breakfast Inn
Route 7, Box 180
Greeneville, TN 37743
(615) 639-8202

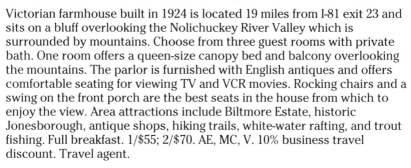

Type of B&B: B&B inn.
Rooms: 3 with private bath.
Rates: 1/$55; 2/$70.

Rating: B+ or ♛♛ Good, exceeds basic requirements.

Victorian farmhouse built in 1924 is located 19 miles from I-81 exit 23 and sits on a bluff overlooking the Nolichuckey River Valley which is surrounded by mountains. Choose from three guest rooms with private bath. One room offers a queen-size canopy bed and balcony overlooking the mountains. The parlor is furnished with English antiques and offers comfortable seating for viewing TV and VCR movies. Rocking chairs and a swing on the front porch are the best seats in the house from which to enjoy the view. Area attractions include Biltmore Estate, historic Jonesborough, antique shops, hiking trails, white-water rafting, and trout fishing. Full breakfast. 1/$55; 2/$70. AE, MC, V. 10% business travel discount. Travel agent.

Monteagle

Edgeworth Inn
Box 340
Monteagle, TN 37356
(615) 924-2669 or 924-2476

Type of B&B: Inn.
Rooms: 9 with private bath.
Rates: 1 or 2/$55-85.

Rating: A or ♛♛♛ Excellent, far exceeds basic requirements.

Historic Victorian inn built in 1896 has been totally restored and is located on the grounds of famed Monteagle Assembly, 1 mile from I-24, exit 134. There are nine guest rooms with private bath. One large suite offers a king-size bed, living room with double sofa bed, and full kitchen. A large parlor on the main floor has a large collection of books and an inviting fireplace. Area attractions include South Cumberland State Recreation Area with 120 miles of hiking trails, University of the South, (a Gothic replica of Oxford University), and spectacular scenery at Cathedral Falls and Fiery Gizard Trail. Continental breakfast. Families welcome. 1 or 2/$55-85. A fee is charged to enter Monteagle Assembly during several weeks in the summer. Travel agent.

Guests write: *"I particularly enjoyed the original art collection. Even in the bathroom, the walls were covered with lovely original etchings. The library was filled with shelves and shelves of diverse reading materials and the fireplace and cushy, comfortable chairs made this a delicious place to read away the evening. The porch has many wonderful rocking chairs for just sitting and visiting. "(B. McLure)*

"The huge king-size beds are the most comfortable beds I have ever slept in. Wendy makes a wonderful sourdough bread and when I told her how much I like it, she gave me a loaf and some of her starter dough to take home so I could bake my own." (K. Hessinger)

Townsend

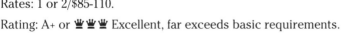

Richmont Inn
220 Winterberry Lane
Townsend, TN 37882
(615) 448-6751

Type of B&B: Large inn.
Rooms: 10 with private bath.
Rates: 1 or 2/$85-110.

Rating: A+ or ♛♛♛ Excellent, far exceeds basic requirements.

Secluded inn built in the style of the Appalachian Cantilever barn is located 35 minutes southeast of Knoxville. Ten guest rooms offer a private bath, spa tubs for two, king-size beds, fireplaces, and balconies with mountain views. Furnishings reflect the local mountain history and culture. The living and dining rooms with 13-foot-high beamed ceilings, are decorated with 18th-century English antiques and French paintings. The Smoky Mountains National Park is a ten minute drive and offers hiking, fishing, bicycling, scenic drives, and tours of historic Cades Cove. Full breakfast and evening candlelight dessert are served overlooking the meadows of Laurel Valley and Rich Mountain. Wheelchair access. No smoking. 1 or 2/$85-110. Travel agent.

Houston

Durham House B&B
921 Heights Boulevard
Houston, TX 77008
(713) 868-4654

Type of B&B: Inn.
Rooms: 5, 4 with private bath.
Rate: 1/$45-60; 2/$60-75.

Rating: A or ♛♛♛ Excellent, far exceeds basic requirements.

Victorian style home with gingerbread trim is listed on the National
Register of Historic Places and located in an urban setting just five
minutes from downtown Houston, a half mile north of I-10, or less than a
mile south of loop 610 east. Choose from five guest rooms which feature
antique furnishings and claw-foot tubs; four have a private bath. The main
parlor offers a player piano and exits onto a large front porch with swing.
Area attractions include NASA, Texas Medical Center, Astrodome, five
museums, Memorial Park, hiking, golf, and tennis. Full breakfast is served
in the romantic dining room or in bed. Families welcome. Weddings can
be accommodated in a garden gazebo. No smoking. 1/$45-60; 2/$60-75. AE,
MC, V. Travel agent.

Jefferson

McKay House Bed & Breakfast Inn
306 East Delta Street
Jefferson, TX 75657
(903) 665-7322, or
from Dallas (214) 348-1929

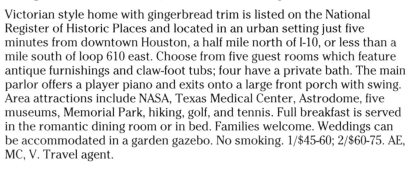

Type of B&B: Inn and cottage.
Rooms: 5 rooms or suites
with private bath.

Rate: 1 or 2/$70-125.

Rating: AA or ♛♛♛♛ Outstanding.

Historic Greek Revival inn with Victorian cottage was built in 1851 and is
located 3 blocks east of Highway 59, 16 miles north of I-20. Each of the five
guest rooms offers a private bath, antique furnishings, fresh flowers, and
selection of Victorian night clothes guests can use. Area attractions and
recreation include lakes, forests, Louisiana bayou, antique shops, boat
tours, theaters, golf, and fishing. Full breakfast specialties include Chicken

a la McKay, shirred eggs, and strawberry soup served in the garden conservatory. Families welcome. No smoking. 1 or 2/$70-125. MC, V. Travel agent.

Guests write: *"Furnished in antiques from the period of the house, guests may often sleep in the Victorian gowns and sleep shirts provided in each room. A full plantation breakfast is served in the conservatory with the ladies encouraged to choose a hat to wear to breakfast. The hosts are happy not only to recommend restaurants and things to see and do, but will also make reservations and purchase tickets for guests." (N. Cox)*

"Every corner of the inn is filled with interesting antiques and unique decorating touches that delight your senses and stir your memories. Breakfasts are satisfying presentations including homemade muffins, unique juices, local jams and jellies, and McKay House original main dishes, all blended with lively conversation among guests and hosts." (L. MacNeil-Watkins)

San Antonio

Bullis House Inn
621 Pierce Street
San Antonio, TX 78208
(512) 223-9426

Type of B&B: Small inn.
Rooms: 8, 2 with private bath.
Rates: 1/$36-55; 2/$40-59.

Rating: B or ♛♛ Good, exceeds basic requirements.

Neoclassical, white-columned mansion is located 2 miles northeast of downtown San Antonio off I-35. Choose from eight guest rooms which feature fourteen-foot ceilings, color TV, and air conditioning. Each room has been individually decorated in soft colors with antique reproductions and period pieces. Deluxe rooms offer a working fireplace, French windows, and brass beds. The inn's original architectural features have been preserved and include oak stairways, parquet floors, marble fireplaces, and crystal chandeliers. The inn has a swimming pool on the premises. Area attractions include Old Army Museum, Fort Sam Houston, Alamo, Sea World, Fiesta Texas, and missions. Continental breakfast. Function rooms are available for weddings and meetings. Families are welcome in special second floor rooms that can accommodate parties of six. 1/$36-55; 2/$40-59. AE, MC, V. Travel agent.

Waxahachie

The Bonnynook Bed and Breakfast Inn
414 West Main Street
Waxahachie, TX 75165
(214) 937-7207

Type of B&B: Inn.
Rooms: 4, with private bath.
Rate: 1 or 2/$60-90.

Rating: A or ♛♛♛ Excellent, far exceeds basic requirements.

Turn-of-the-century Victorian inn with wide porches and gingerbread accents is located 30 miles south of Dallas on I-35. Four antique furnished guest rooms offer a private bath and feature unique antiques such as a sleigh bed, Belgium antique bed, and 1920's Art Deco pieces. Several rooms have Jacuzzi tubs. Walk two blocks to the historic Town Square with its 1850 Courthouse. Nearby attractions include the largest concentration of Victorian gingerbread homes in the state as well as several antique shops, malls, and fine restaurants. Full breakfast. Function rooms are available for meetings and social occasions. Families welcome. Restricted smoking. 1 or 2/$60-90. AE, MC, V. Travel agent.

Guests write: *"The room made us feel the romance of the last century and the bubble bath was great. They've added so many unique touches. We'll never forget the delicious breakfasts." (S. Peak)*

"I can't think of a better way to spend a birthday than going away with the man you love and have been married to for almost fourteen years and coming to such a wonderful place as Bonneynook. We had a great time relaxing, taking a bubble-bath in the old claw-foot tub and just enjoying each other without the kids." (C. Parga)

"This was a wonderful retreat from the everyday hustle and bustle and we didn't hear a phone ring once!" (B. Burns)

"We ended our Christmas holiday with dinner at the Bonneynook. This stay was our first experience at B&Bs and it's just the prescription for two busy professionals from the big city. Bonneynook allowed us to imagine and experience what life was like when the world wasn't so busy faxing a report or E-mailing a memo. We'll carry the Bonnynook's grace and charm with us as we enter 1992." (P. Borchardt)

"We appreciated all the amenities, the sample menus from local restaurants, the fresh fruit tray, the tea and coffee service, the decanter of wine after our return from dinner, the three-course breakfast, the charming hospitality, and the Frank's Room with the beautiful Jacuzzi tub." (M. Matthews)

Park City

Washington School Inn
P.O. Box 536, 543 Park Avenue
Park City, UT 84060
(801) 649-3800

Type of B&B: Inn.
Rooms: 12 guest rooms and 3 suites, all with private bath.
Rate: 1 or 2/$75-225.

Rating: AA or ♛ ♛ ♛ ♛ Outstanding.

Grand Victorian mansion built in 1889 has been completely restored and is now listed on the National Register of Historic Places. It's location is an urban residential area of Park City, 25 miles east of Salt Lake City. Each of the twelve guest rooms and three suites has a private bath and phone. A large suite on the third floor can easily accommodate families or couples traveling together. Popular attractions at the inn include the hot tub, sauna, and steam showers. This is a year-round recreation area with lit night skiing, hiking in the mountains, lakes, fly fishing, wind-surfing, golf, tennis, and mountain biking. Full breakfast. Facilities available for small weddings and meetings. Restricted smoking. 1 or 2/$75-225. AE, MC, V. Travel agent.

Alburg

Thomas Mott Bed & Breakfast
Blue Rock Road, Route 2, Box 149B
Alburg, VT 05440
(802) 796-3736 or (800) 348-0843

Type of B&B: Inn.
Rooms: 4 with private bath.
Rates: 1 or 2/$50-65.

Rating: A- or ♕♕♕ Excellent, far exceeds basic requirements.

Historic farmhouse built in 1850 is located near the junctions of Route 78 and 2 on Northwestern Lake Champlain. There are four guest rooms with private bath, lake views, and homemade quilts. Popular attractions in the area include Missisquoi Wildlife Refuge, Auction House, Shrine of St. Anne, antique shops, and major ski areas of Montreal, Burlington, Stowe, Lake Placid, and Jay Peak. Year-round recreation includes ice fishing, snowmobiling, ice boating, cross-country skiing, golf, swimming, hiking, canoeing, and bicycling. Full breakfast is individually prepared for each guest. Gourmet catered dinners are available on advance notice. No smoking. 1 or 2/$50-65. MC, V. Travel agent.

Arlington

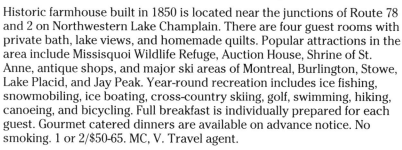

Hill Farm Inn
R.R. 2, Box 2015
Arlington, VT 05250
(802) 375-2269 or (800) 882-2545

Type of B&B: Inn.
Rooms: 13, 8 with private bath.
Rates: 1/$40-75; 2/$60-95.

Rating: B or ♕♕ Good, exceeds basic requirements.

Hill Farm Inn has served as a farm vacation for guests for over eighty-five years and is located in the southwest corner of the state on land which was once part of a historic land grant. There are thirteen rooms in the main inn or guest house; eight offer a private bath. The decor of each room captures the simplicity and charm of a traditional New England farmhouse. A large living room offers comfortable chairs, sofas, and a fireplace. Battenkill River borders the farm and is fun for canoeing and fly-fishing. Other attractions in the area include Bennington Museum, Green Mountain National Forest, antique shops, hiking, bicycling, and skiing. Full country breakfast is included in the rates and a four-course dinner is available at an additional charge by advance reservation. Homemade jam is a complimentary take-home gift. Families welcome. 1/$40-75; 2/$60-95. AE, MC, V. Travel agent.

Guests write: *"I am a manufacturer's representative traveling through Vermont every two months and I stay at Hill Farm Inn. My room is always warm and comfortable. The basket of apples is great for snacking and the jam to take home is appreciated long after my stay. The living room is special in winter with a roaring fire where you can relax with cheese, crackers, and a beverage before dinner. The meals are wonderful and always presented in a very appealing manner. The savings over local hotels is very important to me."* (M. Kelsey)

"Going to Hill Farm Inn is like going to our second home. Several years ago my husband and I switched from our comfortable room in the main inn to a cozy cabin overlooking the Battenkill Valley and Mt. Equinox. Our porch, complete with two lounge chairs, allows us to relax in the clear Vermont air as we watch buffalo graze in the pasture and listen to the crickets and birds chirping around it. It is truly idyllic. Both the countryside and inn itself are unspoiled and possess a gentle spirit that quietly renews the soul." (D. Giaimo)

"As a skier and big eater, I find breakfast and dinner, with fresh baked muffins and bread, to be pleasingly diversified, very good and more than adequate for an active life. Discount tow tickets are available at the inn which saves money and standing in line at the slopes. We feel Hill Farm is more than a place to sleep because the spacious public areas provide opportunities for socializing, reading, watching TV, and playing games." (G. Noble)

"To have your children see a bird hatch its eggs in a tree outside their window and watch her feed the little birds, or have them chase little rabbits, or walk down to see the cows nearby is what we love for our children to experience here. You can't get these experiences just anywhere." (L. Ryan)

Arlington

Inn at Sunderland
R.R. 2, Box 2440
Arlington, VT 05250
(802) 362-4213

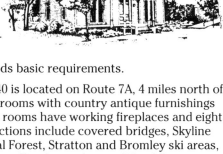

Type of B&B: Inn.
Rooms: 10, 8 with private bath.
Rates: 1 or 2/$70-105.

Rating: B+ or ♛♛ Good, exceeds basic requirements.

Historic farmhouse built in 1840 is located on Route 7A, 4 miles north of Arlington. There are ten guest rooms with country antique furnishings and mountain views. Six of the rooms have working fireplaces and eight offer a private bath. Area attractions include covered bridges, Skyline Drive, Green Mountain National Forest, Stratton and Bromley ski areas, and antique shops. Full breakfast. Families welcome. Wheelchair access. 2/$70-105. AE, MC, V.

Arlington

Shenandoah Farm
Battenkill Road
Arlington, VT 05250
(802) 375-6372

Type of B&B: B&B home.
Rooms: 5, 1 with private bath.
Rates: 1/$40; 2/$65.

Rating: B or ♛♛ Good, exceeds basic requirements.

Historic Colonial home located on Route 313 is 5 miles from Route 7A and near the Battenkill River. There are five antique-filled guest rooms and one offers a private bath. There are several common rooms on the main floor including a formal living room, dining room, and large family room with fireplace. Area attractions include Norman Rockwell Museum, antique shops, fishing, canoeing, and inner-tubing on the Battenkill River nearby, and downhill and cross-country skiing. Full breakfast is served on china and usually offers fresh cinnamon rolls with the main hot entree. Families welcome. Restricted smoking. 1/$40; 2/$65. Travel agent.

Barnet

The Old Homestead
Box 35
Barnet, VT 05821
(802) 633-4100

Type of B&B: B&B home.
Rooms: 5, 2 with private bath.
Rates: 1/$35-45; 2/$45-55.

Rating: C+ or ♛ Acceptable, meets basic requirements.

1850's Colonial-Federalist style home first opened to the public in 1919 and is set in a rural area convenient to the interstate. Choose from five guest rooms, two with private bath. Visit nearby attractions in "Vermont's Northeast Kingdom," or just relax in this traditional Vermont bed and breakfast which emphasizes a quiet and friendly atmosphere. Continental breakfast includes muffins or scones, fruit, and cheeses. 1/$35-45; 2/$45-55.

Barre

Woodruff House
13 East Street
Barre, VT 05641
(802) 476-7745 or 479-9381

Type of B&B: B&B home.
Rooms: 2 with private bath.
Rates: 1/$50; 2/$65.

Rating: A or ♛♛♛ Excellent, far exceeds basic requirements.

Historic Queen Anne Victorian home is situated across from a quiet park near the village center and located halfway between Boston and Montreal at I-89, exit 7. There are two guest rooms available with private bath. Each is individually decorated with antiques, eclectic furnishings, and collectibles. There are two large common rooms which offer comfortable seating for viewing TV, quiet nooks for reading or conversing, and a large collection of interesting books. Area attractions include state capitol, tour of the largest granite quarries in the world, and leaf peeping. Full breakfast is served with fine china, crystal, and silver in the formal dining room. No smoking. 1/$50; 2/$65.

Guests write: *Robert and Terry prepared tea, crackers, cheese, and sliced fruits for us when we arrived very tired and hungry. They also prepared a late night snack for us before we went to bed. This was our first opportunity to stay at a B&B and we're now convinced if they're all like the Woodruff House we shall be customers for life."* (R. Sunday)

"We are the family of Dr. John H. Woodruff who brought his family back here to visit his brother and family. We were privileged to get to stay in his family home. It had been restored and was in great shape. The whole Woodruff family feels very fortunate to have our house in such beautiful shape and in such friendly hands." (J. Woodruff)

"Bob & Terry's sincere concern for our comfort and pleasure was unmatched by any other experience we've had in a B&B. The table was set with the finest details in this most authentic Victorian home. I stepped back in time." (B. Pivnick)

"After sleeping soundly under down comforters, we enjoyed warm conversation by candlelight over breakfast in an elegant dining room. We would choose this delightful bargain over a hotel or a condominium for any of our Vermont ski vacations." (G. Hills)

Brandon

The Moffett House
69 Park Street
Brandon, VT 05733
(802) 247-3843 or (800) 752-5794

Type of B&B: Small inn.
Rooms: 6, 4 with private bath.
Rates: 1/$65; 2/$95.

Rating: A or ♕♕♕ Excellent, far exceeds basic requirements.

Victorian home in a traditional New England village setting is located at the junctions of Routes 7 North and 73 East. Six guest rooms are available, four with private bath. Special features of some rooms include Jacuzzi tubs, four-poster beds, and sitting areas. The house is filled with a collection of Teddy Bears, Franklin Mint books and soldiers, Waterford crystal, and Oriental rugs. A living room on the main floor offers a fireplace, game table, and piano. It is a short walk from the inn to the village center. Nearby recreation includes Killington and Pico ski areas, Lake Dunmore, hiking, golf, tennis, and antiquing. Full country breakfast features homemade muffins, seasonal fruits, and homecooked hot entree. Dinners are available upon request and by advance reservation. Families welcome. Wheelchair access. Restricted smoking. 1/$65; 2/$95. MC, V. Travel agent.

Chester

Henry Farm Inn
Green Mountain Turnpike
P.O. Box 646
Chester, VT 05143
(802) 875-2674

Type of B&B: Inn.
Rooms: 7 with private bath.
Rates: 1/$35-53; 2/$50-80.

Rating: B+ or ♕♕ Good, exceeds basic requirements.

Historic Colonial farmhouse situated on fifty forested acres of foothills was built in 1750 and is located ten miles from I-91 near Routes 103 and 11. There are seven guest rooms with private bath and several of the rooms feature working fireplaces. There are two fireplaced sitting rooms on the main floor for reading, conversing, and relaxation. Area recreation includes skiing, hiking, fishing, golf, and tennis. Full breakfast. Families welcome. No smoking. 1/$35-53; 2/$50-80. MC, V.

Craftsbury Common

Inn on the Common
Main Street, P.O. Box 75
Craftsbury Common, VT 05827
(802) 586-9619 or (800) 521-2233

Type of B&B: Country inn with restaurant.
Rooms: 16 with private bath.
Rates: 1/$130-235; 2/$200-260.

Rating: A+ or ♕♕♕ Excellent, far exceeds basic requirements.

Inn on the Common consists of three white clapboard, Federal-style buildings surrounded by landscaped gardens and offering a panoramic view of the village and Green Mountains. There are sixteen guest rooms available and each features a custom quilt, antique furnishings, warm wallpaper, original artwork, and private bath. The library and living room offer areas for quiet reading or conversing. The inn offers clay tennis courts, lawn croquet, swimming pool, mountain biking, skiing, and a structured walking tour on the premises. Several golf courses are nearby. A full breakfast and five-course dinner are included in the daily rates. Function rooms are available for meetings and weddings. Families welcome. Restricted smoking. 1/$130-235; 2/$200-260. MC, V. Travel agent.

Fairlee

Silver Maple Lodge
R.R. 1, Box 8
South Main Street
Fairlee, VT 05045
(802) 333-4326 or
(800) 666-1946

Type of B&B: Inn with cottages.
Rooms: 12, 10 with private bath.
Rates: 1/$38-58; 2/$42-62.

Rating: B or ♛♛ Good, exceeds basic requirements.

Historic Victorian country inn, circa 1855, is on Route 5, half a mile south
of I-91, exit 15. Choose from twelve antique-furnished guest rooms, ten
with private bath. Private cottage accommodations offer knotty pine
walls and wide board floors of lumber cut on the property. Relax on the
wrap-around porch or play horseshoes, croquet, badminton, or
shuffleboard on the lawn. Visit nearby Lake Morey, Lake Fairlee, Maple
Grove Museum, St. Johnsbury, Quechee Gorge, and Saint Gaudens
National Historic Site. Local recreation includes golf, tennis, fishing,
boating, skiing, hiking, and hot air ballooning. Continental breakfast.
Families welcome. 1/$38-58; 2/$42-62. AE, MC, V. Travel agent.

Guests write: *"We have stayed at the Silver Maple for several years and
have never had a complaint except that the stay was always too short. The
owners really care about their guests and always go out of their way to make
us happy. We enjoyed everything immensely - the lovely room, good
breakfasts, fabulous weather, interesting people, use of their video,
comfortable lawn chairs, perfect location for everything we wanted to do
and see."* (B. Solomon)

Jeffersonville

The Smuggler's Notch Inn
P.O. Box 280
Jeffersonville, VT 05464
(802) 644-2412

Type of B&B: Country inn.
Rooms: 11 with private bath.
Rates: 1/$40; 2/$60-75.

Rating: B- or ♛♛ Good, meets basic requirements.

Historic country inn is located right in the village near Routes 108 and 15. Eleven guest rooms are available, each with private bath. Carefully restored, the inn boasts a brick fireplace, tin ceiling, hardwood floors, and an old-fashioned swing on the front porch. Stroll the wide streets in the village. Year-round activities include antique festivals, skiing, hiking, canoeing, swimming, and biking. Experience the New England fall foliage and watch a maple sugar house in production. Full breakfast frequently features pancakes, eggs, French toast, and muffins. Meeting and wedding facilities are available in the converted ballroom. Families welcome. 1/$40; 2/$60-75. AE, MC, V. 10% auto club, business travel, and senior discounts. Travel agent.

Jericho

Homeplace Bed & Breakfast
RR 2, Box 367
Jericho, VT 05465
(802) 899-4694

Type of B&B: B&B home.
Rooms: 3 share 2 baths.
Rates: 1/$40; 2/$50.

Rating: A- or ♛♛♛ Excellent, far exceeds basic requirements.

Modern farmhouse is situated on one-hundred acres of woods and located 1.5 miles from Route 15 and 8 miles from I-89 exit 12. Choose from three guest rooms which share two baths and feature crewel-style spreads and embroidered pillowcases. The home is filled with European antiques, Vermont craftwork, and a large collection of books. Animals on the farm include horses, sheep, pigs, ducks, chickens, cats, dogs, and donkeys. Explore miles of cross-country or hiking trails. Area attractions include University of Vermont, Shelburne Museum, Stowe ski areas, and Lake Champlain. Full country breakfast may feature eggs, bacon or sausage, homemade rolls, and fruit. No smoking. 1/$40; 2/$50.

Killington

Inn at Long Trail
PO Box 267
Route 4
Killington, VT 05751
(802) 775-7181

Type of B&B: Country inn.
Rooms: 25 with private bath.
Rates: 1/$46-120; 2/$56-148;
Suite/$76-200.

Rating: C or ♛ Acceptable, meets basic requirements.

Traditional New England ski lodge situated in the Green Mountains is located east of Rutland and one mile west of Route 100 North. There are nineteen guest rooms or suites. Each offers a private bath and the suites feature working fireplaces. Popular activities here include relaxing in the living room, choosing a good book from the library, enjoying the hot tub, and watching TV. Area attractions include historic tours, antique shopping, skiing, hiking, horseback riding, and golf. Full breakfast. Function rooms are available for meetings, weddings, retreats, and family reunions. Families welcome. 1/$46-120; 2/$56-148; Suite/$76-200. MC, V. 10% senior, auto club, and family discounts. Travel agent. Open Summer, Fall, and Winter.

Ludlow

Andrie Rose Inn
13 Pleasant Street
Ludlow, VT 05149
(802) 228-4846 or (800) 223-4846

Type of B&B: Country inn and guest house.
Rooms: 10 with private bath.
Rates: 1/$85-100; 2/$100-115; Suites 2/$185.

Rating: A+ or ♛♛♛ Excellent, far exceeds basic requirements.

1829 Country Village Inn is located at the base of Okemo Mountain Ski Resort. Choose from ten uniquely decorated, antique-filled guest rooms that offer designer linens, down comforters and pillows, and private baths. Some rooms feature sloping ceilings and skylights, while others boast whirlpool tubs. Luxury suites offer marble fireplaces, whirlpool baths, king or queen-size canopy beds, and color cable TVs with VCR and stereos. Borrow bicycles to tour back roads and antique shops. Later, sip fireside cocktails and enjoy complimentary hors d'oeuvres in the sitting rooms. Area activities include downhill and cross-country skiing, horseback riding, fishing, swimming, canoeing, tennis and golf. Full breakfast buffet often features blueberry pancakes, buttermilk waffles with Ben and Jerry's Vermont ice cream, or a fresh broccoli and mushroom quiche. Saturday night dinner available by advance reservation. Facilities available for small weddings and meetings. No smoking. 1/$85-100; 2/$100-115; Luxury Suites 2/$185. AE, MC, V. 10% senior discount.

Manchester

The Inn at Manchester
Route 7A, Box 41
Manchester, VT 05254
(802) 362-1793

Type of B&B: Large inn.
Rooms: 20, 14 with private bath.
Rates: 1 or 2/$65-130.

Rating: B+ or ♛♛ Good, exceeds basic requirements.

Historic Queen Anne Victorian inn is located in the village on Route 7-A. There are eighteen guest rooms or suites with views of the Green Mountains. Several rooms feature working fireplaces, queen or king-size beds, stained-glass windows, original artwork, antique furnishings, and one room has a special star-gazing window in a vaulted ceiling. The inn has a swimming pool and is within an easy walk to the village's restaurants and specialty shops. Popular attractions in the area include Southern Vermont Art Center, Bromley and Stratton ski areas, Norman Rockwell Museum, flea markets, antique shops, auctions, concerts, art shows, and year-round recreation. Full breakfast. Function rooms available for small meetings and weddings. Restricted smoking. 1 or 2/$65-130. AE, MC, V. 10% senior and 20% business travel discounts. Travel agent.

Guests write: *Surprising us with a bottle of wine for our anniversary was absolutely super! We were sent off with delicious cookies which was a sweet touch." (R. Kaplan)*

"I enjoyed my very relaxing vacation in Manchester at the inn. All of my needs, even the need to use the washer and dryer, were met during my stay with a smile." (D. Fairchild)

"We enjoyed our stay so much, the company, the cozy rom, the big country breakfast. How many couples do you know who've already had a second honeymoon after only four months of marriage. What a tradition!" (M. Brindle)

Middleton Springs

Middletown Springs Inn
On the Green, Box 1068
Middletown Springs, VT 05757
(802) 235-2198

Type of B&B: Country inn.
Rooms: 9 with private bath.
Rates: 1/$50-80; 2/$60-120.

Rating: B or ♛♛ Good, exceeds basic requirements.

Historic Victorian mansion is listed on the National Register of Historic Places and located near the junctions of Routes 140 and 133 on the village green. There are nine guest rooms with private bath and antique furnishings. Several common areas are offered for playing games, reading interesting books selected from the library, playing the grand piano in the music room, or quietly relaxing and they are centered around a gracious entrance hall with curved staircase. Area attractions include major ski areas, nearby cross-country trails, country auctions, and craft shows. Some of the best bicycling, hiking, and country walking in the state can be found in this area. Full breakfast. Dinner is also available and features Vermont country cooking. 1/$50-80; 2/$60-120. MC, V. Travel agent.

Orwell

Historic Brookside Farms
Route 22A
Orwell, VT 05760
(802) 948-2727

Type of B&B: Inn.
Rooms: 8, 5 with private bath.
Rates: 1/$50-80; 2/$85-150.

Rating: B+ or ♛♛ Good, exceeds basic requirements.

Historic estate built in the 18th-century is located 15 miles north of Fairhaven and 2 miles south of Route 73. There are eight guest rooms available; five offer a private bath. Popular activities at the inn include browsing through the 10,000-volume library, enjoying board games in the den, and watching TV. Guests can observe the farm's maple syrup production in action and several kinds of livestock are bred and raised here. Area attractions include Sheldon Museum, antique shops, tennis, golf, swimming, and skiing. Year-round recreation includes cross-country skiing, ice skating, hiking, fishing, and boating on the premises. Full breakfast includes homegrown bacon and eggs. Facilities available for social functions. Families welcome. Wheelchair access. Restricted smoking. 1/$50-80; 2/$85-150. 10% senior discount. Travel agent.

Rutland

The Inn at Rutland
70 North Main Street
Rutland, VT 05701
(802) 773-0575

Type of B&B: Inn.
Rooms: 12 with private bath.
Rates: 1/$55-140; 2/$65-140.

Rating: A or ♛♛♛ Excellent, far exceeds basic requirements.

Victorian mansion built in 1890 is located on North Main Street (Route 7), 1 block north of the junction of Routes 7 and 4 East. Twelve guest rooms are available and each includes a private bath, telephone, and TV. Area attractions include Killington and Pico ski areas, Wilson Castle, New England Maple museum, Hubbarton Battle Museum, Vermont Marble Exhibit, and Norman Rockwell Museum. Continental breakfast features homemade muffins, coffee cakes, and biscuits. Small wedding and meeting facilities available. No smoking. 1/$55-140; 2/$65-140. AE, MC, V. 10% business travel discount. Travel agent.

Stockbridge

Stockbridge Inn B&B
P.O. Box 45
Route 100 North
Stockbridge, VT 05772
(802) 746-8165

Type of B&B: Inn.
Rooms: 6, 2 with private bath.
Rates: 1/$40-60; 2/$50-90.

Rating: B or ♛♛ Good, exceeds basic requirements.

Historic inn was originally built in 1860 for the grandson of the famous horse breeder, Justin Morgan and it's located in the country on Route 100-North also known as the Skier's Highway. Each of the six guest rooms is named after offspring of the first Morgan horse and two rooms offer a private bath. Popular activities here include strolling through the fields, bicycling down winding roads, hiking, seeing local plays, and year-round recreation. Full country breakfast. 1/$40-60; 2/$50-90. MC, V.

Stowe

Baas' Gastehaus
180 Edson Hill Road
Stowe, VT 05672
(802) 253-8376

Type of B&B: B&B home plus cottage.
Rooms: 3, 1 with private bath.
Rates: 1/$30-40; 2/$40-56.

Rating: B+ or ♛♛ Good, exceeds basic requirements.

Historic Early American estate is situated in a pastoral setting located off
Route 108, 10 miles north of exit 10 off I-89. There are three guest rooms
in the main house and a separate guest cottage on the grounds which
offers complete privacy. A comfortable living room on the main floor
offers good views of the surrounding mountains and is a popular place for
reading, relaxation, and meeting other guests. Area attractions include
skiing, hiking, golf, Trapp Family Lodge, canoeing, fishing, tennis, art
center, and Mt. Mansfield. Host speaks German. Continental breakfast
offered or full breakfast available by request. Families welcome. 1/$30-40;
2/$40-56. Travel agent.

Stowe

Hadleigh House
Route 100 North,
1386 Pucker Street
Stowe, VT 05672
(802) 253-7703

Type of B&B: B&B home.
Rooms: 3 with private bath.
Rates: 1 or 2/$55-65.

Rating: B+ or ♛♛ Good, exceeds basic requirements.

Colonial farmhouse in a rural setting was built in the early 1800's and
offers views of Mount Mansfield. Choose from three guest rooms, each
with private bath. Furnished with family memorabilia, the living room
offers quiet reading before the fireplace and board games. Friendly
horses live on the property. Area recreation includes downhill and cross-
country skiing, sleigh rides, snowmobiling, hiking, and bicycling. Full
breakfast. Families welcome. Restricted smoking. Resident dogs and cat. 1
or 2/$55-65. MC, V.

Stowe

Inn at the Brass Lantern
717 Maple Street
Stowe, VT 05672
(802) 253-2229 or (800) 729-2980
Type of B&B: Inn.
Rooms: 9 with private bath.

Rates: 1 or 2/$70-120.

Rating: A or ♛♛♛ Excellent, far exceeds basic requirements.

1810 Colonial farmhouse is located off Route 100, a half-mile from the center of the village at the foot of Mt. Mansfield. Choose from nine guest rooms with private bath, antique furnishings, and homemade quilts. Several of the rooms feature working fireplaces. Each evening, guests are invited to sit by the fire in the living room where tea and dessert are offered. Area attractions include craft and antique shops, buggy and sleigh rides, skiing, fishing, hiking, and golf. Full breakfast. Facilities are available for weddings and small meetings. No smoking. 1 or 2/$70-120. AE, MC, V. Travel agent.

Stowe

Spruce Pond Inn
1250 Waterbury Road
Stowe, VT 05672
(802) 253-4236

Type of B&B: Country inn
with restaurant.
Rooms: 6 with private bath.
Rates: 1/$40-50; 2/$45-90.

Rating: B or ♛♛ Good, exceeds basic requirements.

Spruce Pond Inn is an historic Colonial home built in 1820. There are six guest rooms with private bath and cable TV. Popular activities here include skating on the pond near the inn and sitting in front of the fireplace after a full day of skiing. Nearby attractions include Ben & Jerry's Ice Cream Factory, hiking, biking, and cross-country skiing. A full breakfast features homemade pastries and granola and is served in front of the bay windows in the dining room. The dinner menu includes heart-healthy entrees. Function rooms are available for large meetings and weddings. No smoking. 1/$40-50; 2/$45-90. AE, MC, V. 10% senior discount. Travel agent.

Stowe

Ye Olde England Inne
433 Mountain Road
Stowe, VT 05672
(802) 253-7558

Type of B&B: Country inn.
Rooms: 20 with private bath.
Rates: 1 or 2/$74-125.

Rating: A or ♛♛♛ Excellent, far exceeds basic requirements.

Historic Tudor-style country inn was built in 1890 and is located minutes from I-89 on Route 100. There are a total of twenty guest rooms with private bath, English prints, four-poster beds, interesting brass and copper accessories, and private phones. Area attractions include the Stowe-Learn-to-Ski program, polo tournaments, fishing, golf, tennis, and hiking. Full breakfast features breakfast chef's specials. Function rooms are available for meetings and weddings. Families welcome. Restricted smoking. 1 or 2/$74-125. 10% auto club discount. Travel agent.

Underhill

Sinclair Towers B&B Inn
RD 2, Box 35
Underhill, VT 05489
(802) 899-2234

Type of B&B: Inn.
Rooms: 6 with private bath.
Rates: 1/$45-55; 2/$55-70.

Rating: A- or ♛♛ Excellent, far exceeds basic requirements.

Historic Queen Anne Victorian inn built in 1890 has been fully restored and is located in the village, 15 miles northeast of Burlington, and west of Smuggler's Notch. Six guest rooms are available, each with private bath, individual decor, and air conditioning. A living room on the main floor offers a fireplace and the parlor has a collection of books and games. Area attractions include several major ski areas, Burlington-Shelburne Museum, Smuggler's Notch, Underhill State Park, and Ben & Jerry's Ice Cream Factory. Seasonal outdoor activities nearby include apple picking, leaf peeping, antique shows, sleigh rides, maple sugaring, scenic train rides, tennis, and hiking. Afternoon tea is offered daily as well as a full breakfast that features waffles, eggs, pancakes, or French toast. Function rooms are available for meetings and social occasions. Wheelchair access. No smoking. 1/$45-55; 2/$55-70. MC, V. Business travel discount. Travel agent.

Vergennes

Emerson's Guesthouse B&B
82 Main Street
Vergennes, VT 05491
(802) 877-3293

Type of B&B: Guesthouse.
Rooms: 4, 1 with private bath.
Rates: 1 or 2/$35-65.

Rating: B or ♛♛ Good, exceeds basic requirements.

Historic guesthouse built in 1850 is located a half-mile from the junctions of Route 7 and 22A, and is surrounded by landscaped lawns and gardens. There are four spacious guest rooms and one offers a private bath. Guests enjoy strolling the garden areas, relaxing on the porch or in the common rooms. Area attractions include Shelburne Museum, Morgan Horse Farm, and Kennedy Brothers Marketplace, golf, tennis, swimming and bicycling. Full breakfast includes homemade jams, jellies and breads. 1 or 2/$35-65.

Waitsfield

Knoll Farm Country Inn
RFD 179, Bragg Hill Road
Waitsfield, VT 05673
(802) 496-3939

Type of B&B: Country inn.
Rooms: 5 with shared baths.
Rates: 1/$60; 2/$100

Rating: C+ or ♛ Acceptable, meets basic requirements.

Historic country farm and inn situated on one-hundred-fifty hilly acres in the Green Mountains offers spectacular views and is located 14 miles south of I-89, exit 9 on Route 100. Choose from five guest rooms with shared baths which are decorated with family heirlooms, including a 100-year-old four-poster pineapple bed. Relax in one of the two living rooms, the well-stocked library, or in front of the wood stove in the kitchen. There is much to do on the property including exploring the outdoors, visiting farm animals, hiking or sledding on mountain pastures, swimming or skating on the pond, and nature trails. Hosts have operated Knoll Farm since 1957, raise their own food ,and offer a full breakfast featuring fresh eggs, whole wheat muffins, sausage, and bacon, as well as family-style dinners, both included in the daily rate. No smoking. 1/$60; 2/$100. 10% senior discount.

Guests write: *"My hosts were sensitive to our vegetarian food request and we loved meeting, talking, and laughing with interesting guests around the dinner table. The wonderful trails for walking combined with the incredible views is a constant reminder that you're in the heart of the Green Mountains. We especially enjoyed meeting the magnificent Highland cattle, horses, pig, chicken, and of course the dog and cat." (J. Dean)*

"During nine of the past thirteen years, often for seven consecutive weeks, I have enjoyed the informal cordiality of both hosts and guests at meals, and between meals, the serene solitude of the upper pasture, and the inspiring views in almost every direction." (W. Cobb)

"Our most delicious meal of all was a special dinner Ann prepared - fresh vegetable soup with veggies from her own organic garden and a melt-in-your-mouth eggplant casserole. Needless to say, the breakfasts were inventive and healthy. There was a different whole grain hot cereal every day, plus homemade breads, farm fresh eggs, homemade jams, and lots of maple syrup. Knoll Farm is for the tourist who wants to forget that she/he is a tourist. It's for people who want to embrace Vermont as it truly is." (J. Peter)

"While I know that inn books so often speak of the physical - and I have always delighted in the special touches in the rooms such as fresh wildflowers, family quilts, spreads, and furniture, extra books, magazines, brochures - I hope you will mention something about the atmosphere and the genuine interest in people which is evident at Knoll Farm." (J. Howard)

Waitsfield

Mad River Barn
Box 88, Route 17
Waitsfield, VT 05673
(802) 496-3310

Type of B&B: Large inn.
Rooms: 15 with private bath.
Rate: 1/$40; 2/$75.

Rating: C+ or ♛ Acceptable, meets basic requirements.

Classic Vermont ski lodge in operation for forty-four years is adjacent to 1,500 private acres and located 17 miles west of I-89, exit 9. There are fifteen guest rooms with private bath, homemade quilts, cable TV, queen-size beds, and small kitchens. The inn boasts a game parlor, fireplace pub, and breakfast and dining rooms. Popular activities here include exploring the nearby mountain streams and swimming in the heated, landscaped pool. Nearby attractions include hiking, golf, biking, rock quarries, Shelbourne Museum, Ben & Jerry's Ice Cream Factory, and Cabot Cheese factory. Full breakfast. Function rooms available. Families welcome. Wheelchair access. 1/$40; 2/$75. AE, MC, V. Travel agent.

Waterbury/Stowe

Black Locust Inn
R.R. 1, Box 715
Waterbury Center, VT 05677
(802) 244-7490 and (800) 366-5592

Type of B&B: Inn.
Rooms: 6 with private bath.
Rates: 1/$60-75; 2/$70-95.

Rating: A or ♛♛♛ Excellent, far exceeds basic requirements.

Historic farmhouse built in 1832 is situated in the hills near Stowe and located 5 miles north of I-89, exit 10. There are six guest rooms featuring brass beds, private baths, antique furnishings, and polished wood floors. A common room on the main floor offers a wood stove and game table is situated by a large bay window. Area attractions include major ski areas, Cold Hollow Cider Mill, Ben & Jerry's Ice Cream Factory, and outdoor recreation. Full breakfast is served on linen and snacks are offered each afternoon. No smoking. 1/$60-75; 2/$70-95. MC, V. 10% senior discount. Travel agent. Open year-round except for two weeks in April and November.

Waterbury/Stowe

Inn at Blush Hill
R.R. 1, Blush Hill Road
Box 1266
Waterbury, VT 05676
(802) 244-7529

Type of B&B: Inn.
Rooms: 6, 2 with private bath.
Rates: 1 or 2/$55-110.

Rating: B+ or ♛♛ Good, exceeds basic requirements.

Historic Cape Cod country inn built in 1790 is situated in the country on five acres and located near I-89, exit 10. There are six guest rooms furnished with a selection of Colonial antique accent pieces. One room offers a working fireplace and two have a private bath. Downstairs common rooms provide plenty of space and comfortable furnishings which invite conversation, quiet reading, or playing board games. Area attractions include Bolton Valley, Sugarbush and Stowe ski areas, Ben & Jerry's Ice Cream Factory, Cold Hollow Cider Mill, hiking, fishing, tennis, and golf. Full country breakfast is served in the rustic kitchen which offers a panoramic view of the Worcester Mountain range. Tea and cookies are offered each evening. Facilities available for outdoor weddings and social functions in warm weather. Restricted smoking. 1 or 2/$55-110. MC, V. Travel agent.

Weathersfield

Inn at Weathersfield
P.O. Box 165, Route 106
Weathersfield, VT 05151
(802) 263-9217 or (800) 477-4828
Fax: (802) 263-9219

Type of B&B: Country inn.
Rooms: 12 with private bath.
Rates: 1/$117.50-120; 2/$175-205.

Rating: A or ♛♛♛ Excellent, far exceeds basic requirements.

Large country inn located 5 miles north of Springfield was built in 1795 and is rich in history. Each of the twelve guest rooms offers a private bath, period antiques, working fireplace, and views of the surrounding countryside. There are five common rooms at the inn including the library with a collection of 4,000 books and a game and exercise room on the lower level. The restaurant and lounge on the premises serves a five-course dinner and offers live piano music nightly. A full breakfast and afternoon tea are served in the library or on the pleasant sunporch. Recreation in the area includes tennis, fishing, hiking, and skiing. A pond on the premises offers ice-skating in winter. Several function rooms are available for meetings and weddings. Rates include breakfast, tea, and dinner. 1/$117.50-120; 2/$175-205. AE, MC, V. Business travel and package discounts. Travel agent.

West Dover

Austin Hill Inn
Route 100
West Dover, VT 05356
(800) 332-7352 or
(802) 464-5281
Fax: (802) 464-1229

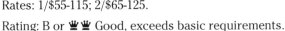

Type of B&B: Large inn.
Rooms: 12 with private bath.
Rates: 1/$55-115; 2/$65-125.

Rating: B or ♛♛ Good, exceeds basic requirements.

Newly renovated Country Colonial inn is located outside the village of West Dover just off Route 100. Choose from twelve guest rooms, each with private bath and individual decor; several offer a private balcony. For moments of relaxation there are several common rooms with a fireplace as well as a swimming pool. Area attractions include fishing, boating on Lake Whitingham, Mt. Snow Ski Resort, golf at Haystack or Mt. Snow championship courses, designer outlet stores, antique malls, and the Marlboro Music Festival. Full New England country breakfast and afternoon tea served daily. Candlelit dinners are available on weekends. There are several function rooms on-site for meetings and social occasions. No smoking. 1/$55-115; 2/$65-125. AE, MC, V.

Guests write: *"You dream of the perfect New England inn and you come to Austin Hill, and there it is! Roaring fires in cozy, beautifully appointed sitting rooms, country-style bedrooms complete with rocking chairs, afghans, candlelight, and chocolates at bedtime, and a friendly, courteous and eager staff. It all sounds like a movie set and it's like a movie set come to life."* (R. Seider)

"I have grown accustomed to the efficiency of modern hotels but Austin Hill Inn has spoiled me. Their friendly dogs, charming and comfortable appointments, and most of all the gracious warmth of the staff have set better standards." (H. Levy)

"Although our stay at the inn was very brief, for two weary travelers, it brought needed relief. Their cheery warm welcome as we entered the door, was like that of a good neighbor, who could ask for anything more? Seriously, the inn is lovely. With four married children and seven grandchildren, we on occasion look for a hideaway. We'll be back." (B. Ford)

"Another bright star has been added to the twinkling Vermont sky, the Austin Hill Inn. Walk through the door and step into a world of warmth and charm from days gone by. Once you arrive you're treated like a special guest but feel like part of the family." (P. Kerantzas)

Wilmington

Nutmeg Inn
West Molly Stark Trail
Route 9
Wilmington, VT 05363
(802) 464-3351

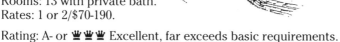

Type of B&B: Large inn.
Rooms: 13 with private bath.
Rates: 1 or 2/$70-190.

Rating: A- or ♕♕♕ Excellent, far exceeds basic requirements.

Early-American farmhouse built in 1777 stands near a mountain brook near the junctions of Routes 9 and 100 in the village center. There are thirteen guest rooms or suites and each offers a private bath, cable TV, brass or iron bed, quilts, and antique dressers. Nine of the rooms feature a working fireplace and one suite has a private balcony overlooking Haystack Mountain and the surrounding meadows. Several of the older rooms feature exposed beams and slanted ceilings which reflect the rich history of the inn. The original carriage house offers a living room with fireplace, TV, and piano, and there is a small library with a collection of books. Recreation nearby includes skiing, leaf peeping, scenic drives, hiking, antiquing, fishing, boating, and golfing. Full breakfast. Families welcome. Wheelchair access. Restricted smoking. 1 or 2/$70-190. AE, MC, V.

Guests write: *"This is the most beautiful and gracious inn we've ever stayed in. Excellent French toast! The inn had all of the luxury of being away, yet the comfort of being home." (P. Quasius)*

Wilmington

Trail's End, A Country Inn
Smith Road
Wilmington, VT 05363
(802) 464-2727

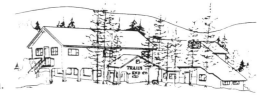

Type of B&B: Inn.
Rooms: 18 with private bath.
Rates: 1/$70-110; 2/$70-160.

Rating: A or ♕♕♕ Excellent, far exceeds basic requirements.

Rustic country inn in a tranquil setting is located in the heart of Deerfield Valley, a half mile east of Route 100 North. Choose from eighteen guest rooms or suites, each with private bath, individual decor, and family heirlooms. Available to guests are an outdoor swimming pool, clay tennis court, stocked trout pond, and English flower gardens. Four-season recreation includes canoeing, horseback riding, hiking, golfing, sleigh rides, and downhill or cross-country skiing. Full breakfast includes homemade granola and a varied choice of entrees such as pancakes, waffles, egg dishes and breakfast meats. Afternoon refreshments are served daily. Families welcome. Facilities available for meetings and social functions. 1/$70-110; 2/$70-160. MC, V.

Guests write: *"Friendly smiles, warm hospitality, and a make-yourself-at-home feeling, are always present. My wife and I have returned every year since our first visit." (P. Diana)*

"Mary and Bill treat us like family. Their warmth permeates the inn in the rooms, the food, and the total ambiance of Trail's End. This is our fifth year at the inn and the only check that I look forward to writing all year." (P. Marier)

"My wife and I return with friends each year to this comfortable refuge. Mary and Bill preside with gracious concern for our comfort and subtle attention to detail while including us in the extended family that shares this happy hearth." (J. Batson)

"There are always cookies and lemonade in the summer and hot cider in the winter plus bowls of nuts and apples for nibbles. The rooms are charming and each one furnished differently." (W. Gross)

"We have visited Trail's End for four years in a row and it is always a treat. Bill and Mary are terrific hosts and they are enormously proud of their inn. They continue to improve the rooms. The Saturday night dinner is always fun and Bill's poached eggs are famous." (D. Celani)

Woodstock

Charleston House
21 Pleasant Street
Woodstock, VT 05091
(802) 457-3843

Type of B&B: Inn.
Rooms: 7 with private bath.
Rates: 1 or 2/$75-135.

Rating: A or ♕♕♕ Excellent, far exceeds basic requirements.

Greek Revival townhouse built in two sections is listed on the National Register of Historic Places and located 150 miles north of Boston. Choose from seven antique-filled guest rooms with private bath in the Charleston House or additional accommodations at the Canterbury House just two blocks east which features authentic antique Victorian furnishings in an

100-year-old setting. Many rooms offer canopy beds and all are well-coordinated in color fabric and decor. Visit nearby Billings Farm, Killington ski area, golf, tennis, boating, hiking, and swimming. Full breakfast is served with recipes featured in the inn's own breakfast cookbook. Resident dog. 1 or 2/$75-135. MC, V, AE.

Guests write: *The breakfasts were outstanding. The atmosphere was warm and inviting and Jan and Mark were terrific and easy to get to know. There was an impromptu wedding here one night and the hosts were more than accommodating." (J. Pritchard)*

Woodstock

Deer Brook Inn
HCR 68, Box 443
Woodstock, VT 05091
(802) 672-3713

Type of B&B: Inn.
Rooms: 4 with private bath.
Rates: 1/$50-60; 2/$65-85.

Rating: B+ or ♛♛ Good, exceeds basic requirements.

Historic Colonial farmhouse built in 1820 was once a working dairy farm and is located on Route 4, four miles west of the village. There are four large guest rooms and each offers a private bath, homemade quilts, and polished wide pine floors. The front porch offers views of the Ottauquechee River meandering by and there's a living room with fireplace for warming up after a day of skiing. Recreation in the area includes skiing, bicycling, golf, hiking, swimming, and fishing. The area is also known for its numerous antique shops. Full breakfast features home baked muffins and is served in the family-style dining room. Families welcome. Restricted smoking. 1/$50-60; 2/$65-85. MC, V.

Guests write: *"This was a warm and welcoming place to return to after some rather cold and un-welcoming ski slopes. We've been having breakfast withdrawal since we left! Cereal and grapefruit aren't making it and Gary (my husband) is after me to make quiche." (J. Maffie)*

"We had a wonderful stay and the breakfast was wonderful. There was only one other inn we stayed at during our month of traveling that could match the feeling of welcome ad the sense of home that Deer Brook Inn offers." (A. Muratet)

Woodstock

Woodstocker B&B
Route 4, 61 River Street
Woodstock, VT 05091
(802) 457-3896

Type of B&B: Inn.
Rooms: 9 with private bath.
Rates: 1/$60-110; 2/$65-115.

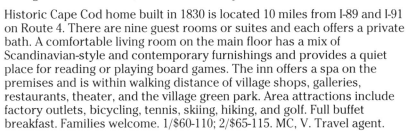

Rating: B+ or ♛♛ Good, exceeds basic requirements.

Historic Cape Cod home built in 1830 is located 10 miles from I-89 and I-91 on Route 4. There are nine guest rooms or suites and each offers a private bath. A comfortable living room on the main floor has a mix of Scandinavian-style and contemporary furnishings and provides a quiet place for reading or playing board games. The inn offers a spa on the premises and is within walking distance of village shops, galleries, restaurants, theater, and the village green park. Area attractions include factory outlets, bicycling, tennis, skiing, hiking, and golf. Full buffet breakfast. Families welcome. 1/$60-110; 2/$65-115. MC, V. Travel agent.

Guests write: *"I have stayed in numerous B&B establishments and have found this one to be unique. Perhaps it is the sincere friendliness of the charming host and hostess, Liza and Romano. This couple is professional and at the same time presents a family-like environment. The accommodations are comfortable, clean, and homey - like a visit to Grandmother's house." (D. Lepore)*

Blacksburg

Sycamore Tree Bed & Breakfast
P.O. Box 10937
Blacksburg, VA 24062
(703) 381-1597

Type of B&B: B&B home.
Rooms: 6 with private bath.
Rates: 1/$50-105; 2/$55-110.

Rating: A- or ♛♛♛ Excellent, far exceeds basic requirements.

Farmhouse nestled at the foot of Hightop Mountain is located four miles east of Blacksburg's city limits. Six guest rooms with private bath are furnished with antiques and country accessories. Common rooms on the main floor include a living room and family room with fireplace and the porch offers views of the mountain meadow. Area attractions include golf, hiking, antique stores, fine restaurants, museums, historic buildings, and nightly entertainment in the neighboring towns and universities. Full Southern-style breakfast. No smoking. 1/$50-105; 2/$55-110.

Boyce

The River House
Route 2, Box 135
Boyce, VA 22620
(703) 837-1476.

Type of B&B: Inn.
Rooms: 5 with private bath.
Rates: 1 or 2/$75-119.

Rating: B or ♛♛ Good, exceeds basic requirements.

Historic farmhouse is situated on fifteen acres of open woodlands and river frontage on the Shenandoah River near Route 50 in northwestern Virginia. There are five guest rooms, each with individual decor and private bath. The original 1780 kitchen is now the Hearth Room with walk-in fireplace, queen-size bed, double sofabed, and a collection of books and prints from the theater. The spacious master suite features polished floor boards, an antique double bed, and a romantic atmosphere. The fireplaced parlor on the main floor offers a relaxed setting for reading, board games, toasting marshmallows, and readings of stories and poetry. The hosts hold regular theater weekends in the country which feature the comedic works of great humorists and playwrights. Area attractions include Appalachian Trail, historic landmarks, antique shops, mountain hiking, and local vineyard tours. Full breakfast/brunch served. Facilities are available for small meetings and social functions. 1 or 2/$75-119. MC, V. 10% auto club, business travel, and senior discount. Travel agent.

Bumpass/Lake Anna

Rockland Farm Retreat
Lake Anna
3609 Lewiston Road
Bumpass, VA 23024
(703) 895-5098 or (301) 384-4583

Type of B&B: Country inn.
Rooms: 6 with shared baths.
Rates: 1 or 2/$50-60.

Rating: C+ or ♛ Acceptable, meets basic requirements.

Victorian plantation with seventy-five acres was built in 1820 and is located 15 miles south of Fredericksburg off I-95. There are six guest rooms with shared bath. Relax on the large front porch and in the living room, or explore the 75 acres of farmland with its wildlife, farm buildings, livestock, and vineyard. The inn is near Lake Anna water sports, horseback riding, hunting, golf, hiking, and bicycling. Host speaks French and Spanish. Full breakfast. Facilities are available for weddings, family reunions, retreats, and meetings. Families and pets welcome. Restricted smoking. 1 or 2/$50-60. AE. 10% family discount. Travel agent.

Charles City

North Bend Plantation B&B
12200 Weyanoke Road
Charles City, VA 23030
(804) 829-5176

Type of B&B: Inn.
Rooms: 3 with private bath.
Rates: 1 or 2/$95-110.

Rating: A- or ♕ ♕ ♕ Excellent, far exceeds basic requirements.

General Sheridan used this historic plantation home on 250 acres as his headquarters during the Civil War. The home was built in 1819 and is located halfway between Williamsburg and Richmond in Virginia Plantation country, off Route 5. There are three guest rooms on the second floor and each has a private bath, family antiques, and pleasant decor. There are several common rooms at the inn including a billiard room and parlor which boasts a collection of rare books. Popular activities here include walks on the property, bike riding on country roads, plantation home tours, antique shops, and Colonial Williamsburg attractions. Full country breakfast. 1 or 2/$95-110.

Guests write: *"Our stay was delightful! They walked us through history and served a delicious breakfast and we enjoyed the breakfast chats with George." (A. Southworth)*

"The setting, the books, the room, the breakfast, and especially the Coplands was delightful." (W. Canup)

"It's wonderfully peaceful here. We really enjoyed traversing the field with Ridgely and looking at the Civil War trenches. The fox hunt was splendid!" (A. Bedwell)

"Our accommodations were historic and comfortable and the girls were right at home playing around the farm. Ridgley gave us a wonderful trip down to the river during which we met a herd of llamas. Both hosts are tireless in sharing their knowledge of the area and their enthusiasm for the history of their property and families. The hospitality of the Coplands is exceptional and privacy is a much appreciated option after a day of sightseeing." (N. Engeman)

Charlottesville/Scottsville

Chester Bed & Breakfast
Route 4, Box 57
Scottsville, VA 24590
(804) 286-3960

Type of B&B: Inn.
Rooms: 5, 1 with private bath.
Rates: 1 or 2/$65-90.

Rating: A- or ♛♛♛ Exellent, far exceeds basic requirements.

Historic Greek Revival home built in 1847 is located 17 miles south of Charlottesville near Routes 726, 20, and 6. There are four second-floor guest rooms with shared baths or a downstairs guest room with four-poster bed and private bath. The entire inn is air-conditioned and each guest room features a woodburning fireplace. The first floor living room has a fireplace and fine art collection and the second-floor library offers informal seating and an interesting selection of books. The extensive grounds include an unusually large number of tree specimens. Bicycles and a kennel for pets are available. Area attractions include Monticello, Ashlawn, University of Virginia, winery tours, canoeing and tubing on the James River, skiing, and golf. Full breakfast. Dinner is available by advance reservation. 1 or 2/$65-90. AE. Travel agent.

Charlottesville/North Garden

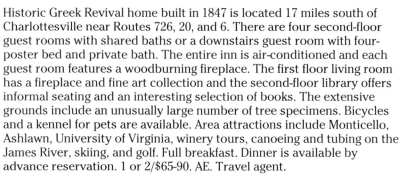

Inn at the Crossroads
Route 2, Box 6
North Garden, VA 22959
(804) 979-6452

Type of B & B: Inn.
Rooms: 5 with in-room sinks
and shared baths.

Rates: 1 or 2/$59-69

Rating: A- or ♛♛♛ Excellent, far exceeds basic requirements.

Historic landmark tavern built in 1820 is located 9 miles south of Charlottesville off Route 29 at Route 692. Named for different facets of art and litcrature, each of the five guest rooms are designed to be as close to what they might have been in the original days of the tavern. Take time to unwind with a book and explore the grounds which open to the foothills of the Blue Ridge. The inn is ideally located near Monticello, Ash Lawn, Michie Tavern, and Montpelier. Full breakfast. Small meeting facilities available. Restricted smoking. 1 or 2/$59-69. MC, V. Travel agent.

Guests write: *"Even six months pregnant, we still felt as pampered as newlyweds. We appreciated their helpfulness and hospitality and the breakfast - wow!" (R. Plant)*

"The house has a great feeling of being at home. I thank them for allowing me to bang on their piano and for those tasty blueberry pancakes." (A. Morris)

Charlottesville/Palmyra

Palmer Country Manor
Route 2, Box 1390
Charlottesville, VA 22963
(803) 589-1300 or
(800) 253-4306

Type of B&B: Country inn with restaurant and cottages.
Rooms: 12 with private bath.
Rates: 1/$80-115; 2/$95-125.

Rating: B or ♛♛ Good, exceeds basic requirements.

Colonial plantation home is situated on one-hundred-eighty acres of wooded wilderness twenty miles southeast of Charlottesville on Route 640. There are two guest rooms in the main house. Five newly-built modular duplex units with ten more guest accommodations are referred to as cottages and each has a private bath, fireplace, and separate deck. Relax in the inn's library, main parlor, or screened-in porch. Child-care is available on-site as well as hot-air ballooning, fishing, hiking and swimming. Area attractions include the homes of Thomas Jefferson, James Monroe, and Texas Jack. Full breakfast and dinner are included in the rates. Function rooms are available for meetings and weddings. Families welcome. Restricted smoking. 1/$80-115; 2/$95-125. AE, MC, V. 10% auto club discount. Travel agent.

Guests write: *"Here are some of the many pleasures we experienced here: the dining was exquisite, choice of wine super, accommodations were spacious and very romantic. The past holds many memories and it now holds one very special time at Palmer House." (J. Lobdell)*

Christiansburg

The Oaks B&B Country Inn
311 East Main Street
Christiansburg, VA 24073
(703) 381-1500

Type of B&B: Inn.
Rooms: 4 with private bath.
Rates: 1 or 2/$65-95.

Rating: AA- or ♛♛♛ Outstanding.

Classic Queen Anne Victorian built in 1889 is the focal point of the East Main Historic District and located just 2 miles off I-81 and 24 miles from the Blue Ridge Parkway. The main inn has four guest rooms with private bath and two offer working fireplaces. Special features of the inn include a wrap-around porch with Kennedy rockers, patio with comfortable chairs, sundeck, and several common rooms including two formal parlors with fireplaces and fine antique furnishings, and a pleasant sunroom with wicker furnishings, collection of games, and TV. A garden gazebo attached to a small cottage houses a new hydrojet spa. The private cottage has a sauna, bathroom and efficiency kitchen as well as two beds, one in a small loft area. Area attractions include Blue Ridge Parkway, Appalachian Trail, historic sites, wineries, antique and craft shops, boating, fishing, hiking, golf, and tennis. Full gourmet breakfast. Smoking restricted. 1 or 2/$65-95. Business discount. Travel agent.

Fairfax

The Bailiwick Inn
4023 Chain Bridge Road
Fairfax, VA 22030
(703) 691-2266 or (800) 366-7666.

Type of B&B: Inn.
Rooms: 14 with private bath.
Rates: 1 or 2/$95-175.

Rating: AA or ♛♛♛ Outstanding.

19th-century restored Federal home is located in a historic area fifteen miles west of Washington, DC and one mile south of I-66 on Highway 123. Choose from fourteen guest rooms with private bath. Most of the rooms feature queen-size featherbeds and all are furnished with fine antiques. Deluxe rooms offer working fireplaces and Jacuzzi tubs. Common areas for relaxation include the book-filled parlors and Colonial brick-walled garden. Fairfax offers numerous quaint shops and restaurants and area attractions include Civil War battlefields, George Mason University, Wolf Trap Park for the Performing Arts, and Washington, DC sites. A full breakfast features specialties such as Robert E. Lee Eggs served with sticky buns, cornbread, and assorted fruit. Afternoon tea is served daily and offers scones, tarts, and a variety of tea sandwiches. Function rooms are available for weddings and meetings. Families welcome. Wheelchair access. No smoking. 1 or 2/$95-175. AE, MC, V. Senior, family, and business discounts. Travel agent.

Guests write: *"The Bailiwick Inn is one of the most charming and elegant inns we've ever seen. Our room, the service, and the food were just wonderful." (Y. Harvey)*

"All was so well executed, the handwritten welcome note, the red apples on the dining room table, the grapes growing in the arbor. All was so well appointed and well thought through." (J. Rex)

"I enjoyed the murder mystery weekend. Having never been to one before, choosing the Bailiwick Inn as my initial beginning was the best thing I could have done. I was made to feel welcome and at home which was so very thoughtful. The staff was very courteous and having the special attention by one and all was wonderful." (E. Barnes)

Gordonsville

Sleepy Hollow Farm B&B
16280 Blue Ridge Turnpike
Gordonsville, VA 22942
(703) 832-5555

Type of B&B: Inn.
Rooms: 4 rooms and 2 suites with private bath.

Rates: 1/$50-75; 2/$60-95.

Rating: A or ♛♛♛ Excellent, far exceeds basic requirements.

Historic Colonial farmhouse is located 25 miles northeast of Charlottesville and 3 miles north of Gordonsville on Route 231. There are six guest rooms available with private bath in the main house or in a separate cottage. One room in the main inn offers a whirlpool and working fireplace. The cottage rooms are all two-room suites which feature either a working fireplace or wood-burning stove. Area attractions include Montpelier, Monticello, museums, national park, historic areas, antique and craft shops, wineries, tennis, fishing, swimming, canoeing, bicycling, and horseback riding. Full breakfast. Facilities available for meetings and weddings. Families welcome. 1/$50-75; 2/$60-95. MC, V. Travel agent.

Leesburg

Fleetwood Farm B&B
Route 1, Box 306-A
Leesburg, VA 22075
(703) 327-4325

Type of B&B: B&B home.
Rooms: 2 with private bath.
Rates: 1 or 2/$95-120.

Rating: A or ♛♛♛ Excellent, far exceeds basic requirements.

Plantation Manor home built in 1745 is a Virginia Historic Landmark on the National Registry of Historic Places and is located in Loudoun Hunt Country, 15 minutes from Dulles Airport. Choose from two unique guest rooms, each with private bath (one with large Jacuzzi), fireplace, and air-conditioning. Enjoy the use of the living room, cook-out facilities, horseshoes, croquet, and gardens. A canoe and fishing equipment are also available. Explore this working sheep farm and grounds with its Colonial herb garden, apiary, and several spoiled cats which live on the property. Area attractions include Manassas Battlefield, Harper's Ferry, festivals, and horseback riding. Full breakfast includes homemade jams, jellies, and honey. Restricted smoking. 1 or 2/$95-120.

Lexington/Clifton Forge

Firmstone Manor B&B Inn
Route 1, Box 257
Clifton Forge, VA 24422
(703) 862-0892

Type of B&B: Inn with cottage.
Rooms: 8, 4 with private bath.
Rates: 1 or 2/$65-125.

Rating: A or ♛♛♛ Excellent, far exceeds basic requirements.

Historic English Manor home built in 1873 is surrounded by mountains and located 18 miles from Lexington near I-64, exit 35. Choose from eight guest rooms with antique and wicker furnishings and quilted comforters whose individual decor themes include Hungary and Santa Fe rooms. A separate cottage on the property offers complete privacy and a fully equipped kitchen. There are several common areas on the main floor including a solarium with wicker furnishings, parlor with Victorian decor, and library with comfortable seating for viewing VCR movies and TV. Popular area attractions center around the mountain and lake recreation including hiking, swimming, boating, golfing, and fishing. This area is also known for its numerous antique shops and country auctions. Guests have a choice of full or continental breakfast and afternoon refreshments are also served. Dinner is available by advance reservation on Friday and Saturday evenings. 1 or 2/$65-125. MC, V.

Lynchburg

Lynchburg Mansion Inn B&B
405 Madison Street
Lynchburg, VA 24504
(804) 528-5400 or
(800) 325-1199

Type of B&B: Small inn.
Rooms: 4 with private bath.
Rates: 1/$84; 2/$89-109.

Rating: A+ or ♕♕♕ Excellent, far exceeds basic requirements.

Nine-thousand square-foot Spanish-Georgian home built in 1924 is listed on the National Register of Historic Places and stands on a half-acre in the Garland Hill Historic District of Lynchburg. Four guest rooms each offer a private bath, air conditioning, cable TV, and phone. Some of the rooms offer four-poster beds with steps and working fireplaces along with whimsical wicker and bamboo accents. The restored master bedroom suite offers a king-size bed, working fireplace, queen-size sleep sofa, private entry and solarium. Common rooms on the main floor include the fifty-foot grand hall featuring high ceilings and cherry and oak staircase, and a living room with over-stuffed chairs and fireplace. Area attractions include Poplar Forest, Appomattox, Point of Harbor, Blue Ridge Parkway, Blue Ridge Mountains, Red Hill, antique malls, outlet stores, and surrounding universities and colleges. Full breakfast. 1/$84; 2/$89-109. AE, MC, V. 10% senior, business, and auto club discounts.

Reedville

Cedar Grove Bed & Breakfast Inn
Route 1, Box 2535, Fleeton Road
Reedville, VA 22539
(804) 453-3915

Type of B&B: B&B Inn.
Rooms: 3, 1 with private bath.
Rates: 1 or 2/$55-85.

Rating: A- or ♛♛♛ Excellent, far exceeds basic requirements.

Colonial Revival inn built in 1913 is situated on Virginia's Northern Neck right on the Chesapeake Bay at Fleet on Point, and located three miles from Reedville near the junctions of Routes 657 and 360. Three antique-filled guest rooms are available. The suite offers a private bath and balcony with water views. Guests are invited to relax in the Victorian parlor or in the casual sunroom where books and TV are available. Borrow bicycles for a countryside ride, play tennis or croquet on the property, or just relax watching the fishing boats going by on the Bay. Nearby are the Tangier and Smith Island cruises, charter fishing excursions, and historical attractions. Full breakfast is served on china in the formal dining room. Restricted smoking. 1 or 2/$55-85. Travel agent.

Guests write: *"The hosts are gracious, the food is excellent, and one feels as though they have gone back in time to a more relaxed and elegant way of living, yet with all the conveniences of today. I loved the porch and the room made me feel I was a special guest. It is lovely, so clean, and beautifully decorated." (S. Ramos)*

Guests write: *"My husband and I appreciated the well-kept rooms, tidy and thoroughly clean with added touches such as a fresh flower, an interesting book or magazine, cookies or refreshments to enjoy - all giving the impression that we were not just a paying guest but they wanted our stay to be special." (D. Amsl)*

"Cedar Grove was so relaxing; from the first moment we arrived and spent some time sipping wine on the sunporch to the walk where I became engaged. The food was outstanding and the hospitality exceptional." (S. Snader)

Roanoke/Smith Mountain Lake

Manor at Taylor's Store
Route 1, Box 533
Wirtz, VA 24184
(703) 721-3951

Type of B&B: Inn with cottage.
Rooms: 6 with private bath.
Rates: 1/$65; 2/$65-95.

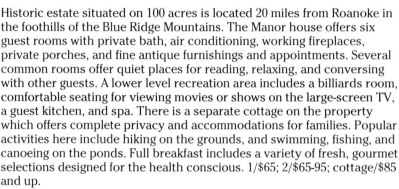

Rating: AA- or ♛♛♛♛ Outstanding.

Historic estate situated on 100 acres is located 20 miles from Roanoke in the foothills of the Blue Ridge Mountains. The Manor house offers six guest rooms with private bath, air conditioning, working fireplaces, private porches, and fine antique furnishings and appointments. Several common rooms offer quiet places for reading, relaxing, and conversing with other guests. A lower level recreation area includes a billiards room, comfortable seating for viewing movies or shows on the large-screen TV, a guest kitchen, and spa. There is a separate cottage on the property which offers complete privacy and accommodations for families. Popular activities here include hiking on the grounds, and swimming, fishing, and canoeing on the ponds. Full breakfast includes a variety of fresh, gourmet selections designed for the health conscious. 1/$65; 2/$65-95; cottage/$85 and up.

Guests write: *"For us, going here is like taking a very deep breath and seeing the beauty of the world all over again. The grounds are breathtaking, the animals friendly and fun, and the hosts always kind and smiling. This is a place that gets richer at each return. This is a place to take off your too tight shoes and walk barefoot and free with beauty all around. We'd move in if they'd have us." (S. Shields)*

Smithfield

Isle of Wight Inn
1607 South Church Street
Smithfield, VA 23430
(804) 357-3176

Type of B&B: Inn.
Rooms: 12 with private bath.
Rates: 1/$49; 2/$59-99.

Rating: A- or ♛♛♛ Excellent, far exceeds basic requirements.

Newly-built Colonial reproduction inn located 1 mile from Smithfield
National Historic District is near Routes 10, 258, and the south end of the
James River Bridge. Choose from twelve guest rooms, each with private
bath and cable TV. Three spacious suites with fireplaces and Jacuzzi tubs
are ideal for special occasions. There are over 60 historic homes and
buildings dating from 1632 in this old Riverport Town and guided tours
can be arranged for groups of ten or more. Hampton, Norfolk, Virginia
Beach, and Fort Story are nearby and Williamsburg or Jamestown are just
30 minutes and a short ferry ride away. Full breakfast features Smithfield
ham biscuits. Restricted smoking. Wheelchair access. 1/$49; 2/$59-99. AE,
MC, V. 10% senior, business travel, and auto club discounts. Travel agent.

Stanley

Jordan Hollow Farm Inn
Route 2, Box 375
Stanley, VA 22851
(703) 778-2285 or 778-2209

Type of B&B: Country inn with restaurant.
Rooms: 21 with private bath.
Rates: 1 or 2/$78-130.

Rating: A- or ♛♛♛ Excellent, far exceeds basic requirements.

Restored Colonial horse farm nestled on 45 acres of rolling hills and
meadows and surrounded by the Shenandoah National Park is located six
miles south of Luray. Two separate lodges on the property offer twenty-
one guest rooms with private bath, handmade furniture, and family
heirlooms. The top rooms feature whirlpool tubs and working fireplaces.
There is a mini-barnyard with farm animals, and pony rides for children
are available by appointment as well as horseback rides into the
mountains. Popular activities here include hiking mountain trails, relaxing
on the porch, and nearby fishing, skiing, swimming, and golfing. Area

attractions include Luray Caverns, Skyline Drive, and the New Market Battlefield Museum. The prices listed here do not include breakfast which normally costs between $3-6/person. Dinner is also available and box lunches can be made up for hikers or horseback riders with advance notice. Function rooms for weddings and meetings are offered. Families welcome. 1 or 2/$78-130. MC, V. Travel agent.

Strasburg

Hotel Strasburg
201 South Holliday Street
Strasburg, VA 22657
(703) 465-9191

Type of B & B: Hotel and
inn with restaurant.
Rooms: 25 with private bath.
Rates: 1 or 2/$69-149.

Rating: B+ or ♛♛ Good, exceeds basic requirements.

Victorian hotel and adjacent inn built in 1895 are located 2 miles off of I-81 in downtown Strasburg. The entire hotel has been renovated and features a collection of art and antique period pieces throughout the restaurant and parlor as well as in the guest rooms themselves. Each room offers a private bath, telephone, and TV. Special suites in the small inn next door offer lots of privacy, unusual decor and architectural features, and whirlpool baths. There is a restaurant and intimate pub on premises. Area attractions include Skyline Drive, Strasburg Emporium antique market, Wayside Theaters, Belle Grove Plantation, caverns, and Wayside Wonderland's beach. Continental breakfast. Facilities are available for small meetings and social functions. 1 or 2/$69-149. AE, MC, V. 10% auto club and senior discounts; 25% business travel discount. Travel agent.

Williamsburg

Applewood Colonial Bed & Breakfast
605 Richmond Road
Williamsburg, VA 23185
(800) 899-2753 or (804) 229-0205

Type of B&B: Inn.
Rooms: 4 with private bath.
Rates: 1 or 2/$55-99.

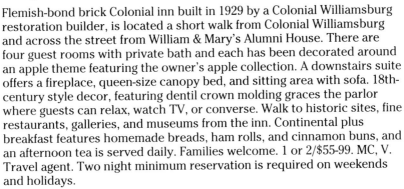

Rating: A- or ♕♕♕ Excellent, far exceeds basic requirements.

Flemish-bond brick Colonial inn built in 1929 by a Colonial Williamsburg restoration builder, is located a short walk from Colonial Williamsburg and across the street from William & Mary's Alumni House. There are four guest rooms with private bath and each has been decorated around an apple theme featuring the owner's apple collection. A downstairs suite offers a fireplace, queen-size canopy bed, and sitting area with sofa. 18th-century style decor, featuring dentil crown molding graces the parlor where guests can relax, watch TV, or converse. Walk to historic sites, fine restaurants, galleries, and museums from the inn. Continental plus breakfast features homemade breads, ham rolls, and cinnamon buns, and an afternoon tea is served daily. Families welcome. 1 or 2/$55-99. MC, V. Travel agent. Two night minimum reservation is required on weekends and holidays.

Williamsburg

Colonial Capital Bed & Breakfast
501 Richmond Road
Williamsburg, VA 23185
(804) 229-0233 or (800) 776-0570

Type of B&B: Inn.
Rooms: 5 with private bath.
Rates: 1/$65; 2/$85-125.

Rating: A or ♕♕♕ Excellent, far exceeds basic requirements.

Walk three blocks to Colonial Williamsburg from this Colonial Revival home built in 1926. Five pleasant guest rooms are located on the second and third floor and each has individual decor and offers a private bath. A large parlor area with fireplace offers a comfortable spot for meeting other guests, playing board games, or watching movies and TV. The backyard patio, deck, and side porch offer relaxation after a full day of seeing the sights. Borrow bicycles to explore the area. Walk to Colonial

Williamsburg, College of William and Mary, fine restaurants, and galleries from the inn. Full breakfast and afternoon tea and wine are served daily. Facilities are available for small weddings and meetings. Restricted smoking. 1/$65; 2/$85-125. MC, V. Travel agent.

Williamsburg

The Legacy of Williamsburg Bed & Breakfast
930 Jamestown Road
Williamsburg, VA 23185
(804) 220-0524 or (800) WMBGSBB

Type of B&B: Inn.
Rooms: 2 with private bath.
Rates: 1 or 2/$80-125.

Rating: A or ♛♛♛ Excellent, far exceeds basic requirements.

Reproduction Early American-style clapboard structure is located just six blocks from the historic Williamsburg area. Choose from two suites or two rooms which feature tall poster canopy beds, random pine floors, eighteenth-century furnishings, and private bath. The inn offers six fireplaces, a rare collection of eighteenth-century furniture, and walls adorned with oil paintings and samplers. Relax in the library and on the screened-in deck, or play billiards or eighteenth-century games in the Tavern room. Area attractions include the College of William and Mary, restaurants, outlet malls, and Busch Gardens. Full breakfast includes hearty farm-style specialties and a nightly glass of sherry or wine is offered. No smoking. 1 or 2/$80 for room; $125 for suite. MC, V.

Guests write: *"Staying at the Legacy with its 18th-century atmosphere and 20th-century conveniences was the best of both worlds. Mary Ann and Ed's love and knowledge of antiques made us feel right at home in Colonial Williamsburg." (P. Molony)*

"Hosts make it an adventure with 18th-century settings, featherbeds, antique furniture, and best of all - no TVs. This past Christmas something happened that makes her exceptional in our eyes. Our car broke down while we were there and being it was a weekend, we had to wait till Monday for repairs. I wanted to rent a car but the innkeeper would have none of it and lent us her car for the time we were there." (C. Ellmers)

Williamsburg

Liberty Rose Bed & Breakfast
1022 Jamestown Road
Williamsburg, VA 23185
(804) 253-1260 or
800-545-1825

Type of B&B: Inn.
Rooms: 3 with private bath.
Rates: 1 or 2/$95-155.

Rating: AA- or ♛♛♛♛ Outstanding.

English Colonial home built in 1922 and recently renovated is situated on a hilltop acre of stately oak and beech trees near the historic area. Three guest rooms are furnished with queen-size beds, French, English, and Victorian antiques, papered walls, silk fabrics, lace, and goose-down appointments. All have private baths. Combining these main rooms with small twin-bedded extra rooms, makes spacious suites for two, three, or four persons. A large guest parlor features woodburning fireplace, grand piano, and unexpected treasures. Full breakfast is served on the porch with wrap-around windows. Ask about those famous chocolate-chip cookies. Families welcome. No smoking. 1 or 2/$95-155. MC, V.

Guests write: *"Many B&Bs excel at displaying Colonial or Victorian artistic flair in decor. Somewhat less of them also offer little personal touches that put guests quickly at ease and make them feel especially pampered. Few of them however, can pass our bed test. Liberty Rose excels in everything." (J. Blackmore)*

"The little tray of homemade oatmeal-raisin and chocolate-chip cookies found in our room after a full day of touring Williamsburg made us feel special. Breakfasts on the sunporch were delightful and delicious - gracious service." (C. McDuffie)

"The restoration and decoration is just spectacular. Each room has its own character. Each corner holds its own surprise. The breakfasts eliminate the need for lunch and were totally unique each morning." (B. Willett)

Williamsburg

Newport House
710 South Henry Street
Williamsburg, VA 23185-4113
(804) 229-1775

Type of B&B: B&B home.
Rooms: 2 with private bath.
Rates: 1 or 2/$90-120.

Rating: A- or ♕♕♕ Excellent, far exceeds basic requirements.

Newport House is a careful reproduction of an original 1756 house and it is located within a five minute walk of Colonial Williamsburg. There are two spacious guest rooms with private bath, four-poster bed, period American antiques and reproduction furnishings. There is a large parlor on the main floor with fireplace and a collection of books. Guests are invited to stroll through the flower, herb, and vegetable gardens or join in a Colonial dance in the upstairs ballroom. Hostess is a registered nurse who enjoys making eighteenth-century clothing. Host is former captain of an historic full-rigged ship and is now an author and publisher of history books. Area attractions include historic sites in Jamestown and Yorktown, the James River Plantations, and Busch Gardens. Full breakfast specialties often include apple-cinnamon waffles, specialty breads, and baked apples. Families welcome. 1 or 2/$90-120. Travel agent.

Guests write: *"John and Cathy Millar have created an establishment which truly enhances a visit to Williamsburg. The house and the beautiful furnishings perfectly combine 20th-century comfort with 18th-century elegance and taste. The facilities are superb, the breakfasts delightful, and the conversation uncommonly pleasant." (B. Smith)*

"The two rooms that are set aside for guests, the Philadelphia Room, and the Newport Room, make other accommodations in Williamsburg look shabby. Each morning, breakfast is enlivened by delightful conversation and the antics of Sassafras, the rabbit, and Ian, the Millar's little boy. For those visitors who wish to be close to the center of the restored area, but far from the maddening crowd, Newport House is perfectly located. It is but a short walk from Duke of Gloucester Street, but the quiet that surrounds it is always welcomed." (C. Potter)

Williamsburg

War Hill Inn
4560 Long Hill Road
Williamsburg, VA 23188
(804) 565-0248 or (800) 743-0248

Type of B&B: Inn.
Rooms: 5 with private bath.
Rates: 1 or 2/$60-90.

Rating: A- or ♛♛♛ Excellent, far exceeds basic requirements.

War Hill Inn is a quiet country farm located 4 miles from Colonial Williamsburg. Enjoy complete privacy in the newly built Colonial cottage with whirlpool or in one of four rooms with private bath in the 18th-century style farmhouse. After a full day of touring the many local sights, guests enjoy unwinding in the swing and watching and petting the farm animals. Full breakfast is served in the dining room. Families welcome. No smoking. 1 or 2 $60-90. AE, MC, V.

Wintergreen/Nellysford

Meander Inn
Routes 612 and 613, Box 443
Nellysford, VA 22958
(804) 361-1121

Type of B&B: Inn on a farm.
Rooms: 5 with private bath.
Rates: 1 or 2/$60-95.

Rating: A- or ♛♛♛ Excellent, far exceeds basic requirements.

Historic farmhouse built eighty years ago is situated on fifty acres of pasture and woods in the foothills of the Blue Ridge Mountains near the Wintergreen Resort and thirty miles south of Charlottesville. Five guest rooms offer a private bath, panoramic view, queen-size four-poster beds or twin sleigh beds, and Victorian or country antiques. Popular activities here include soaking in the hot tub, swimming in the pool, relaxing on the porch, and listening to the turn-of-the-century player piano. Guests who wake up early can help feed the horses and gather the fresh morning eggs. Area attractions include Charlottesville, Wintergreen, Appalachian Trail, Crabtree Falls, wineries, and fishing and hiking in the Blue Ridge Mountains. Full country breakfast. Facilities are available for small retreats and meetings. Families welcome. No smoking. 1 or 2/$60-95. MC, V. Travel agent.

Wintergreen/Nellysford

Upland Manor
Route 1, Box 375
Nellysford, VA 22958
(804) 361-1101

Type of B&B: Inn.
Rooms: 10 with private bath.
Rates: 1 or 2/$85-115.

Rating: A- or ♛♛♛ Excellent, far exceeds basic requirements.

Restored historic manor is located between Charlottesville and the Blue Ridge Parkway near the Wintergreen Resort. Choose from ten guest rooms or suites with private bath and period furnishings. Several rooms offer a whirlpool tub or claw-foot tub with shower. Guests enjoy exploring the fourteen acres that surround the inn and have spotted deer and a wide variety of bird species. Area attractions include University of Virginia, Blue Ridge Parkway, Skyline Drive, historic sites, skiing, fishing, and golfing. Full breakfast features specialties such as peach cobbler, apple pancakes, and strawberry French toast. Function rooms are available for small weddings and meetings. No smoking. 1 or 2/$85-115. MC, V. 10% senior and auto club discount. Travel agent.

Coupeville

The Inn at Penn Cove
702 North Main Street
Coupeville, WA 98239
(800) 688-COVE or
(206) 678-8000

Type of B&B: Inn.
Rooms: 6 with private bath.
Rate: 1 or 2/$75-125.

Rating: A or ♛♛♛ Excellent, far exceeds basic requirements.

The Inn at Penn Cove is comprised of two historic 1887 Victorian homes
that are located seven blocks off Highway 20 in the town of Coupeville.
There are three guest rooms at the main inn. Each offers a private bath,
fireplace, and antique furnishings. The Coupe Gillespie House next door
offers three additional accommodations. Area attractions include Ebey's
Landing, National Historical Reserve, Fort Casey, Deception Pass, Puget
Sound, Penn Cove, specialty shops, fine restaurants, bicycling, and hiking.
Full breakfast. No smoking. Function rooms for meetings and weddings
are available. 1 or 2/$75-125. MC, V. 10% senior discount. Travel agent.

Port Angeles

Domaine Madeleine
1834 Finn Hall Road
Port Angeles, WA 98326
(206) 457-4174

Type of B&B: B&B home.
Rooms: 2 with private bath.
Rates: 1/$69-99; 2/$79-125.

Rating: A+ or ♛♛♛ Excellent, far exceeds basic requirements.

Waterfront contemporary home overlooking the Strait of Juan de Fuca is
located just outside Port Angeles on Washington's Olympic Peninsula.
There are two guest rooms with private bath, water views, and European
featherbeds. The deluxe second-floor room offers a private 30-foot
balcony, Jacuzzi tub, and stereo system. A comfortable living room on the
main floor features a 14-foot high basalt fireplace, antique furnishings,
and a hand-built harpsichord. Guests are welcome to explore the
surrounding five acres and the waterfront. Area attractions include
Olympic National Park, Hoh Rain Forest, Lake Crescent, Wild Game farm,
Sol Duc Hot Springs, and recreation such as skiing, fishing, and hiking. A

full breakfast includes freshly baked bread, entree, dessert, and French roast coffee. Facilities are available for small weddings and meetings. 1/$69-99; 2/$79-125. MC, V. 10% senior discount. Travel agent.

Port Townsend

Bishop Victorian Guest Suites
714 Washington Street
Port Townsend, WA 98368
(206) 385-6122

Type of B&B: Inn.
Rooms: 13 with private bath.
Rates: 1/$54-79; 2/$63-89.

Rating: B- or ♛♛ Good, exceeds basic requirements.

Victorian hotel built in 1890 has been completely restored and is located right in the heart of downtown Port Townsend near the ferry terminal. The lower floor of the building is used as a storefront and a flight of steps leads to the inn's lobby. Thirteen guest suites are furnished with some period pieces and offer private bath, sitting area, full kitchen, and one or two bedrooms. Walk to area shops, restaurants, and the ferry terminal. Area attractions include Olympic National Park (40 minutes by car), Mt. Baker, the Cascades, Admiralty Bay, and Fort Worden State Park, known for its use in the movie, "An Officer and A Gentleman". Continental breakfast. Families welcome. Restricted smoking. 1/$54-79; 2/$63-89. AE, MC, V. Senior discount.

Port Townsend

Holly Hill House B&B Inn
611 Polk
Port Townsend, WA 98368
(206) 385-5619 or (800) 435-1454

Type of B&B: Inn and cottage.
Rooms: 5 with private bath.
Rate: 1/$71-129; 2/$76-134.

Rating: B+ or ♛♛ Good, exceeds basic requirements.

Historic 1872 Victorian home is within walking distance of the downtown shops and restaurants. There are three guest rooms with private bath in the main house. The carriage house, adjacent to the inn, offers two additional rooms with private bath. The home has been well preserved and features stippled woodwork, authentic Victorian plantings, and an unusual towering holly tree. Area attractions include Fort Worden State Park, Centrum, downtown shopping, fishing, hiking, tennis, and golf. Full breakfast. 1/$71-129; 2/$76-134. MC, AE, V. Travel agent.

Sequim

Greywolf Inn
177 Keeler Road
Sequim, WA 98382
(206) 683-5889 or 683-1487

Type of B&B: Small inn.
Rooms: 6 with private bath.
Rates: 2/$50-90.

Rating: B or ♨♨ Good, exceeds basic requirements.

Newly-constructed contemporary inn is situated atop five wooded acres in the Olympic Peninsula, a scenic two hour drive from Seattle via Highway 101. Choose from six guest rooms with private bath and themes such as Bavaria, the Orient, the Deep South, and French Provincial. Popular activities here include sitting on the deck or patio, hiking five miles of trees, fields, and stream, or relaxing by the fire in the living room with a good book from the inn's well-stocked library. Area attractions include Olympic National Park, Hurricane Ridge, Hoh Rain Forest, Dungeness Spit, or the Juan de Fuca Straits. The ferry at Port Angeles is less than thirty minutes by car. Full breakfast includes assorted pastries and breads, fresh fruit, and a special hot entree. Restricted smoking. 2/$50-90. AE, MC, V. Travel agent.

Guests write: *"Greywolf Inn was a delightful discovery. All linens, furniture, and appointments are top-of-the-line. Rooms have the warmth of home by displaying family mementos. This warmth and attention to detail was extended to breakfast that was served on the glass-walled porch overlooking fields and woods. The meal was so attractively presented my husband took a photo of our plates!" (D. Clarke)*

"Staying at the Greywolf was like a touch of home with their full library of books and a roaring fireplace. You really felt like more than a guest, almost like a member of the family. They personally took us and our daughter to an unusual outdoor zoo that was the highlight of our visit." (J. Miller)

"Our stay at Greywolf Inn has been a thoroughly delightful and refreshing experience. The comfortable bed in our room provided us with the best sleep we have had in years. We are very impressed with the quiet beauty of this place, its immaculate cleanliness, and the impeccable good taste and graciousness of our hosts." (E. Nordstrom)

"Since spending three nights at Greywolf Inn in August, we have sent three other parties there to enjoy the gourmet breakfasts and country atmosphere with wonderful hospitality. Each group found Greywolf far exceeded their expectations." (J. Dunham)

"Peggy's tasty orange muffins and fresh brewed coffee kept us longer than necessary at the table all the while gazing through the windows across meadows full of wildflowers that crept toward wooded vistas in the distance. Walking paths are everywhere. Travelers looking for comfort, beauty, restful ease far from the maddening crowd, will find Greywolf Inn the place to seek out and enjoy." (V. Caisse)

Yakima

37 House
4002 Englewood Avenue
Yakima, WA 98908
(509) 965-5537 or 965-4705

Type of B&B: Inn.
Rooms: 6, 4 with private bath.
Rates: 1 or 2/$65-120.

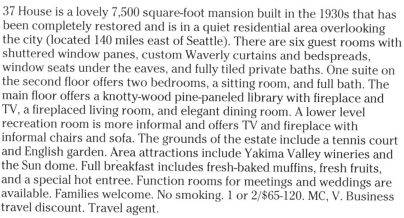

Rating: A or ♛♛♛ Excellent, far exceeds basic requirements.

37 House is a lovely 7,500 square-foot mansion built in the 1930s that has been completely restored and is in a quiet residential area overlooking the city (located 140 miles east of Seattle). There are six guest rooms with shuttered window panes, custom Waverly curtains and bedspreads, window seats under the eaves, and fully tiled private baths. One suite on the second floor offers two bedrooms, a sitting room, and full bath. The main floor offers a knotty-wood pine-paneled library with fireplace and TV, a fireplaced living room, and elegant dining room. A lower level recreation room is more informal and offers TV and fireplace with informal chairs and sofa. The grounds of the estate include a tennis court and English garden. Area attractions include Yakima Valley wineries and the Sun dome. Full breakfast includes fresh-baked muffins, fresh fruits, and a special hot entree. Function rooms for meetings and weddings are available. Families welcome. No smoking. 1 or 2/$65-120. MC, V. Business travel discount. Travel agent.

Guests write: *"The breakfast of Eggs Benedict was cooked to order and we've never tasted better. I can't say enough about the 37 House. It is what I*

always thought B&Bs should be like but never experienced."
(D. Williamson)

"This was my husband's first experience at a B&B and he was surprised he liked it so well. I have stayed in B&Bs before but this one is first rate. We thoroughly enjoyed ourselves. I think perhaps we shall make it an annual anniversary event and I'm so glad they saved this wonderful house from the wrecker's ball." (F. Webb)

"This was a home I had often admired during my growing-up years in Yakima and it was fun staying there as a guest. The manager graciously moved us to another room when we expressed a concern about noise from the traffic during the night. We were given the master suite at no added expense and appreciated this courtesy very much. Our breakfast was delicious and attractively presented." (S. Parkhill)

"The accommodations were wonderful. The hospitality was especially warm and the house was very beautiful. It was like being at home because we could use the kitchen and there was fresh fruit and homemade cookies for us to enjoy." (S. Albers)

Charles Town

Hillbrook Inn
Route 2, Box 152
Charles Town, WV 25414
(304) 725-4223

Type of B&B: Country inn.
Rooms: 5 with private bath.
Rates: 1 or 2/$150-240

Rating: A+ or ♛♛♛ Excellent, far exceeds basic requirements.

Historic English Tudor country estate on seventeen acres of sweeping lawns, unspoiled woodland, streams, and ponds, is located just 5 miles west of Charles Town. There are five guest rooms with private bath and handsome furnishings. The mansion is decorated throughout with a fine collection of antiques, Oriental rugs, and original art, and features many working fireplaces. Area attractions nearby include Harper's Ferry, horse races, outlet and antique shopping, and white water rafting. The dining room serves a full country breakfast and a seven course dinner with wine. Facilities are available for weddings and meetings. 1 or 2/$150-240. MC, V.

Petersburg

Smoke Hole Lodge
P.O. Box 953
Petersburg, WV 26847
(304) 242-8377
(winter phone only,
no phone in summer)

Type of B&B: Mountain lodge.
Rooms: 7 with private bath.
Rates: 1/$85; 2/$155.

Rating: A or ♛♛♛ Excellent, far exceeds basic requirements.

Spacious newly-rebuilt mountain lodge and ranch on 1,500 remote wilderness acres is 12 miles south of Petersburg, close to Monongahela National Forest. Five rustic guest rooms are available, each with private bath, or two dormitories that together can sleep nine. The ranch runs on kerosene, wood, and bottled gas as it has neither electricity nor phones. This makes for a fascinating turn-of-the-century experience. The ranch is an angus cattle operation, and many other animals live there as well. The property abounds with deer and on occasion a bear is sighted. This is a relaxing, get-away-from-it-all spot for the whole family. Enjoy bass fishing, swimming, inner-tubing, and hiking on the property. Hearty full breakfast, lunch, and dinner are included in the rates, as is round-trip transportation from Petersburg where hosts will meet you for the hour-and-a-half trip up the mountain by four-wheel drive. Families and pets welcome. 1/$85; 2/$155. Travel agent or write above address. Open May through October.

Valley Chapel/Weston

Ingeberg Acres
Millstone Run Road
P.O. Box 199
Valley Chapel, WV 26446
(304) 269-2834

Type of B&B: Farm B&B.
Rooms: 3 with shared baths.
Rates: 1/$39; 2/$59.

Rating: B or ♛♛ Good, exceeds basic requirements.

Ingeberg Acres is a 450-acre horse and cattle breeding farm located in the heart of West Virginia. There are three second-floor guest rooms which share a bath and offer air conditioning. Popular activities here are watching and helping with the farm chores, hiking on marked trails, birdwatching, swimming in the pool, and relaxing on the patio and deck. Hunting is allowed on the property with special permission. Full breakfast is served family style. Families welcome. No smoking. 1/$39; 2/$59. 10% auto club, business travel, family, and senior discounts.

Baraboo

Pinehaven Bed & Breakfast
E13083 Highway 33
Baraboo, WI 53913
(608) 356-3489

Type of B&B: Small inn.
Rooms: 4 with private bath.
Rates: 1/$50-60; 2/$55-65.

Rating: B+ or ♛♛ Good, exceeds basic requirements.

Chalet-style contemporary inn surrounded by pines and overlooking a two-acre lake is located three miles east of Baraboo on Highway 33. Each of the four guest rooms offer a private bath and distinctive decor with features such as homemade quilts, crocheted coverlets, or matching comforters and shams. The view of the lake and Baraboo Bluffs is outstanding from the inn's upper veranda and lower decks. Guest enjoy strolling the grounds, crossing the river on the 1890s bridge, and seeing the host's Belgian horses. Area attractions include Circus Museum, Devil's Lake State Park, Wisconsin Dells, and International Crane Foundation. A full breakfast includes specialties such as broccoli-rice quiche, morning glorious muffins, raspberry cream-cheese coffee cake, and peach French toast. No smoking. 1/$50-60; 2/$55-65. MC, V.

Burlington

Hillcrest Bed & Breakfast
540 Storle Avenue
Burlington, WI 53105
(414) 763-4706

Type of B&B: Small inn.
Rooms: 3, 1 with private bath.
Rates: 1 or 2/$60-75.

Rating: A- or ♛♛♛ Excellent, far exceeds basic requirements.

Edwardian home built in 1908 is situated on the crest of a hill with panoramic view of the valley and waterways below and is located off Highway 11 West. There are three guest rooms with individual decor and one offers a private bath. Special features of the room include queen-size carved oak or walnut beds, river views, period antique furnishings, lace curtains, and Oriental rugs. The lower porch offers antique wicker furniture and views of the surrounding lakes and rivers. Guest enjoy exploring the landscaped grounds and restored gardens where weddings are often held. Area attractions include antique shopping, golfing, skiing, swimming, and boating. Full breakfast. No smoking. 1 or 2/$60-75.

Cedarburg

Washington House Inn
W62N573 Washington Avenue
Cedarburg, WI 53012
(414) 375-3550 or (800) 369-4088

Type of B&B: Inn.
Rooms: 29 with private bath.
Rates: 1 or 2/$59-139.

Rating: A or ♕♕♕ Excellent, far exceeds basic requirements.

Historic Victorian urban inn is centrally located in the town's Historic District, 3 miles west of I-43, exit 17. There are twenty-nine guest rooms throughout the complex and each features a private bath, antiques, cozy down quilts, fireplaces, and fresh flowers. Deluxe suites offer Jacuzzi tubs and unique architectural features. Area attractions include historic Cedar Creek Settlement, antique shops, and Pioneer Village. Continental breakfast includes fresh-baked muffins and fresh-squeezed juices. Function rooms are available for weddings and meetings. Families welcome. Wheelchair access. 1 or 2/$59-139. AE, MC, V. 10% senior and auto club discounts. Travel agent.

Guests write: *"It was the most wonderful romantic place we've ever been. The interior was beautiful, the atmosphere was perfect. It was truly everything I thought it would be and more." (C. Urbanek)*

Hayward

Lumberman's Mansion Inn
P.O. Box 885
Hayward, WI 54843
(715) 634-3012

Type of B&B: Small inn.
Rooms: 7 with private bath.
Rates: 1/$50; 2/$85.

Rating: B or ♕♕ Good, exceeds basic requirements.

Historic Queen Anne Victorian mansion built in 1887 is located about one hour south of Duluth. There are seven guest rooms with private bath, down comforters, period antiques, fine linens, and lace curtains. Several of the larger rooms offer a Jacuzzi tub. The mansion is being fully restored and its original elegance has been preserved in the maple floors, fireplaces with decorative tile and wood mantels, pocket doors, and carriage stoop. The McCormick Library on the main floor offers a fine selection of books and historical documents. Homebaked goods and hot apple cider are served in the adjacent parlor. Year-round recreation in the area includes skiing, skating, snowmobiling, biking, and hiking. Full breakfast offers such house specialties as waffles, wild rice pancakes, or baked egg specialty, along with muffins, fresh fruit, and homemade jams. Function rooms are available for weddings and meetings. Families welcome. No smoking. 1/$50; 2/$85. MC, V. 10% business discount. Travel agent.

Guests write: *"The hosts were so cheerful and accommodating. We enjoyed a long talk over a beautifully served breakfast and left feeling as though we had made new friends. I was really impressed by the use of china, silver, crystal, and linen for the breakfast meal. The attention to detail helped make it a memorable visit. Our biggest regret is that we could stay only one night."* (B. Petersen)

Janesville

Jackson Street Inn B&B
210 South Jackson Street
Janesville, WI 53545
(608) 754-7250

Type of B&B: Inn.
Rooms: 4, 2 with private bath.
Rates: 1/$40-55; 2/$50-65.

Rating: A- or ♛♛♛ Excellent, far exceeds basic requirements.

Historic Victorian home built in the four-square style in 1899 is located 1.5 miles west of I-90 on Highway 11. There are four second-floor guest rooms and two offer a private bath. The original architectural features of the home have been preserved and include a glass prism chandelier, brass lighting fixtures, glass pocket doors, oak cross-beam ceilings, leaded beveled glass windows, Italian marble mantels, and intricately carved oak paneling. Outdoor games set up at the inn include a small putting green and shuffleboard game. Area attractions include the Lincoln-Tallman Museum, three historic districts, top-rated golf courses, and bicycle and ski trails. Full breakfast includes specialties such as blueberry pancakes or egg custard. Families welcome. Restricted smoking. 1/$40-55; 2/$50-65. AE, MC, V. 10% auto club, business travel, and senior discount. Travel agent.

Kenosha

The Manor House
6536 3rd Avenue
Kenosha, WI 53143
(414) 658-0014

Type of B&B: Small inn.
Rooms: 4 with private bath.
Rates: 1 or 2/$90-130.

Rating: A+ or ♛♛♛ Excellent, far exceeds basic requirements.

Historic Georgian manor house built in the 1920's is in the heart of the Lakeshore Historical District of Kenosha and overlooks Lake Michigan, yet is only four miles from I-94. There are four second-floor guest rooms with private bath, cable TV, rich fabrics, Oriental carpets, and 18th-century antiques. A small sitting area found between two bedroom wings offers a private corner for relishing breakfast or viewing the lake. The first floor common rooms are spacious and opulent with unusually fine antiques and appointments. A lower level offers special conference facilities. The grounds include a swimming pool, fountain, rose garden, gazebo, and many varieties of trees. Area attractions include the nearby Historic District, museums, beaches, golf courses, and county parks. Continental breakfast includes seasonal fruits. Restricted smoking. 1 or 2/$90-130. AE, MC, V. Business discount available.

Guests write: *This was the best place to enjoy our 11th Anniversary. It was truly relaxing with super, gracious hosts." (B. Mooney)*

"The Manor House is very pretty and comfortable, elegant, and cozy - a relaxing weekend get-away and wonderful one-year wedding anniversary." (A. Kelman)

Lake Delton

The Swallow's Nest B&B
141 Sarrington, P.O. Box 418
Lake Delton, WI 53940
(608) 254-6900

Type of B&B: B&B home.
Rooms: 4 with private bath.
Rates: 1/$50-60; 2/$55-65.

Rating: B+ or ♛♛ Good, exceeds basic requirements.

Contemporary home in a wooded setting is located just off I-90 and I-94. There are four second-floor guest rooms with private bath and air conditioning. Several common areas on the first floor feature monastery windows, a two-story atrium with skylights, library with fireplace, decks overlooking the lake, wildflowers, and a gazebo by a waterfall. The host's photography studio and gallery are on the premises. Area attractions include Wisconsin Dells, Lake Delton, Devil's Lake State Park, downhill skiing, Circus World Museum, antique shops, and restaurants. Full breakfast. No smoking. 1/$50-60; 2/$55-65. MC, V.

Racine

Lochnaiar Inn
1121 Lake Avenue
Racine, WI 53403
(414) 633-3300

Type of B&B: Inn.
Rooms: 8 with private bath.
Rates: 1 or 2/$70-165.

Rating: A or ♛♛♛ Excellent, far exceeds basic requirements.

Lochnaiar Inn is an impressive lakeside English Tudor structure which is situated on a bluff overlooking Lake Michigan and located in the downtown Historic District. There are eight guest rooms which offer a variety of size, decor, and amenities, but each offers a queen or king-size beds, fresh cut flowers, telephone, and TV. Several rooms offer Jacuzzi tubs and cozy fireplaces. Two common rooms on the main floor offer areas to converse with other guests or read a good book. Downtown restaurants, shops, and marina area with outdoor recreation and year-round festivals is within walking distance of the inn. Continental breakfast. Function rooms are available for meetings and social occasions. Restricted smoking. 1 or 2/$70-165. AE, MC, V. 10% business travel discount. Travel agent.

Alberta
Didsbury/Calgary

Ausen Haus B&B
R.R. 2
Didsbury, AL Canada T0M 0W0
(403) 335-4736 or 335-4053

Type of B&B: B&B home.
Rooms: 3, 1 with private bath.
Rates: 1 or 2/$45-75.

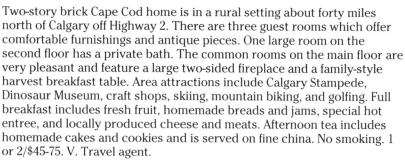

Rating: B or ♛♛ Good, exceeds basic requirements.

Two-story brick Cape Cod home is in a rural setting about forty miles north of Calgary off Highway 2. There are three guest rooms which offer comfortable furnishings and antique pieces. One large room on the second floor has a private bath. The common rooms on the main floor are very pleasant and feature a large two-sided fireplace and a family-style harvest breakfast table. Area attractions include Calgary Stampede, Dinosaur Museum, craft shops, skiing, mountain biking, and golfing. Full breakfast includes fresh fruit, homemade breads and jams, special hot entree, and locally produced cheese and meats. Afternoon tea includes homemade cakes and cookies and is served on fine china. No smoking. 1 or 2/$45-75. V. Travel agent.

British Columbia
Victoria

Prior House B&B Inn
620 St. Charles Street
Victoria, BC, Canada V8S 3N7
(604) 592-8847

Type of B&B: B&B home.
Rooms: 5 with private bath.
Rates: 1 or 2/$65-160.

Rating: AA or ♛♛♛♛ Outstanding.

Historic Edwardian mansion built in 1912 is located in a quiet neighborhood near downtown Victoria. There are five guest rooms located throughout the inn. The ballroom on the lower level and the 3rd floor suite have been converted into accommodations especially suited for families. A large master bedroom on the second floor boasts a bathroom almost as large as the bedroom and features wrap-around mirror walls and ceiling, three marble sinks and vanities, Jacuzzi tub, and separate shower. Originally built for the King's representative in British Columbia, no expense was spared in the quality of materials used in building the inn whose special features include rich oak paneling, stained-glass windows, antique furnishings, and carved stone terraces overlooking a large garden. Area attractions include Government House, Empress Hotel, Parliament Buildings, and Royal British Columbus Museum. Full gourmet breakfast and evening refreshments are served daily. Families welcome. Function rooms are available for meetings and social functions. No smoking. 1 or 2/$65-160. MC, V. 10% auto club, business travel, and senior discounts. Travel agent.

New Brunswick
Fredericton

Happy Apple Acres
R.R. 4
Fredericton, NB, Canada E3B 4X5
(506) 472-1819

Type of B&B: Inn.
Rooms: 3 with private bath.
Rates: 1/$45; 2/$60.

Rating: B+ or ♛♛ Good, exceeds basic requirements.

Happy Apple Acres is situated in a rural area atop a hill with water views and it's located about ten minutes from downtown Fredrickton which is the capitol of New Brunswick province. The main inn offers a two-room suite with private bath and sauna. A separate cottage offers two guest rooms. The special Honeymoon Room is quite popular for its heart-shaped whirlpool bath and when the Honeymoon package is requested, this room is outfitted with fresh flowers, chocolates, fruit basket, and terry robes. Area attractions include parks, beaches, skating ponds, skiing, camping, and hiking. The property includes orchards of apples which guests are welcome to pick in season. The breakfast menu features fresh fruit, apple pancakes with apple syrup, chunky apple muffins, or fruited French toast with maple syrup. 1/$45; 2/$60 (Canadian). Honeymoon packages and business travel discounts available.

Guests write: *"The sweetheart tub is a unique experience and the accommodations and hospitality excellent. We still have very pleasant memories of our stay with the Hamilton's." (S. Eiseman)*

"We loved the dogs, the fireplace, the sauna, blueberry pancakes, and the warm hospitality." (S. Munger)

Quebec

Montreal

Manoir Ambrose
3422 Stanley
Montreal, QC, Canada H3A 1R8
(514) 288-6922
Fax: (514) 288-5757

Type of B&B: Guesthouse.
Rooms: 22, 15 with private bath.
Rates: 1/$30-60; 2/$55-75.

Rating: C+ or ♛ Acceptable, meets basic requirements.

Turn-of-the-century Victorian brownstone is located in the heart of the city. There are twenty-two guest rooms between the two buildings that are adjoined in the center. While there is a wide variety in the size, decor, and quality of the guest rooms, each offers a TV, radio, and phone; fifteen have a private bath. A breakfast room on the lower level is a pleasant area where guests help themselves to a continental breakfast and beverages. From the inn, it's a short walk to restaurants, theaters, shopping, and convenient public transportation. Continental breakfast. 1/$30-60; 2/$55-75. MC, V. Travel agent.

St-Marc-sur-Richelieu

Auberge Handfield
555 Chemin du Prince
St-Marc-sur-Richel, QC,
Canada J0L 2E0
(514) 584-2226

Fax: (514) 584-3650
Type of B&B: Country inn.
Rooms: 55 with private bath.

Rates: 1/$46-105; 2/$55-145.

Rating: A or ♛♛♛ Excellent, exceeds basic requirements.

Auberge Handfield is comprised of a large historic country inn built in 1800, a maple sugaring camp, several cottages, and a newly built lodge and is located 35 minutes north of Montreal near exit 112 of Highway 20. There is a wide variety in the size, decor, quality, and amenities of each room but they all offer a private bath, phone, TV, and air conditioning. In the summer, guests relax on the outside terrace with swimming pool and view yachts in the marina. The most recent addition to the inn is a new indoor health spa with exercise equipment, spa, and professional health advisors. The inn owns a large ferry boat docked on the river nearby which comes alive with summer theater from June through September. Area recreation includes mountain hiking, golf, swimming, and horseback riding. Continental breakfast is included in the rates. Lunch, dinner, and Sunday brunch are available at additional charge. Families welcome. There are numerous function rooms available for meetings and social occasions. 1/$46-105; 2/$55-145.

Tear Out This Page!

**It won't ruin your book. And we really
want to hear comments on your B&B
travels (good or bad). Won't you write us?**

Your Name: _____

Address: _____

City: _____

State: _____Zip: _____

Where did you stay? _____

_____

Comments: _____

_____

_____

_____

_____

_____

_____

_____

*May we reprint your comments in the next edition of
the guidebook?*   ☐ *Yes*   ☐ *No*

Return to:
Director, American B&B Association,
1407 Huguenot Road, Midlothian, VA 23113

Tear Out This Page!

It won't ruin your book. And we really want to hear comments on your B&B travels (good or bad). Won't you write us?

Your Name: _____

Address: _____

City: _____

State: _____ Zip: _____

Where did you stay? _____

_____

Comments: _____

_____

_____

_____

_____

_____

_____

_____

May we reprint your comments in the next edition of the guidebook? ☐ *Yes* ☐ *No*

Return to:
Director, American B&B Association,
1407 Huguenot Road, Midlothian, VA 23113

Tear Out This Page!

It won't ruin your book. And we really want to hear comments on your B&B travels (good or bad). Won't you write us?

Your Name: _____

Address: _____

City: _____

State: _____ Zip: _____

Where did you stay? _____

_____

Comments: _____

_____

_____

_____

_____

_____

_____

_____

May we reprint your comments in the next edition of the guidebook? ☐ *Yes* ☐ *No*

Return to:
Director, American B&B Association,
1407 Huguenot Road, Midlothian, VA 23113

Tear Out This Page!

It won't ruin your book. And we really want to hear comments on your B&B travels (good or bad). Won't you write us?

Your Name: _____

Address: _____

City: _____

State: _____Zip: _____

Where did you stay? _____

_____

Comments: _____

_____

_____

_____

_____

_____

_____

_____

May we reprint your comments in the next edition of the guidebook?   ☐ *Yes*   ☐ *No*

Return to:
Director, American B&B Association,
1407 Huguenot Road, Midlothian, VA 23113

Tear Out This Page!

It won't ruin your book. And we really want to hear comments on your B&B travels (good or bad). Won't you write us?

Your Name: _____

Address: _____

City: _____

State: _____Zip: _____

Where did you stay? _____

_____

Comments: _____

_____

_____

_____

_____

_____

_____

_____

May we reprint your comments in the next edition of the guidebook? ☐ *Yes* ☐ *No*

Return to:
Director, American B&B Association,
1407 Huguenot Road, Midlothian, VA 23113

Tear Out This Page!

It won't ruin your book. And we really want to hear comments on your B&B travels (good or bad). Won't you write us?

Your Name: _____

Address: _____

City: _____

State: _____ Zip: _____

Where did you stay? _____

_____

Comments: _____

_____

_____

_____

_____

_____

_____

May we reprint your comments in the next edition of the guidebook?   ☐ *Yes*   ☐ *No*

Return to:
Director, American B&B Association,
1407 Huguenot Road, Midlothian, VA 23113